de Granada Luis, Mary E Herbert

Life of Dom Bartholomew of the Martyrs

Religious of the order of St. Dominic and archbishop of Braga, in Portugal

de Granada Luis, Mary E Herbert

Life of Dom Bartholomew of the Martyrs
Religious of the order of St. Dominic and archbishop of Braga, in Portugal

ISBN/EAN: 9783742814630

Manufactured in Europe, USA, Canada, Australia, Japa

Cover: Foto ©Lupo / pixelio.de

Manufactured and distributed by brebook publishing software (www.brebook.com)

de Granada Luis, Mary E Herbert

Life of Dom Bartholomew of the Martyrs

LIFE

OF

DOM BARTHOLOMEW

OF THE MARTYRS.

Religious of the Order of St. Dominic, and Archbishop of Braga, in Portugal.

TRANSLATED BY

LADY HERBERT,

FROM

THE ORIGINAL OF FATHER LOUIS OF GRENADA, AND FOUR OTHER BIOGRAPHIES.

NEW EDITION.

LONDON:
THOMAS BAKER, SOHO SQUARE.
1890.

Contents.

	PAGE
Preface to the French Translation	1

BOOK I.

CHAPTER I.

The birth of Bartholomew—why he took the surname of "The Martyrs"—of the virtue and charity of his parents … 11

CHAPTER II.

Bartholomew determines to renounce the world and become a religious—he enters the Order of St. Dominic, and becomes the model of the Noviciate … 15

CHAPTER III.

Bartholomew's work after his profession—the opinions of Louis of Grenada as to the studies of young religious—Bartholomew is chosen as preceptor of the son of the Infanta—his love of solitude … 20

CHAPTER IV.

Bartholomew joins prayer and meditation on Holy Scripture to his theological studies—he exercises the functions of Apostolic Preacher with singular holiness—he is elected Prior of Benefico—his disinterestedness, charity and wisdom in the guidance of his monastery … 25

CHAPTER V.

The pre-eminence of the Cathedral of Braga and its prelates—the intrigues at court to procure the archbishopric—the Queen offers it to Louis of Grenada, who refuses it … 29

CHAPTER VI.

Father Louis of Grenada proposes Dom Bartholomew to the Queen as Archbishop of Braga—the Queen consents, and appoints him, but cannot prevail upon him to accept it ... 34

CHAPTER VII.

Dom Louis of Grenada tries to persuade Dom Bartholomew to receive the archbishopric, but in vain—finally, he forces him to accept it by threatening him with excommunication ... 41

CHAPTER VIII.

Dom Bartholomew, finding himself forced to accept the bishopric, falls into such sadness that he becomes very ill—many speak against his election—that he was called to the archbishopric as Cardinal Ximenes was to that of Toledo 46

CHAPTER IX.

Bartholomew's dangerous illness—after his recovery he goes to salute the Queen—his election is praised by one of the greatest nobles in Portugal, and one who had been the most indignant at his promotion 50

CHAPTER X.

Dom Bartholomew is consecrated Archbishop—his entry into Braga—his regulations for his own conduct and his daily life 53

CHAPTER XI.

The Archbishop retrenches all the magnificence of his predecessors—he puts his house in order, and reforms the administration of his revenues 57

CHAPTER XII.

The way the Archbishop judged in civil causes, and the Christian manner in which he exacted that justice should be administered by his officers 59

CHAPTER XIII.

The Archbishop preaches in his cathedral church, and of the solidity and fruit of his sermons 65

CHAPTER XIV.

The Archbishop commences his visitation in the middle of winter—he encourages his followers by the example of a little shepherd 69

CHAPTER XV.

Of the zeal, prudence, and charity of the Archbishop in his visitation 72

CHAPTER XVI.

The Archbishop labours to instruct himself the priests and people of his diocese 79

CHAPTER XVII.

Of his extreme care in the selection of those who aspired to Holy Orders, and his desire that all his priests should be fully occupied 81

CHAPTER XVIII.

The Archbishop's friends, seeing him overwhelmed with work, implore him to appoint a coadjutor, which he refuses to do 84

CHAPTER XIX.

Of the great charity of the Archbishop towards the poor, the sick, and all who needed his help 87

CHAPTER XX.

Father Louis of Grenada proposes to the Archbishop greater magnificence in his palace—the Archbishop justifies his conduct by the canons of the Church, and Grenada is compelled in the end to agree with him 92

BOOK II.

CHAPTER I.

	PAGE
Origin and progress of Luther's heresy—commencement and continuation of the Council of Trent, until the pontificate of Pius IV.	103

CHAPTER II.

Bull of Pius IV. for the re-assembling of the Council of Trent—Dom Bartholomew prepares to obey the summons—the charity required of bishops towards the Universal Church ... 111

CHAPTER III.

The Archbishop starts for Trent—he lodges on his way at different monasteries of his Order, where he tries to pass as a simple religious—he is, however, discovered on several occasions 115

CHAPTER IV.

Description of the town of Trent—the Archbishop's agreeable reception by the Cardinal Legates—his holy and useful occupations—he cuts off all superfluous visits 120

CHAPTER V.

The Archbishop writes from Trent to his vicar-general—he describes his reception—he bears an unconscious witness to his own charity towards the poor, by describing that of the Bishop of Modena ... 124

CHAPTER VI.

The Archbishop's primacy is contested—the Pope desires him to precede the other Archbishops, and then orders that all should rank according to the date of their promotion 127

CHAPTER VII.

In what manner the Council of Trent was opened under Pius IV. ... 130

CHAPTER VIII.

The Archbishop induces the fathers in council to treat first the question of the reform of the clergy, beginning by the Cardinals—his generosity is revered by every one .. 132

CHAPTER IX.

The Cardinal of Lorraine arrives at Trent with the French Bishops—he relates the evils and sacrileges caused by heresy in France—letter from the Archbishop on this subject.. 138

CHAPTER X.

The Archbishop proposes that the council should treat the question of residence, and induces Father Peter of Soto to write his feelings on the subject to the Pope before his death 142

CHAPTER XI.

The holy prelate persuades the Council to re-consider the question of residence—the decree on this matter—the character of D. Guerero, Archbishop of Grenada .. 144

CHAPTER XII.

The Archbishop exhorts the Fathers of the Council to warn kings of the importance of the choice of bishops—the decree of the Council on the subject 154

CHAPTER XIII.

The feelings of the Archbishop, and the decree in council regarding the modesty and exemplary life required in bishops 157

CHAPTER XIV.

Of the wise conduct and the reputation of the Archbishop among all the prelates—his feelings, and those of the Council, on episcopal generosity 163

CHAPTER XV.

Decree of the Council of Trent, whereby all the ancient canons are renewed touching the life and morals of the clergy 168

CHAPTER XVI.

The Archbishop speaks strongly in the Council on the abuses current in the matter of Church patronage—ordinance of the Pope, and conduct of St. Charles on the subject .. 168

CHAPTER XVII.

Letter from the Archbishop to his Vicar-General, in which is shown his love for religious poverty, and the care he took of the young clergy whom he had brought up, and of the virgins consecrated to God 172

CHAPTER XVIII.

The Archbishop leaves Trent to go to Rome with the Cardinal of Lorraine—how he behaved during his journey .. 175

CHAPTER XIX.

The arrival of the prelate at Rome—The Portuguese ambassador pays him great honour, and obtains from the Pope an order that he should live in his palace .. 178

CHAPTER XX.

The holy prelate has an audience of the Pope and of St. Charles, and is most favourably received by both .. 181

CHAPTER XXI.

The Cardinals receive the Archbishop with great honour—he shows them his horror of luxury, and speaks his mind plainly to the Pope as to the magnificence of his buildings 184

CHAPTER XXII.

The Archbishop, having seen with great regret that the bishops in Rome remained standing and bare-headed, while the Cardinals were seated, persuades the Pope to change this custom 189

CHAPTER XXIII.

St. Charles consults our prelate on the wish he had to retire into a monastery—the Archbishop dissuades him, but he advises him to repair to his diocese as soon as the affairs of the Church will allow him 194

CHAPTER XXIV.

Of the holy prelate's aversion for human and secular things —of the influence he had with the Pope, and the liberty with which he spoke to him 200

CHAPTER XXV.

The Archbishop implores the Pope with great earnestness to consent that he should resign his Archbishopric—the Pope refuses him—the conversation between St. Charles and the Archbishop on this subject 203

CHAPTER XXVI.

The holy prelate leaves Rome, and returns to Trent—he finds that certain points had been altered in what had been resolved upon by the Council, and has them reinstated as before 208

CHAPTER XXVII.

The winding up of the Council of Trent—declaration made by the Cardinal of Lorraine in the name of all the bishops of the Gallican Church—the holy prelate takes leave of the cardinal and the French bishops 212

BOOK III.

CHAPTER I.

The Archbishop, returning to his diocese from Trent, learns a curious particular regarding the Council—he goes to pay his respects to Philip II., by whom he is very well received 215

CHAPTER II.

The Archbishop, hearing that great preparations were being made for his arrival at Braga, cheats them all by suddenly appearing in his cathedral church—the joy of the people at his return 218

CHAPTER III.

The Archbishop founds his seminary, according to one of the ordinances passed by the Council 220

CHAPTER IV.

The chapter claiming the right of visitation in the town, the Archbishop declares to his council that he is resolved to dispute this right, and visit himself 223

CHAPTER V.

The Archbishop commences his visitation of the town despite the remonstrances of the chapter—letter of St. Charles on the subject—conclusion of the affair 227

CHAPTER VI.

The Archbishop visits the churches of the military Knights Commanders—with what firmness he represses the insolence of Commander Poyarez, who was converted by hearing his Mass 234

CONTENTS.

CHAPTER VII.

The Archbishop goes into the wildest corner of his diocese—how his suite escape a great danger—the manner in which he provided pastors for these abandoned peasants .. 241

CHAPTER VIII.

The extraordinary conversions of the Archbishop, and with what force and authority he repressed vice 246

CHAPTER IX.

On the Archbishop's treatment of ecclesiastics who led irregular lives, and their conversion 250

CHAPTER X.

Of the great charity of the Archbishop during the famine, and the way he exhorted the rich to give alms and help the poor 256

CHAPTER XI.

A priest from Braga accuses the Archbishop to the Pope—the secret animosity felt by many at his conduct—the calumniator, being condemned, implores forgiveness of the prelate 260

CHAPTER XII.

With what moderation the Archbishop bore the injuries which passionate persons said or did publicly against him 264

CHAPTER XIII.

The holy prelate returns to Braga during the plague, in spite of the entreaties of every one that he should not expose himself to the danger of infection—with what charity and devotion he cares for the dying and the dead—the Cardinal of Portugal and the King implore him to leave the scene of danger—he excuses himself by a letter .. 268

CHAPTER XIV.

The Archbishop excommunicates the president of the court of assizes, who usurped the rights of the Church—he justifies this action on his part in a letter to the king, and finally obtains all that he wishes 277

CHAPTER XV.

Dom Sebastian, King of Portugal, undertakes a crusade in Africa against the Moors—the Archbishop, and all his counsellors, oppose and dread this expedition 285

CHAPTER XVI.

Dom Sebastian, in spite of the advice of his officers, offers battle to the King of Morocco—the Archbishop offers up continual prayers for him throughout his diocese—his defeat and death—admirable piety of Thomas of Jesus, of the Augustinian Order, taken prisoner in this battle .. 290

CHAPTER XVII.

Dom Henry, Cardinal, reigns in Portugal after Dom Sebastian—his affection for our holy prelate—his conduct and death—all the kingdom of Portugal being in confusion, the Archbishop finds himself obliged to retire for a time from Braga 299

CHAPTER XVIII.

Philip II. takes possession of the kingdom of Portugal, and selects the Archbishop of Braga to receive his oaths .. 302

CHAPTER XIX.

The Archbishop obtains leave from Gregory XIII. to resign his Archbishopric, and retire to Viano 305

CHAPTER XX.

Occupations of Dom Bartholomew after his retreat in the monastery—his love of prayer and meditation on holy Scripture—his extreme charity towards the poor .. 310

CHAPTER XXI.

The holy prelate falls ill of a malady which ends in his death—his extreme patience in suffering—Dom Augustine, his successor in the Archbishopric of Braga, comes to visit him ... 314

CHAPTER XXII.

Happy death of Dom Bartholomew—the town of Braga pleads for his body—the inhabitants of Viano take up arms to keep it—he is finally buried in the monastery ... 317

CHAPTER XXIII.

Of the miracles wrought by the servant of God during his life and after his death ... 320

CHAPTER XXIV.

How the body of the venerable prelate was taken up nineteen years after his death, and put in a rich tomb ... 324

BOOK IV.

CHAPTER I.

The intention of this book is to pourtray the feelings of Dom Bartholomew by his own words, and to make reflections on his life—that the instructions it contains will be useful to all the faithful ... 327

CHAPTER II.

Dom Bartholomew proposes St. Gregory's pastoral as a rule for all prelates—the qualities which that great Pope required for the episcopate are specially found in our holy Archbishop ... 329

CHAPTER III.

That the repugnance felt by Dom Bartholomew to his election as bishop, arising from his extreme humility, was exactly in accordance with the rules laid down by St. Gregory ... 333

CHAPTER IV.

Dom Bartholomew shows, by the teaching of the fathers, how pastors should devote themselves to prayer and to meditation on holy things—that this advice is useful to all the faithful, and how they are to practise it 338

CHAPTER V.

Of the obligation laid upon pastors to instruct their people, and preach to them the word of God 347

CHAPTER VI.

How Dom Bartholomew laboured to show the necessity of bishops residing in their dioceses—that his opinions were in exact conformity with those of St. Charles 353

CHAPTER VII.

How pastors should set a good example by the regulation of their household and servants—opinions of Dom Bartholomew as to the visitation of bishops.. 355

CHAPTER VIII.

The holy prelate proves how pastors should follow the rules of Jesus Christ, and of the apostles and saints, without listening to the judgments or lax spirit of the age .. 360

CHAPTER IX.

Of the zeal which pastors should show in opposing the scandals and disorders of the age, and in labouring for the conversion of sinners 366

CHAPTER X.

Dom Bartholomew shows, by the example of St. Gregory, with what firmness bishops should defend the Church, and maintain truth and justice 369

CHAPTER XI.

Of the zeal which bishops should have in admitting to Holy Orders, and to benefices in the Church, those only who were worthy of serving her 373

CHAPTER XII.

That a bishop should conduct himself in a spirit of gentleness, without using his authority in an imperious manner—of the tenderness and charity shown by Dom Bartholomew to win souls 377

CHAPTER XIII.

Of the prudence necessary to a bishop—that according to St. Gregory it should be shown principally in not anticipating judgment, and by using great reserve in ecclesiastical decisions 384

CHAPTER XIV.

How pastors should love and help the poor, and how Dom Bartholomew excelled in that virtue 390

CHAPTER XV.

With what care Dom Bartholomew exhorted his people to give alms, following in this matter the spirit of the Fathers of the Church 395

First Point.—Of the strict obligation under which all Christians lie to give alms 396

Second Point.—that charity should only be given out of property legitimately acquired 399

Third Point.—That in giving alms we should strive to atone for and free ourselves from sin 401

Fourth Point.—That we should give liberally, and in proportion to our wealth 403

Fifth Point.—That we must give with discretion, according to the diversity of times, seasons, and persons .. 407

SIXTH POINT.—That we must avoid vanity in giving alms, and accompany them with humility 410
SEVENTH POINT.—That we should give with joy, and have the utmost tenderness and compassion towards the poor .. 414

CHAPTER XVI.

With what care bishops should abstain from luxury, and employ conscientiously the property of the Church—of how this rule should be applied to their relations .. 418
Letter of Pope Clement IV. to one of his nearest relations .. 425

CHAPTER XVII.

Of the patience pastors should show in the persecutions and troubles of this life—what the virtue of the Archbishop was on this point 426

CHAPTER XVIII.

What ought to be the humility of bishops, and what was that of the holy prelate 434

CHAPTER XIX.

Of the resignation of the holy prelate—six reasons why a bishop may leave his bishopric 442

CHAPTER XX.

That the humility of the Archbishop was the real cause of his resignation—example of several saints who have done the same—wisdom of Philip II. in his choice of bishops 450

CHAPTER XXI.

Of the mistrust, scruples, and anxieties, which frequently prevent pious souls from making progress in the ways of God 462

CHAPTER XXII.

That peace and joy should find themselves in the truly faithful—that human sadness and disquiet come from the temptations of the devil, and of the bad effects they create ... 467

CHAPTER XXIII.

What an amount of learning Dom Bartholomew possessed—his affection for Holy Scripture, and for the doctrine of the Fathers, and for a spiritual comprehension of the Psalms ... 478

CHAPTER XXIV.

How the holy Archbishop loved prayer—how he practised and recommended it to others ... 482

CHAPTER XXV.

That a recognition of God's benefits is necessary to an advance in piety—what the virtue of the Archbishop was on that point ... 489

CHAPTER XXVI.

On the special devotion of the holy prelate towards the Passion of our Lord—of the labours and austerity of his life ... 494

CHAPTER XXVII.

Of the profound respect of the holy prelate for the Sacrifice of the Mass—of the special graces he received during its celebration—how he honoured the Virgin and the Saints ... 501

CHAPTER XXVIII.

The great wish our holy Archbishop had for death—of his extraordinary ardour to receive the holy Viaticum—of his patience in his illnesses ... 509

CHAPTER XXIX.

What were Dom Bartholomew's merits as a monk—a memorandum written by him when dragged from his monastery to be made a bishop—his feelings on the principal points of a religious life 514

CHAPTER XXX.

Parallel of Dom Bartholomew with St. Charles Borromeo—
—Conclusion of this Biography 522

Preface to the French Translation,

WHICH WAS PUBLISHED AT PARIS, IN 1663.

We do not think it is necessary to represent here what was the life of Dom Bartholomew of the Martyrs. It is enough to say that since his happy death he has been honoured by many miracles; that his memory is held in veneration throughout Spain and Portugal, and in the French provinces adjoining. Therefore, several Bishops eminent for their learning and piety, and for the indefatigable vigilance with which they have devoted themselves to the salvation of the souls whom God has confided to them, and having an intimate knowledge of his actions and virtues, have earnestly desired that the life of so holy a man should be written, and become as widely known in the Church of France as in his own country. They admired the rare qualities which were combined in his person; and the love they have for the Church made them ardently wish that a prelate who has so guided and enlightened his diocese during his life, should become by his example the model of bishops in that great kingdom. For although saints are born each in his or her particular country, and are attached to a special church or diocese, they are nevertheless destined by God for the good of the whole earth, and participate in this way in the glory of the Catholic Church which is their mother; and so the odour of their virtues communicates itself to all the world.

and is spread over all places, and to the end of time. If this blessed archbishop has not been, till now, well known in France, he has been renowned in other Christian kingdoms, and his life has been written by five different authors.

The first was Father Louis of Grenada, of the same Order of St. Dominic, a man noted for his eminent virtue, and for his pious writings. He was Provincial when Dom Bartholomew was Prior of one of the houses of his Order; and it was he who compelled him, in spite of his resistance, to accept the Archbishopric of Braga. As he was linked in the closest friendship with Dom Bartholomew, and that he knew him intimately, both from his own intercourse with him, and from those who afterwards lived with him, he began, even during the Archbishop's life-time, to write an abridged account of his virtues, and of the principal events of his life. He could not finish it, however; for he did not live as long as Dom Bartholomew, having died in 1588, at the age of 84, while the holy prelate did not close his mortal career till two years later, namely, in 1590.

After the death of Grenada, F. Louis of Cacegas, also a Religious of St. Dominic, undertook to continue the biography of Dom Bartholomew. He searched carefully for every detail which should serve to illustrate his actions and virtues. But he, again, died before his labours were completed.

The fathers of the Order, determining to finish what these two eminent men had begun, chose for the purpose Father Louis of Souza. This father was held in great reputation for his eminent qualities, and God had called him to enter the Order of St. Dominic in so marvellous a manner, that we will give an account of it in a few words.

In 1578, the King of Portugal, Dom Sebastian, having been defeated and killed in Africa by the Moors, and a great number of the Portuguese nobility having been either killed or taken prisoners in the same battle, it happened that one who was well known at court was reported as dead, and the news was brought to his wife. She wrote at once, and sent emissaries empowered to treat with the Moors for the ransom of the prisoners, hoping that her husband would, after all, be discovered among the latter. But the messengers returned, and assured her that every possible inquiry had been made; but that there was no doubt that her husband had been killed in the fight. Several years after, Souza, who was a man of high rank, sought out this lady, whom he thought, and as she herself believed, was a widow, and made her an offer of marriage. She was at first very much opposed to the idea, and was a long time before she could make up her mind. At last, more than ten years having elapsed since the supposed death of her husband, and seeing that all her relations strongly urged Souza's suit upon her, from his high birth and great merits, she yielded and married him. Some years after, the first husband of that lady, who had not been killed as was supposed, but had been made a slave by the Moors, accidentally found a merchant who had been ransomed and was returning to Portugal. He implored him to find his wife, and let her know the pitiable situation in which he was placed. This merchant lost no time, on his return to Portugal, in finding out the lady, and assured her that he had discovered her husband among the Moors, and that he had implored her to leave no stone unturned to facilitate his deliverance. The poor lady was greatly surprised at this intelligence, and doubted whether she ought to attach any credence to the stranger's words, seeing they were entirely contrary to the repeated assurances she had received of the death of one whom he maintained was still living. Souza, who was a man of great wisdom, and one who feared God, seeing his wife in such great distress and agitation, told her that he knew a way to relieve her from this terrible uncertainty. So he took the merchant up into a gallery in their house, where there were a number of portraits, and among them that of the poor nobleman who was supposed to be dead, and told the stranger that if he knew him so well, he begged him to point out to him which was the portrait of that lady's husband. At first the merchant excused himself from the proposed test, saying that so many years had elapsed, and the hardships he had suffered as a slave must have so altered him that in all probability he would be unrecognisable. Nevertheless he came into the gallery, and directly pointed out among the pictures the portrait of the gentleman in question. . Souza was at once convinced of the truth of his statement, and, returning to his wife, told her that he had made up his mind to leave her and the world, and enter the Order of St. Dominic. Fortunately they had no children. She, on her side, resolved to retire into a nunnery of strict observance in Lisbon, with the determination to stop there always if her husband would allow her to do so. At the same time she laboured with all her might to deliver her husband from his captivity, in which she eventually succeeded.

Souza, having become a Dominican, was soon noted in the Order for his extraordinary fervour and exemplary piety. It is reported of him that he so loved solitude, that, while living at the Convent of Benefico—of which Dom Bartholomew was Prior when he was made Archbishop—he never stirred out of it except to get information on certain points which he thought necessary for the perfection of his biography. For he was not contented with the memoirs of Grenada and Cacegas, but went himself into all the towns and villages of the diocese, to verify all the most important events in his life by the testimony of eye-witnesses. He thus entered into conversation with many persons of undoubted veracity and position as to the conduct and miracles of the holy prelate; some of whom had accompanied him in his visitations, while others had lived a long time with him. After these exact details had been obtained, he began this life in Portuguese, in "*a grave, noble, and elegant style,*" as other authors remark, and published it in 1619, under the name of Cacegas, who was its beginner, and of his own likewise, while those who had been eye-witnesses of what he related, were still alive.

The fourth author of a Life of this holy prelate is Dom Rodriguez de Cunha, Archbishop of Lisbon, who, in his history of the Archbishops of Braga, gives an abridged account of the virtues and principal actions of Dom Bartholomew. He confirms the miracles wrought by him during his life and after his death; and amidst the many eulogiums passed upon him, he calls him: "*the father of the poor, and an illustrious example to all prelates.*"

The fifth person who wrote his life, was Louis de Mougnoz, licentiate in theology, who gives us, in six volumes, the history of Souza, and says he had never read anything more edifying and pious than this biography. But his principal object was to translate it from Portuguese into Castillan, so that the example of such rare sanctity should be known and revered throughout Spain.

We have, in the following pages, therefore, drawn our materials from all these five sources, while attaching special value to the words of Father Louis of Grenada, whose great reputation entitles him to the first place. But as it is to the Order of St. Dominic that we are indebted for the details we have tried to render in our own language, so it is to these Fathers that all the fruit of this holy life will be due, should God deign to give it His benediction. The Church owes a double obligation to this Order: first, for having given her so holy a bishop, and then for having made his memory immortal by writing the history of his life. And although Dom Bartholomew was indeed the glory of the disciples of St. Dominic, he was not the only one; for on the day of the feast of their holy founder, when Dom Bartholomew, at the Council of Trent, officiated pontifically, there were present of the same Order, six archbishops, seventeen bishops, and twenty-eight doctors, besides the Father General of the Order, some of whom were the most eminent theologians at the Council. Rarely can a more authentic life be written than this one, compiled, as it was, by five authors, who were all, save one, personally acquainted with him, and eye-witnesses to much that they relate. But all that has reference to the Council of Trent deserves special credence, because it has been taken from a journal written at the time, and on the spot, in Latin, by the holy prelate himself, in which he has marked all the most important events which took place during the Council. This journal begins with these words: "*Concilium apertum est*, 18 *die Januarii anno* 1562."

In quoting his words we have endeavoured to keep to their exact substance, without any change but that required by the difference of language. But remembering what was said at the Council of Trent, "*that his speeches were vigorous and full of common sense*," we have been sometimes obliged to abridge portions of phrases evidently added by his biographers, and which are not conformable to his spirit.

The events of his life are related in the first three volumes of this biography. But we have thought it advisable to add a fourth volume, filled with meditations on his special virtues, and to show what was his mind on the duties of pastors, and of all Christians, by giving copious extracts from his own writings, which hitherto has never been done. We hope that those who have really studied this fourth book, and will thus have learnt from this holy prelate what ought to be the true spirit of Christianity, either in bishops or in any other condition of life, will read with another eye, and with fresh interest, the three first books which represent his actions and daily life. For they will then see how conformable these actions were to the maxims of the greatest saints; and that what he did is only a living picture of what he taught. This is one of the principal advantages in the lives of the Saints; that one can read them over and over again with pleasure, as the second reading is generally more useful than the first. Profane and frivolous stories often disgust one; for having nothing real or solid about them, they cease to please when they do not strike one by their novelty; and the same curiosity which tempts one to read them, makes one indifferent to or despise them when one knows them. But the lives of those persons who have been led by the Spirit of God have this advantage, that they mingle usefulness with a holy pleasure, and that they nourish the heart without wearying the spirit, because one finds in them at the same time amusing incidents, touching examples, and edifiying instructions.

This is enough to give our readers some idea of the following biography. We feel ourselves, however, bound to own that once or twice we have called Dom Bartholomew not only a holy man, and a holy prelate, but a *Saint*. In so doing we had no intention of placing him in that category, knowing well that it rests with the Sovereign Pontiff alone, as the Vicar of Jesus Christ, to declare good men "Saints" when he judges it advisable for the faithful, and when their sanctity has been proved by miracles. Thus, when we have used the term, we have only wished to do so in conformity with the ordinance of Pope Urban VIII., so that in calling him a "saintly" bishop, we mean it in the sense in which, during his lifetime, all the people declared "*that he was a Saint*," that is, that his life was pure and perfect, and superior to that of the generality of men.

In this way one of the authors of his life remarks, that Dom Augustine de Castro, the second successor of Dom Bartholomew in the archbishopric of Braga, who is looked upon as a prelate of great and distinguished merit, and who assisted Dom Bartholomew on his deathbed, said of him soon after to Father Louis of Cacegas: *" That he had such a veneration for Dom Bartholomew of the Martyrs, his predecessor, that he invoked him in his prayers with the same confidence as he did St. Fructuosus, and the other holy Bishops who had governed before him the See of Braga: but that, nevertheless, he only honoured him privately in this way, knowing that we can only offer public worship to those who have been canonized and placed in the rank of the Saints by the authority of the Holy See."*

THE LIFE

OF

Dom Bartholomew

Of the Martyrs,

A RELIGIOUS OF THE ORDER OF ST. DOMINIC, ARCHBISHOP OF
BRAGA, IN PORTUGAL.

FIRST BOOK.

The words of Jesus Christ, in which He promises to remain for ever in His Church, and that all the powers of hell shall not prevail against it, are not merely verified by the secret aid imparted by Him continually to His faithful people; but by His raising up, from time to time, prelates eminent for their ability and piety, to combat the errors which strike at faith, as well as the laxity which corrupts discipline. It was with this design that He brought into the world, in the sixteenth century, the blessed archbishop whose life, by the grace of God, we have undertaken to write. He was born at a time when the Church sorely needed such a champion; for it was besieged on the one hand by a deluge of heresies, and on the other by the disorders and immorality which had crept even into the lives of those consecrated to the altar. God gave him truly Christian parents, whose chief care was to maintain him in his baptismal purity; and in order that no worldly contact should stain his soul, they persuaded him very early in life to enter the Order of St. Dominic, which he did with wonderful fervour, and where, having daily increased in every Christian grace and virtue, he remained until dragged away, in spite of his resistance, to fill the most important episcopal throne in Spain. But He who thus designed to promote him did not destine him to be merely the light of one particular diocese. He wished him to shine in the face of the Universal Church, so that his zeal and piety should serve as a model to all future bishops. For this reason he was summoned to the Œcumenical Council of Trent, under the pontificate of Pius IV., where he showed such an amount of knowledge, wisdom, and firmness, that he became an object of esteem and veneration to all the cardinals and bishops there present, beloved by the Sovereign Pontiff, and, which is still more remarkable, honoured by the great St. Charles Borromeo himself, who treated him with special confidence and affection.

May the same Holy Spirit, which animated this saintly prelate, deign to assist us in the work we have now set before us, to endeavour to give a faithful record of his actions and virtues. We believe that such a life may be of great advantage to all the faithful.

Those who are engaged in the world, and in the care of their families, will see in his education how children should be brought up, for God alone, with a view to a final consecration to His service. Those who are called to the Religious Life will here find a perfect model of holy exercises. Kings and queens may learn, by the Christian manner in which a great and holy princess raised this saintly man to the episcopal throne, what zeal and discretion they should exercise in the choice of those on whom they confer ecclesiastical dignities. And all those who are called upon to serve the Church in the guidance of souls, and especially bishops, will see in this history what is expected of those who are charged with such important functions, and what amount of piety and vigilance is required of them, while meditating on the life of a prelate who resembled one of the saints in the earlier ages of the Church; for he was always absorbed in the glory of God and the good of his people; indefatigable in his labours; inflexible in his zeal for discipline and justice; intrepid in danger, braving the plague and even death itself for his flock; humble and tender towards the poor; firm though courteous towards the rich; inflexible towards the great; severe only towards the unjust; and at the same time so wise and so temperate in word and deed that he acquired the love and esteem of men of every class and condition of life.

CHAPTER I.

THE BIRTH OF BARTHOLOMEW.—WHY HE TOOK THE SURNAME OF "THE MARTYRS."—OF THE VIRTUE AND CHARITY OF HIS PARENTS.

Bartholomew of the Martyrs was born in the month of May, 1514, in the town of Lisbon, the capital of Portugal. Pope Leo X. was then at the head of the Church. The kingdom of Portugal was governed by Dom Emmanuel I., who was called "The Happy." We may add that it was not the least of his blessings that so holy a man should be born during his reign. His father's name was Dominic Fernandez; his mother's, Maria Correa. They were both natives of that suburb of Lisbon called Verdella, and of an old and respectable family. They had not, it is true, much of this world's goods; but they were rich in piety and good works, and filled with the love and fear of God. Amongst the many qualities which endeared them to God and man, one was remarkable above all others, and that was their devotion to the poor and their generosity in relieving their wants. They continually bore in mind the advice of Tobias to his son: *"Give alms of thy substance, and turn not away thy face from any poor person; for so it shall come to pass that the face of the Lord shall not be turned away from thee. According to thy ability be merciful. If thou have much, give abundantly; if thou have little, take care even so to bestow willingly a little."* In truth, this virtue may be looked upon as the most essential to people who are engaged in the world and in the married state; and hence arose that admirable saying of a holy doctor of the Church to the father of a family: "Have you two children? Take our Lord Jesus Christ, in the person of one of His poor, as a third; and by thus making yourself the father of one of His members He will look upon your children as His own." God, who deigns to reveal Himself specially to simple souls, had imprinted this deep love of the poor in the hearts of Bartholomew's father and mother; and their reward, even in this life, was their son, who may be called the embodiment of divine charity.

He received baptism and the name of Bartholomew in the Church of our Lady of Martyrs, which was the parish church of his parents. But later on, when he dropped his family name to enter into Religion, he took the title of this little Church of the Martyrs, which he loved to the end of his life; so that it will not be irrelevant here to give a short account of the origin of the name of this church, and the memorable events concerning it.

In the year 1147, Dom Alphonsus Henry, King of Portugal, having re-conquered the greater portion of his dominions from the Moors, resolved to rescue, likewise, his capital city of Lisbon, or perish in the attempt. He assembled his army and soon became master of all the neighbouring country. But not being strong enough to lay siege to the town, our Lord facilitated his enterprize in an unexpected manner. For, one morning, the whole bay appeared covered with ships, and the king discovered that these vessels contained an army of chosen men, under the command of William, Prince of Anjou, who were on their way to the conquest of the Holy Land. King Henry felt that these were allies, sent specially to him from heaven, and despatched at once messengers to Prince William to ask his assistance. He represented to him that as he and his noble army were about to wage a distant war on the infidels, it was meet and right that they should begin with those who were nearer at hand. That the taking of Lisbon would be easy if besieged both by sea and land; and that they would arrive with still greater renown in Syria if they could assert that they had already triumphed over the infidels in Europe. It was not difficult to persuade this brave and generous prince to enter into his reasoning; so that immediately casting anchor in the Tagus, he landed his whole force and laid siege to the town.

This joint operation was begun in the month of May of that same year, and was protracted till October, the despair of the besieged adding to their courage. A great number fell on both sides, but especially on that of the besiegers, they being less protected than the infidels, who fought behind their walls. Their brethren in arms styled them "martyrs," and revered them as such, so that it was resolved to erect two little chapels, one in each camp, which should be consecrated to their memory. At last, after five months siege, the city was taken on the 25th of October. The king instantly set to work and built the Church of St. Vincent; while Prince William and his army erected that called "Our Lady of Martyrs," to serve as a perpetual memorial of those good and brave men who had lost their lives in fighting against the infidels.

This is the identical church of which Bartholomew took the name, and which his eminent virtue has rendered still more celebrated.

The child was evidently destined from his birth to be something remarkable. He had an excellent natural disposition, being gentle, obedient, and sweet tempered. From a boy he showed the greatest love of purity. His mother took him early to church and impressed upon him all the respect due to sacred places. Like St. Basil, he knew but of two roads, one to the church and another to the schools, save when his mother sent him to carry alms or provisions secretly to the sick and suffering, and especially to those of a higher station of life, who would sooner die than ask an alms. His mother had a special devotion to such persons, and would often go without necessaries herself in order to relieve them. In this way was the child formed by his pious mother to works of charity, unselfishness, and thoughtfulness for others. She preached to him not by words but by her actions, and accustomed him to do good by seeing it done around him. God, who foresees all things, had chosen for him parents who were worthy of the precious deposit entrusted to them. And no adverse influence arose to mar an education and training which were so eminently Christian.

CHAPTER II.

BARTHOLOMEW DETERMINES TO RENOUNCE THE WORLD AND BECOME A RELIGIOUS;—HE ENTERS THE ORDER OF ST. DOMINIC, AND BECOMES THE MODEL OF THE NOVICIATE.

The childhood and youth of Bartholomew were passed in this manner without any striking events; but as he daily grew in grace and virtue, so the Holy Spirit put into his mind holy inspirations and a desire to consecrate himself solely to the glory of God. He represented to himself continually the emptiness of everything on earth, and the immutability of the promises of God, till he was ready to exclaim with St. Bernard: "How do the pleasures of this world vanish like shadows! How full of misery is this life! How quickly does death surprise us, when our eternal destiny will be fixed for happiness or misery!"

God made him understand, at the same time, what great happiness could be found in the religious life, and what security he would there enjoy for the fulfilment of his holy desires. This soul, which had always preserved its baptismal innocence, at once obeyed the voice of heaven, and yielded without difficulty to the earliest inspirations of divine grace.

The Order of St. Dominic was then, as it has ever been, one of the most fervent in the Church, and was held in high reputation, especially in Spain. Father Louis of Grenada was one of the greatest preachers of that day, and edified the whole world by his writings and piety.

Bartholomew, who had often heard him preach, felt himself strongly attracted to that Order, and was only deterred by his humility, which made him fear that he was unworthy to join it. But at last he summoned courage to open his heart to his parents, trusting that their piety would prevent their throwing any difficulties in the way, if they were once convinced of the reality of his vocation. His mother, who loved him tenderly for his many good and amiable qualities, was at first much surprised and startled at the idea. But finding that he had really no other end in view than the glory of God and the good of souls, and that he only proposed leaving them because he preferred heaven to earth, both his parents consented, looking upon his decision as a reward for the care with which they had nourished pious feelings in his heart from a child. They had always looked upon him as a direct gift from God, and so could not refuse to give back to Him what they had received. Unlike those fathers and mothers who force their children into the secular careers they have chosen for them, Bartholomew's parents left him free to follow the inspirations of God's grace, and were thus examples to those who think of nothing but the worldly interests of their children; who drag from the service of the altar those whom God has chosen, and make them embrace states of life for which they have no taste or disposition. Hence arise dissensions in families, maledictions on parents, and often signal misfortunes to the children themselves, who may well say, according to the words of St. Cyprian, "*Parentes sensimus parricidas.*"

Bartholomew, more and more strengthened in his resolution by his parents' kindness, often went to the Dominican monastery to talk to the fathers, and one day, on the Feast of St. Martin, 1528, he felt himself so moved by the strong desire he had to leave the world, that he went straight to the prior of this house and opened his whole heart to him.

The prior's name was Father George Vogado, a doctor of theology, and for many years preacher and confessor to the king, Dom Emmanuel. He was a man of great ability and experience in the guidance of souls. From the first moment that he saw Bartholomew he felt that he was one touched by the Spirit of God; but wishing, as a wise director, to test him still further, he represented to him the austerity of the rule, the perpetual fasts and watchings, the continual silence, the excessive poverty, the hair shirts and disciplines, in addition to the necessity of arduous study to fit him for the work of preaching. "If, therefore," he added, "these severities are trying to the most robust natures among us, what will it be to you, who, in addition to your youth, seem to be of a delicate constitution?"

But the representation of all he would have to suffer seemed only to inflame Bartholomew's ardour still more; while his sole fear was that his delicate appearance would prevent his being accepted. Summoning up courage, he therefore replied: "My Father, I wish to enter Religion to fly from the pleasures of a world which I hate, and to embrace all the pains and sufferings, which I desire with my whole heart, and which I feel to be necessary for my salvation. No human obstacle can daunt me, because I expect to conquer all that is human by divine strength, placing all my confidence in Him Who has invited me to carry His cross. I do not therefore dread the labours and sufferings that you have represented to me, because the body is never weak when the will is strong; and with the grace of God, we can conquer all things."

The prior, not being only satisfied, but edified, by this answer, sent for the master of novices and some other fathers, who examined him rigorously as to his habits and way of life; but all were equally delighted with his understanding and answers. Several of the Religious, who had known him in the world, bore witness likewise to his excellent character, and the Christian way in which he had been brought up; so that the prior, after having collected the votes of the community, gave him the habit that very day after compline, as he considered that such extraordinarily fervent dispositions deserved a dispensation from the ordinary rules.

No sooner had he entered the noviciate than he gave sensible proofs of how completely his call was from God. He looked upon the world as a prison, from which he had escaped, and his cell as a paradise. He was continually marvelling at the mercy of God, which had called him to the Religious state, and his tranquil happiness showed itself in his face, and in all his actions. He was modest in appearance, circumspect in his words, punctual and exact in the performance of all duties, whether great or small, and particularly in observing the hours of Divine Office, leaving all other employments with a holy haste, that he might be the first in singing the praises of God.

His love of silence was extraordinary: he avoided all but necessary intercourse with men, so as to commune with God more frequently in his own heart. He obeyed his superiors with his whole will, respecting all equally, as he never attached himself to persons, but to God, Whom he considered he was listening to in the persons of his superiors. His fervour in all holy exercises was continually renewed by his meditations on the infinite love of our Lord Jesus Christ, and he entered Religion with the hearty desire to love Him as He had done, and to follow Him in His humility and His labours for souls.

Possessed with these ideas, he loved religious poverty as the rich love their riches; and would always choose the lowest and most menial offices in the house. He felt as if to himself especially were these words of the Evangelist addressed: "*When thou art invited, go, sit down in the lowest place.*" For he really believed that the lowest place should always be his, and so would treat as his superiors the novices who had entered long after him, ever considering himself the last in the house. His tenderness for his brethren was mingled with great respect; and as he loved them all in God, so was he much loved by them. He lived as a stranger in the monastery, except as far as his own office was concerned, neither meddling with anything else, nor asking questions, nor judging of any matter, but trying to die so completely to his own will as to live alone for the will of God. His courage in, and love for, mortifications were as great in his noviciate as during his whole life, uniting all his sufferings to those of our Lord Jesus Christ, and hiding himself, as it were, in His sacred wounds as in a place of safety. If ever he fell into some venial fault, he listened to reproof with such sweetness and gentleness, that though grieved at having in the smallest degree offended God, he was neither discouraged nor troubled; and so his little falls, instead of diminishing his perfection, only served to render him more humble, more firm, and more vigilant. His continual mistrust of himself, and the perfect confidence he had in God, whom he considered as his sole strength, sustained him in all his labours, and made him taste of that peace which passeth all understanding, and of that interior joy which Jesus Christ has promised to the meek and humble of heart.

At last, the year of his noviciate being at an end, God would not allow him to be deprived any longer of that for which he had so ardently longed. On the 20th November, 1529, he made his Profession in the hands of Father George Vogado, who had given him the habit. He was then only fifteen years of age and seven months; for the law had not then come into force, which was wisely decreed by the Council of Trent, that no Religious should be allowed to make his Profession till he had completed his sixteenth year. He chose the name, in Religion, of "Bartholomew of the Martyrs," in remembrance of the little church of which we have spoken, where he had first been made a child of God in holy baptism.

CHAPTER III.

BARTHOLOMEW'S WORK AFTER HIS PROFESSION.—THE OPINIONS OF LOUIS OF GRENADA AS TO THE STUDIES OF YOUNG RELIGIOUS.—BARTHOLOMEW IS CHOSEN AS PRECEPTOR OF THE SON OF THE INFANTA.—HIS LOVE OF SOLITUDE.

Soon after Bartholomew's profession, a course of philosophy was given in the Dominican convent at Lisbon, which he was desired to follow. But they were careful not to let pagan sciences injure his natural piety; and for fear lest the study of letters and human reasonings should absorb him too much, he was specially recommended to study with still greater earnestness the Word of God, and to draw down His grace by constant prayer and meditation on sacred subjects.

This is the spirit of the Order of St. Dominic, which is very much insisted upon by Father Louis of Grenada, in his "*Treatise on Prayer:*"

"*The wisdom of this world,* writes St. Augustine, (part 2, parag. 8, chap. 4,) *inflames the mind with vanity; that of God fills it with His love. It does not make men proud and talkative, but humble and silent. If, then, when God teaches me Himself by His word, I turn away from Him to have recourse to human and earthly masters, do I not do injury to that Divine Teacher? Do I not despise His doctrine when I think less of that than I do of the teaching of men? If the number of persons who fall into this error were not so great, the evil would be less serious. But what am I to say when almost every one in the world falls into this snare? It is said that in the Straits of Magellan, out of three vessels which strive to pass through them, one is always lost. But in this dangerous moral passage of which we are speaking, there is hardly one in a hundred who escapes. How many students are there not in the world, while our Lord and Master Jesus Christ has so few true disciples? And what is still more to be deplored, even those who leave the world to go into Religion, at the very time when they ought to be striving with all their might to throw off the old man and put on the new, as if this were an affair of a few days, or of minor importance, hardly have they begun to open their eyes and to know God, than they give themselves up to the study of pagan philosophers and human letters, where, during many years, they do not hear the name or one single word of Jesus Christ.*

"*And although such studies, by the necessities of the times and the importunities of heretics, may be necessary in some measure, we should look upon them as a great pest and evil in our lives, as they take up so much of our time, and make us walk so many years as strangers to the knowledge of Jesus Christ.*

"*Listen to the words of St. Gregory of Nazianzum, who says: 'That the sciences and reasonings of the pagan philosophers resemble the plagues of Egypt, which have come into the Church as a punishment for our sins. That if our miserable position in this life reduces us to this necessity, we ought, at least, to wait till the foundations of virtue in the learners be so well laid that they can bear the extra weight. But who can see without profound sorrow that when a soul is still tender, and a young man is just beginning to taste of the sweetness of the milk of Jesus Christ, he is forcibly dragged away from the breasts to feed on pagan philosophy, where he can find no other pasture than sophisms and false arguments!' Tell me, I beg of you, whether those who encourage such a system do not act like the cruel King Pharao, when he wanted to destroy the people of God, and so commanded that all male children should be drowned in the Nile? Is not this what we see every day; that hardly has a soul begun to live anew in Jesus Christ, and before it has had time to gain strength in its new birth, it is plunged into these pagan waters, and drowned, so that it loses all the spirit of devotion which it had before conceived?"*

As Bartholomew, however, only applied himself to these human studies through obedience, without feeling any particular inclination for them, it was easy for him to avoid this danger. In fact, the best part of his time was given to spiritual exercises, and the rest to study; so that if philosophy partly filled his mind, piety alone took possession of his heart. He succeeded, however, wonderfully in his studies; his quickness and application enabling him to overcome difficulties which cost others years of toil.

After passing through this course of philosophy, Bartholomew began the study of theology. And during this time a Chapter of his Order was held at Quimarais, and he received the commands of his superiors to go there, as being one of the most able men in his province. He fully justified the high opinion which had been formed of him, and in a short time was judged capable of teaching others what he had himself learned. He was consequently appointed Professor of Philosophy in the Lisbon College, founded by the King, Dom Emmanuel. He fulfilled the important duties of this office in the most able as well as the most Christian manner, his one aim being to make his pupils as pious as they were learned. He offered continual prayers to God for this one end, that his disciples might advance as steadily in divine as in profane philosophy. Soon after, he was selected by the fathers of the province to accompany the Father Provincial, Francis Bobadilla, to the general chapter which was to be held at St. Stephen's in Salamanca. There he showed such extraordinary wisdom and knowledge in the public disputes which he was desired to hold in the name of his province, that the Father General, Francis Romen, was delighted, and created him on the spot a doctor of theology. Another chapter in that same year being held at Lisbon, he was elected definitor.

Bartholomew suffered from these different degrees of honour which were showered upon him, and which were more a burden to him than a subject of joy. He loved his cell more than ever, and was not less humble and modest than before. He never failed to assist at the choir as he had always done, omitting no community exercise, and preserving the same recollection of mind in spite of his multifarious occupations. One of the consequences of his new dignities was the perpetual interruption caused by the visits of great personages, who were attracted towards him by his high reputation for sanctity and learning. These visits were a real penance to him, and he used to complain that not only were they a terrible waste of time, but that they interrupted his communion with God, and forced him to have continual intercourse with men, to which nevertheless he was compelled to submit.

Another honourable employment was soon after thrust upon him, greatly against his will. The Infanta, Dom Louis, son of Dom Emmanuel, King of Portugal, and brother of the King, Dom John III., having destined his second son, Dom Antonio, for the Church, earnestly begged the Dominican Fathers to give him Bartholomew as a master in theology. It was impossible to refuse this favour to the prince, so that Bartholomew was sent by his superiors to Ebora, where the court and the young princes then resided. He accepted this office with extreme repugnance; and that which made him an object of envy to many, was looked upon by him as a source of deep regret. For, being possessed solely by the love of Jesus Christ, and remembering his religious profession, he continually had the words of the apostle St. James in his mind: "*Whoso will be a friend of the world is an enemy of God.*" And he dreaded lest he should soil the purity of his soul by the mere sight of the luxury and pomp which that century displayed in the courts of kings. He submitted himself, however, to the orders of his superiors, and lived for some time as preceptor of the young princes. It is not known how long he remained in this position; but to him it was a time of real imprisonment, in spite of the esteem and affection of his pupils. He sighed for solitude and his cell, because he had proved that it was only there he could enjoy peace of mind. And as he had a special reverence and affection for St. Bernard, he used often to quote the following words of his, when that saint, too, was compelled to live in courts and among the great ones of this world. "*My distracted life and unquiet conscience cries to Thee, and implores Thy aid. I am like that fabulous beast in heathen mythology, composed of different parts and materials, being neither a layman nor an ecclesiastic; neither do I live any longer as a Religious, though I still wear the habit. How unhappy I am! like a little bird, who, being scarcely fledged, is all day long out of the nest, exposed to all the winds and storms.*" (Epistle 112 and 249.)

CHAPTER IV.

BARTHOLOMEW JOINS PRAYER AND MEDITATION ON HOLY SCRIPTURE TO HIS THEOLOGICAL STUDIES. — HE EXERCISES THE FUNCTIONS OF APOSTOLIC PREACHER WITH SINGULAR HOLINESS. — HE IS ELECTED PRIOR OF BENEFICO. — HIS DISINTERESTEDNESS, CHARITY AND WISDOM IN THE GUIDANCE OF HIS MONASTERY.

During the twenty years that Bartholomew taught scholastic theology, with general esteem and approbation, he was far from neglecting that divine theology which consists in prayer and meditation on Holy Scripture, and of which the Holy Spirit is the only Master. This knowledge of God does not consist in reasoning, but in loving. It is acquired by the heart and by the will; and, as is wisely said by Father John of Jesus and Mary, a barefooted Carmelite: "*The more we search through the subtlety of the schools to know the greatness of God, the more the will is drawn away from His love; unless we mingle our studies with that wisdom which descends from above, and which, as the Apostle St. James says, is 'modest' and 'peaceable,' and only granted to the humble of heart.*"

The same feeling was expressed by Father Louis of Grenada, the great friend of Bartholomew, in his "Treatise on Prayer." He writes: "*True wisdom is acquired by the fear of God, by a good life, by the practice of virtue, and a continual meditation on the law of God. It is impossible to learn it in any other way, as St. Augustine teaches in these words: 'Many desire eagerly the light of wisdom, while they* *despise virtue and justice; and they should be warned that they will never obtain what they desire if they be not careful to practise what they despise, according to the words in Holy Writ:* 'My son, if thou desirest wisdom keep justice, and God will give it you.' *For wisdom is a gift of the Spirit, which is obtained more by prayer than by arguments. For that reason St. Augustine says again:* 'Those who have learned from Jesus Christ to be meek and humble of heart make greater progress in the knowledge of God by prayer and meditation, than by study and reading.' "*

Bartholomew was filled with thoughts like these. Knowing that God is a God of purity itself, and can only be seen by the pure in heart, he strove to purify his soul by the exercise of all Christian virtues, so that he might behold the light of God, and receive that interior unction which teaches all things.

For this reason he made a little collection of the words of holy persons and saints, especially of those who seemed the most likely to inspire others with the fear and love of God. This book was published later, under the title of "*Abridgment of the Spiritual Life.*"

In speaking of this book to the Cardinal of Lorraine, when he was with him at the Council of Trent, Bartholomew said that it was the burning charity and piety of St. Bernard which had induced him thus to try and record his actual words, for that he considered him a master in the spiritual life, and the best interpreter of the Holy Spirit.

He was not content with quoting him continually in his book, but he took several long extracts from his works, especially from his Sermons on the Canticles, and calls these sentences "*words of fire,*" "*pearls and diamonds,*"-

---

* " Qui à Jesu Christus didicerunt mites esse et humiles corde, plus cogitando et orando proficiut quàm legendo et audiendo."—Aug. Ep. 112.

"*and the most delicious food of the soul.*" For, according to St. Bernard's words: "*The Spouse of Christ, which is holy Church, striving to know her Beloved, does not trust in the deceptions of human learning, nor indulge herself in vain reasonings or human curiosity; but invokes the Holy Spirit, so that grace may be imprinted in her heart, and impart to her, at the same time, the light of knowledge and the ardour of charity.*"—(In Cant. Serm. 8, No. 5.)

In his task of Apostolic Preacher, to which he had been appointed by his superiors, and which obliged him so continually to preach the Word of God to the people, Bartholomew made every one feel that he spoke out of the abundance and fulness of his heart; so that the humble disciple of Jesus Christ became, unconsciously to himself, the master of his hearers. He was careful, before preaching, to prepare himself by earnest prayer; and ever bore in mind those words of our Lord of the holy Precursor: "*Lucerna ardens et lucens,*" knowing that to shine usefully, and to bring home the truth to the hearts of his hearers, he must himself be filled with the love of God, and with zeal for the salvation of souls. For this reason he adopted later for his motto these two words: "*ardere et lucere.*"

Whilst he was at Ebora, teaching theology to the young prince, without a thought beyond his daily duties, he was elected Prior of the Convent of Benefico, by the unanimous votes of the Religious, who received him with extraordinary satisfaction and joy. This convent was at half a league from Lisbon, and in a very agreeable position. It was one of the reformed monasteries in the province, and had the glory of producing men of great ability, whose holiness had been proved by many miracles.

The only fear was lest the Infanta should disapprove of this election. But as the prince was a wise man, he, on the contrary, testified his hearty approval, and sent his son to the monastery, in order to be still under Bartholomew's care. The new prior devoted himself at once to his duties, and especially to the spiritual government of his house. Nothing was too minute to escape his vigilance. His most anxious wish was to detach his monks from themselves, and to lead them to a stronger love of God by continual prayer and watchfulness. He used to say to them that he did not exhort them to be grave and modest in speech and manner, but always to remember the presence of God, and to worship Him in spirit and in truth: "for all those external things," he would add, "have their root in the soul; and when that is well regulated within, all that is without will follow of itself, according to the words of Jesus Christ: '*Munda prius quod intus est calicis, ut fiat id quod deforis est mundum.*"—(Matt. 23.)

He did not care about increasing the buildings of the monastery, and was indifferent as to the food and clothing of the monks; but his main object was to inspire them with humility and true charity. For being persuaded that nothing would be wanting to those who serve God in spirit and in truth, he showed no anxiety to increase the revenues of the monastery; and was so liberal in the distribution of alms that on one occasion of famine, when a number of poor people were gathered round the gates to beg for food, he gave them all the fish which had just been dressed for the community, saying that in such a moment of necessity herbs and fruits must suffice for Religious who had made a vow of poverty.

The princes who were then in Portugal, and especially Cardinal Dom Henry and the Infanta Dom Louis, often came to the monastery to see the holy prior, whose life and conversation edified them more and more. As they knew how poorly he and his monks lived in that house, they never failed to leave behind them abundant alms.

But the prior, who had no idea of heaping up treasures on this earth, seeing that the scarcity was still so great, and that all the country was swarming with poor who had no means of subsistence, distributed all the money the princes left amongst them, while he consoled them by his loving words and counsels, not reserving anything for his monastery but the providence of God.

Perhaps this might be the proper place in which to relate the extraordinary virtues of this holy man before he was raised to the episcopal throne. But in truth, what he was then he continued to be to the end of his life; only increasing day by day in all Christian graces and virtues. For he did not show more piety in his cell than, later on, in his episcopal palace, nor more poverty as a monk than in the midst of riches; and what he was to his Religious, that he became towards all his flock. In fact, while the greater portion of men when leaving their monasteries leave also their discipline, and run the risk of losing their souls in the world, this man, on the contrary, was only thereby confirmed in virtue, and grew daily in wisdom and grace, both in the sight of God and men.

CHAPTER V.

THE PRE-EMINENCE OF THE CATHEDRAL OF BRAGA AND ITS PRELATES.—THE INTRIGUES AT COURT TO PROCURE THE ARCHBISHOPRIC.—THE QUEEN OFFERS IT TO LOUIS OF GRENADA, WHO REFUSES IT.

We have described Dom Bartholomew's life in his monastery, where he was only intent on guiding the souls entrusted to him, as a wise and faithful servant, and nourishing them with the divine word. But whilst he avoided the world with the utmost care, and kept himself as far as possible hidden in his solitude, God had decreed to bring him forth in the eyes of men, for the benefit of countless souls and the edification of the whole Church.

Towards the end of March, in the year 1558, the episcopal see of Braga fell vacant, owing to the death of Dom Balthasar Limpo. This church, though not the richest, is nevertheless the most important in the kingdom of Portugal, whether one considers its antiquity, or its extent, or the great saints who have governed it. Its bishops have been as illustrious for their holiness and science as for their high birth. Twenty-two of them have been canonized; and more than one hundred others were so eminent for their virtues and ability that their biographies would fill a library. They showed the greatest firmness in maintaining the purity of the faith, when threatened by the barbarians on the one hand or the heretics on the other. Many of these prelates sealed their faith with their blood, and died martyrs. Princes of the blood and sons of kings have filled this episcopal chair; and for more than four hundred years the primacy of the churches of Spain and Portugal has been contested at Rome between the Archbishop of Braga and that of Toledo. Honorius III. at last decided that, their claims being co-equal, two briefs should be prepared, giving to each primate an equal dignity; so that their respective claims remain, as it were, undecided to this day. We have only mentioned these facts to show the dignity and importance of the see in question, which will explain the intense anxiety shown by many to obtain it.

The kingdom of Portugal was at that time governed by Queen Catherine, widow of Dom John III., King of Portugal, daughter of Dom Philip I., and sister of the Emperor Charles V., both of them Kings of Spain. This queen was a woman of admirable qualities and really royal virtues, which never shone more than since the death of the king her husband. For during all the time of the minority of the young king, Dom Sebastian, who was her grand-son, she governed the kingdom with a prudence and gentleness which excited the admiration and love of all her subjects. In fact, the affection of her people was such towards her, that when she wished, after some time, to give up the reins of government, to finish her days in greater tranquillity and peace, the Chambers of the town of Lisbon came, in the name of the whole people, and implored her to change her resolution, representing to her the great wisdom and virtues with which God had enriched her, and the deep love her subjects bore her, which ended by compelling her in a way to retain the authority in her own hands.

But what was most admirable about this queen was her purity of conscience and her deep piety. She chose Dom Louis of Grenada as her confessor, who henceforth resided altogether in Portugal. For the Cardinal, Infanta Dom Henry, Archbishop of Ebora, who was full of zeal for the Church, had invited Louis of Grenada to Ebora on account of his great reputation; and having proved his eminent virtues and witnessed the influence he exercised for the good of his flock, the Cardinal obtained from the Father General of the Order a promise that he should always be attached to that province, of which he was elected provincial in the month of October, 1557.

Dom Louis was therefore employed in the visitation of his province, when the see of Braga fell vacant by the death of the archbishop. The queen, who knew the extreme necessity of filling aright this important see, was most anxious to find a man worthy of the promotion, and at the same time to act according to her conscience as before God. There were at court many persons, who, from their high birth, or from the services they had rendered to the crown, thought themselves entitled to the vacant see. Interest and ambition, therefore, combined to try and shake the firmness and integrity of the queen, and to conquer her resolution to ignore all human considerations, and seek only for one who should the most worthily fill so responsible an office. These intrigues continued day by day, yet without shaking the queen's resolution. The great reputation of Dom Louis of Grenada, and the esteem in which he was held by the whole court and people, made every one believe that he would be selected for the vacant post, especially as his election would be approved by men of all shades of opinion.

The press, which generally is beforehand with public and private intelligence, announced first that the queen was going to offer him the bishopric; and then that she had done so. Dom Louis, in the meantime, was quietly at Santarran, where he was detained by a wound he had received in the foot, from a dangerous fall which he met with during his visitation.

However, the rumour of his election spreading far and wide, it came to the ears of Dom Bartholomew, who was Grenada's great friend. It touched him very much, for he loved him deeply; and he wrote to him at once, saying how anxious he had been about his accident, but that he had just heard a report which made him more anxious still, for that there was far less risk in a bad fall than in being overwhelmed by the burden of an archbishopric. He ended by imploring him to pray heartily that he might be delivered from so great a danger, adding that he wished him every possible good and blessing save that of the episcopate.

Although the people had anticipated the queen's intentions, they were not wrong in believing that she had determined to offer the vacant see to her holy confessor;

for in a day or two she summoned him to her presence, and spoke as follows.

"You know that I offered you, not long ago, a bishopric, which you refused: and although I was vexed at this refusal, I accepted your excuses. But now the case is different. You know that the archiepiscopal see of Braga is vacant. This church has been for a long time in a most deplorable state. Its deep wounds demand a skilful physician, and I know none better than yourself. Receive then this charge, in the name of God. I should give it to another in fear and trembling; but to you I should confide it with joy, knowing that you would acquit yourself of it worthily. Render then this service to Jesus Christ. Deliver this diocese from so many evils, and me from the anxiety and disquiet I have on this account, by relieving my conscience from the burden of a choice at once so important and so difficult."

Grenada, seeing the extreme anxiety of the queen, replied at once: "That her highness did him only too great an honour in judging him so favourably; but that he knew himself to be utterly incapable of such an office; that he had proved his insufficiency too often to entertain for a moment the idea of accepting such a charge. That if he had refused a smaller bishopric before, so much the more reasonably should he refuse the archbishopric of Braga. That all he was fit for was to write some little pious books, and try and save a few souls, and serve the Religious of his own Order. That to pass from this humble state to an archbishopric would be to raise himself from earth to heaven. That he therefore implored her to cast her eyes on some one who would be more fit for this dignity; and that, as for him, he only prayed to live and die in his cell."

The queen was greatly distressed at Grenada's resolution, which she despaired of being able to conquer, because there was no one in the kingdom who could impose submission or obedience on him as superior. Yet she could not but admire his decision, and finally told him: "That since he would not do what she so earnestly desired, he was at least bound to find her some one else who would be worthy of the archbishopric." Grenada, too thankful to have escaped the threatened honour, replied to the queen: "That an affair of such importance could not be settled in a moment. That he must consult God and pray much, so that he might discover His will."

The queen gave him three days in which to think it over; after which she desired him to return and let her know the name of the person he would suggest.

CHAPTER VI.

FATHER LOUIS OF GRENADA PROPOSES DOM BARTHOLOMEW TO THE QUEEN AS ARCHBISHOP OF BRAGA.—THE QUEEN CONSENTS, AND APPOINTS HIM; BUT CANNOT PREVAIL UPON HIM TO ACCEPT IT.

The refusal of the vacant see by Dom Louis of Grenada was quickly made public; and all those who hoped to obtain it redoubled their eagerness and their intrigues about the court. His example, so far from inclining them to imitate it, only filled them with an unholy joy; as now that he was out of the way, they thought they could the more easily satisfy their ambitious views. Persons without either piety or ability, and plunged in worldliness, coveted beyond anything a dignity which had made a saint tremble: so blinded are men when they judge the things of God with human eyes. Grenada had prayed much during these three days, and finally resolved to propose Dom Bartholomew to the queen. But he heard also that she had been overwhelmed with more urgent solicitations than ever to give the see to one of the nobles of the court, and that reasons of state had been brought to bear upon her; some of her councillors having represented to her that during her grandson's minority it was vital to keep things quiet at court, and especially not to arouse the discontent of the most powerful personages in the kingdom. Grenada foresaw that if the archbishopric were given to one of these men the rest would speedily console themselves with the feeling that it had been bestowed on one of their own order, according to the ordinary rules of the world; but that to see it given to an obscure monk like Dom Bartholomew, would enrage them all, and be looked upon as a direct insult offered to the whole body of the nobility.

Therefore, having found the queen, he spoke to her frankly as follows: "That he knew no one more worthy of the dignity than Dom Bartholomew of the Martyrs; that he was a very learned man, and that his virtue was equal to his knowledge; and that, being his intimate friend, he could answer for him to her highness that he had all the necessary qualities to form a great bishop." Then, knowing how people had tried to force the queen's better judgment, and that although she had sufficient courage and firmness to resist such importunities, she yet needed some stronger light to expose their weakness and falsehood, he added: "I know well, madam, what great difficulties you have had in this matter. I am aware of the violent solicitations which have been made to your royal highness by great personages, to obtain this archbishopric. And I can well understand that you might fear the consequences of giving it to a humble and obscure religious, without high birth or great connections. But, madam, permit me to speak boldly to your highness in this matter, as I do so for your own sake. If you fear to displease these great people, how much more should you fear to displease God, by preferring the gratification of an unjust ambition to the interests of Jesus Christ and of His Church? If it were a question of an earthly charge, a mere worldly dignity, it would be just and right for your royal highness to consider the high birth, the noble services rendered to the state, and other considerations in the candidates for the office. But when it is a question of a charge in God and for God, it is God alone, madam, and the divine qualities required for the post, which you are bound to consider. The election of prelates, properly speaking, rests with our Lord Jesus Christ. It is He Himself who calls them, and "*His Holy Spirit who places them,*" as saith the Scriptures, "*to rule the Church of God, which He hath purchased with His own Blood.*" (Acts xx. 28.) Those, therefore, to whom the nomination of bishops is entrusted, should, as St. Gregory the Great exhorts, seek only for men whom God has called, so as to choose those whom He has elected. And in holy writ He tells us what manner of man he should be who is called upon to govern the Church. He does not ask that he should be a great or noble man according to this world; but that he should be humble and charitable; that he should have knowledge kindled by piety, and piety enlightened by science. Above all, that he should have courage and firmness, and an ardent zeal for the glory of God and the salvation of souls, without which all other qualities in a bishop are useless and dead. Illustrious birth, madam, cannot ensure these qualities; on the contrary, it is often an obstacle, as the same Pope says: '*Human nobility often makes souls mean and common-place before God;*' (In cap. 9, 1 Reg. ver. 6) because it makes them proud and induces them to despise others. For as what is great before God is often held in contempt by men, so, as St. Luke has it, '*that which is high to men, is an abomination before God.*' (Luke xvi.) If, however, these great and divine qualities could be found united in the person of one of the great personages we have alluded to, then your highness would do well to select him. But when it is a question of giving to God a pontiff, a defender of the Church, and a pastor of souls, how is it possible that your highness should prefer those who have none of the qualities which God asks for in a bishop, and on the contrary, all those which He despises, to one who possesses every one of those virtues in an eminent degree, and to whom the only thing needed is, what was wanting to the apostles themselves, and to some of the greatest bishops in the Church? For whatever may be said of the low birth of him whom I venture to name to your highness, it is certain that he is of a much better family than was St. Peter and the apostles, and of as good a one as the great St. Augustine. This, madam, is what I have felt it my duty to represent to your highness. If it should surprise you, I may say that it likewise astonishes me. But I am only the mouth-piece of what is said by God Himself, and by the greatest saints in their writings. I should be utterly unworthy, madam, of the great honour which your highness has done me by asking my advice in a matter of such grave importance, and which concerns both your salvation and mine, if I did not speak to you as before God; trampling under foot all human considerations, and only looking to the immutable Truth, which is one day to judge us all, not according to the rules of this world, but according to the just judgment of the Most High God."

The queen listened to Grenada's words with deep and earnest attention, and then replied: "I think your words are good and true, and I thank you for them with my whole heart. For I am persuaded that it is only for the love of God, and from the great anxiety you have for my salvation and your own, that you have spoken as you have done. You know I have often said that I wished with all my heart that during my regency the bishops of Portugal were immortal, so that I might have no archbishoprics or bishoprics to give away. It is enough to have to answer for myself and for the state, without being responsible for the salvation of souls. Therefore it is sufficient that I have your assurance that Dom Bartholomew is thoroughly worthy of this onerous charge. Send him to me and I will give it to him. Let the great personages of my court take offence if they will; I fear more the anger of God: for He is my judge, which they are not."

At these words Grenada hastened away, and sending for Bartholomew, told him "that the queen wished to communicate a matter of great importance to him." He went, therefore, straight to the palace, without the smallest suspicion of the reason for which he was sent. After the usual salutations, the queen opened the subject as follows: "You know how many people have importuned me to obtain the vacant see of Braga; but I have made my choice, and it has fallen upon you, who, I know, are far from thinking of anything of the sort. So I have sent for you to give you this dignity in the name of the king, my grandson, feeling convinced that you will worthily fulfil the important charge committed to you."

We may imagine the utter surprise and amazement of the humble monk at these unexpected words. The multitude and confusion of his thoughts at first choked his speech; but in a few seconds, recovering his calm of mind, he replied to the queen as follows: "Madam, your highness confers upon me an honour all the more surprising as it is disproportioned to my merits, although nothing can add to my gratitude for such a proposal. Your highness offers me a post revered by every one and desired by many.

But you must allow me to say, madam, that I cannot forget the words of God, who warns me by His written word and through the mouth of His saints, that this burden, far from being a desirable one, would be dreaded even by the angels. We may think differently, but we cannot go against the opinion of holy writ. Therefore, the perils of such a position being so great, your highness will not be surprised that, considering the height of the elevation which she proposes to me, I should apprehend at the same time the depth of the precipice below into which I should almost inevitably fall. I fully believe, madam, that with the great knowledge you possess of such matters, you would not imagine you were placing me in such peril, because you fancy I have the qualities necessary for a bishop in so onerous a charge. But I, madam, am entirely persuaded that the contrary is the truth; and that I possess none of the qualities necessary for a bishop. And even had I any such virtues, I should always think myself obliged to fly from such heavy responsibilities, having had so many examples of men who appeared worthy of the episcopal charge before their promotion, and then lamentably changed and became quite different to what they were before."

At these words the queen, who had a great deal of wisdom and penetration, interrupted him, and said: "That she did not believe that men who could so change when they became bishops were really different before; that no doubt they had sought the office from motives of ambition, and that thus it was not their dignity which had changed them, but which had served to reveal the real natures of these men. That as for himself, he had nothing to fear on that score, as he showed plainly by his resistance how far he was removed from seeking such a charge." She added: "That his provincial had borne such a witness to his fitness for the post that he was bound to defer to his opinion."

Bartholomew replied: "Your highness will persist in believing me better than I am: but I implore her not to be offended if I persist also in knowing myself better than she does. Your highness employs the authority of Dom Louis of Grenada to persuade me to accept her offer: and it is this very same authority which compels me to refuse it. For if your highness has deigned to believe him when he spoke of me, it is only fair and just that you should believe me when I speak of him. His wisdom and sanctity are well known to you. His ability is as public as his writings. And yet your highness has accepted his refusal, first of a bishopric, and then of this very archbishopric of which there is now a question. I implore you, madam, to be as just to me. If he considers himself incapable, I am infinitely more so than he is. Your highness has the power of conferring this dignity upon me, but not that of giving me the qualities necessary for me to bear it. The prince of the apostles commands us in the same breath to '*fear God and honour the king.*' (1 Peter ii. 17.) I render to your highness, madam, all the honour and gratitude I owe her for the unexpected offer she has made me. But at the same time I show my fear of God by my refusal." And after having spoken these last words, with a profound bow he left the audience chamber.

The queen remained surprised and astonished at the humble and Christian firmness of Bartholomew's reply. She began to esteem him more highly than ever, and desired the more to conquer his modesty and determination, which appeared to her invincible. She was equally struck with the contrast between men of this world and men actuated by the spirit of God. She felt herself importuned in a hundred ways by some of the greatest people in her court to obtain this charge, and yet found all her persuasions fruitless to persuade a humble religious to accept it; so that while some were ready to carry heaven and earth by storm to be made bishops, it would be necessary to use violence to compel this unknown man to become one.

Being resolved to bring the matter to an issue she at last sent again for Grenada, and told him: "That she had found Bartholomew all and more than all that he had said. That she now esteemed him, not only from his report, but from what she had seen and heard herself." And so she ordered him either to persuade or to constrain Bartholomew to accept the archbishopric: which Grenada gladly promised to do.

CHAPTER VII.

DOM LOUIS OF GRENADA TRIES TO PERSUADE DOM BARTHOLOMEW TO RECEIVE THE ARCHBISHOPRIC, BUT IN VAIN.—FINALLY, HE FORCES HIM TO ACCEPT IT BY THREATENING HIM WITH EXCOMMUNICATION.

Grenada, in obedience to the queen's command, went at once to find Dom Bartholomew; and, with all the authority which his affection and his position as provincial gave him, he strove to persuade him to yield to what he considered was the call of God. Bartholomew replied: "That he implored him to believe that he knew himself better than anybody else did; and that being incapable of guiding himself, he was still more so of guiding a large flock. That he entreated him to consider how he himself would not yield to the queen's entreaties to accept it. That if he considered himself incapable, much more so was his poor servant Bartholomew. That he implored him to allow him the same liberty he himself had used, and to follow his example more than his words." After that he held his tongue. But seeing that Grenada pressed him more and more, to make him change his resolution, he was extremely moved, and cried out with a deep sigh: "What, my Father! is it possible that a person like you, whom I have always looked upon as a real father, a charitable superior, and a true friend, should now have so little compassion and charity for your son, your friend, and your Religious? Truly, our Father General Hubert gave far other proofs of his perfect love for Albert the Great, when the Pope wanted to make him bishop, by replying that he would sooner see Albert dead and carried to the cemetery, than raised to the pontifical dignity and exposed to all its perils! If you do not choose to take pity on my weakness, you should at least consider that if I were unfortunate enough to yield to your entreaties, you would take upon yourself, and on your own soul and conscience, all the faults and grave evils which my insufficiency would certainly make me commit in so great and difficult a charge."

This conference took place in the Lisbon Convent; and Bartholomew, hoping that Grenada would yield to his reasoning, asked him at once for leave to return to his own monastery at Benefico. But Grenada ordered him on no account to leave Lisbon without his express permission, adding that he would think seriously over what he had said; but that he must not think him unkind if, after all, he was forced to act towards him as his superior, as he would not yield to his persuasions as a friend. He gave him however, a little time to think over the matter before God, because he wanted him to accept the archbishopric quietly, without being forced to exercise his authority as provincial. However, after having allowed him some days reflection, finding him determined to keep to his original resolution, he was compelled to take a more stringent line to overcome his modesty.

On the 8th of August, 1558, he caused the great chapter bell to be rung after compline, and all the monks being assembled in choir, he called Dom Bartholomew and spoke to him as follows:

"My Father, you know how long and how patiently I have represented to you that it was your duty to cease your resistance and to accept the Archbishopric of Braga, to which the queen has nominated you. You know enough of the piety of this princess to be aware that she would not have preferred you to such a charge if she did not think, as we do, that God had called you to it. I do not blame you for the difficulty you have had to make up your mind in this matter. We are living in an age which sadly needs good examples. Every one knows how the holiest persons in the Church have dreaded the episcopate, even in times of greater peace and purity of morals than now; and yet we see too many men in these days, who love and intrigue for the very honours from which saints fled, and *who bring no other dispositions to be bishops*'—as St. Gregory of Nazianzum writes—'*than the wish to be so;*' (Orat. 20.) that is, the very qualities of ambition and pride which render them unfit for, and unworthy of it. By the grace of God you are far removed from that state of mind, and, on the contrary, very much opposed to it. Had it been otherwise, I should not have thought of pressing this dignity upon you. And that you may feel the more convinced that it is God Himself who calls you to this charge, I solemnly declare that if I had known any other monk or ecclesiastic of whom I was as well assured as I am of you, and whom I thought more fitted for the post, I should have indubitably preferred him, and done my utmost to persuade the queen to give it to him. I know too well the importance of those words of St. Gregory: '*That he who is chosen for a bishop should be the man who is most worthy before God.*' After this sincere protest you must consider that I have as much to fear as you in this matter, which ought to reassure you; as, by forcing you to accept this archbishopric, I lay the charge likewise on my own shoulders, as my conscience must answer for yours.

"You know that this same Pope, who speaks so strongly against those who enter the episcopate by the door of ambition and self-interest, sets bounds, likewise, to the modesty of those who are legitimately called to it. He says that '*their humility will be only true in the sight of God when they do not oppose His will, or reject any honour that may be offered them with inflexible obstinacy.*' (Pastor. part 1, cap. 8.) Therefore he concludes that in such matters he who is really humble, and not too much attached to his own will and opinion, though '*shrinking in his heart from the dignity imposed upon him, nevertheless submits to the voice of obedience: ex corde debet fugere, et invitus obedire.*' (Ibid.) It was thus that S. Augustine suffered himself to be made priest and then bishop, though with much grief and many tears. And yet, to encourage those who are in your present state, he adds: '*that as there is nothing in the Church more difficult, more dangerous, and more laborious, than the charge of a priest or a bishop, there is nothing also happier before God, if one fights in this holy army according to the orders of Him who is our general commander in chief. Si eo modo militetur, quo noster imperator jubes.*' (Epist. 148.) Therefore, my beloved father, seeing in you all the marks it appears to me that one can have, that you are called of God to this charge, strengthen yourself in Him, and in the all-powerful help of His grace. And as it is He who has engaged you to serve others, it is He also who will give you that which you must impart to them. You will be

His mouth, and He will speak by you; you will be His eye, and He will lead others through you; you will be His arm, and He will act in you. He will be your light in your doubts, and your consolation in your toils. And so that you may be able one day to say to Him that it is not you who have undertaken this office, but His own order which constrained you, I command you, in virtue of the obedience that you owe me as your provincial, and under the pain of major excommunication if you refuse, to show me your submission at once by accepting the charge I hereby lay upon you."

At these words, Bartholemew, thunderstruck, yet overwhelmed by the authority of the speaker, felt himself unable to resist any longer, and in spite of his extreme repugnance, threw himself on the ground at the feet of the provincial, as is the custom of the Religious of that order when their superior gives them a command. After which, having asked permission of the father provincial to speak, he rose and said: "From the earliest years of my life I sought obedience in religion, so that it might shelter me from the perils of this world; and now that I am getting old this same obedience throws me, as it were, out of the nest, and forces me to mix again in the world. This same obedience makes me do violence to my inclinations, stifle my thoughts and resolutions, and blind myself, as it were, by persuading me that in an employment in which I foresee my ruin, I shall, on the contrary, ensure my salvation and that of many others.

"I yield then, my father, not to men, but to God, to whom I am vowed by obedience. And I protest that it is from Him alone that I can accept this dignity, and not from any prince on earth. For I take God to witness that only the power of religion, which is the power of God Himself, and no other authority under heaven, could have obliged me to receive so terrible a burden."

CHAPTER VIII.

DOM BARTHOLOMEW, FINDING HIMSELF FORCED TO ACCEPT THE BISHOPRIC, FALLS INTO SUCH SADNESS THAT HE BECOMES VERY ILL.—MANY SPEAK AGAINST HIS ELECTION: THAT HE WAS CALLED TO THE ARCHBISHOPRIC AS THE CARDINAL XIMENES WAS TO THAT OF TOLEDO.

The chapter being over, the archbishop-elect left the choir and went to pray before the Blessed Sacrament, there to try and find some consolation in his great sorrow. He stayed there a long time, making the offering of his will, which had been overcome by obedience. He could do nothing in his present state but annihilate himself, and, as it were, lose himself in God, at the sight of the many perils which surrounded him, and address himself to Him as did the apostles in the storm, crying out: "*Domine, salva nos, perimus!*" (Matt. viii. 25.) When he had gone back to his cell the Religious all hastened to express the joy they felt at his election, which only gave him fresh sorrow and served to increase his grief. Then, being left alone, he set himself once more to consider his position. He felt that however impossible it had become for him to escape, the risks he ran were just as great. That he was going to be exposed on a sea where he should encounter a thousand storms, and where he feared many others which he could not foresee. That many holy men had been called to the episcopate, who, nevertheless, had thus been lost; and that it was perhaps a secret judgment of God to punish him for some hidden fault in his heart. He passed the whole night in this kind of agitation without being able to sleep. In the morning he had a raging headache, followed by a violent fever, which the agitation of his mind greatly increased, so that very soon he was in great danger.

The news of this novel election, with all the circumstances attending it, quickly spread through the town, where it caused intense surprise and astonishment in men's minds. The world, whose maxims had been entirely disregarded, were loud in their disapproval. At court it was the subject of unmixed ridicule; and those who had intrigued to get the appointment for their own friends were extremely offended. They could not bear that a humble Religious, of whom they scarcely knew the name, had been dragged out of the obscurity of his cell to be raised to the first dignity in the kingdom; and all the more because he had not taken a single step to bring it about; he had not uttered one word of flattery to any one, nor had he taken the trouble to see a single person of influence about the person of the queen. They were extraordinarily piqued that this election should have been brought about in such a manner, so contrary to the usual mode of selecting bishops, which is unhappily but too common in the present day, and of which St. Jerome complained even in his time, saying: *"That there are many who do not care to appoint as columns of the Church those who are the most capable of supporting it: but rather those for whom they have a personal preference; or who have won them over by their flatteries; or for whom interest has been made by some rich or powerful personage."* (Heiron. lib. i. advers. Jovinian.) Their envy, in fact, had been changed into mortal hatred; and they drew up and published a libellous paper filled with false statements, to make the election ridiculous and dishonour the character and reputation of Dom Bartholomew. They then contrived to let the libel fall into the hands of the Infanta. But this prince, who perfectly knew the piety and the entire disinterestedness both of Grenada and the archbishop-elect, treated the libel with the contempt it deserved, rightly looking upon it as the result of a furious and disappointed ambition.

Other people, with more piety and light, having seen the way in which the election had been brought about, felt that great advantage would thereby accrue to the Church of God, and especially as the devil was so irritated by it, that having failed to put a stop to it in other ways, he had resorted to insolent and public calumnies, which were however too easily refuted to do much harm.

The clamour having after a short time subsided, a great revulsion of feeling set in, and all the world began to admire and talk of the piety, wisdom, and firmness of the queen, who had shown in this important matter that when it was a question of God and His Church, she was a servant of one and a daughter of the other, and only remembered that she was queen to maintain their interests with all her authority and power. She proved, on this occasion, that she was an inheritor of the virtues of her illustrious ancestor Isabella, Queen of Castille, who is still held in veneration throughout Spain for her generosity and wisdom. For in 1495 the archbishopric of Toledo falling vacant by the death of Cardinal Dom Peter Gonzales, of Mendoza, this pious princess, with whom the next nomination rested, as being the proprietor of the kingdom, was most anxious to find a man wise and holy enough to deserve such a dignity, which was the first in Spain. The King, Dom Ferdinand, her husband, pressed her to give it to his natural son, Dom Alonso of Arragon, who was already archbishop of Sarragossa. But the piety and zeal of the queen were above such considerations, so that she never would yield to the king in this matter.

She had as a confessor, F. Francis Ximenes, of Cisneros, a Religious of the Franciscan Order, who hid under his

brown habit an extraordinary amount of wisdom and
ability, and a still more eminent piety. The queen resolved to invest him with the archbishopric; and without
saying a word to him or to any one else on the subject,
privately sent to Rome for the necessary bulls, which she
duly received. One day during Lent, as he was going
back on foot from Madrid to his convent, to assist, as was
his custom, at the Offices of Holy Week, the queen sent
for him, and having spoken to him for some time on indifferent matters, suddenly drew out of her pocket the bulls of
Pope Alexander VI., and said to him: " Will you be good
enough to take this packet and see what his Holiness sends
us by these apostolic letters?" Francis read on the outside the address, which ran as follows: *" To our Venerable
Brother, Francis Ximenes, Archbishop-elect of Toledo."*
For the first moment he was extraordinarily troubled; but
then, quietly kissing the papal missive, he gave back the
letters to the queen without opening them, saying, simply:
"Madam, these Apostolic letters are not for me." And
directly leaving the audience chamber he started for his
convent. Fearful of being pursued even there he hastened
on, but was overtaken by some of the queen's ministers,
with orders to bring him back and persuade him to accept
the charge. But all their efforts were fruitless; and only
a positive command from the Pope overcame the resistance
of a mind as humble as it was grand and heroic.

With great reason, therefore, did Queen Catherine prefer
Dom Bartholomew to the most illustrious nobles in her
kingdom; having before her eyes the example of her great
ancestress, who, by thus promoting a humble and unknown
monk, obtained for Spain one of the best and greatest
statesmen the world had produced, i.e., the great Cardinal
Ximenes, whose wisdom, justice, generosity and piety,
made him a model to all succeeding ages.

CHAPTER IX.

BARTHOLOMEW'S DANGEROUS ILLNESS.—AFTER HIS RECOVERY HE GOES TO SALUTE THE QUEEN.—HIS ELECTION IS PRAISED BY ONE OF THE GREATEST NOBLES IN PORTUGAL, AND ONE WHO HAD BEEN THE MOST INDIGNANT AT HIS PROMOTION.

The illness of Bartholomew became so serious that every one thought he was going to die. Even his enemies were compelled to acknowledge how great must have been the violence done to his wishes to reduce him to such an extremity; and the irritation against him was changed to pity and regret. Pious persons were deeply grieved at his dangerous state, having conceived great hopes from an election where flesh and blood had had no part, and where the finger of God was clearly visible.

The holy man, however, found nothing but consolation in the thought which was afflicting others. His peace of soul increased in proportion to the increase of his illness; for he dreaded his future life, and looked upon death as a haven from the dangers which threatened him. In fact, one might say of him as people did of St. Antoninus, that he went to the bishopric as to a martyrdom; but with this difference, that, having so vivid a faith, he would have embraced martyrdom with the utmost joy and goodwill, while he undertook the labour of the episcopate with an obedience filled with fear.

But God, who had designed him for great things, had determined to prolong a life which was to be so holy a one in His sight, and contribute so much to the advantage of the Church. So the violence of the disease began to abate; and as soon as he had a little regained his strength, he was sent to his monastery at Benefico to complete his cure, so that after a few weeks his health was completely re-established.

As soon as he was able to walk he came on foot to Lisbon with one of his monks, to present his homage to the queen, and kiss hands on his appointment to the archbishopric. At the same moment the Duke d'Avero came to the palace, to complain to the queen that she had refused the archbishopric to his brother. And whilst he was waiting for his audience, and leaning over a balcony, one of the gentlemen of his suite asked him if he would like to see the man who had been appointed, and at the same time pointed out to him Dom Bartholomew, who, having come into the court of the palace, and being weary with his journey in consequence of his illness, had sat down on a stone to rest himself.

The duke looked at him with great curiosity, and, seeing the modesty and gravity of his appearance, was touched in spite of himself; and could not help admiring such great humility in one who had been raised to so high a dignity. So when Dom Bartholomew came up the stairs, the duke came forward, and, bowing very low, kissed his hand as that of an archbishop; and being in a few minutes admitted to his audience, together with Dom Bartholomew, he spoke to the queen as follows:

"Madam, I came to complain of your highness' refusal to appoint my brother to the archbishopric of Braga, which I had asked for, as you know. But having now seen the man to whom your majesty has given it, I come, on the contrary, to tender my humble thanks to your highness for having bestowed it on one so worthy of the charge. In truth, madam, I think my brother would make a better governor of a province than Dom Bartholomew: but there is no doubt that Dom Bartholomew is far more worthy of being made an archbishop. For it appears to me that humility is one of the qualities the most becoming in a prelate. And, as for our house, we have always carried our heads so high that we hardly know the name of the virtue! Therefore, instead of complaining to your highness of your choice, I reverence it, on the contrary, and blame myself for having ever condemned it, even in thought. If I may be permitted to hope for any grace or favour, it would be that I might have as much credit with your highness as I feel sure Dom Bartholomew has with God."

The queen's face, during the utterance of this compliment, showed how gratified she was at the revulsion of feeling on the part of the duke. But the archbishop, replying, said: "I know, madam, the deep respect I owe you; and yet I do not fear to say to your highness, that I find myself in a totally different mind from the Duke d'Avero; and that I am come to do exactly the reverse of what he has done. For, instead of coming to complain, he has thanked your highness: whereas I, who ought to come and return thanks, am disposed, on the contrary, to complain. Your goodness and gentleness, madam, are known and appreciated by all your subjects; it is only I who have to complain of the violence you have done me. You have set a father against a son, and a friend against a friend, to condemn me to the episcopate, as you condemn others to exile, to prison, or to death. And certainly, if the choice were in my own power, I would gladly have embraced all these three evils, rather than fall into the one where I now find myself. I beseech of God, madam, to forgive your highness for this act. But I fear that He will one day call you to a terrible account for it!"

The queen replied, with a smile: "Monseigneur Archbishop, if, when I come to die, I have nothing more serious on my conscience than your appointment, I shall feel assured of dying in great peace."

The duke, having heard the archbishop's words, conceived a still higher respect and esteem for his virtue. And the queen was delighted to find that her choice was not only accepted, but even praised by those who had been the most violently opposed to it.

This illustrious example shows us, that when those in authority despise the complaints and criticisms of the world, in order to do an action which is both just and right, and remain firm in their resolution, they end by winning the esteem and approval even of those who were the most active in their opposition. For, as prejudice and self-interest cloud the minds of men and prevent their being able to judge things rightly, so when the proper thing has been done, and they have lost all hope of succeeding in their pretensions, they feel in themselves the equity of the sentence; and often their reason approves and admires that which their passions had at first prompted them to condemn.

CHAPTER X.

DOM BARTHOLOMEW IS CONSECRATED ARCHBISHOP.—HIS ENTRY INTO BRAGA.—HIS REGULATIONS FOR HIS OWN CONDUCT AND HIS DAILY LIFE.

When the bulls sent by Pope Paul IV. had arrived, the archbishop-elect sent Dr. Martin Salvator to Braga, with power to take possession, in his name, of that secular and ecclesiastical dignity. The following Sunday, which was the third Sunday in September, he was consecrated in St. Dominic's Convent, at Lisbon. It was in that same convent that, thirty years before, he had taken the habit of his Order. It was remarked that St. Gregory the Great, who had been forced, like himself, to exchange his monastic cell for the pontifical dignity, was consecrated on the same day.

On the 8th of September, the Feast of the Nativity of the Blessed Virgin, he received the pallium from the hands of the Archbishop of Lisbon, Dom Ferdinand Vascon:ales of Manesa.

As Braga had been for more than a year without a chief pastor, the archbishop felt he must not delay any longer to undertake the care of his flock. Accordingly, on the 22nd of September, he left his Lisbon convent with many tears, the monks accompanying him to the gates. He departed without any escort or followers, silently and noiselessly; as poorly, as far as outside show was concerned, as he was rich in piety within. His carriage resembled that of the apostles more than the equipage of bishops now-a-days. He took but one single companion with him, Father John of Leyra, a learned and ancient father of his Order, for whom he had a particular esteem. Having arrived on the frontiers of his diocese, the news of his advance spread rapidly, in spite of his care to prevent it, and from all sides men hastened to meet and do him honour. The villages emptied themselves of their whole population, and ran in crowds to welcome him and receive his episcopal blessing. He gave it them with a countenance beaming with such love, modesty, gentleness, and charity, that the enthusiasm for him knew no bounds. He arrived at Braga on the 4th of October, and the whole municipal body, with the principal inhabitants of the city, came out to receive him, and that with a joy and satisfaction which seemed universal. When he set foot in the episcopal palace he found himself in a magnificent mansion, enriched with the most beautiful pictures, furniture and gilding, and a splendid suite of apartments. All this vain show and luxury, however, instead of pleasing him filled him with sorrow and compassion for those who had introduced such secular taste into a bishop's house, and who had made use of the patrimony of the poor to heap up riches only suited to a worldly court. Considering within himself, however, that this palace had been the abode of so many holy prelates and saints, his predecessors, he lifted up his heart to them with respectful fear, imploring them to protect him and to intercede for him with God that he might revive, in that house, their spirit of holiness and mortification, and become their successor, not only in rank but in piety.

After the necessary formalities had been gone through, and every one had paid him the homage due to his ecclesiastical dignity, he began seriously to consider what he could do to diminish the splendour of his palace and edify his people by regulating his manner of life after a soberer fashion.

He determined to close the magnificent suite of apartments used by his predecessors, and chose a humble little set of rooms, which he furnished according to his own taste. In his bedroom there was but a little trestle bed with a couple of mattresses, and this bed was so short and narrow, that, as the archbishop was very tall, he had to curl himself up to lie in it, and could neither turn nor move. He placed near his bed a basin of water to wet his eyes when he woke, and so conquer sleep. He always went to bed without attendance, which was very unusual in those days. He wore no linen, and never gave up his habit under his episcopal robes. The walls of his room were bare, and without hangings, even in winter. He had a plain wooden writing table without a cloth on it, only a crucifix, and no carpets, winter or summer. He rose every morning at three o'clock, prayed, said his Office, and spent the rest of the time till eight, in the study of the Holy Scriptures and the fathers of the Church. At eight o'clock he said his Mass, and directly afterwards held his audiences, always admitting the poor first. Then he went into his business-room with his auditors and council, and worked with them till twelve o'clock, which was his dinner hour. In the afternoon he would open his doors again and receive those who came to him for counsel or advice, or on whatever business they had, until the evening.

In a general way he always retired to his own rooms when the Angelus bell sounded, and leaving temporal affairs, would then devote himself anew to prayer and meditation, which was the nourishment of his soul in all his labours. For though he was scrupulously exact and conscientious in the discharge of all business transactions, he had that peculiar power of being able to put it all aside when the hour came for him to go back to his room; and God gave him the grace never to be disquieted, or bothered, or anxious at the thoughts of the multifarious affairs in which he was engaged, whether as archbishop, or as temporal lord over so large a diocese; but having done his best, to leave the issue quietly in God's hands. If during the time of rest, when, as he said, he was striving before God "to make up the waste and losses of the day," some one came to interrupt him on urgent business, he would despatch it as quickly as possible, saying gently: "*Sufficit diei malitia sua;*" and would sometimes add "that after having given all his day to his neighbour's business, it was but fair that the evening should be for God and his own soul." Sometimes, when he shut himself up in this way in his own room, or in his little oratory adjoining, he would pray with such fervour as to be heard by those outside. This went on till ten or eleven o'clock at night, when he went to bed. His high position and his extraordinary labours did not prevent his practising his ordinary mortifications, and wearing constantly a hair shirt, as in his monastery.

As to the rules and regulations of his table, he practised

exactly the orders of the African council as regards the temperance and frugality of bishops. For in a general way he would only have one dish, either of beef or mutton, and if any scarce or delicate food were put before him, he would send it away directly to some sick person. When his dinner was brought to him he always divided it in half, and sent the other half to the poor; and the same with his wine. He continued this practice to the end of his life. For he always considered, when he sat down to dinner, that he had likewise invited Jesus Christ, and felt himself honoured to be allowed thus to share the gifts he had received from Him, and to treat Him in the persons of His poor.

Thus did this holy man regulate his own hours and daily life. Let us now see how he managed his household.

CHAPTER XI.

THE ARCHBISHOP RETRENCHES ALL THE MAGNIFICENCE OF HIS PREDECESSORS.—HE PUTS HIS HOUSE IN ORDER, AND REFORMS THE ADMINISTRATION OF HIS REVENUES.

The archbishop thoroughly understood S. Paul's words to Timothy when he said: "*If a man know not how to rule his own house, how shall he take care of the Church of God?*" (1 Tim. iii. 5.) Therefore he determined so to regulate his household that it might serve as a model to all others. He would only have persons of exemplary lives, and not one more than was absolutely necessary. He chose for his chaplains and almoners men of proved wisdom, charity, and piety, selecting also some of the Religious of his own Order to help him in the arduous functions of his ministry. He added some young men to serve the others, but whom he took great care to bring up strictly and well, insisting also on their wearing cassocks, as destined for the ecclesiastical profession. His stable consisted of one mule, which he used when he went out, but which at other times he employed for all sorts of useful purposes. That was all his establishment! He would not hear of chamberlains, or house stewards, or grooms, or pages, or footmen, or gentlemen in waiting, who had always hitherto formed part of the archbishop's retinue. He said that "he must leave such worldly pomp to seculars; and that a bishop who feels himself the representative of Jesus Christ, who was poor, ought to glory in imitating His poverty, and not to try and rival the great of this world in vanity and luxury.

Having chosen his servants with extraordinary care, he laboured incessantly to render their lives holy and exemplary. As they were so few, it was easier to avoid the licence and irregularities common in great households. He insisted that they should be examples of regularity in their religious exercises, of modesty in dress and conversation, and of charity towards one another. In his palace gambling and swearing were unknown. If it happened that any offended against purity in word or deed, he was instantly reprehended, and if necessary dismissed. No one was allowed to sleep out of the house. Although he had full confidence in those whom he had placed at the head of his house, yet so great was his fear of any sin creeping into his establishment, and so disgracing it, that he had his own eye upon them all, and often would go himself and see that his servants were all in, and the doors of his palace closed at the appointed hour.

As to the administration of the revenues of his bishopric, he entrusted it to men of proved honesty and conscientiousness, without either cupidity or avarice, and who were gentle and courteous in reclaiming the monies due. He chose for his treasurer the man he found most charitable to the poor, and most inclined to give alms. His old friend Father John of Leyra had the care of all the temporalities of the house, but was obliged to render an exact account of the expenditure to the archbishop himself. Thus, all superfluous expenses being cut off, and the property administered with such care and fidelity, after having taken what was necessary for the person and household of the archbishop, a very large sum was left for works of charity to the poor.

CHAPTER XII.

THE WAY THE ARCHBISHOP JUDGED IN CIVIL CAUSES; AND THE CHRISTIAN MANNER IN WHICH HE EXACTED THAT JUSTICE SHOULD BE ADMINISTERED BY HIS OFFICERS.

Having taken such pains in the regulation of his household and his revenues, the holy archbishop next devoted himself to the reform of the administration of justice in civil causes, an innumerable number of which came before his court, not as archbishop, but as lord of Braga. But to understand this, it is necessary to say a few words of the peculiar position of this town, and of the temporal power possessed by its archbishop.

The town of Braga is one of the noblest and most ancient, not only in the kingdom of Portugal, but also in Spain. Situated between two great rivers, the Douro and the Migno, in a beautiful and fertile country, the Portuguese look upon it as a terrestrial paradise. The beauty of the town had been enhanced by its previous archbishops, who were not at all like the saint whose life we are relating, but spent a great part of the episcopal revenues in the embellishment of their capital. The cathedral is venerable, not only from its antiquity, but from the magnificent relics it possesses. There are likewise a great many monasteries belonging to different Religious Orders. The Kings of Portugal had conferred on the Archbishops of Braga territorial rights, both over the city and the provinces adjoining. In this way they hold a civil as well as a religious jurisdiction over the people, and have a seneschal (or judge) and a court of justice composed of fourteen counsellors, whose business is to try and to pronounce judgment both in civil and criminal cases.

Now the archbishop, having much at heart to reform the administration of justice in this court, spoke to each of the council separately. He found that in many cases trials were allowed to languish for an indefinite time, to the great detriment of the parties concerned. Then he made inquiries secretly of some persons of known integrity, as to what were the lives and morals of these judges, and how each acquitted himself of his duties.

Having thus obtained all the information he required, he gave notice to the officers of the court that on a certain day he should come himself to the chambers, and preside at the sitting. The judges were very much surprised, yet at the same time pleased at the idea, as they anticipated great amusement at the sight of a monk, so little accustomed to worldly affairs, taking part in matters requiring acute legal knowledge, and in which they flattered themselves he would be utterly at fault.

The day came, and the archbishop walked into the council chamber with a calm and dignified manner, in which assurance was mingled with modesty; and having taken the chair addressed them as follows:

"Had God listened to my wishes and prayers He would have allowed me to remain in the hidden life which I had chosen, and you would have had an archbishop more worthy than myself to bear the heavy burden thrust upon him. But as it has pleased Him to lay upon me these difficult duties, contrary to my own will, He obliges me at the same time to use every effort to acquit myself of these onerous functions to the best of my ability. You know that the Archbishop of Braga is likewise the temporal sovereign of this city and its neighbourhood, and that in that capacity he is bound to see that justice is done towards all men.

"I wish with all my heart that this should be carried out with the greatest exactness and impartiality. But I can only do this through your aid. I conjure you, therefore, to help me to fulfil the solemn charge which God has thus entrusted to me. I am not come here to complain of your conduct. Of some amongst you I know many things which give me satisfaction as regards the past, and hope as regards the future. But the pastoral charity I have towards you, and towards all those to whom you administer justice, obliges me to set before you what a solemn thing it is for one man to judge another; still more for one Christian to judge another Christian. The Pagans themselves have taught us this first lesson, and holy writ teaches us the second. The Holy Spirit, speaking to Moses, whom God had made the lawgiver of His chosen people, shows us, in a few words, how great should be the virtue and integrity of judges, when He says: '*Provide out of all the people, able men, such as fear God, in whom there is truth, and that hate avarice; and appoint them rulers, who may judge the people at all times.*' (Exod. xviii. 21.) He commands them to fear God, because, without that, they could not be firm in resisting injustice and violence, and might be more afraid of displeasing men than of offending God. He wills them to 'love virtue and justice,' as without that they could not hold the scales of justice fairly, and might yield to the interest and solicitations of persons who were dear to them. He orders them to 'hate avarice,' not only lest they should prefer a shameful gain to the duty of their state, and that they might escape a snare into which no honest or conscientious man would fall, but also for fear they should yield to a more subtle and dangerous temptation, namely, one which persuades judges that they are justified in receiving presents. Thus God speaks to them again by the mouth of the same legislator: '*Non accipies munera, quæ etiam excœcant prudentes et subvertunt verba justorum.*' The reason why presents 'blind the wise' is because they do not perceive that such gifts bind them to those from whom they receive them. I trust in the mercy of God, who has called you to this employment, which renders you the arbiters of the property, the honour, and even the life of a man, that He will likewise give you the light of knowledge and discernment of the truth; and a spirit of equity and justice, that you may fulfil these grave duties as He desires. It is true that you are the judges of your brethren, but God is your Judge. They have to give an account of their actions to you; but you have to render an account of yours to Him from Whom no secrets are hid. Your judgments will be judged by Him. Therefore, as those you try, and who come before you in this court, fear you, so should you far more fear Him and invoke Him often, that He may enlighten your understandings and strengthen your hearts, so that you may be, as it were, the mouthpieces and organs of His justice. Who is the man who will not tremble when he considers, in a criminal case, for instance, that his evidence, or one word of his, may deprive a fellow-creature of life? I know that sometimes you are constrained to do this; and that we dare not encourage licence by a hope of impunity. But God forbid we should strip ourselves of humanity or charity, even when called upon to exercise the severities of justice!

Thus a holy doctor says with great justice: '*Facile est atque prociive malos odisse quia mali sunt; rarum autem et pium eosdem ipsos diligere quia homines sunt; ut in uno simul et culpam improbes et naturam approbes; ac propterea culpam justius oderis, quod eâ fœdatur natura quam diligis.*' (August. Epist. 54.) When, then, you are compelled to resort to this extremity, it must be only from respect for the law, for the orders of the sovereign, or from the care necessary for the public safety, which should induce you thus to do violence to mercy and pronounce a sentence of death. But there are other occasions, of less importance, but of more every-day occurrence. I mean those which relate to the property and honour of men, in which I conjure you to exercise the most scrupulous fidelity. Strive, I entreat of you, to shorten as much as possible the time of lawsuits, which so fearfully eat up the fortune of those who plead, and which sometimes outlive the very men whom they are intended to help. How often do we see the rich tyrannising over the weak because the latter have not the means to plead the law, which otherwise would be in their favour. Do not, therefore, permit these long and interminable lawsuits, which ruin all concerned in them, weary those who are compelled to take part in them, and, above all, often constrain the poor to abandon their just rights and give a triumph to an unjust cause.

"The fathers of the Church have said that each father of a household should be a bishop in his own house. But this saying is still more applicable to all of you in the important charge which God has entrusted to you. For bishops should be like God Almighty, the protectors of the poor and the widows, and the father of the orphans; they should maintain their cause against the rich, who oppress and calumniate them; and should defend their rights and do justice to all. Acquit yourselves, then, I entreat you, of this solemn duty as in the sight of God. Do for us in civil causes what we are obliged to do in ecclesiastical matters, or wherever our ministerial duties call us. We ask this of God for you with our whole heart. And we conjure you, with all episcopal tenderness and charity, to take heed to our words. You may be assured that you will always find in us a father who loves you, a friend who will serve you, and an archbishop who will uphold you, if you fulfil, as before God, all the functions of your responsible charge."

The archbishop delivered this speech with the eloquence which was natural to him, heightened by the ardour of his charity, the authority of his position, and the dignity and gravity which in him were habitual. The judges were thunderstruck; for they never expected anything of the sort from him, and had, on the contrary, been very much prejudiced against him. For, as men judge by outward appearances, they could not imagine that any one could be a great archbishop who was not surrounded with that pomp of retinue and crowd of officers, and all that magnificence which had previously accompanied the lords of Braga. Many of them, seeing him in his religious habit, had laughingly said: "He was only a shadow of an archbishop:" and "being only a poor monk, had forgotten that he had been made a prince of the Church:" and "that he had changed his palace into a monastery," &c., &c.

But all these men were struck dumb at the archbishop's manner and words, and felt, by the wisdom of that speech, and the firm determination with which it was uttered, that they had an archbishop to deal with who would not only be the protector of the good and the terror of the bad, but who would also be their master; that his integrity would render him incorruptible; and that his vigilance would allow nothing to escape him. Therefore, all those who were good, honourable, and conscientious, rejoiced at having found so firm a friend, and so powerful a protector in his person; but those whose intentions were not so pure, and who had hitherto abused their trust, felt that they must turn over a new leaf with such a master, and that they could never hope to deceive one who had such a clear discernment of human character and human faults; while he was likewise invested both with the justice which would condemn, and the authority which would punish them.

CHAPTER XIII.

THE ARCHBISHOP PREACHES IN HIS CATHEDRAL CHURCH, AND OF THE SOLIDITY AND FRUIT OF HIS SERMONS.

The archbishop, having thus set his house in order, determined to apply himself mainly to the essential functions of his ministry. He knew that a bishop was not only the minister, but the living image of Jesus Christ, and must, like Him, engender souls by the word of life, and nourish them with the like food: that for this reason St. Paul considers himself sometimes* "*the father*," sometimes "*the mother*," sometimes "*the nurse*," of the children of God, dispensing to them either milk or solid food, according to their wants; thereby teaching us that bishops should foster and develop the divine life in their people's souls by the preaching of the Word. Therefore preaching, according to the teaching of the Council of Trent, has always been considered "*as the principal function of bishops.*" (Sess. 5, cap. 2, de Refor.) And Jesus Christ, who is their model, has given them the example when He

---

* I. Cor. iv. 15; Gal. iv. 19; I. Thessal. ii. 7.

says: "*Me oportet evangelizare, quia ideo missus sum.*"
(Luke iv., v. 43.) Which the apostle confirms in these
words: "*Non misit me Christus baptizare sed evangelizare.*"
(I. Corinth. i. v. 1.) Our holy archbishop being, then,
thoroughly persuaded of this truth, laboured hard to
nourish himself continually with the divine words of holy
writ, and with those of the holy doctors and fathers who
are its interpreters, so as to pour into the souls of his
flock that living water which comes from heaven. He
next determined to preach continually in his cathedral
church, and especially during Advent and Lent, and on
all the great feasts and most of the Sundays of the year.
And he began his course of sermons with admirable fervour of spirit, and amidst an immense concourse of people.

He preached both as a bishop and as a father, uniting
the tenderness and paternal love of the latter with the
dignity and authority of his sacerdotal office. As there
was nothing low or familiar in his expressions, neither
was there anything studied or affected. Everything he
said was grave, judicious, and solid, and conformable to
the majesty of the divine word, with which his whole heart
and mind were filled. And we may, therefore, truly say
that he was one of those wise men of whom St. Augustine
speaks, when he applies to them those words of Solomon:
"*The multitude of the wise is the welfare of the whole
world.*" (Wisdom vi. v. 26.) For, according to the excellent
rule of this same father: "A preacher speaks with the
more or the less wisdom, as he is more or less advanced
in the love and knowledge of holy Scripture." "*Sapienter
dicit homo tantò magis, vel minus, quantò in Scripturis sacris
magis, minusve profecerit.*" (De Doct. Chr. L. 4. cap. 5.)

His great anxiety, therefore, was to stir up his congregation; to wake them from the state of profound ignorance
in which many of them were plunged; to root out abuses
and vices; to strike the minds of the careless and indif-

ferent by bringing before them the judgments of God, and so to persuade them to think seriously of their salvation; in a word, to try and touch them, so as to soften the hardness of their hearts and lead them to a real and solid conversion, and a total change of life. He proposed to himself, as a model, those wise words of St. Bernard: "*The dove should be the image of a preacher. She moans more than she sings, and teaches us how we should sigh during this our exile. I like to hear a preacher who does not think of pleasing me that I may applaud what he says; but who touches my heart, so that I begin to weep over myself. You will become indeed one of those holy doves if you thus teach men to enter into themselves and groan over their own miseries: and you will teach them this, not by mere words, but by identifying yourself with them and groaning over yourself. For in this, as in so many other things, example is incomparably more powerful than words.*" (In Cant. Serm. 59. no. 3.) This rule was followed by our holy prelate. He prayed and sighed much before God before going into the pulpit, remembering the words of St. Augustine addressed to preachers of the Gospel: "*Let him love to pray before he speaks, so that he may give that which he has received from on high: and let him ask of God, amid the multitude of explanations or expressions which may come into his head, that he may choose those which He, who knoweth the heart of man, may see to be the most likely to touch the souls of those that listen to him.*" (De Doctr. Chr. L. 4, cap. 15.) In the same way the apostles of old reserved to themselves the duty of "*prayer and the ministering of the word,*" (Acts vi. v. 4) to teach us that those two things are inseparable; and that both one and the other belong specially to the bishops, who are their successors.

Having, then, taken the utmost care to draw down the blessing of God on his words, they were listened to by everybody with the greatest respect and attention; for all knew that his own heart was in perfect accordance with his tongue, and that his actions bore witness to the truth of his words. He taught fathers of families to look upon the Christian education of their children as the most important affair they had in this world, and the principal means of their own salvation, if we are to believe St. Paul; and that the same apostle exhorts them to have a particular care of their servants and household. And, at the same time, those who heard him knew that his episcopal palace was a model of perfect regularity, and that all belonging to, or dependent on him, were examples of piety and exemplary modesty.

He taught the rich to beware of avarice and luxury, and to despise the perishable goods of this world to gain heaven; and they saw that the bishop himself trampled underfoot, with the most entire disinterestedness, all the riches of the earth, with its pomps and vanities.

He pictured in strong colours to the sensual and voluptuous, that, being enslaved by their passions, they would pay, for transitory delights, the cost of eternal torments. And his hearers felt that, notwithstanding his high position, his magnificent palace, and the example of other prelates, nothing had been able to weaken the rigour or austerity of his mortified and penitent life.

He preached a zeal for justice to all who had to administer it: and every one knew how firm and inflexible he was himself in that virtue. Finally, he brought every one to make large alms, each according to his ability, saying, that the salvation or damnation of Christians mainly depended on their fidelity or negligence in obeying this precept. And his hearers were well aware, that, although archbishop, he lived himself as a poor man, and laboured day and night, in public and in private, to be the nursing-mother of the poor, and the helper and protector of the weak and miserable. Thus one could say of his sermons, as of those of Jesus Christ: "*In potestate erat sermo ipsius;*" (St. Luke iv. v. 32,) for he taught nothing to others which he had not first practised himself: "*Cœpit facere et docere.*" (Acts i. v. 1.)

CHAPTER XIV.

THE ARCHBISHOP COMMENCES HIS VISITATION IN THE MIDDLE OF WINTER. — HE ENCOURAGES HIS FOLLOWERS BY THE EXAMPLE OF A LITTLE SHEPHERD.

Three or four months were spent as we have described; but at the beginning of the following year the archbishop determined to make a visitation of his diocese. He knew that the bishops had learnt from the apostles to exercise this function with the utmost care, being one of the most important in their ministry. Thus, in the Acts of the Apostles, we find St. Paul saying to Barnabas: "*Let us return and visit our brethren in all the cities wherein we have preached the word of the Lord, and see how they do.*" (Acts xv. v. 36.) Following this rule and example, the councils have insisted on the necessity of this visitation by the bishops, as the same apostle says to the bishops of Asia: "*Take heed to yourselves and to the whole flock, wherein the Holy Ghost hath placed you bishops, to rule the Church of God, which He hath purchased with His own blood.*" (Acts xx. v. 28.) This can only be done, say the Council, by personal visitation: "*ut episcopus nemini desit,*" (Conc. Provinc. Colon. ann. 1549,) so that the bishop may, by his vigilance, supply the wants of all. And they add that it is in this manner that he learns to know, to stop, and to prevent, even the greatest disorders. That is why it is said in the Gospels, that "*while men* were asleep the enemy came and oversowed cockle among the wheat, and went his way." (St. Matt. xiii. 25.) Which means, the evils which creep in from false doctrine. And again the Councils: "*Dormiunt prelati qui non visitant. Soli vigilant et servant custodias noctis super gregem suum, qui mala quæ matuuntur, visitatione præcidunt.*" (ibid.)

The archbishop, filled with this spirit, and burning with zeal for souls, resolved to commence his visitation in the middle of winter. His chapter and council strongly opposed this resolution. They represented to him that the weather was very bad; that the country he was about to visit was subject to heavy falls of snow and horrible cold; that he would thus be exposing his own health to great danger as well as that of his suite; and that he had infinitely better postpone his holy intention till Lent was over, and spring had brought about a milder temperature. But the archbishop replied to all these reasons, that a good pastor did not think either of the cold of winter, or the heat of summer, when it was a question of looking after and serving his sheep; and that, on the contrary, it was in such seasons that his presence was the more necessary. That since he had been made archbishop, his life no longer belonged to himself, but to his flock; and that he would not be doing his duty to his people if he thought, for one moment, of sparing his own health, when it was a question of saving their souls.

It was useless to argue with one who was guided by a purer and higher light than that of mere human reason. So that, encouraging his priests as much as he could, and urging them to take part in his apostolate, and be the co-operators in his ministry, he set out in the very middle of winter, and began his visitation.

His only anxiety during this journey was for those who accompanied him; for hard as he was towards himself, he was tender and compassionate towards every one else. He would have liked to suffer himself what all had to share alike. He was always the first to confront any danger, and the last to accept any alleviation in their position: and with his wonderful sweetness and cheerfulness he bore every discomfort without a word of complaint, so that his companions were ashamed to grumble, and his example encouraged them to make every sacrifice for the good of souls.

One day, passing from one village to another, they were overtaken by a tremendous storm of very cold rain, followed by so biting a wind that they were almost frozen with cold. The archbishop was marching on in front, on his mule, preferring thus to travel alone, that he might occupy himself with holy thoughts on the way. Whilst, then, he was struggling on in spite of the weather, he perceived a little shepherd boy all in rags and wet through, who was watching some sheep on the hill side. At the bottom of this hill there was a cavern which would have sheltered him from the storm. Filled with pity for the poor child, he stopped his mule, and told him to come down and take shelter under the rock. The shepherd boy replied: "I should not dare, sir; for if I were not to watch over my flock the wolf would come and carry off one of my sheep, or a fox might strangle one of my lambs." "Well, what difference would that make to you?" replied the archbishop. "O sir," answered the boy, "it would make all the difference in the world to me, for I am responsible for these sheep to my father, who is at home, and he would scold me well, and I should be in great luck if I came off even as cheaply as that. I watch over my flock, and he over me."

The archbishop, charmed with his answer, waited till his companions came up, and then, pointing to the child, said: "Look, my brethren, some of you think we are doing too much; yet we do less than this poor little shepherd boy. He suffers as we do, and more than we do; yet he has only the care of beasts, and we of souls; he watches against the wolves, and we against the demons; he does it to please his father, and we to please God; his reward is the poor food he gets, ours is paradise. I think God Himself must have sent us this little child, for his example speaks volumes to us, and his patience is a lesson to us all."

His companions were touched by the child, and by the instruction he had drawn from so slight an incident. But it was impossible not to admire the vigour of his piety and courage, which, in spite of all the difficulties which surrounded him, kept him ever on the alert for the teaching of God, seeing His Hand in every object, and following Him in all things.

CHAPTER XV.

OF THE ZEAL, PRUDENCE, AND CHARITY OF THE ARCHBISHOP IN HIS VISITATION.

Great as had been the archbishop's zeal in undertaking this visitation, he had not the less care and vigilance in carrying it out. This is the way he set to work.

After getting up very early in the morning, and repeating his usual prayers, he said Mass in the church of the place where he was, and administered the Sacrament of Confirmation. He then preached, in a clear and simple manner, so that his words might be within the comprehension of the poorest of his hearers. He spoke principally against impurity, a vice which was deplorably common in that country, and his horror of it made him speak with unusual force of sins "more worthy" (as he said) "of beasts than men."

A very pernicious custom had slipped into the churches in that neighbourhood with regard to immorality, of which the devil himself must have been the inventor. For when any scandal of that sort had been perpetrated, the parties were asked if they would marry or not. And if they would not consent, a certain sum of money was exacted, which was looked upon as an equivalent for the sin, and no more notice was taken of the matter. The archbishop, whose mind was pure, and whose judgment was clear, had a horror of anything which savoured of self-interest or condoning of sin, and was consequently greatly shocked at this abuse. It seemed to him that thus to sell the impunity of crime was an infamy which dishonoured, not only the episcopal dignity, but the Christian religion itself. He knew that this shameful traffic encouraged the vicious in their sinful courses; and that those whose business it was to reprove them would say nothing if sufficiently paid for their silence. To remedy this great evil, therefore, he resolved to forbid the church to such persons, and sent orders all round the country that none should be permitted to hear Mass in any place whatever who persisted in such conduct. This strong measure had its effect. The fear of being altogether excommunicated and rejected by both God and man had great weight in those days, and the archbishop had the consolation of seeing many repent of their crimes, and return as true penitents to the fold.

But he did not limit his zeal to the reformation of great and crying evils. He took equal care to heal differences in families; to bring about peace in households, and a better understanding between husbands and wives, parents and children, servants and masters; to reconcile all who were at variance, and give them openings whereby little heartburnings could be soothed, and love take the place of hatred. But his chief care was to raise and watch over the conduct of the pastors of each church. He examined carefully into the accusations made against them, or into the praises they received. He watched their method of instructing the poor and ignorant; their reverence in administering the holy sacraments, or celebrating the divine office; and their conduct both within and without the church. Those whom he found worthily fulfilling the duties of their important charge he treated with the greatest honour, making them dine at his table, and feel that he would always be their friend and protector. He exhorted them to labour with still greater fervour in the work of saving souls bought with the Precious Blood, and for whom they would have to give so strict an account. Thus he encouraged the good and strengthened the weak; while he was not wanting in vigour and severity towards those of whom he had received just complaints, menacing them with extreme measures, and making them feel the full force of his displeasure. He put down in a little memorandum book all that he had remarked in his visitation; and in order that it might remain more secret he made marks known only to himself, representing the qualities of each priest. Round the good he would draw a white circle; round the bad a black one; and those he suspected would have a line half white and half black. This little book he took with him in all subsequent visitations, which he found most useful, as he could not then be imposed upon by false reports, either for or against the persons concerned.

One day, having found out an instance of grave irregularity in an ecclesiastic of high degree and position, he frankly reproved him for it. The accused, taken by surprise, could not answer the charges brought against him, and so had recourse to the common excuse "that the archbishop was his enemy, and so, ready to believe anything said against him." The archbishop replied with great sweetness and gentleness: "My brother, how can I be your enemy when I bear you always on my heart?" and at the same moment opened his breast and showed him a paper on which his name was inscribed; and then began speaking to him with such exceeding love and sweetness that the culprit's heart was touched to the quick, and he not only confessed his past sins, but ever after led a most holy and mortified life, and looked upon the archbishop as his greatest friend, and the best physician of his soul.

During this visitation, likewise, he made a memorandum of all the most earnest and holy priests he met, so that when an opportunity occurred he could promote them to more important cures in his diocese. Having found out that many persons, at their death, had left large sums to the Church in order to obtain the suffrages of Masses and prayers, which money had been quietly appropriated by the clergy for other purposes, he insisted upon the most minute restitution being made, so that the wishes of the dead should be punctually fulfilled.

Another incident happened during this journey, proving the charity and prudence which this holy pastor evinced in the care of his flock. He found out that a certain rich lord of high birth was living a most scandalous life. He did not see how he could pass over such conduct; and yet his high position entitled him to some respect. Having recommended the affair with earnest prayer to God, it came about that this man was urged out of civility to come himself and pay a visit to the archbishop. The latter received him with great honour, and having begged him to be seated, he placed himself by his side. Then, every one having left the room, and finding themselves alone together, the archbishop suddenly rose and threw himself at his feet, exclaiming: "Forgive me if I tell you of the sorrow which is in my heart. Love may be importunate, but is always excusable, as it is only prompted to speak from pure affection. God has entrusted me with the care of your soul, and I cannot look on calmly while I see it on the point of perishing. I am your friend, and I wish that God should be so too. But He cannot be so unless you change your way of life. I conjure you, therefore, to have pity on yourself and on me, for I shall never know a moment's rest or peace as long as I see you in such danger." The gentleman was so astonished at the excessive tenderness and humility of the archbishop, that, having conjured him to rise, he rushed out of his presence. But the words the holy pastor had spoken bore immediate fruit: he entered into himself, conceived a horror of his previous sins, was entirely converted to God, and, from that moment, led the most exemplary life. He said afterwards, that the ardent zeal the archbishop had shown for his soul, combined with the extreme humility of one he looked upon as a saint, had worked a revulsion of feeling in him which all menaces, or severity, or representations of the judgments of God, had hitherto failed to effect.

The paternal charity of the archbishop was shown quite as strongly in his reception of the poor and ignorant; and his patience and gentleness were so great that no cloud came across his face, no matter how wearisome or importunate his visitors might be. Often, when he arrived at a place, for confirmation or other matters, many would come late and oblige him to begin all over again; but he was never disturbed or put out, and left whatever else he might be doing to attend to them. So that it became a saying amongst them that no one could come to the archbishop at a wrong moment; for his time always belonged to others, and his will to the will of God.

After having visited all the country in the neighbourhood of Valentia, he made a détour by Varcelos, which was at seven or eight leagues distance, and there discovered, while looking over the list of his parishes, that one little church on his way had not been visited. He instantly retraced his steps in that direction, telling his servant that he had forgotten something very important. When they arrived at this church he was almost tired to death, and excused himself to his companions for the trouble he had given them, stating the cause of his return, and adding: "You see, my children, that I am like the head physician of fourteen hundred hospitals, which is the number of parishes I have in my diocese. If, then, there were only one sick man in this little parish, which is one of these hospitals, do you think I should be excusable, in the sight of God, if I were to let him die without coming to see him, this being a clear obligation on my part? It is true that I have provided each hospital with a doctor— i.e., a rector, a vicar, or a curate,—but, as the principal physician, I have the superintendance of them all; and it is my business to see that they take proper care of their sick; for, if they should fail, their negligence would be laid to my charge. It is well, also, to teach them, by example, what the charity of pastors should be, so that they may devote themselves heart and soul to their duties, seeing how precious a single soul committed to us is in the sight of God."

This visitation lasted rather more than a month, and as it was continually renewed throughout the diocese, few, if any, evils could escape his vigilance. For, besides insisting upon seeing everything with his own eyes, and inquiring minutely into the character of his priests, he set his face so vigorously to reform the scandals which had arisen in previous times, that, whereas evils formerly went on with unchecked impunity, his wholesome severity awoke the most indifferent to a sense of their duty, and raised the whole tone of public opinion, so that those who persisted in wrong-doing were visited with universal reprobation.

Before concluding this chapter I will mention another anecdote worth remembering. As he visited every village, however poor and miserable it might be, he was one evening obliged to stop for the night in a hamlet which was so wretched and ruinous that there was only one single house with a tiled roof, which, in consequence, was pompously called the "castle." All the rest were built of earth and mud, and covered with branches of trees. His servants went to the "castle" accordingly, to prepare his bed. But he absolutely forbid them to go there, saying that he would not be lodged better than his people. They represented to him that in these mud cabins he would not even be sheltered from the rain, which fell in torrents. But he would not yield to their entreaties. Whilst they were talking together that night of his humility, and of his determination not to be better treated than any one else, his servants heard a great noise, of which they could not guess the cause. But the next day they found that it was this very castle, where they had so wished to lodge their master, which had fallen in, and had become a heap of ruins. The archbishop, having heard this, returned thanks to God for His visible protection, and said to his followers: "Learn from this incident, my children, that the poverty of Jesus Christ is useful, not only for a future life, but also very often for this one; for one lodges more safely in a humble hut than in a castle: and those who love what appears to be the most magnificent in this world, are often overwhelmed in its ruins."

CHAPTER XVI.

THE ARCHBISHOP LABOURS TO INSTRUCT HIMSELF THE PRIESTS AND PEOPLE OF HIS DIOCESE.

The archbishop hastened, after his visitation, to return to Braga, so as to be there during Lent. He preached through all this holy season regularly and daily to his people, and with the same edification as in previous years.

Easter-time being one of comparative rest, he began seriously to consider what could be done for the improvement of his diocese, and to remedy some of the serious evils he had discovered during his visitation. He felt that the majority of his people were sunk in the most profound ignorance, which frequently resulted in shameful and horrible crimes; and that the origin of the mischief often was the insufficiency of their pastors, and sometimes the scandalous lives they led. He saw plainly that, according to the word of the Son of God, the body of his diocese would always be in darkness so long as its pastors, who should be its eyes, were thus blinded, as St. Gregory the Great fully explained in his commentary on the text: *"If then the light that is in thee be darkness, the darkness itself how great shall it be!"* (St. Matt. vi. *v.* 23.) Wishing therefore to supply the needs of so many abandoned souls, nominally Christians, without having either faith or the knowledge of Jesus Christ, he composed a little Catechism in the vulgar tongue, explaining in simple terms the principal mysteries of our religion, and he imposed upon all such curates as were unable to preach to their people the duty of reading this book to them after the Gospel, so as to instruct them in the faith. He wrote also some short and simple sermons, for the different feasts of the year, and for the Sundays in Lent and Advent, which he gave orders should be read on those days when there was no preacher, so as to teach the people the meaning of the Church's year, and encourage them in the practice of all Christian virtues. Knowing also the effect which the Lives of Saints have in touching the hearts of men, he caused a book to be printed in the vulgar tongue, containing the histories of all the saints mentioned in the Church Calendar, which he published at his own cost, and distributed throughout his diocese.

He summoned also some of the most able religious of his Order, to instruct those who should hereafter be called to the cure of souls. And he established a seminary in his own palace at Braga, which he endowed in perpetuity, so that those who had a vocation for the priesthood might there be trained free of cost, and pursue their studies under his own eye. He chose a wise and virtuous priest to be at the head of this seminary, of whom he exacted a rigorous supervision of the students, lest any vice or irregularity should creep into the house, taking care to impress upon his mind that he cared far less for their progress in their studies than for the holiness and purity of their lives, without which all learning would be worse than useless.

In fact, there was no stone left unturned by the archbishop to strive to improve the education and morality of his diocese, especially among his priests; and being full of this idea, he addressed himself to the Society of Jesus, whose college at Coimbra for the training of missionaries for the East had produced such wonderful fruits.

The eagerness which God had put into his heart for the extension of the kingdom of Jesus Christ throughout the world, had inspired him with the deepest veneration for

S. Francis Xavier and his companions; and for that reason his most earnest wish was to be assisted in the reformation of his diocese by the disciples of the great S. Ignatius, who, having so admirably formed and directed his Society, had died only five or six years before. The archbishop wrote, therefore, to the new General, Father John Lainés, setting forth his difficulties, the extreme ignorance of his people, and the necessity of doing all in his power to raise the tone of his priesthood, which had fallen so low in those degenerate times; and ended by imploring him to send at least twelve of his fathers to teach and preach to the people, while he prepared a suitable college for their reception. The chapter of the town somewhat objected to the proposal of this new foundation; but the archbishop, with his consummate prudence, removed by degrees every obstacle, and those who had been most opposed to the introduction of the Jesuits, came round to his way of thinking, when they found the impossibility of finding any other persons equally reliable for the important missions with which the Society was to be entrusted.

CHAPTER XVII.

OF HIS EXTREME CARE IN THE SELECTION OF THOSE WHO ASPIRED TO HOLY ORDERS, AND HIS DESIRE THAT ALL HIS PRIESTS SHOULD BE FULLY OCCUPIED.

This great servant of God, as we have before said, spent every moment of his time which could be spared from his laborious functions, in studying Holy Scripture and the Fathers of the Church. Hence arose his extraordinary reverence for the priesthood of Jesus Christ. The idea he had conceived of it was so grand, and so profoundly engraved in his heart, that when candidates for Holy Orders were brought before him, he could not help examining them in the light of God's word, and weighing them in the balance of the sanctuary, with what some considered almost an undue severity. It surprised those around him to see that, great as was his anxiety to obtain a larger number of priests for his vast diocese, and deeply as he had deplored the lack of pastors during his visitation, he yet was so difficult in the selection of the men who presented themselves for ordination. The truth was, that looking only to God in this matter, he did not dare admit any one to fulfil these high functions unless fully persuaded that they were directly called by the Holy Spirit Himself. In consequence, nothing could be more rigorous than his inquiry into every detail of their past lives. Not content with their proficiency in learning, he exacted positive proofs of their love towards God, and their zeal for the salvation of souls. And if he found reason to doubt anything in their antecedents, he would delay their ordination until fully satisfied of a thorough change of heart; and no prayers or interest from any quarter could make him yield. On this point alone he was inexorable. Many would bring foreign recommendations to back up their requests; but he would always reply, that the very fact of their having obtained these was a proof that they had little merit of their own, and that the only passport to his favour was true personal holiness. For those who came to him filled with an ardent love of God and their neighbour were always warmly received; and if their humility made them shrink from the thought of the priesthood, he encouraged them in every possible way. But he indignantly rejected all those who sought to lead others, without being able to guide themselves, and "who wished to *rise, from ambitious motives alone, to the ministry of humility.*" *(S. Greg. Past., part 1, cap. 1.)*

He had the strongest aversion for those who, instead of earning their living in an ordinary manner, strove by a horrible sacrilege to make a traffic of holy things, and sacrifice the priesthood to their avaricious views, by looking upon it as any ordinary profession. Abuses of this sort had crept in everywhere, which he scourged with the utmost severity, and drove from the altars all men, however high in position, in whom he found these shameful dispositions. This gave great offence in many quarters, of which, however, the archbishop took no sort of heed. He was especially anxious regarding those who were admitted to the sub-diaconate, for, as that is the first step in Holy Orders, and, failing in that, a man is still free to enter into any other profession, the archbishop expected great things of those who thus presented themselves, and made them give up altogether the idea of the priesthood, if they were unable to maintain the purity and perfection of life which he considered indispensable. It was remarked that when he administered the Sacrament of Ordination, he did it with such dignity, and with exhortations of so fervent a nature, that everyone was filled with a holy fear and reverence. He made a rule in his diocese, which he considered very advantageous for those aspiring to the ecclesiastical state, remembering the words of the Wise man: "*Idleness hath taught much evil*" (Ecclesiasticus xxxiii. verse 29); and that was only to receive those who knew some trade, or had some occupation which should prevent their falling into lazy habits, and then into other disorders. For not only would their work be a safe-guard, but it would enable them to support themselves in case of any reverses, without being obliged to have recourse to alms. And as he had a great respect for all the ordinances of the Church, and always tried to form his conduct by those rules, he took this idea from the Fourth Council of Carthage, which ecclesiastical authorities call *the treasure of the Church's discipline,* and which orders in its fifty-first Canon, " *that clerics, however learned they may be in the word of God, should learn some trade whereby they might, if needful, earn their bread.*" (Clericus quantum libet verbo Dei eruditus, artificio victum quærat) ; and in the fifty-second Canon : " *Let clerics earn something wherewith to clothe and feed themselves, either by some light trade, or by cultivating the ground, without interfering, however, with their holier functions.*" (Clericus victum et vestimentum, sibi artificiolo, vel agriculturâ absque officii sui detrimento paret.) He wished to put these holy regulations in practice, suggested, as they were, by the Church, under the inspiration of the Holy Spirit; but he would not oblige his ecclesiastics to follow them against their own inclinations, such practices having unfortunately fallen into disuse.

CHAPTER XVIII.

THE ARCHBISHOP'S FRIENDS, SEEING HIM OVERWHELMED WITH WORK, IMPLORE HIM TO APPOINT A COADJUTOR, WHICH HE REFUSES TO DO.

While the archbishop was thus labouring with might and main to fulfil the arduous duties of his ministry, the Devil was preparing a snare for him; and one all the more dangerous, as it was cloaked with an appearance of prudence and charity. Some of his friends, seeing the heavy responsibility of his office, the multiplicity of his cares, the anxiety of his mind, together with the austerity of his life, were touched with compassion, and fancying they had found a remedy for these evils, addressed themselves to him as follows : " That it appeared to them that the work he had undertaken exceeded his strength ; that at Braga his whole days were occupied in judging and hearing secular cases, and his whole nights in prayer, composition, and study; that on his visitations all these labours were redoubled: yet, that in spite of such superhuman labours, he never relaxed the austerity of his life; that it was impossible any human frame could stand such fatigues; that though he was a bishop, he was still a man; that he should consider the weakness of human nature, and measure his labours accordingly; that God, while He enjoins charity, enjoins also prudence and discretion, and wishes that zeal should be tempered with both; that if he did not value his life for himself, he owed it to his flock, to whose welfare he had vowed it; in a word, that in order that his life should be prolonged, without giving up any of the obligations of his charge, he should appoint a titular bishop as a coadjutor, who should relieve him from a portion of his work. That this was the invariable custom in so extensive a diocese as his own; that his predecessors had done it; and that thus he would preserve his life, and be an example and guide to his flock for a longer period."

The archbishop, whose soul was enlightened by the Spirit of God, considered that flesh and blood had inspired these thoughts in persons otherwise good and virtuous, and, in consequence, he replied to them with his usual tranquillity: "That he was very grateful to them for the care they showed for his body; that he thought their intention was kind and praiseworthy; but that as to the advice they gave him, he begged them to consider that we have a very subtle enemy, who frequently makes use of those who are the servants of God, to speak to men who are likewise in His service, but in whom he has no part; that as they had implored him to remember that he was a man, he would likewise beg them to consider that he was a bishop; that no one would dream of warning the general of an army that he might be killed if he exposed himself to the chances of war, because every one knew that it was a general's business to expose himself to danger, as a leader of his troops; that no one considered whether he lived or died, but whether he led his troops bravely.

"In the same manner, that it was not necessary that he, as bishop, should live; that the salvation of his people did not depend on his life; that the great God needed no one; that having preserved the Church of Braga many centuries before him, He would equally care for it after he was dead; that as to appointing a coadjutor, he knew well that the Church allowed it, but that it could only be granted when absolute necessity or the infirmities of age demanded it, and not if asked for from idleness or softness; that he was resolved, with the grace of God, and as long as his strength lasted, to go on as he had begun; that labour without ceasing was the portion of a bishop, and that with this feeling, he ought never to fear shortening his days, as he could neither look for rest nor reward till the hour of death."

His friends were completely silenced by his answer, and could only admire the unshakeable firmness with which the love of God inspired him. They felt like the friends of S. Paul, when they conjured him not to go up to Jerusalem, where it had been prophesied he should have to suffer terrible things; and who, when they found him inflexible in his resolution, and willing to face death itself, submitted themselves to the will of God, exclaiming: "*Domine voluntas fiat.*" (Acts xxi., verse 15.)

CHAPTER XIX.

OF THE GREAT CHARITY OF THE ARCHBISHOP TOWARDS THE POOR, THE SICK, AND ALL WHO NEEDED HIS HELP.

This holy prelate, striving to imitate S. Paul in all the functions of his ministry, imitated him equally in his charity and in his tenderness and compassion towards the poor. He considered that his position as archbishop made him their father and nursing mother. He was always devising fresh schemes for their relief, and looked upon all their wants as his own. The following is the rule he adopted in the distribution of his alms.

In his first visitation he demanded an exact return of all those in real distress in each parish, not only of those who sought relief, but of others who hid their poverty from all human eyes to suffer in secret; and having received these returns, he drew up a memorandum, in which he entered the names, ages, sex, and state of all these poor people, and then caused the necessary relief to be given to each, according to their need. The numbers thus relieved were enormous; for before he had visited a third part of his diocese, he had already sent clothes and necessaries to four hundred poor people. He made a similar inquiry into the condition of all his poor people at Braga, and took particular care of the orphans and widows, and of young girls who had no means of living. His vigilance in this respect was so great, that there was no need, however hidden, of which he was not informed. And because he was always afraid of sinning against charity, lest the delicacy of some people who had known better days should induce them to hide their distress, he employed a number of good and virtuous persons to hunt up those who would rather suffer any amount of misery than make their circumstances known; and to them he secretly sent assistance in various ways, so as to fulfil the obligation which he considered was laid upon him, to come to their relief.

If, for instance, he discovered, on inquiry into the lives and habits of any of these poor people, that their poverty was accompanied by great virtue and piety, he would instantly enter their names in a memorandum-book kept for this purpose, and desire his almoner to send them every week a certain quantity of wheat, meat, and fish, according to their families. If they were of a higher class, he would give them a certain sum of money every month. And all these charities were managed with such regularity and exactitude, that each one knew the very day when he would receive it, and that there would never be the smallest retrenchment or diminution in the gift. The archbishop also paid the rent of a great many of the poor people's houses, especially if they were old or sick. He maintained a doctor, at his own expense, to visit the poor only; and he used to say that we should look upon the poor as our bankers, who will give us high interest for our money in heaven.

Besides these charities, the archbishop gave food or money every Wednesday and Friday to all the poor who came to his palace, and sometimes there were upwards of a thousand persons thus relieved. But as he knew that spiritual alms were more important than corporal, he employed a good and earnest priest to preach to them the word of God before distributing their bodily food.

He always had some little money about his person, as he could not bear to refuse any one who asked him for an alms, wishing to fulfil to the letter the command of our

Saviour: "*Give to every one that asketh thee.*" (S. Luke vi., verse 30.)

He was also most liberal in the sums he awarded to different monasteries and convents, for he felt that, according to the words of many holy doctors, we gave specially to eat and drink to Jesus Christ when we gave alms to those whose pure, holy, and disinterested lives prove that they are really members of His body, and faithful imitators of His poverty. These charities cost him a great deal, because they were perpetual. And another great expense to him was the general hospital, which he had founded on his first arrival at Braga, and of which he had the whole charge. He had also established infirmaries in the different parishes, both for men and women, which he had provided with everything necessary for the sick, and whom he constantly visited himself.

But there was another form of alms which he exercised, and that was the virtue of hospitality, recommended by S. Paul to all bishops. He used to say that he considered himself the guest in his own house, and the poor as its legitimate owners. As a great many religious of different orders, and poor priests, came on business to Braga, or passed through it on their way to their respective houses, the archbishop bought some property adjoining his palace, and built there a home to receive them, considering himself aggrieved if any went to an inn.

He placed in this house a respectable married man as a steward, and gave him means to furnish it with every necessary and comfort, and with a fixed income to defray the expenses of his guests. Every day their dinner and supper was sent, ready cooked, from the archbishop's palace, and however great the number might be, the servants were never taken by surprise; for a large quantity of food was always supplied, and what was not wanted for the guests, was distributed among the poor.

Neither seculars nor sick were received into this house, nor could the ecclesiastics themselves, for whom it had been founded, remain there more than a certain number of days, for fear that they should take advantage of the comforts they there enjoyed, and thus be induced to lose their time in idleness. But those who had real business to detain them, could always obtain permission to do so.

In the palace itself, the archbishop received three classes of persons. The first were the rectors, vicars, and curates of his whole diocese, who came to him on business regarding their parishes or churches. He received them with extreme joy, looking upon them as his brothers and coadjutors, without whose aid he could not acquit himself of the duties of his office. So that he would have his palace doors always open to them, both to board and lodge, and to provide them with everything they required.

The second class consisted of those who had at some former time been in his household, or living in his house. If they came for lawsuits, he only let them stay a few days, because he considered it would be unfair to let them live free of expense, and prolong a suit which might be the ruin of the opposite party. But if it were not a question of a lawsuit, he let them stay as long as they liked.

The third class to whom his palace was always open, was the Religious of his own Order, who came to Braga. He had set apart a wing of his palace on purpose for them, where no one else was admitted, and which was fitted up like the monasteries of their order. The way in which he forestalled and thought of every one's comfort and convenience was the astonishment of all; and, in truth, there was no need, corporal or spiritual, which was not relieved by the fatherly hand of the archbishop.

But he did not only give alms of his abundance, like the

rich; he retrenched absolute necessaries for himself, (like the widow in the Gospel,) so as to have more to give, and thus to exercise the most perfect form of charity.

One day, the procurator of his house, seeing that he was still wearing the habit he had when prior of his order, which was getting very old and ragged, sent the tailor with a piece of new, fine stuff, to make him a fresh one. The archbishop took out his memorandum-book, and asked the tailor if he knew three young girls, whom he mentioned to him, who were living with their widowed mother in great poverty, but who were noted for their goodness and piety. The tailor replied that he knew them. "Then go to them," replied the archbishop, "and make them out of this stuff three nice gowns, without letting them find out where it came from."

Another time, when they had given him a new cloak to wear on Easter Day, he called his almoner, who was entirely in his confidence, and told him to take it to a tradesman of the town, who was very old and sick, and to tell him to make himself a coat out of it.

One day, he heard by chance that a poor woman, who was very ill, and to whom he daily sent a dinner, had a wretched bed, and that the greatest part of her sufferings arose from the cold which she felt, having no blankets or anything to cover her, though it was in the depth of winter. No sooner did he hear this, than he ran to his own bed, and taking off one of the two blankets, he rolled it up, and calling a boy whom he was training as a cleric, told him to take it directly to the woman, without any one knowing anything about it.

On another occasion, a very old woman came into his room, whose extreme poverty, in the midst of winter, was shown by the thinness of her clothes. The archbishop was alone at the moment, and could not find anything to give her; so he tore down a piece of cloth which made a "portiere" to his room to keep out the draught, and after having folded it up, gave it to her.

We have entered into all these little details, because they give a real idea of the extraordinary charity of one whose whole life was a series of similar acts. He had the firm conviction that all his goods belonged to the poor; that he was only the dispenser of them; and that they were always to be preferred before himself, so that he had even a scruple about taking the most necessary things for his own use. In fact, he verified in his own person a saying attributed to another saint: "That he was avaricious for himself, liberal towards his friends, and only extravagant in dealing with the poor."

CHAPTER XX.

FATHER LOUIS OF GRENADA PROPOSES TO THE ARCHBISHOP GREATER MAGNIFICENCE IN HIS PALACE.—THE ARCHBISHOP JUSTIFIES HIS CONDUCT BY THE CANONS OF THE CHURCH; AND GRENADA IS COMPELLED IN THE END TO AGREE WITH HIM.

Towards the beginning of the summer of 1560, Father Louis of Grenada came to Braga, bringing with him Dom Bernard of the Cross, a Religious of his Order, who had been bishop of S. Toma, and had then resigned his bishopric, and retired to his monastery. The apparent reason for Louis of Grenada's visit to Braga was, that as he was making a visitation of the convents of his order, civility required him to come and see the archbishop on his way, even without regard to his old friendship.

But the secret reason of his visit was the report which had reached Lisbon of the extreme poverty of the archbishop's palace and household. As his election had given such offence to so many persons of high rank, who envied his position, they watched every detail in his conduct, to find, if possible, some matter for reproach. The ambition which had previously blinded them to their own unfitness for so solemn a charge, now made them shut their eyes to all the rare qualities of this excellent and holy archbishop, and try to find out every imaginable defect in him, although such defects existed only in their own imaginations. They saw everything he did in a wrong light; and published far and wide that he was a bishop only in name,—that he would never even wear the episcopal dress. They called his frugality, shameful meanness; his careful management of his revenue, in order to relieve a greater number of poor, was only the result of avarice; his assiduity in all the functions of his office was degrading to episcopal dignity; and lastly, his humility and moderation were only a sign of his mean origin and unworthiness for the post.

Grenada was pained at the malignity of these persons, and at the effect of their calumnies in throwing a cloud over the zeal and virtue of so eminent a prelate. He also felt how these reproaches fell tacitly back on himself, as every one knew that he had been one of the main instigators of the election.

To be able, therefore, more thoroughly to refute these calumnies, he determined to go to the archbishop's palace, and judge with his own eyes if the accusations, so freely brought against him, had any foundation in fact.

The archbishop received his guests with a joy and gladness not to be told, but made no further change in his table than that of having one dish more.

The provincial, after watching narrowly everything that went on in the house, became more and more convinced of the falseness of the charges brought against the archbishop. He found that his household was small, it was true, but thoroughly well organised. He could not find one who was idle; but all were hard at work, and imitating the zeal, prudence, and diligence of their master. Some acted as secretaries, others prepared provisions and food for the poor and sick; in a word, all were busily and usefully employed, and equally careful not to lose a moment of time.

He was much struck by the liberality, and yet exact order with which the revenues of the archbishopric were administered; and above all, with the inviolable fidelity of the dispensers and administrators of so much wealth. But most of all was he struck by the archbishop himself, and the marvellous way in which he added to the austere life of a monk the arduous and wearying duties of his episcopal charge; so that the falsehood of the judgments which had been passed upon him by his calumniators became hourly more and more apparent.

He thought, nevertheless, that it would be well to propose to him to increase in some way the number and state of his household, so that the mouth of calumny might be stopped once and for ever.

One evening, therefore, the conversation fell upon his election as archbishop, which was always a sore subject with the holy prelate, who sighed, and said: "I pray God to pardon my friend Grenada, who, though so good and virtuous, was not afraid of dragging one he professed to love from a quiet and safe retreat to plunge him into a sea of storms and tempests." Then, pointing to the provincial, he turned to the bishop, and added: "This man made a buckler of my poor head to defend his own from the blow which threatened him. I cannot think of this, or speak of it, even now, without being pierced with sorrow."

The bishop answered, "That he thought the father provincial had, in reality, very little to do with the election. That he had only been the instrument of that of which God alone was the author. That the designs of providence ought not to be less recognized and adored because they were executed by the hands of men. That the proof that God had Himself called him to this charge, was the extraordinary ardour and charity he had shown in the supervision of his diocese. That it was impossible not to be struck with admiration at the extreme care he took of the poor and suffering among his flock, and the exactness he had shown in retrenching all superfluities in his house, in order to have more to bestow on the needy and destitute. That the only doubt he had in his mind was, whether the archbishop had not gone a little too far in this direction. That he should not have dared say even so much as this, if he did not know that the father provincial shared in this opinion."

Grenada, turning towards the archbishop, added immediately: "That, as to his election, he was quite easy in his mind before God, if he really had had any part in it, on that score; that all he ventured to beg of him was, that he would do something to justify it before men. That he had been delighted with all he had seen of the regulations of his household, with the wisdom and modesty of his servants, and above all, with their ardent zeal and charity towards the poor and afflicted. That the only thing he wanted him to consider a little more, was his position as archbishop, and especially as archbishop of Braga, and that a certain respect for appearances was necessary in so eminent a charge. That he was very far from wishing to inculcate luxury of any kind. That he condemned, as strongly as the archbishop himself could do, those prelates who went about more as governors of provinces than as successors of the apostles, and who, by their extraordinary magnificence, seemed to wish to bring the pomp of the age to the very foot of the altar. But that the archbishop must consider that we are not living now in the days of those great saints whose poverty was sustained by miracles.

That the Christians of this age are weak in faith; that they need something which strikes the eye before they will show their bishops the reverence due to them. That it had annoyed him very much to hear him decried at court, on this very account, as one unworthy of his position, and as throwing discredit on the wise and judicious choice of the queen. That, in a word, he wished to concert with him some measures whereby he might so regulate his family, his household, and his person, that all pretext of calumny or scandal might be taken away, without in any way transgressing the laws of God."

The archbishop listened to Grenada's reasoning with respectful and attentive silence, and then, looking gravely at both him and the bishop, he replied as follows: "I am very much obliged to you for your goodness towards me, and I look upon your admonition as one of the graces God has vouchsafed to me. But forgive me if I own that I am rather surprised to hear those from whom I expected nought but counsels of perfection, speak to me in so human a manner; so that, instead of trying to induce me to be more faithful in fulfilling the functions of my ministry, you endeavour, on the contrary, to persuade me to relax in my efforts. I am not in the least surprised at what is said of me at court. I am only astonished that, in this matter, courtiers and religious should hold the same language, and that persons as holy and estimable as yourselves should become the defenders of such a cause. Let us sum it up in a few words. The world complains that my house and my retinue are too simple, and that I do not know how to show the magnificence required of an archbishop of Braga. This language is worthy of those who use it. But is it then necessary that a minister of God should yield his dignity to their caprice, or that he should relinquish his principles to conform himself to theirs? Those great saints whom the Church reveres as her chiefs and princes, S. Nicolas,

S. Basil, S. John Chrysostom, and particularly the great S. Martin, whose poverty and charity were so truly apostolic, without speaking of many others,—were they ignorant of the fact that the world only reveres what is called outside show? and that they would gain far more human esteem and consideration if they would show a little more human magnificence?

"Of course, they knew this as well as we do; but they said with S. Paul: '*Do I seek to please men? If I yet pleased men, I should not be the servant of Christ.*' (Gal. i., verse 10.) They thought that, having to announce the Gospel of the humility and poverty of Jesus Christ, they could not do so better than by making themselves poor to preach a crucified God. What has happened since those days to make us suspicious of their conduct and wisdom? and what prevents our imitating them? Is it because the world mocks at us? But it mocked equally at them. As, then, they despised its ridicule and sarcasms, we should despise them too. I cannot for a moment imagine that you think their conduct in this respect was not worthy of imitation, as you know that it was formally prescribed by the Church, in an express ordinance of the Fourth Council of Carthage: 'Let the bishop have common furniture and a poor table, and let him live like a poor man; and let him win the authority and dignity due to his office by the purity of his faith, and the holiness of his life.' *(Episcopus vilem supellectilem et mensam ac victum pauperem habeat; et dignitatis suæ autoritatem fide et vitæ meritis quærat.)*— (Can. 16.)

"This is the voice of the Holy Ghost, speaking to us by the mouth of the whole Church of Africa. I invite you, then, to be my judges and my counsellors.

"The Holy Ghost orders me, as a bishop, to have *poor furniture and a poor table.*

"The world, on the contrary, exhorts me to fly from poverty, and to seek for splendour and luxury in everything.

"To which of these authorities am I to defer?

"The world pretends to justify, and even to sanctify in some way, this reasoning, by affirming that such magnificence is necessary to sustain and keep up the episcopal dignity.

"The Holy Spirit, on the contrary, teaches us that a bishop is *only to be recommended* by this apostolic poverty, joined to holiness of life; because it is not outside show, but piety and goodness, which are to impress on the hearts of men the respect and veneration which are his due.

"This is our rule. It is for us to follow it. If, as a religious, I have tried to keep the rule of our order, now, as bishop, I must try and keep the rule which the Church has prescribed for bishops. Therefore, do not imagine, I entreat of you, that I am an enemy to outward pomp and show only because I am a religious. It is true that I have been a poor religious, as S. John was poor, who is the model for all religious; but now I am bound to be equally poor as a bishop, as was my master Jesus Christ, when He preached the Gospel; as all the apostles and their successors the saints have been; and as the Church enjoins of all her prelates. So that, if God had called me from the ranks of the clergy, and not from a religious order, to be bishop, I should not certainly have worn my habit, but I should have thought it my duty to regulate my household and my table in the same economical manner, and I should equally have despised the world's opinion to the contrary. For who is to observe inviolably the rules of the Church, if the bishops do not? Do not, therefore, I entreat of you, try by human concessions to content men. One cannot serve God and mammon, for God forbids all that the world commands.

"If I am to think more about the luxury of my household, I must necessarily retrench something in the nourishment of my poor. Could I be so hard-hearted as to take the bread out of the mouths of those who are starving, in order that my own table may be more delicately served? Could I be so pitiless as to leave the members of Jesus Christ naked in this severe cold, in order to hang my dead walls with fine tapestries, and cover my floors with beautiful carpets? Is it thus that you wish me to be more prudent, more subservient to human opinion? God preserve me from such blind discretion, or from such cruel complaisance! My goods belong to the poor, and not to me. I am bound to love them as my own children, and to respect them as being one day my judges. I should be far more afraid of saddening them than I should desire the approval of the rich. God forbid that I should buy that vilest of things,—the vain esteem of men,—at the price of the tears and the blood of the poor. If, after all, the world mocks at our conduct, its scorn should be our glory and our joy, and we should exclaim with S. Paulinus: 'O! blessed injury, to be despised of men for the sake of obeying Jesus Christ! We ought far more to dread their esteem, as we cannot please them without displeasing God.' (O beata injuria, displicere cum Christo! Magis timendus est a mortalium, quibus sine Christo placetur.)" (Epist. 29.)

The archbishop paused, and the bishop, turning to the father provincial, said: "We were rather in trouble, when we arrived here, to know how to justify his grace the archbishop before the court and the world; but I think now our hardest task will be to attempt to justify ourselves before him."

Then Grenada, who had been deeply touched by the archbishop's words, now spoke: "You complained, just now, that I had not treated you as a true friend, when I thrust you, in my place, into the archbishopric. But you have, with your own mouth, justified my act. It is true that I dreaded this dignity for myself, and that I felt assured that God had called you to it, because I remarked in you a firmness and a courage of which I was myself utterly incapable. I knew that these qualities in a bishop are the foundation of all others. For, if he should be less learned than another, he can obtain help from science and the works of clever men; but if he have no heart, no power on earth can give it to him. This quality must be found in himself. It cannot be borrowed; and if it be not there, all is wanting. Therefore, S. Chrysostom, in his book on the Priesthood, said that, 'having fled from a bishopric offered to him, he made the election fall on his friend S. Basil, because his courage and his love of justice made him thoroughly worthy of that dignity.' (Chrys. de Sacerd., lib. 2, cap. 3.) As for me, I was always entirely persuaded of the firmness and charity with which God had inspired you. But I am now more and more convinced that I was right, seeing the courage which you have shown in asserting your principles, contrary to the opinion of two persons for whom I know you have the deepest reverence and affection. And so far from thinking you are to blame in this matter, I bless and praise God, on the contrary, for the feelings which He has implanted in you, and I beseech of Him to confirm you in them more and more.

"It is true that the world's scandal had shaken me a little, for it is vexatious to see men making a pretext of some small external things, which are apparently non-essential, to tarnish the actions and character of the holy and just. But after what you have said, and considering that your conduct in all these points is so episcopal, according to the judgment of the Church, I cannot wish that you should alter it in any one particular, or that you should diminish the portion of the poor, to yield either to human respect, or to the criticisms of the rich. Therefore, I say to you, go on boldly as you have begun. When the life of a bishop is thus regulated in the sight of God, and is thoroughly consistent, it wins of itself the approbation of all honest men. Those who might at first be disposed to find fault, will end by praising it, and envy, with its bitter tongue, will be reduced to silence, seeing that conduct so holy and unimpeachable is beyond the reach of calumny."

The bishop expressed the same sentiments as the father provincial, so that the archbishop was filled with joy and consolation at being thus acquitted by two persons whom he held in such affection and veneration.

He took this opportunity to propose to Grenada a plan he had had for some time in his mind. He had lately visited Viano, a city famous for its commerce and great riches. He felt that these two things, together with the great concourse of strangers and foreign merchants of all countries, who flocked into the town at the time of the annual sales, made this place a centre of luxury and vice; to counteract which he was anxious to found a convent of the religious of his own order, so that by their preaching and example, they might inspire men to practise charity, and flee from avarice.

He proposed then, to the father provincial, to establish such a house, if the order would accept it. To which Grenada replied, " That he accepted the proposal gladly, provided there were any means of making a foundation: but that he could not contribute much himself, being so overwhelmed with other claims."

The archbishop, who knew exactly the cost of his own establishment, replied, " That he had already thought the matter over, and that he found he could give a considerable sum every year towards this foundation."

The father provincial having agreed, the archbishop added, smiling : " Well, my father, you see, if I had done as you wished, and spent my money in decorating my palace, and having a more pompous equipage, where should

I have found the sum necessary for this work, which you feel yourself will be of the greatest service to this portion of my people, and contribute so much to the glory of God?"

The provincial could not reply; and soon after, the monastery was founded, and became a centre of piety, and the greatest joy to the good people in that town.

Grenada and the bishop stayed a few days longer with their saintly host, being more and more edified at his holy conversation, and at all they had seen in his house. Finally, they were compelled to leave him; and as they talked over his charity, his generous and episcopal hospitality, and all the other qualities which had so struck them during their visit, they could only bless and praise God for having permitted that their order should have produced so great a bishop, not only for the reformation of the Church in Portugal, but for the glory of the whole Catholic body throughout the world.

END OF THE FIRST BOOK.

SECOND BOOK.

CHAPTER I.

ORIGIN AND PROGRESS OF LUTHER'S HERESY.—COMMENCEMENT AND CONTINUATION OF THE COUNCIL OF TRENT, UNTIL THE PONTIFICATE OF PIUS IV.

Hitherto we have only considered this holy bishop in the exercise of his ministry and the government of his diocese.

But now the providence of God, who designed him for great purposes, brought him forward on the most important of all occasions, namely, that of a General Council, assembled for the purposes of defending and defining the Faith, destroying heresy, and re-establishing Church discipline throughout the world.

Scarcely had the archbishop been a year, and a half in his see, than he was summoned to take part in the Œcumenical Council of Trent, by apostolic letters from Pope Pius IV.; and as upwards of sixteen years had elapsed since this council had been assembled, we will now speak of the reasons why it was convoked, and the progress it had made before the arrival of our holy prelate.

Every one knows that a schism broke out in the Church at the beginning of the sixteenth century, which, born from a slight cause, in a short time made extraordinary progress, and was followed by the ruin of a multitude of souls. Pope Leo X., having issued certain indulgences in order to excite Christians to undertake a crusade against the Turks, the duty of publishing them throughout Germany was committed to the Dominicans, contrary to the usual custom, which gave this charge to the Augustinians. These last were very much offended, and their vicar general, after sending a remonstrance to Rome, ordered one of his monks, named Luther, to preach against the Dominicans.

This monk, till then unknown, but whose name has ever since been held in abhorrence by the whole Church, was one of those of whom a saint has said, "that there are persons whom the Devil chooses and forms from infancy, so that, by inspiring them with his own venom, he may make them the instruments of his malice, and do through them what he would be unable to accomplish by himself."

Luther began preaching accordingly with the greatest vehemence against the fathers of the Dominican Order; then he turned his abuse on the ministers of the Church, whom he vilified in every possible manner. It was unhappily but too true that the licentious lives of many amongst them dishonoured their holy profession. For Luther was not alone in exposing these vices; they had been already stigmatised with the utmost severity by a holy religious of the Franciscan Order, called "Brother Thomas," (called by the people, on account of his great virtues, the "holy friar,") who went up and down the country preaching penance, and threatening those unworthy priests with the very judgments which afterwards befel them.

But this man of God only reprehended the immorality of certain men, (as other saints have done,) showing how they disfigured the body of Christ, which is His Church; for, loving her as he did, the stains on her purity were the more painful to him. Luther, on the contrary, only made use of his invectives as a favourable pretext for making the

Church itself odious, so as to justify his own apostasy, on which he had already determined. From abuse of immorality, he went on to denounce doctrines, especially that of indulgences, and the power vested in the Holy See to grant them. From thence he proceeded to throw doubts on papal authority; and finally attacked the sacraments, and all the principal articles of the Christian Faith.

His superior, who had sent him to preach in the first instance to vent his animosity against the Dominicans, repented very soon of his imprudence, and endeavoured to silence him. But the evil was beyond remedy. He found out too late that he had given arms to a furious enemy, and that he had contributed, by his selfish indiscretion, to kindle a fire which neither his order nor the Church has ever since been able to extinguish.

The Pope, Leo X., having desired his legate in Germany, Cardinal Caïetan, to speak to Luther, and to try by every kind of gentle means to bring him to a sense of his error, finding all his efforts vain, then resorted to more vigorous measures, and in 1520 published a bull, denouncing his heresies, which he maintained with inflexible obstinacy.

And to show to what lengths this heresiarch pushed his impiety, we have only to read what the Emperor Charles V. said of him, in a solemn edict, at the Diet of Worms, in 1521, which was translated into all languages, and sent to every court in Europe: "*This child of iniquity and disobedience,*" he says, speaking of Luther, "*after his heresies had been justly condemned by the bull of Pope Leo X., not only has not repented of his impiety, but has published, and goes on publishing, day by day, books full of error, in which he attacks the sacraments, purgatory, prayers for the dead, and all the religious Hierarchy of the Church. He lifts himself up against the Sovereign Pontiff, successor of S. Peter, and Vicar of Jesus Christ, and vilifies him with unheard of blasphemies and infamous outrages. He turns* into ridicule the authority of the holy Fathers of the Church, and tramples the reverence due to them under his feet. He resuscitates from the depths of hell all the heresies which previous councils have condemned, and boldly declares that if those who maintain them are heretics, he is ten times worse."

This same Emperor adds: "*That this Luther had reached such a summit of impiety, that he had publicly burnt the holy canons and decrees of the Church; and that, when spoken to with great gentleness about his opinions, he had replied, 'that not only he would not defer to any authority, but that if an Œcumenical Council were assembled, he should look upon its proceedings with suspicion, as matters of faith had never been properly treated in these councils.*"

Finally, having represented "*that this heretic was introducing confusion, not only in the ecclesiastical, but in the civil state, exciting his subjects to rebellion, murder, and arson,*" the Emperor declares, "*that this man is not a man, but a devil, who, under the semblance of a man and of a religious, has come upon earth to cause the ruin of souls, to divide kingdoms, and to corrupt the Faith of Christ.*" He concludes, therefore, by "*banishing his person from every portion of his empire, and condemning his writings to the flames.*"

The holy doctors who treat upon the subject of heretics, have often remarked, that, as true children of the serpent-enemy of man, they glide skilfully into the minds of their victims, filling them secretly with their venom, and wrapping up their lies in many folds, to give them the semblance of truth. But Luther was not like this. The Devil, who inspired him, had filled him with more rage than skill. He attacked God Himself in His immutable truth, the Church in her tradition, the Sovereign Pontiff in his authority, and all Christian princes in their dominion over their subjects; so that a general confusion was introduced in all orders and degrees of men.

Not content with rejecting the holy doctors, as the Emperor had said in his edict, he even ventured to affirm: "*That they had written with pre-occupied minds, that their works were full of obscurities, and that, if they had not changed their opinions before their deaths, they did not deserve the name of saints.*" "*As for Papists,*" he wrote elsewhere, "*they are always crying out, 'The Church, the Church! the Fathers, the Fathers!' but if they were to quote a thousand Augustines, or a thousand Cyprians, I should not believe them the more. These men were dreamers, and had always a veil before their eyes.*" In this way he spoke of the fathers in general, and of those in particular he would add: "*That Ireneus was a blasphemer; that Chrysostom was a rebel and a chatterbox, that his writings were nothing but a confused waste of words; that Jerome should be erased from the category of doctors as a heretic, that he was an impious man without any judgment, who had gone mad upon the subject of fasting and virginity; that if God had not shown him mercy, he would have deserved hell rather than heaven; and that he would not for a thousand crowns run such a risk as Jerome of being damned.*"

Strange to say, these gross and palpable heresies were so contagious that many provinces were infected by them. But our surprise diminishes when we remember the state of the Church in Germany at that time. Luther found the Church verily "sitting in darkness," and both priests and people plunged in every kind of disorder. Thus, preaching to men who were Christians only in name, and Pagans in their habits—a Christianity of flesh and blood—he found little difficulty in corrupting their minds, and assimilating their creed to their lives.

But the blindness of the people was the more astonishing when this heresiarch married, and that in the most scandalous manner; and yet this fact did not make him lose the absolute authority he had acquired over certain men's minds. For after the death of his patron, the Duke of Saxony, who never could tolerate the idea of this infamous marriage, on which Luther was nevertheless resolved, the world witnessed the spectacle of a priest and a monk publicly espousing a consecrated virgin,—a nun,—whom he had seduced to follow him in his apostasy, and whom he had carried out of her convent, with eight of her companions, all girls of high rank; and although many of the heretics themselves were scandalized at this shameful and brutal proceeding in one who professed to be a Church reformer, still his insolence and effrontery made him glory in this double sacrilege, execrable alike in the sight of God and men.

Those to whom he held out the bait of licence and libertinage, which he openly preached instead of the Gospel of Jesus Christ, continued to uphold both his person and doctrines. After having lived so scandalous a life, he died in the same manner, held in reputation by the souls he had deluded and depraved, who erected statues to his memory in the churches, with the inscription: "*Divus et Sanctus Doctor Martinus Lutherus, Propheta Germaniæ.*"

Such was the beginning, the career, and the end of this apostate. But the evils he occasioned did not die with him. Not only did his heresy continue, but it became the source of constant fresh heresies, which sprang up in every direction. For, having insolently upset the fundamental rule of faith, and refused to recognise the Church as the interpreter of Holy Writ, or tradition as contained in the writings of the fathers and councils, or the authority of the Holy See, he became a precursor of all future heresies, and opened the door to every species of error. In fact, very soon after his death, there sprang up a sect called Sacramentarists, whose doctrines were promulgated by Zwinglius in Switzerland, and by Calvin in France, and although differing in many fundamental points from Luther, and from each other, they were united in their determination to destroy the Catholic Faith, and to start a church of their own, which they pretended was founded on the Gospel alone, and on the simple word of God.

The Church being consequently afflicted with such great evils, and menaced on all sides, those who had her interests most at heart, earnestly prayed for that most powerful of all remedies, the convoking of a General Council. The Emperor Charles V., and all the princes of Germany who had remained staunch in their faith, demanded it eagerly, and at the Diet of Spires, in 1529, ordered, that until such an Œcumenical Council should be assembled, no change should be tolerated in the Catholic religion, and that the services should be resumed according to the old faith in all such places as had been invaded by the Lutheran heresy. But the Duke of Saxony, and fourteen towns in the empire, remained obstinately in their errors, and protested that they should appeal to the Council, while at the same time separating themselves from the Church. Hence arose the word *Protestant*, which they have kept to this day.

Leo X. having died, Adrian VI., a Dutchman by birth, who had been tutor to the Emperor Charles V., was elected Pope by the Cardinals, who did not know him; so that it appeared that their choice had been directed by God Himself, as they had not considered his person, but only his virtue and merits. All Christendom hailed his promotion to the papal throne with joy and hope, and he himself was resolved not to disappoint their expectations, but to labour with all his might to defend the Church from the heresies which were attacking her on all sides.

As he attributed these errors to a relaxation of discipline, he strove to re-establish everywhere the old rules, quoting often those excellent words: "*Observe the canons, and there will be no heretics.*" Unhappily, his pontificate was of

very short duration; and he passed it in the deepest
anxiety and sorrow at his inability to remedy the evils
around him. The following inscription was put on his
tomb: "*Hic situs est Adrianus VI., qui nihil sibi infœlicius
in vita, quàm quòd Imperaret, duxit.*" (Here lies Adrian
VI., who thought that the greatest misfortune in all his
life was that of having been obliged to rule.)

Pope Clement VII. succeeded him, and seeing the
extreme peril which threatened the Christian world, held
a Consistory in Rome, in which he represented to the
cardinals, that all these evils resulted from ecclesiastical
disorders, and that he should commence by reforming their
morals, beginning by his own house. He added that he
hoped to unite all Christian princes in the calling of a
General Council to re-establish Church discipline, and
exterminate heresy and schism. But he also died before
he had been able to carry out his design. Paul III.
succeeded him, and resolved at once to summon the desired
council. The bull of convocation was sent out in 1542,
and the place of sitting determined upon was the town of
Trent. Its first meeting was held in the year 1545, on the
13th December. In 1547 the plague broke out in Trent,
and the Council was consequently transferred to Bologna.
In the interval Pope Paul III. died, and Cardinal de Monte,
who had acted as legate at the council, was created Pope
under the name of Julius III., and decided to re-commence
the deliberations of the Council once more at Trent. In
1552 it was again suspended, on account of the war which
had broken out in Germany, and imperilled its safety.
Three years later, Julius III. also died, and Marcellus II.
became Pope, an election which filled all the Christian
world with joy, on account of his great reputation for
holiness and purity of life. When asked if he would not
change his name at his election, he replied: "*Nec nomen
meum, nec mores mutabit pontificatus.*" (The papacy will

change neither my name nor my habits.) He would not allow even his own brother to come to Rome, not being able to bear the idea that the wealth and authority of the Church should be employed to further the ambitious views of his family. But in the midst of his schemes to re-establish innocence and integrity in the whole of the papal court, he died, twenty-two days after his election, to the despair of all those who really loved the Church, but to the secret joy of those who had feared too rigid an inquiry into their scandalous and luxurious lives.

Paul III. succeeded him, but during his short pontificate the sittings of the Council were still suspended. He died in 1559, and Paul IV., uncle of the great S. Charles Borromeo, was elected in his room, and at once issued a bull, re-opening the council at Trent on Easter Day, 1561. This bull was sent to all the Catholic kingdoms, and so reached Portugal, where our archbishop prepared immediately to obey its summons.

CHAPTER II.

BULL OF PIUS IV. FOR THE RE-ASSEMBLING OF THE COUNCIL OF TRENT.—DOM BARTHOLOMEW PREPARES TO OBEY THE SUMMONS.— THE CHARITY REQUIRED OF BISHOPS TOWARDS THE UNIVERSAL CHURCH.

When the summons to attend the Council first reached the archbishop, he hesitated. He looked to his own flock, and saw that only a portion of his diocese had been visited; that the new rules he had set on foot in the other part were scarcely yet firmly established; that his absence for any length of time might lead to their neglect or imperfect observance; and that things might fall back into the same disorder in which he had found them.

On the other hand, he felt himself bound to consider the importance of the summons he had received, the grandeur of the occasion, and the measure in which it would affect the whole of Christendom. His episcopal charity, which was as Catholic and universal as his faith, inspired him with the same feelings of affection and tenderness for the whole Church as he felt towards his own diocese. Seeing her attacked in her faith, torn by schism, and dishonoured by the irregular and often scandalous lives of her priests, he felt that an Œcumenical Council had become the only possible remedy for such grave disorders, and was delighted to sustain, by his voice and authority, the faith which he would gladly have sealed with his own blood.

This truly pastoral zeal has always been shown by the prelates of the Church. However dear might be their respective flocks, they have not hesitated to leave their dioceses to defend the cause of faith and justice in council, and such conduct has always been held up to respect and veneration among saints.

Thus S. Chrysostom praises S. Eustatius, patriarch of Antioch, who appeared at the Council of Nice, as the champion of the orthodox faith against Arianism: "*For he had learnt*," he writes, "*from the Holy Spirit Himself, that a bishop should not simply have an eye to the church which God has confided to him, but should interest himself in all the rest, so that, as he offers his prayers to God, not for his own diocese alone, but for the whole Church throughout the world, he should likewise extend his charity to all the countries where the Church exists, and to all the faithful who compose it.*" *(S. Chrys. hom. de S. Eustat. Antioch.)*

S. Chrysostom himself eminently possessed that boundless charity which he commends in others, for Sozomen says of him, "*that his episcopal magnanimity moved him to employ every means for the re-establishment of faith and morals, not only in his own diocese, but among all the faithful." (Sozom. Hist., lib. 2, cap. 8.)* And Theodoret praises him for having *"imitated S. Paul, and embraced, like him, the care of all the Churches." (Theodoret, lib. 5, cap. 29, c. 31.)* In the same spirit, S. Basil, as it appears by his letters, took the same interest in the Church of Antioch as in his own, instructing and exhorting the people to preserve the faith inviolate, and to defend themselves from all the snares of the heretics (Basil, Ep. 5, 7, 9, c. 6); and S. Gregory of Nazianzum speaks highly of this quality in him, saying: *" That he had established the laws of truth and equity among all Christians throughout the world, and that he had not contented himself, as some did, with restricting his vigilance to the narrow circle of his own diocese, but, raising himself above human considerations, he had illumined with his great mind and heart every corner where Jesus Christ had shed the light of His grace and truth." (Gregory Nazianz. Orat. 20.)*

Pope Celestine also commends this same general and apostolic charity to all the bishops of the Œcumenical Council assembled at Ephesus. *"The duty of upholding and defining the faith of God,"* he writes, *" has been laid upon all bishops. It is an indispensable and hereditary obligation, to which we have all engaged ourselves, we who are scattered all over the face of the earth, to preach the Gospel of Jesus Christ, in the place of the apostles to whom it was said, 'Go and teach all nations.' We must consider,"* (he adds,) *" that we have received a general command, which must be executed by all, as it has been given to all." (Ep. Celest. Pap. ad Syn. Ephes., part 2, art. 2.)*

This same spirit of God, which had taught this important truth to all these holy prelates, had impressed the like thoughts in the mind of the Archbishop of Braga.

The sorrowful sight of the public evils ever growing in the body of the Church, outweighed his feeling for his own diocese. He felt he could no longer act as the pastor of his own flock alone, but that he must raise his thoughts to the higher function of the episcopacy, which obliges its bishops to act as true successors of the apostles, by joining those august assemblies, where, as the mouthpieces of the Holy Ghost, the rules of faith may be confirmed, and those sacred laws enforced, which are the oracles of the truth of God in all ages of the world.

Convinced, therefore, of the duty and importance of the summons, his only thought henceforth was to make every arrangement for his journey. At that moment he was suffering from violent pains in his legs, which at first sight would seem to prevent his departure. But as he was used to despise and overlook all such bodily sufferings, rather than let them interfere with the smallest duties of his charge, he determined that on so important an occasion nothing but positive inability to move should stop him.

He first devoted himself to arrange everything for the government of his diocese during his absence, so that only his own person being wanting, every rule should be as exactly observed as when he was present, and no change should be allowed in any particular.

He appointed Father John of Leyra as his vicar-general, a man of whose wisdom and piety he had had long experience; and associated with him persons whose knowledge and virtue had been sufficiently proved to put his own zeal and conscience at ease.

As to his equipage and court, we have seen before how utterly he despised all outward show or human respect. Although he was to appear at the Council as Archbishop of Braga, who bears the title of Primate of all Spain, (which is disputed by the Archbishop of Toledo,) he still insisted on arriving at Trent with the same simplicity and modesty as he showed in his own diocese. He took as companion in his journey, Father Henry of Tabora, whom he looked upon as his son, having brought him up when he was Prior of his Order. And this father was so worthy a disciple of so great a master, that he was subsequently elected Bishop of Cochin China, and afterwards Archbishop of Goa, and Metropolitan of Oriental India.

He took as secretary a certain doctor of great learning and piety, whose humility was equal to his science. He added to his suite an almoner, and one or two servants, who were indispensable for such a long journey, and thus started on his important mission. His eyes being always fixed on God, and thinking only of how he could best please Him, he had no regard for appearances or for the judgments of men, and measured everything by a higher standard than that of human opinion.

CHAPTER III.

THE ARCHBISHOP STARTS FOR TRENT.—HE LODGES ON HIS WAY AT DIFFERENT MONASTERIES OF HIS ORDER, WHERE HE TRIES TO PASS AS A SIMPLE RELIGIOUS.—HE IS, HOWEVER, DISCOVERED ON SEVERAL OCCASIONS.

Having earnestly commended his diocese and himself to God, our holy archbishop set forth for Trent the Monday after Passion Sunday, that is, on the 24th of March, 1561. As he had no object in view but the glory of God, he thought that his prompt arrival at Trent might perhaps induce other prelates to attend likewise, and so, though the season made it inconvenient, he would not delay his departure a single day. Having come to the limits of the town of Braga, he got off his horse, and walked the rest of the way to the frontier of his diocese, which is separated by a river from the bishopric of

Miranda. Then, having turned round in the direction of his diocese, he knelt down and prayed with episcopal love and fervour for his flock, beseeching our Lord to preserve it, and to become Himself its pastor during his absence. He finished his prayer with these words, which Jesus Christ addressed to His Father: *"I pray for them. I pray not for the world, but for them whom Thou hast given Me, because they are Thine; keep them in Thy name."* (S. John xvii. verse 9.) Then, having solemnly blessed his diocese, and implored once more the blessing of God, he rose, shedding an abundance of tears, which he could not restrain, and which made even his companions weep with him.

He then mounted, and went on his way, following a certain rule in his progress, which he observed all the way from the kingdom of Castille to Trent. Before arriving at the town where he was to pass the night, if he knew that there was a Dominican convent there, he left his suite, hid his pectoral cross, and went alone with the father who was his companion to the monastery, after having given strict orders to his people to go and lodge at some inn, but on no account to divulge who he was on any pretext whatever. They were only to rejoin him outside the gates of the town the following day. By this pious ruse he contrived to be received in several convents of his Order as a simple religious, which was infinitely pleasing to his humility.

The first house where he was received in this way, without being recognised, was at Zamora, where he stopped for Palm Sunday, and took part in all the offices.

When he arrived at Palentia, he went in the same way to the convent of his order, with his companion. Being admitted, they were brought to the prior's cell, where they both prostrated themselves at his feet, asking for his blessing. Now this prior was a very severe man, and extremely exact in the observance of the rule; so that he instantly demanded to see the licence, which they should have received from their superiors, to visit foreign countries. The archbishop, who was not prepared for this question, being full of wit, tried to turn the conversation, and to amuse the prior, hoping he would forget the matter or pass it over. But he had to deal with a man of a stern and inflexible nature, and seeing that they could not produce any letters, he ordered them to be confined in separate cells, until he had made up his mind what to do with them.

Then the archbishop was a good deal puzzled what to say or do; but his companion, feeling that the zeal of the worthy prior might lead him to do things which he would afterwards very much regret, replied, smiling: "As for me, father prior, I have no trouble in justifying myself, for I have received my licence from the venerable Archbishop of Braga, and he it is who is now standing before you."

The prior was so taken aback that he remained for a moment silent; then, when he was going to entreat the archbishop's pardon and forgiveness, the latter interrupted him by saying: "Father prior, you did your duty, and I only esteem you the more for it. I thank God for your zeal for the observance of holy discipline. My only regret is, that I thus lose the occasion of being treated as a poor religious. Love me always as a brother, and believe me that I should never have appeared before you in any other character had God so allowed it." The prior made him a thousand excuses nevertheless, and was overjoyed to have so great a saint as his guest.

He passed incognito in several other convents; partly because the superiors were not all so strict as the one we have just mentioned, partly because his dignified presence prevented their exacting the ordinary formalities in his case. For they believed him to be at least a doctor of theology on his way to the Council, as many passed that way with the same object.

When he arrived at Burgos, he was received with great consideration, although they had not an idea who he was; and being very tired, he decided to stop here a couple of days to rest, dining with the community, and then spending the recreation hour in the cloister, talking with the prior and some of the fathers. But soon after a great knocking was heard at the door, which the porter having opened, a courier appeared in hot haste, desiring to know where the Archbishop of Braga was, as he had certainly arrived in the town, and was supposed to be in this convent. The porter was very much surprised, but said that they had no one in the house but two poor Portuguese monks, who had arrived the day before. The messenger did not ask any further questions, but went straight into the cloister, and seeing the archbishop, made him a low obeisance, and pulled a letter out of his pocket, saying: "Your Grace, this is a letter from the King, who has sent me to search diligently until I had found your lordship, and bring him back an answer as soon as possible."

The prior was stupefied, and the archbishop not less so. But, taking the letter very sadly, he replied to the messenger: "My friend, how came you to hunt for the Archbishop of Braga among these good humble monks?" Then, turning to the prior, he said: "I was beginning to enjoy life, and now this man has come and taken all my pleasure away."

The prior, delighted at this unexpected discovery, said, "He was very much indebted to the King's messenger, or rather to the providence of God, which had revealed to him who was his guest, for the welfare and consolation of the whole house. That before they had possessed a treasure without knowing it; but now they could glory in their riches."

The archbishop, opening the King's letter, found that he had written to him regarding the Council, insisting particularly on one point, i.e., that he should maintain his right to take precedence of other archbishops, as Primate of all Spain, which was a title due to the see of Braga, and considered by the king as adding glory to the whole of Portugal. The archbishop simply replied: "That the orders of his royal highness should be obeyed," and then resumed his conversation with the monks. But the prior and every one in the house came to pay their respects to him, and ask his blessing. And seeing that he had thus lost the liberty and rest he had hoped to find in that house, and which his humility delighted in, he refused to stay any longer, and declared he felt himself nothing but a stranger, since the religious had ceased to treat him as a brother.

Finally, having passed through several other convents of his order, where he was received as simply as he wished, he arrived at Trent. He would have preferred to live in the Dominican monastery in that town. But as he had been told that his doing so would be a great inconvenience to the monks, on account of the great number they had to lodge during the Council, he changed his mind, and sending on his suite, desired them to find a suitable lodging for him, while he himself came into the town on foot, with only the father who accompanied him, hoping thereby to keep his arrival a secret. But scarcely had he set foot in the place when two bishops came, whose only dispute was as to which should have the joy and honour of receiving him under their roof. One was the Bishop of Modena, the other the Bishop of Verona, and both were members of his own Order. The first had such a reputation for charity that he was called "*The*

Father of the Poor"; and knowing the feelings of the archbishop on that score, it was not possible that he should not be attracted by one who so closely resembled him. It was at his house, therefore, that he consented to lodge that night; but the next day the archbishop insisted on removing to the house which had been prepared for him, and where he felt he should live more as a poor religious, which was always the object of his ambition.

CHAPTER IV.

DESCRIPTION OF THE TOWN OF TRENT.—THE ARCHBISHOP'S AGREEABLE RECEPTION BY THE CARDINAL LEGATES.—HIS HOLY AND USEFUL OCCUPATIONS.—HE CUTS OFF ALL SUPERFLUOUS VISITS.

The town of Trent is situated on the frontiers of Germany and Italy, and in the country of Tyrol. It is a very fine town, and would not yield to the most beautiful cities in Germany in the splendour and comfort of its houses and hotels. Its situation is very advantageous, and it abounds in every kind of merchandise. The river Athesis passes at the foot of its walls, waters part of Italy, and finally flows into the Adriatic.

The town is peculiarly healthy, although surrounded by high mountains, called by the ancients the Trent Alps, because the freshness of the air blowing over the snow mountains, and the thickness of its great trees, temper the extreme heat of the sun, which in summer seems to concentrate its rays in this little valley.

It was impossible to have fixed upon a better site for the Council, for it is as the centre of three kingdoms: Germany, Italy, and France; and as it is an independent town, subject neither to king nor any other sovereign, it was reassuring to heretics, who had pretended to fear the undue influence of the secular power, and hid, under this vain pretext, the real aversion they had to appearing before so august an assembly.

The bishop of this town is its spiritual and temporal head, and administers both jurisdictions. But they acknowledge some kind of suzerainty in the Counts of Tyrol, who are likewise archdukes of Austria.

At this time, Cardinal Louis Madruccio Alleman had been elected Bishop of Trent; and Cardinals Hercules Gonzagua, of the house of the Dukes of Mantua, and Jerome Seripando, a Neapolitan, had arrived to open the Council as legates of his Holiness. They had been very much annoyed at the tardy response of the bishops to the papal summons. For Italy alone had as yet sent any of its representatives, and of these only ten had arrived; so that when they heard of the advent of an archbishop from the extreme west, and of so illustrious a see, they were very much rejoiced.

The archbishop hastened to pay them his respects the very day after his arrival, looking upon them as holding the place of the chief pastor of the Church, and the Vicar of Jesus Christ. The cardinal legates received him with every kind of affection and respect, and assured him that his arrival was the best news they could send to the Pope, as he was the very first bishop that had come to the Council from Spain. That his Holiness was displeased at the delay in the arrival of the other prelates; and that they hoped that the example of the Archbishop of Braga would induce the others to hasten their proceedings.

In fact, every one was delighted at his arrival, both at Rome and Trent; and the Pope wrote to express his joy at his prompt obedience to his summons, desiring his legates to treat him with the utmost respect and consideration. The Pope likewise wrote to the princes of Christendom, urging them to hasten the departure of their respective prelates for the Council, and citing the good example given by the archbishop in the matter, so that on all sides he found himself loaded with honour and praises. But to such things he was entirely indifferent. And as soon as the necessary courtesies had been exchanged he gave his whole mind to the important subjects which were to come under discussion.

In spite of all the efforts of the Pope, however, the Council made little progress. No French Bishops had yet appeared, and every one felt that many months must elapse before the real deliberations of the Council could commence; so the archbishop, who hated idleness, took advantage of this interval, as of a season given him by God, to make a species of retreat, and purge himself from all the stains he fancied he had contracted in the continual labours and distractions inseparable from the government of his vast diocese. He resolved not to go out except for purposes of devotion, and to keep silence with men so as to hold converse continually with God. If compelled to show civilities to any one, he did so as an ecclesiastic and a bishop, following in all things the rules of faith and charity, but keeping clear of all worldliness and ambition in his intercourse with others. Except on these occasions, which were very rare, he always stayed at home, and no one saw him but at church. In this matter he practised the excellent advice of the Pope S. Gregory, who says: "*That a bishop should rarely appear in society, and that he should spend most of his time in retreat. That he ought to try and free himself from all worldly affairs, in order to occupy himself solely with spiritual, and he ought to show himself in public so seldom, that his appearance should seem to be almost a miracle.*" (*Gregor. in* 1 *Reg., cap.* 16, *v.* 4.)

This man of God looked upon the advice of these holy doctors, not as an object of mere admiration, but as a model which God had given him for his imitation, so that he might follow it with fidelity in his rule of life. His favourite meditation was on the holy Scriptures. He weighed every word with the deepest reverence, and also studied diligently all such passages in the works of the fathers as bore upon the matters which were to be dealt with in the coming Council.

As we see in holy writ how Moses remained on the mountain in fasting and prayer, that he might learn God's will regarding His people, so did our holy archbishop endeavour, by the use of the same means, to obtain the guidance of the Holy Spirit, so that he might propose nothing to the Council which would not strengthen the faith and contribute to the welfare of the whole Church. His edifying life, so worthy of a bishop who was preparing himself for a divine and solemn work, redoubled the esteem and veneration of all around him. We have a proof of this in the following extract from a letter written by Father de Tabora, (afterwards archbishop in India,) to a father of the Society of Jesus:

"As to his grace, the Archbishop of Braga, all I can say is, that he seems to me to grow every day in learning and sanctity. In spite of the vexatious delay in the opening of the Council, I believe he has never employed his time better; and when he returns to Portugal, which I hope in God's mercy he will do, he will come back loaded with graces and blessings for himself and all his flock. He has won for himself in this town a consideration and a liberty to do as he wills, and to live as much alone as he pleases, which no one else has been able to attain. I believe if he had had his own way, he would never willingly have left the monastic solitude in which he finds all the delight of his heart. His reputation for holiness here is extraordinary. The bishops admire him, the poor seek him, and to all he is just the same father and friend as he is to those of his own diocese. I do not think you will receive my praises of him with suspicion, because you already esteem him as much as I do. For he has too many witnesses of his virtue and charity in Braga, to need any from this distant region.—Trent, November 3rd, 1561."

CHAPTER V.

THE ARCHBISHOP WRITES FROM TRENT TO HIS VICAR-GENERAL. —HE DESCRIBES HIS RECEPTION.—HE BEARS AN UNCONSCIOUS WITNESS TO HIS OWN CHARITY TOWARDS THE POOR, BY DESCRIBING THAT OF THE BISHOP OF MODENA.

Although the Archbishop remained in so deep a solitude, (which he had created for himself in the midst of the turmoil of this great city,) he did not, in consequence, forget the diocese to which God had bound him by the strongest ties. He wrote continually to his vicar-general, and we will insert one of his letters here, as it describes both his journey to, and his arrival at Trent, and therefore forms an essential part of his biography.

LETTER FROM THE ARCHBISHOP TO HIS VICAR-GENERAL.

"My dear father,

"I think we are now experiencing, both of us, the truth of that saying of S. Augustine, that the absence of our friends gives us a keener feeling of love for them than we should have felt in their presence. But as God is the author of our separation, I hope He will make it useful to us both, and that He will supplement by His grace all the advantages which we might have derived from more frequent intercourse. I will not weary you with all the details of our journey; it would be too long a story, and I shall leave that to my secretary. We arrived at Trent at the happiest moment possible. For more than six weeks the cardinal legates and a few Italian bishops had been impatiently waiting for the arrival of the bishops from France and Spain. Therefore, having arrived the first of all the latter, and the report being instantly spread that the primate of Spain had come from the most distant point to obey without delay the papal summons, the cardinals and all the people were filled with joy, and augured well for the success of the Council. The legates, in consequence, overwhelmed me with civilities, and joyfully wrote to announce my arrival to the Pope. Among the Italian bishops who are arrived, are two from our own Order, one of whom, the Bishop of Modena, is eminent in science and holiness. We have only known each other a few days, yet we are as intimate, and have become as great friends as if we had lived together for ten years.

"Enough of my proceedings. I should now like to hear something of yours. I do not doubt that the innumerable anxieties inseparable from the care of so vast a diocese, must give you some trouble. But if you will only consider the way in which this labour has been thrown upon you, it will fill you with peace and consolation. Do not devote so much time to exterior business as to rob yourself of the hours you usually set apart for meditation and prayer. For more than ever do you need light and grace from God, so as to receive from Him what you have to render to others. Therefore, the time you spend in these holy exercises, so far from being taken from them, is really expended to their greater advantage. I conjure you to take immense care of the poor, even more than I recommended to you when we parted. For the love of this virtue has redoubled in me since I have had before me the example of the holy Bishop of Modena, who is a shining light in our Order. For his revenue does not exceed a thousand ducats, and yet he does more charity in his diocese than I do in mine. I really cannot conceive how he manages to live. As for me, I think God works miracles on behalf of generous souls, especially such as do all for the love of our Lord Jesus Christ. He told me himself that he had now and then been frightened at the amount of expense he had incurred, and yet he had never run into debt. Therefore, I conjure you again, to be not only liberal, but magnificent, and if I may say so, holily prodigal towards the poor. Let me know how many orphan girls you have provided for. Be sure you do not diminish in any way the sums destined for them. Do you fear to impoverish yourself for God, who holds in His hands inexhaustible riches? You know that in the order of our charities, those who come first are always religious persons, and such as are consecrated to Jesus Christ. God says, in holy writ, *'If I should be hungry, I would not tell thee, for the world is Mine, and the fulness thereof.'* (*Psalm xlix., verse 12.*) But when He is hungry in the persons of His spouses, who are part of Himself, He does not disdain to let us know. And if He should be humble enough to ask our help, should we be so proud as not to make it our glory to come to His aid? Forgive me, dear father, if I be too urgent in pressing this recommendation upon you. I speak to myself in speaking to you; so that, excited by the example of this holy bishop, of whom I have just told you, I may follow in his steps, and do more than I have hitherto attempted. It is not the richest, but the most charitable person who assists the poor the most. I share in all your labours in my daily thoughts and prayers, and I hope that God will strengthen you, and that your very zeal will afford you joy and consolation. For if I dare judge of your great heart by mine, which is so narrow, I do not doubt but that you are on fire, and well nigh consumed by the divine fire of the pastoral charge. I conclude by beseeching you once more to give yourself entirely to the poor, of whom God has made you, at this time, the father and protector."

CHAPTER VI.

THE ARCHBISHOP'S PRIMACY IS CONTESTED.—THE POPE DESIRES HIM TO PRECEDE THE OTHER ARCHBISHOPS; AND THEN ORDERS THAT ALL SHALL RANK ACCORDING TO THE DATE OF THEIR PROMOTION.

Although the archbishops who had arrived at Trent were too few in number for the assembling of the Council, yet they met continually in the public offices of the Church, such as High Mass, Vespers, &c. It was therefore necessary to regulate their order of precedence as regarded their seats. The Archbishop of Braga, as primate of all Spain, was compelled, by the King's orders, to precede all the other archbishops, an honour which the older prelates would not yield to him. It was therefore necessary to write to the Pope on the subject, who confirmed the dignity of the primate, and ordered all the archbishops to go after him. We find this in an extract from a letter of the archbishop's, where he relates what passed, as follows: "I write to the King what I have done to maintain the primacy of my see, according to his express orders. There was some dispute as to precedence, and much to be said on both sides. But it was argued against me, that Rome had not definitely pronounced its opinion between the two primacies of Toledo and Braga. At last, it was decided to refer the matter to the Pope himself, who decreed that I was to take precedence of all the archbishops. Dom Laurenzo Loppez di Tabora, the ambassador, was of great service in this affair. I am, therefore, second in all church functions, such as at the solemn Mass, which to-day was said for the dead, having only before me the Patriarch of Jerusalem."

But this arrangement did not suit the Spanish bishops at all, who declared that the primacy rested, not with the Archbishop of Braga, but with the Archbishop of Toledo, and that by ancient and vested rights.

The legates, seeing the extreme difficulty which had arisen in this matter, again referred the matter to the Pope, who, by a brief drawn up the last day of December, decreed, *"That to avoid contention, the patriarchs should precede the archbishops, and the archbishops the bishops, but as to the precedence of each, it should be decided by the date of their promotion."*

This brief having been read to the assembly, the Archbishop of Braga considered that a further explanation was necessary, lest it should militate against the rights of the primacy which he had sworn to uphold. He therefore represented to the cardinal legates "how important it was not to open the Council by a violation of existing rights; that the zeal of the Pope, in convoking the Council, made him feel sure that the preservation of the dignity of each episcopal see was not less dear to him than his own; and that his Holiness concurred in the views of Pope Gregory the Great, when he said: '*My glory is the glory of the universal Church; my honour consists in the preservation of the honour and rank which are due to each bishop in that Church.*'"

He added, that, "if it were a question of his own person or his own interest, he would yield to the whole world; but when it was a question of the primacy of the see which had been confided to him, he was obliged, by the law of God and the canons of the Church, as well as by the example of the saints in similar matters, to maintain the rights of which he was only the depositor, and to leave them intact to his successors."

The archbishop enunciated these reasons with such firmness, and in so wise and modest a manner, that the whole assembly were very much struck by his speech. The cardinal legates were equally impressed by its substance, and replied: "That the Pope had no intention whatever, by this brief, to prejudice any existing rights; that he did not wish to wound any person either in his position or dignity, and that the primate would remain, after the Council, in precisely the same state, and in possession of all the same privileges as heretofore." They added that they would give him this declaration in writing. The archbishop was contented with this explanation, and answered: "That having thus protected the rights of his see, which he was not allowed to disregard or neglect, he wished for nothing better than to contribute by every means in his power to the peace of the Council, by preventing any disputes which might arise between the bishops." The Pope, having been informed by his legates of the archbishop's wise and temperate remonstrance, expressed himself thoroughly satisfied with his conduct, and wrote himself to him, confirming the declaration which the legates had made in his name.

CHAPTER VII.

IN WHAT MANNER THE COUNCIL OF TRENT WAS OPENED UNDER PIUS IV.

Since the month of April, 1561, when the archbishop had arrived at Trent, to the end of that year, a large number of bishops had come from different parts of the world; so much so, that towards the beginning of 1562 it was decided to open the Council.

The Festival of the Chair of S. Peter, which falls on the 18th of January, was chosen for the occasion, when the first sitting was held in the magnificent church dedicated to our Lady, under the title of S. Mary Major.

The cardinal legates entered first, with the majesty befitting so solemn an occasion, and a great silver cross being borne before them, was placed in the midst of the Council. The legates sat at the top of the church, on a raised bench, and the cardinals on each side. In front of them were the patriarchs, and then the archbishops and bishops, who numbered two hundred and sixty. After them came the abbots and generals of religious orders. The ambassadors were placed on lower seats down the nave of the church, the ecclesiastics being to the right, and the seculars to the left. There were also a great number of doctors and the most learned men in Christendom.

The cardinals and all the members of the Council first knelt and implored the aid of the Holy Spirit in these words:

"*That the greatness of their sins would not have per-*

mitted them even to appear before Him, if it were not in His name that they had met together, and to follow His guidance in all things. They besought Him that He would deign to come down and abide in their hearts, to be the beginning and ultimate end of all their actions. That He would give them His Light, to preserve them from wandering in the wrong paths, and the purity of His Love, to render them firm and incorruptible in the defence of justice. That He would inspire them with the right thoughts, and Himself form their decisions and correct their judgments; so that, being faithful to Him in all things, and conforming their wills to His, they might become His temples and organs upon earth, and receive hereafter the crown and reward of their fidelity in heaven."

This prayer, (which they repeated each day,) being concluded, the Cardinal of Mantua, president of the Council, addressed the fathers, and represented to them how greatly they should praise and bless God, who had put it into the heart of the Sovereign Pontiff to re-open this Council, begun by Paul III., and continued by Julius III., to destroy heresy and schism, to correct disorders and abuses in morals, to re-establish the ancient piety, and to afford the Church in these unhappy times an efficacious remedy against the fearful evils and perils which menaced her. He wound up his speech with these words: "I conjure you, august and venerable fathers, to show in this assembly an ardour and zeal worthy of the ministers of Jesus Christ, and to perform so great and holy an action in a truly holy manner. We are in the sight of the whole world, and in the presence of our enemies. For this reason, we must not only fight for the truth of our doctrines, but give them an example of holy and irreproachable lives. All episcopal virtues should shine forth in us, and the ruling of our persons should extend to our houses. As we are met here to try and reform the Church, do not let the faithful perceive that many things are to be reformed in ourselves. We therefore beseech the help of God without ceasing, and by fasting, prayer, and almsdeeds, implore the Light of His Holy Spirit, that we may know, follow, and teach to others, the paths of truth, virtue, and life eternal."

Thus, after an interruption of ten years, was this solemn Council re-opened. It was in reality the seventeenth sitting, counting from the beginning of the Council under Paul III.

In the following sitting, whilst graver questions were pending, they condemned all bad books spread throughout Christendom, whether impugning the faith, or tending to corrupt the morals of the simple and ignorant. They chose out a certain number of the fathers in the Council, and those most renowned for learning and piety, in order to examine and report upon these books; and the second person selected for this office was our Archbishop. We will continue in the next chapter our account of his manner of dealing with the subjects under discussion, or that were about to be brought before the Council.

CHAPTER VIII.

THE ARCHBISHOP INDUCES THE FATHERS IN COUNCIL TO TREAT FIRST THE QUESTION OF THE REFORM OF THE CLERGY, BEGINNING BY THE CARDINALS.—HIS GENEROSITY IS REVERED BY EVERY ONE.

When it came to the question of which subject should be first discussed in the Council, the Archbishop of Braga held a different opinion from most of his colleagues. For they proposed to deliberate on several minor matters, against which the archbishop, burning with episcopal and apostolic zeal, remonstrated in the following terms:

"We cannot better maintain the dignity of the Council than by continuing in the way it was begun. And the principal end proposed by the originators of the Council was the purification of the morals of the clergy. For that purpose their deliberations turned towards the reformation of the Church, before defining questions of faith; and for this reason, that the heresies which they sought to destroy arose mainly from the disorders and abuses which had crept into the clergy. And these disorders had reached to such a height, that the King of Portugal, Dom John III., sent a letter to Pope Paul III., which was publicly read in the Council, setting forth: *That the ancient discipline of the Church had been so relaxed, that even if there were no heresies to fight against, it would have been necessary to convoke a general council, to correct the disorders and abuses which were patent to all. For it was this very corruption of morals which had given rise to heresy, and if they were reformed, the heresies themselves would be destroyed.*' (Acta. Conc. Trid. Lovanii, 1567.)

"For the same reason, the illustrious Cardinal of Mantua, when opening this Council as the legate of the Holy See, told us in his excellent speech: *That we were not only to overcome the heretics by the truths of faith, but still more by the example of a holy life, and that, intending to labour for the reformation of others, we must be careful that there should not be found occasion of reform in ourselves.*'

"And this Christian and episcopal sentiment is in exact conformity with that of the cardinal legates of Pope Paul III., who originally opened this Council in a speech full of humility and charity, which is recorded at the head of these acts, and in which, speaking in the name of the Pope, they do not shrink from saying, that all the fathers assembled in that Council ought to look upon themselves as the cause, not only of the demoralization of the faithful, but also of the melancholy heresies which, in this century, have risen up against the Church. I will give you their own words, which I beseech of you to weigh seriously:

"'Although, by the mercy of God, it may be true that none of us here present have ever taught error, we cannot deny that the principle and origin of heresy rests with ourselves. For these impious and erroneous doctrines, being like thorns and briars in the fields of the Church, which our Lord had given us to cultivate, we ought to feel guilty of their springing up, and of our negligence in not rooting them out, just as we should accuse a labourer if his field be full of weeds; because, though he may not have sown them, and they may have sprung up by themselves, it was his duty to prevent their growth, and his neglect of proper cultivation which allowed them to increase. And if we are guilty of the rise and progress of these errors, we are still more so of the disorders and abuses which have crept into the Church. For while we have always detested heresy in every form, we cannot deny that the sad relaxation of discipline must be laid to our charge, as we were bound by all the duties of our office, either to enforce it when we saw it menaced, or to restore it where it had fallen away.'

"It is in this truly apostolic spirit that the cardinal legates who opened this Council, (both of whom have since become popes,) addressed this holy assembly. As, therefore, they allow that all the disorders in the Church have arisen from the sins and immorality of its ministers, we must equally believe that such disorders will continue, unless we first set to work to extirpate the cause of all these evils. The Holy Spirit has said: '*The multitude of the wise is the welfare of the whole world.*' (Wisdom vi., verse 26.) We must, then, be these spiritual doctors or wise men, sent by God to heal the wounds of souls.

But if we ourselves are covered with sores, we should, at least, have enough sense to avoid the reproach of the Gospel: 'Physician, heal thyself,' and labour to cure ourselves before attempting the healing of others. A wise doctor, when he sees a body dangerously attacked in various parts, strives first to cure the most important organs, the health of which would affect the whole system. In the same way, God having placed us, as it were, as the heads of the members of His body, (which is His Church,) it is only right that we should labour first to acquire that soundness and health which we might afterwards impart to the rest of the faithful. Besides, what authority over, or what credence can we expect in the minds of men, when we prescribe what we do not choose to follow ourselves? S. Chrysostom has said, with great reason: '*That nothing is colder than the speech of a man who does not carry out his words in his deeds. That this is not acting as a doctor of the Church, but merely imitating a comedian, who is representing a person in a theatre. For this reason,*' (adds the saint,) '*the apostles said nothing which they had not themselves done. And it was not even necessary for them to speak; for their lives were a continual sermon, and a voice which all could understand.*' *(In Act. Apost., hom. 1.)*

"This, then, should be our rule on so solemn an occasion. When we, the pastors, become faithful followers and imitators of Jesus Christ, our sheep will likewise imitate us. When we grow like the holy bishops of old, our flocks will likewise aspire to the piety of the first Christians. Then shall we see fulfilled the prophecy of Isaiah, which, in reality, regards the Church, though figuratively applied to the Jews: '*I will turn My hand to thee, and I will clean purge away thy dross, and I will take away all thy tin. And I will restore thy judges as they were before, and thy councillors as of old. After this thou shalt be called the city of the just, a faithful city.'"* (Isaiah i., verse 25.)

The archbishop concluded his speech with these words, which were full of such ardent piety that the prelates were greatly impressed, and decided at once to treat the reformation of the clergy as the first subject for discussion. Some days after, when the Council met, the question was mooted as to whether the cardinals should be included in this general reform? The prelates who, by their age, preceded the archbishop, and who were very numerous, demurred against this proposal; and all of them, one after the other, said, with the extreme respect and civility which they considered due to their high dignity, *"That their illustrious eminences the cardinals did not need any reformation."*

But when it came to the turn of the archbishop to speak, he said: "The prelates who have given their opinion before me, have all declared that the noble order of cardinals has no need of reform, in consequence of the respect which they bear to their dignity. But as for me, I declare the contrary, and feel that it is this very respect which makes me maintain that so illustrious a body need an equally illustrious reform. *Illustrissimi Cardinales indigent, ut mihi quidem videtur, illustrissima reformatione.* For it seems to me that the veneration which I feel towards them would be more human than divine, and more in appearance than in reality, if I did not wish that their conduct and reputation should be as pure and inviolable as their dignity is eminent. As they are fountains of which others must drink, they ought to be the more careful that nought but the purest water should flow from them: and the first thing I should wish them to deign to change in themselves is, the way in which they generally treat the bishops." He added: "That episcopal authority had been virtually annihilated since the establishment of the order of cardinals, who were unknown in the primitive Church; that formerly they ranked with other priests and deacons, and that it was only since the tenth century that they had begun to raise themselves above their condition. But even then they did not dare compare themselves with bishops; that they had always recognised bishops as their superiors until the twelfth century; but that since then they had so set themselves up above them, that they now trampled them under their feet, and even kept them in their palaces, holding only the rank of servants. That there was no hope of bringing about a real reform in the Church till the bishops were re-established in the position and with the authority which was their due. That in this he only regarded the ordering of God, of whom S. Paul says that He Himself has placed each member of the body of Jesus Christ according to his proper rank. And finally, considering what bishops and cardinals were before, and what they are now, he could only say in groanings before God, and in complaining of the Church to the Church itself: '*Ab initio non fuit sic.*'" (S. Mat. xix., verse 8.)

The archbishop spoke with such firmness and episcopal eloquence, that admiration for his zeal stifled at first in all minds any thoughts which might have led them to consider that he had taken an unwarrantable liberty.

The solidity of his virtue, and the consistency of his conduct, made things appear praiseworthy in him which would have been thought extraordinary in others. For every one felt and knew that he was neither incited to speak in such a manner by ambition nor by passion, still less by envy or caprice. That he had no human ties nor interest with any one in power under heaven, and that the sole aim and end of all his actions was to glorify God, to serve the Church, and to satisfy the dictates of his conscience, so that the cardinals themselves, who were the most interested in the matter, listened to his advice without showing the least displeasure, and always testified as much esteem and admiration for him to the end as they did at the beginning.

Several of the bishops, who were more worldly-wise, and had more regard to human respect, were amazed at his stating so boldly what they would scarcely have dared to think secretly. But by the result and success of this action on his part, it became evident that a bishop who is all for God and His Church, and *"who fears more,"* (according to S. Gregory,) *" the anger of the Sovereign Truth, which is in heaven, than the judgment and power of men, who are on earth,"* is the more generous as he is the more humble, and that he will reject, as an unworthy meanness, the cowardly advice over which human timidity throws the cloak of moderation and prudence, while, leaning only upon God, his sole fear is lest he should offend Him.

CHAPTER IX.

THE CARDINAL OF LORRAINE ARRIVES AT TRENT WITH THE FRENCH BISHOPS.—HE RELATES THE EVILS AND SACRILEGES CAUSED BY HERESY IN FRANCE.—LETTER FROM THE ARCHBISHOP ON THIS SUBJECT.

Towards the end of the year 1562, that is, in the month of November, Cardinal Charles of Lorraine arrived, with the French bishops. He brought the letter written by the King of France, Charles X., to the Council. It was read before the whole assembly, and he then read a speech which has been inserted in the acts of the Council, in which he said, among other things, *" That France was reduced to a deplorable state. That on all sides there were murders, divisions, troubles, and sacrileges, and everything which could foster impiety and heresy; that a worse than civil war was raging with the utmost fury on both sides; that in some places one saw great fires lighted, in which they burnt the Church vestments, the works of the Fathers, the images of the saints, and even their sacred bones and relics, the ashes of which were afterwards thrown into the river. In others the priests were dragged from the altar, and massacred in the most cruel manner. And some did not fear to carry their horrible impiety so far as to defile the Holy of Holies, and to endeavour to abolish entirely the Adorable Sacrifice; thus striving to efface the very traces of the faith of our fathers."* And as to the cause of these deplorable excesses, he adds: *"The hand of God is upon us, and we are justly striken for our sins. We have brought down upon us His anger and His justice, for the morals of all orders of men in the kingdom are corrupted, and even the discipline of the Church has been allowed to fall into ruin."*

He then entreated the fathers of the Council to labour for the reformation of these evils, and particularly those who sincerely desired the welfare of the Church, assuring them that he, and all the bishops of France, were anxious to help them with all their might to carry out these reforms; which the fathers of the Council gladly agreed to. And as the zeal of our archbishop for the discipline of the Church was so great, he conceived a particular affection for these French bishops, and resolved to help them by every means in his power.

But the accounts they had given of the state of France, especially the Cardinal of Lorraine, was a real grief to him, and he shed many tears at the outrages offered to God by these impious and barbarous hands, who, according to the words of the Psalmist, had *"set fire to Thy sanctuary, and defiled the dwelling place of Thy name on the earth."* (Psalm lxxiii., verse 7.) And he poured out all his feelings of sorrow and indignation to his Vicar-General in the following terms:

"My dear Father,

"Though I wish to write to you, yet I do so this time with sorrow, because it appears to me that this is a season more for weeping than for words. But I write to conjure you likewise to lift up your heart with prayers and tears to God, that He may deal with us according to His mercy, and not according to our sins, which are infinite. The Bishops of France are arrived, and with them the Cardinal of Lorraine, who, speaking to the Council in the name of the whole country, described the excesses and malice of the heretics to be such as I cannot think of without horror. Frenchmen persecute Frenchmen, profane the holiest places, break the sacred images, throw down the altars, and burn with fire the most sacred objects of our faith, and the more they strive to put down these heretics, the more they seem to increase. I assure you I am getting alarmed, lest a spark of this abominable fire should reach even to Braga. For I am persuaded, by what I hear and see around me, that a Christian who lives according to the maxims of this world, and forgetful of his own salvation, is not less susceptible of this contagious heresy than dry wood is of fire, because it is an open door for every species of licence and libertinage.

"It is by this bait to the corruption of our poor human nature that the preachers of these unhappy doctrines tempt so many of their disciples, because they teach that every Christian, no matter whether in holy orders or not, should embrace the state of matrimony, and they exempt every one from the laws of the Church, as regards fasting, abstinence or confession. Therefore, there is no doubt that if the smallest entrance be given to these false prophets, they will speedily gain innumerable disciples.

for we know how many persons plunge themselves in licentious lives, although they profess to believe that God has forbidden such things, and that we do our best to warn them of their danger. Unhappily, much of this mischief arises from the relaxation of discipline in the clergy themselves. I entreat you, therefore, my father, to arm yourself with fresh zeal, so as to nip in the bud all disorders and vices in the Archbishopric of Braga. Tear out these tares from the hearts of men, lest they bring forth fruits of sensuality and heresy, and dread nothing so much as false indulgence in such matters. Be, therefore, both firm and vigilant. Despise the judgments of men, and fear that of God alone. Esteem yourself happy if, by acting in this manner, you make enemies, and sharpen the tongues of the slanderers. For it is a sign of predestination if you are persecuted for righteousness' sake. I implore you to admit no one to holy orders without the most rigorous examination, especially as regards morality; and rather to add to my regulations on this subject than to diminish them. It will be quite enough if you ordain three times a year. I entreat you to order public prayers throughout the diocese, especially for the salvation of France, and for the destruction of this terrible heresy, which has already wrought such evil on that country, and which will be the cause of much more. But, above all, labour for the reformation of morals. Vice and licence have sown the seeds of all these errors. Stifle them, and you will destroy the source of the evil. I pray to God to strengthen you with His might, and fill you with His Holy Spirit, which, being both the spirit of love and of truth, will teach you so to bear and keep souls in charity as to preserve them from the snares of the evil one."

CHAPTER X.

THE ARCHBISHOP PROPOSES THAT THE COUNCIL SHOULD TREAT THE QUESTION OF RESIDENCE, AND INDUCES FATHER PETER OF SOTO TO WRITE HIS FEELINGS ON THE SUBJECT TO THE POPE BEFORE HIS DEATH.

In the following meetings of the Council, many subjects were treated, and principally that of residence. It had been already discussed under Pope Paul III., and a decree had been framed on the matter in the sixth sitting. But the bishops were divided on this point. Many wished to shelve the question, because they did not wish to reside near their churches, or for some other reason of self-interest. But others, among whom was our archbishop, thought it was a point of vital importance, and earnestly demanded its re-consideration. The Cardinal of Mantua, president of the Council, and several of the bishops, did not wish the question re-opened. They dreaded the result, and tried to evade it by substituting other subjects which, they said, were of greater importance. But the archbishop, with sixty-eight other bishops, the greater portion of whom were Spaniards or French, represented so strongly the importance of this question, that the cardinal was obliged to consent, only saying that it would be wiser to defer the discussion till they came to treat of the Sacrament of Holy Orders, and as this proposal was just, every one was satisfied.

But the archbishop, who feared endangering anything which concerned the interests of God, went to an old Dominican, Father Peter de Soto, who was theologian to the Pope, and very old and sick, and implored him to use the little strength which remained to him, to warn the Holy Father of the obligation under which he lay to compel prelates to reside in their dioceses. This venerable old man was extremely clever, and looked up to both by the Pope and by all the fathers of the Council. He entirely concurred in the archbishop's views, and feeling his end drawing near, wrote to the Pope in the following terms:

"Most Holy Father,

"Being on the point of appearing before God, and the zeal I feel for the honour of your holiness only ending with my life, I have thought that it would not be displeasing to you that in these, the last moments of my mortal career, I should take the liberty of giving you one word of advice concerning the vexed question of residence. I believe, then, that it would be worthy of your holiness' piety and virtue, to see that not only the Council should clearly define the duty of bishops and other ministers of the Church to reside in their cures, but that when once defined, this duty should be enforced, and inviolably observed by your holiness and all other prelates. And to speak even more clearly, I would decree that no cardinals should hold bishoprics unless they be resolved to reside in their sees. These are the last wishes and the dying words of your very humble and very faithful servant. And as I earnestly pray that your holiness may enjoy a long and happy life, so I believe that when it shall please God to exchange it for a better one, it will be a consolation to you to have done as I entreat in that last hour, in which I find myself at this supreme and terrible moment."

CHAPTER XI.

THE HOLY PRELATE PERSUADES THE COUNCIL TO RECONSIDER THE QUESTION OF RESIDENCE.—THE DECREE ON THIS MATTER.—THE CHARACTER OF D. GUERERO, ARCHBISHOP OF GRENADA.

Several days passed, during which different questions were propounded in the Council. At last, they came to the Sacrament of Holy Orders, which caused a very earnest discussion. But though this was the time, according to the president, when the question of residence was to be discussed, no one had the courage to open the subject.

The archbishop perceived this; and as in the affairs of the Church he never consulted any one but God and his own conscience, without having regard to any human considerations, he went to the cardinal legates in their own palace, accompanied by the Archbishop of Grenada and the Bishop of Segovia, and represented to them in respectful terms that it was for the glory of God that this question of residence should be decided, and that he was sure they would not disappoint the expectation of so many prelates, who earnestly wished for the solution of this matter, which was, moreover, eagerly sought for by the whole Church.

The legates had nothing to oppose to his reasons; and being convinced of the justice of his demands, they promised that they would do what he wished at the next sitting of the Council.

The next day, accordingly, the proposal was made. But the difficulties attending its execution were greatly exaggerated, and other affairs being represented as most urgent, it was put to the vote, and the archbishop's side being the weakest, it was decided to postpone the question for three months.

The archbishop saw plainly that by this postponement they were in hopes of so wearying the patience of those who cared about the matter, that it would finally be allowed to drop altogether. And therefore, filled with indignation at such tampering with an affair which regarded the honour of God, he spoke as follows:

"There are certainly many things to be discussed in this Council, but none are more important than this question of residence, which has been postponed again and again. We are met together here in the name and for the benefit of the whole Christian Church; and we are bound to listen to the voice of the Churches who complain that they are deprived of the presence of their bishops, who treat them like thieves, only passing by to take their goods, and then departing, instead of remaining as pastors and shepherds of the flock, to nourish, guide, and console them. This is not only a great evil in itself, but the source of many others. And if I may be allowed to speak my mind freely on the subject, I would add, that I know only one greater evil than this, and that is, that we who are assembled here, in God's name, to redress so great a scandal, are working, on the contrary, to hide and veil it; and that, instead of removing it by our decisions, we authorise it by our silence. The blood of souls abandoned by their pastors cries out to heaven for vengeance! Do we dare to shut our ears to their cries? We are here in the sight of God, and of all the children of the Church, and of our bitter and heretical enemies. All that we do is seen and judged by all. If such considerations, and respect for our own characters do not move us, let us fear, at least, the menaces of God, who declares that He will judge those who are judges with the utmost severity of His justice. Let us fear, likewise, the tears and groans of desolate and neglected souls, mounting up to heaven, as holy writ tells us; and let us dread also to envenom the tongues of our enemies, by giving them an opportunity of justly ridiculing the reformation of Christendom, which we have published far and wide, and lest God should reproach us, as He did the Jewish people by the voice of His prophet: '*Propter vos nomen meum blasphematur in Gentibus.*'" (Isaiah lv. verse 1.)

The archbishop spoke with such vigour and warmth on this occasion, that his words made a profound impression, and fifty-eight of the bishops who had voted for the postponement rescinded their opinion, so that the very small minority which remained obstinate were compelled to yield; and it was decided that the discussion of the question should be commenced at once.

There were long speeches from all the fathers in turn; and then it came to our archbishop, who spoke again as follows:

"Many of the prelates who have preceded me have amply shown, by the authority of past councils and fathers, and especially of S. Thomas, that the duty of residence is indispensable and of divine right. But if I may be allowed to speak my mind, I should say that we ought really to consider ourselves most unhappy to be compelled to pronounce on this subject at all. For alas! to what state can the Church be reduced, if it has come to be a matter of doubt whether those to whom He has confided His flock are to look after them or not? We should be amazed and horrified if a servant were to neglect the children committed to his care by his master, or a shepherd his flock, or a mother her nursing child. And yet we are not shocked that when God has entrusted to us the care of the souls He has redeemed, and of whom we are at once '*pastors, fathers, and mothers,*' (according to S. Paul in the Thessalonians,) we abandon our charge, and think the obligation of living amongst them a hardship! S. Ambrose says that pastors are *vicars of the love of Jesus Christ, (vicarii amoris Christi,)* and that as He has thus made them heirs of His priesthood, so He wills that they should also imitate Him in His perfect charity. That is why He exacted of S. Peter, and in his person of all the apostles, a *triple pledge of love* before establishing him as pastor of His sheep.

"Dare we, then, doubt for a moment whether we be bound to live with them, when we are obliged to be ready to die for them at any moment? We hesitate to allow that our presence is necessary to them, and yet we are forced to own that our lives are no longer our own, but theirs. How then can any one pretend that in this matter we are asking too much, and carrying things to excess? On the contrary, we can only say on this subject what S. Bernard did to Pope Eugenius: '*Non fortia loquimur, sed possibilia.*'

"Reverend fathers, do not let us flatter or deceive ourselves. It is a great evil, and even, in my opinion, a great crime, for bishops not to reside among their flocks. But even if they do, it does not thereby follow that they are to be highly commended. We do not praise a servant because he performs the duties he owes to his master, nor a governor because he remains in his seat of government, nor a doctor because he stays at the bedside of his patient. The presence of such persons is an obvious necessity if they are to fulfil the duties they have undertaken, but it is not enough to be there. They need many other qualities besides, to perform their duties thoroughly and well. When, therefore, we urge the necessity of residence as an indispensable obligation, we do not pretend thereby to restore the episcopal order to its pristine perfection, as some have affirmed, but only to do away with one of the greatest and most shameful of its scandals. I say one of the greatest of its disorders, because it lowers pastors even below the position of mercenaries, that vilest and most despised of states before God and men. Thus, one of the fathers has said, sighing: '*Our Saviour condemns mercenary pastors, but would to God the Church had now even hirelings to guide her!*' For the hireling, as the Gospel says, remains with his flock *at least till the wolf comes.* But now pastors do not wait for the arrival of the wolf to flee from and abandon their flocks! They leave them to themselves, without ever troubling their minds as to what may become of them, or whether the enemy of souls may ravage and tear them! And even the hireling, as says S. Augustine, though he may fly from fear, does not hesitate to return when the danger is past. For he flies from God when he abandons the innocent through the timidity which keeps him tongue-tied and inactive, when he is bound to defend them. '*Fugisti quia tacuisti; tacuisti quia timuisti.*' Let us then to-day wipe away this reproach from the Church of God. Let us declare positively that residence is indispensable and of divine right. Let us dry the tears of the children whom their fathers have abandoned. Let us put a stop to so grave an evil, lest, should we endeavour to hide it, God should visit us in His wrath, and heretics should mock us with the well-deserved reproach that the wounds of the Church are really incurable, since we will not suffer any remedies to be applied to them."

The archbishop's speech was listened to throughout with the deepest attention; and it was decided to draw up a decree defining the duty of residence. This affair was entrusted to a council, composed of the Cardinal of Lorraine, Cardinal Madruccio, the Archbishops of Acquila, Grenada, and Braga, and twelve others. But the legates charged our archbishop with the principal responsibility in the matter, as it was the one in which he had taken the principal part.

Our holy prelate consequently laboured with all his might to draw up the decree in such terms that residence might henceforth be considered indispensable, since he had not been able to obtain that it should be considered of divine right. After many verbal alterations, it was published, as we find it recorded to this day, in the twenty-third sitting of the Council.

In this decree, allusion is first made to what had passed in the previous meetings on the subject, under Paul III., when the Council had spoken in the following terms:

"The Council, wishing seriously to re-establish the discipline of the Church, which has fallen into great neglect, and to correct the depravity of morals existing both among clergy and people, feels that it must begin with those who have been raised to the highest dignities in the Church. For the integrity of those who command is the safety of those who obey. The Council, therefore, wishes that none shall be entrusted with the government of the Church, (a burden dreaded even by the angels,) but such as are really worthy of the dignity, whose lives from their childhood upwards have been passed in the worthy fulfilment of ecclesiastical functions, and who have earned public respect from their virtue and piety. In which matter the rules and ordinances of the Fathers of the Church should be strictly followed. The Council likewise exhorts all bishops to consider that the Holy Spirit, having entrusted to them the care of God's Church, which Jesus Christ purchased with His own Blood, they must be ever watchful over themselves and their flocks, and spare no labour to acquit themselves worthily of the functions of their ministry. The Council warns them that they will be very far from fulfilling this duty, if, instead of watching over the souls committed to them, and of whom the

Sovereign Judge will hereafter demand a strict account, they should abandon them as hirelings. For it is certain that the pastor is entirely inexcusable if, by his absence or other occupations, he neglects his flock, and leaves it to be devoured by wolves.

"*And as, unhappily, in these sad days there are many (which we say with deep sorrow) who, forgetting their own salvation, prefer earth to heaven, human things to divine, and carry on intrigues at court, mixing themselves up with all sorts of worldly affairs, the Council hereby decrees that the ancient canons against non-resident bishops, which, by the corruption of the times have fallen into disuse, shall be enforced in all their original vigour as renewed by the present decree.*" (Concil. Trid., Sess. 6, c. 1, de Reform.)

So far the question of residence had been already settled under Pope Paul III. But as it had been since considered that this decree might be diversely interpreted, the fathers now added other words to enforce their meaning more clearly:

"*For fear that what was holily and usefully laid down in the decree of residence under the pontificate of Paul III., of happy memory, be misunderstood, or not interpreted according to the intention of its framers, the holy Council hereby declares, that all bishops, patriarchs, primates, metropolitans, even though they be cardinals, will be henceforth obliged to reside in person in their dioceses; and that they may only absent themselves for such reasons as we are about to mention. For, as it may happen that Christian charity, or a pressing necessity, or the duty of obedience, or a visible utility to the Church or the state, may sometimes demand or even exact that a bishop should absent himself for a time from his diocese, the Council ordains that he should put down in writing the reasons which justify his absence, so that they may be approved either by the*

Pope, or by his metropolitan, or by the oldest bishop of his province. And let those who thus absent themselves take the greatest care to provide in the meanwhile for the wants and proper administration of their diocese. And as those who are only absent for a few days are not considered absentees, according to ancient canons, the Council declares that on these legitimate and approved occasions the time of the bishop's absence should not exceed two or three months at the most, and that even then they should take great care that such absence should not be in any way prejudicial to the interests of their diocese. The Council also warns them not to absent themselves from their cathedral churches during such seasons as Advent, Lent, or the Feasts of Christmas, Easter, Pentecost, and Corpus Christi, such being the times when the sheep should draw the most food and consolation from the presence of their pastors, unless the functions of their charge should call them to another portion of their diocese.

"If it should happen, which God avert, that any bishops should absent themselves from their dioceses contrary to the rules laid down in this decree, the Council declares that they will incur the penalties awarded in the ancient canons, and which were renewed by Paul III. That they thereby become guilty of mortal sin; and that, more than this, during the time of their unlawful absence, they shall not be entitled to any portion of their revenues, which they cannot in conscience retain, but which must be applied either to the repair of churches or the relief of the poor.

" The Council also decrees that this rule shall equally be put in force in the case of rectors, curates, and all ecclesiastics entrusted with the cure of souls. And that when they have even a legitimate and important reason for absenting themselves, they should obtain the permission first, in writing, from their bishops. That if any dare to contravene or disobey this decree, the Council requires the

ordinary to compel them to reside, by ecclesiastical censures, and by a withdrawal of their revenues, without any privileges, or exemptions, or pleas of immemorial customs, all of which are in reality only abuses and corruptions; nor shall any appeal, even to the court of Rome, suspend the execution of the bishop's orders."

Thus this grave affair of residence was brought to a close. And it was entirely due to the perseverance, zeal, and firmness of our holy archbishop, who first insisted on the matter being brought forward, and then concluded it in the manner and on the terms which were the best he could obtain for the good of the Church.

He was greatly aided in this affair by the Archbishop of Grenada, Dom Peter Guerero, a man of eminent science and zeal, and who was the intimate friend of our saint.

Among other truly generous and episcopal acts of his during the Council, was his maintaining the divine right of bishops, contrary to the opinion of the president, the Cardinal of Mantua. He wrote to Rome, and the Pope complained of his obstinacy to Philip II., King of Spain, who, in consequence, desired his ambassador to make known to the archbishop his displeasure at his conduct.

The ambassador sent his secretary with the king's letter to the Archbishop of Grenada. The latter, without showing the least surprise, answered: "That he was sure his majesty knew well that he was not wanting in zeal for his service, but that the matter in question was purely an ecclesiastical one. That as in civil affairs he would await with respect the orders of the king, in those of the Church he could only consider his duty to God and the cause of truth, as it was to God alone that he would have to give account. That he was persuaded that the king was too wise and enlightened not to despise him as unworthy of his office, should he appear to change his opinion, and betray his duty by a mean and unworthy compliance.

That this Council, which had been so earnestly desired by the whole Christian world, would be useless if it were not entirely free. And that if they began to importune, trouble, or intimidate the prelates, he would instantly beg for his dismissal, and return to Spain. That the truth he had tried to maintain in the Council was derived from God and from holy writ, and that so far from wishing to weaken anything that he had said, he was, on the contrary, prepared to give his life to maintain it."

The secretary faithfully reported his answer to the ambassador, who wrote to the King, that having made known his wishes to the Archbishop of Grenada, he had received them with every demonstration of respect; but, that, believing himself bound in conscience to maintain the opinions he had held before the Council, not only would he yield nothing to the pressure put upon him, but that he had expressed his determination not to be less firm on other occasions. That, in fact, it was useless to attempt to give advice to this archbishop. The king, Philip II., who had a very great veneration for the prelate, and had learned by his own generosity and firmness to respect these qualities in another, not only was not offended at the apostolic boldness and freedom of the prelate, but conceived a still higher esteem for him than before.

CHAPTER XII.

THE ARCHBISHOP EXHORTS THE FATHERS OF THE COUNCIL TO WARN KINGS OF THE IMPORTANCE OF THE CHOICE OF BISHOPS.—THE DECREE OF THE COUNCIL ON THE SUBJECT.

The matter of residence being settled, the Archbishop of Braga considered that the most important matter next to be brought before the Council was the selection of bishops whose residence would be an advantage to their flocks. That it could not be denied, nor could it be owned without shame and sorrow, that there were many places where it could be wished that prelates were always absent from their dioceses. "For some," he added, "are not only hirelings, but wolves; enemies not of vice, but of piety and innocence. They reward those they should punish, and punish those they should reward: and thus deserve to be ranked among those whom the great Pope Gregory the Great stigmatised '*as usurpers of divine authority, and real tyrants.*'" (Gregory, in Reg. 1, cap. 2, v. 30. Ibid., cap. 7, v. 19.)

"This evil is great," he continued, "for it brings with it the loss of innumerable souls, and we might almost look upon it as incurable, as we see the disease without being able to apply the remedy. For canonical elections, which formerly were in the hands of the clergy and people, according to the primitive order of God and the Church, have now been changed into elections made by kings; and it seems useless to discuss the manner in which these elections are conducted, as it does not rest with ourselves. But it seems to me that the charity which we owe to all Christian princes, compels us to represent to them the extreme peril in which they place themselves each time that they give an unworthy prelate to a diocese as pastor of souls.

"In the book of the Acts of the Apostles, we see that Joseph the Just and S. Matthias, having been presented to the apostles that they might choose between them which should be promoted to the apostolate, they did not dare make the appointment themselves, but drew lots, committing the matter first to God Himself, saying: *Thou, Lord, who knowest the hearts of all men, show whether of these two Thou hast chosen.*' (Acts i., verse 24.)

"If, then, even apostles thought themselves unworthy to choose, and if all the clergy and people gathered together, after the primitive order, did not think it possible to decide till they had implored the light of God's Holy Spirit by fasting and public prayers, how can kings make such an election without fear and trembling? Therefore, considering how impossible it is for princes to weigh sufficiently the spiritual importance of these elections, and considering likewise the great trouble they have to free themselves from the importunity of those who surround them, and who desire such dignities for themselves or their relations, we think it would be very useful, with a view to their eternal salvation, to warn them that they commit a mortal sin, and run the risk of eternal damnation, if they do not choose as bishops those who are really worthy; not regarding high birth or interest, but simply their virtue, science, and piety.

"And we do not say this only from the freedom granted to this august assembly, in which we are to act and speak as judges of the whole Church, but when I return to Portugal, where God gave me birth, I will boldly maintain the same thing, and am sure that I shall meet with the approbation of her most gracious majesty our queen, who is regent for her son, Dom Sebastian, the king. For her wisdom and piety have already anticipated whatever the Council may decree as regards this matter, and all Spain and Portugal know the words she spoke, and which deserve to be engraved in the hearts of all the kings and queens in Christendom : ' *That she earnestly wished that during her regency the prelates of Portugal might be immortal, so that she should never have another bishopric to give. That it was quite enough to have to answer for one's own self and the state, without being responsible for the salvation of innumerable souls.*' "

The fathers of the Council, having taken this matter into deliberation, drew up a decree in the following terms:

" *That if in every estate of the Church it was necessary to use the utmost care lest anything derogatory to the honour of God should be found in His House, it was doutly important that no mistake should be made in the election of one who was to be raised above all the rest. For there will be no order in the family if the good qualities expected in its members do not reign supreme in the head. Therefore, although the Council has already published certain ordinances regarding those who are to be promoted to the episcopacy, yet the subject is of such vital importance, that no precautions can be too great to ensure the selection of men worthy of so grave a charge. Therefore it is decreed, that as soon as a bishopric falls vacant the chapter should meet, and public and private prayers be ordered throughout the diocese, that they may obtain a good pastor from God. And without interfering at present in the election of bishops, the Council exhorts and warns all those who have the right of nomination, or who in any other manner are concerned in such elections, to remember that they can do nothing which will contribute more to the glory of God and the salvation of His people, than by selecting good and holy pastors,—men who are really worthy of guiding the Church ; and that, on the other hand, they will commit mortal sin if, either directly or indirectly, they do not promote the election of men whom, in their conscience, they believe to be deserving, looking solely to their merit, and not to the solicitations or human affections of those who covet such dignities for themselves or others."* (Concil. Trid., Sess. 24, cap. 1, de Reform.)

CHAPTER XIII.

THE FEELINGS OF THE ARCHBISHOP, AND THE DECREE IN COUNCIL REGARDING THE MODESTY AND EXEMPLARY LIFE REQUIRED IN BISHOPS.

As we have before said, we do not intend here to give a chronological history of the Council, or of the exact order in which the different questions were discussed or treated, but to dwell chiefly on those subjects in which the object of our biography took the most leading part.

The two questions of the residence and election of bishops having thus been decided, our holy prelate next brought before the fathers in Council the necessity of condemning with a charitable and holy fervour all that could dishonour the episcopate. And one day, in a speech of great learning and dignity, he set forth the danger of the excessive luxury and sumptuous habits of certain ecclesiastics, as giving scandal to the faithful, and named a particular nation who took the lead in this matter. He complained with apostolic zeal that they shrouded their vanity under the false pretext of giving greater dignity to the episcopate; and he showed that their excuse was as criminal as their fault. He proved that the authority and veneration acquired by bishops over the hearts of their people by the exercise of self-denial and piety were incomparably greater than those obtained by super-

fluous expenditure and a pretended keeping up of dignity of station. He proved his words by several passages from the Fathers, and quoted again the words of the canon, (the sixteenth of the Fourth Council of Carthage):
"*Episcopus vilem suppellectilem et pauperum victum et mensum habeat et dignitatis suæ autoritatem fide et vita meritis quærat.*" He spoke also of other things which disfigured the beauty of the episcopate, and of the best means of reforming them. And one day, after having spoken with unusual warmth of prelates who entered the Church without being called to that dignity save by their avarice and ambition, and who employ the money destined for the poor to satisfy their vanity, or to enrich their relations, he added: "I confess I cannot read without a holy horror what that great Pope S. Gregory says of such prelates, who look upon their sacred charge as on a secular profession, which he says is prefigured in the person of the two sons of Eli, both pontiffs among the Jews, and who were both killed in the same day.

"*These two men,*" writes this holy Pope, "*represent those bishops who, regardless of the obligations of their charge, only think of enjoying the pomps and luxury of the world. For the glory which accompanies a bishop, the respectful deference which he receives, the greatness of his power, the splendour of his dignity, the magnificence of his equipage and court, and the abundance of his riches, being loved in a human and secular manner, have the greatest possible attraction to an ambitious and worldly man. But this very splendour is his ruin. We ought to say of such prelates what the apostle says of certain widows: 'For she that liveth in pleasures is dead while she is living.' (1 Timothy chap. v., verse 6.) But what is still more terrible is, that their example encourages others to imitate them in their luxury and extravagances, so that they fall into the same snare. Thus they do not perish alone, for in destroying themselves, they kill the souls of others; and after having drunk the poisoned cup of vanity and luxury, they pass it on to those who are under their authority, and thus poison all together."* (*Gregor. in* 1 *Reg., cap.* 2.)

These are the opinions of a pontiff whom we may call the greatest of all the successors of S. Peter, and who inherited, with his throne, the same spirit of humility and charity.

S. Bernard, who drew his inspiration from the same source, speaks in a like manner of these scandals:

"*The prince of apostles warned Christian women in old times not to give themselves up to vanity and magnificence in clothes. But now we are compelled to address the same reproach to bishops. If they blush to see themselves included in the same condemnation as the weaker sex, let them blush far more to have needed the same remedy, by being sick of the same disease.*" (*Bern. de Offic. Episcop. cap.* 2, *num.* 6.)

And he speaks even more strongly on this subject in one of his sermons on the Canticles: "*All those who are thus permitted to draw near to the Spouse are not the friends of the Bridegroom. There are very few who do not look after their own interests instead of considering His. They love earthly goods and rich gifts, and they cannot serve Jesus Christ after they have become the slaves of money. Look at them when they go abroad, magnificently dressed, in their sumptuous equipages. Who, on first seeing them, would not take them for rich spouses going to the church, rather than friends of a poor Bridegroom? And where, do you imagine, do they obtain those immense riches, those superb clothes, those magnificently-served tables, groaning under the weight of gold and silver vases, save from the funds of their Divine Spouse? It is this profusion of her goods which is the cause of her remaining herself poor, naked, and miserable, of her having lost all her ornaments, and that we behold her pale and languishing, with her face drawn and disfigured. Certainly it is not thus we should deck our bride: this is not guarding, but losing her; not defending, but exposing her to a thousand perils; not feeding the sheep of Jesus Christ, but strangling and devouring them. 'They have eaten My people,' says our Lord by His prophet, 'as they would eat a piece of bread.' (Psalm xiii. verse 4.) And again, 'They have devoured Jacob, and laid waste his dwelling-place.' (Psalm lxxviii. verse 7.) Where, in these days, shall we find a prelate who does not think more of laying up riches for himself, than of weeding out the vices of his flock? Where shall we find one who, by prayer and mortification, is striving to appease the just anger of God, or leading souls to husband the precious moments of mercy and grace? And yet, when we say this, we are only dwelling upon minor faults. There are graver crimes among them, for which God reserves His heaviest judgments. But it is in vain that we speak of these, for they will not listen; and if we were to write down our thoughts, their anger would only be kindled against the writer, and not, as would be only just, against themselves. Let us leave, then, these persons, who neither find nor watch over their Spouse, as it is said in the Canticles, but who, instead, put her up to auction. True it is that they are the inheritors of the apostolic dignity, but not the heirs of their faith or zeal. Many wish to pass for their successors, but few care to be their imitators. Would to God they had as much anxiety to guard their spouse as they have to mount the steps of the pontifical throne! Then they would watch over their own souls and preserve that which has been confided to them. Then would our Lord have no need to exclaim, in the words of the prophet: 'My friends and My neighbours have drawn near, and stood against Me.' (Psalm xxxvii., verse 12.) This is the just complaint made by the Church, and never was it more just than in the age in which we live. It is not enough for those who should be the guardians of our souls to neglect us; they must needs lose us altogether. For being wrapped in profound slumber, and stricken with lethargy, although God warns them by His word, not even His thunders will rouse them. The extreme peril in which they lie is not enough to fill them with fear. Thus, as they are merciless towards their own souls, they are equally so towards their people, and, perishing themselves, they drag down their flocks in the same destruction.* (Bern. in Cant., serm. 77, numb. 1.)

"There is nothing to add to the words and authority of these two saints," concluded the archbishop. "If S. Gregory or S. Bernard were alive to-day, which of us would not wish to follow in their steps? Let us follow them, then, by carrying out what they recommended, and reforming the scandals they detested. For, if they were alive now, they would say the same things. And as the Holy Spirit, who spoke by their mouth, does not die, but is ever the same, we must believe that if we be faithful to Him, in this solemn assembly, He will inspire us with the same feelings, and put into our hearts the same holy desires, which should be the spirit and rule of the Church throughout all ages."

This wise and important advice was gladly followed by the fathers in Council, and after mature deliberation the following decree was drawn up, which we give *in extenso*, containing, as it does, the most important instruction that bishops can receive:

"*We wish much that those who have been named to the episcopal dignity should recognise the gravity of their duties and their charge, and that they should fully understand that they have not been called to it to satisfy their worldly interests, to enrich themselves, or to live in luxury and magnificence, but to labour diligently with the one object of procuring the greater glory of God. For it is indubitable* that the faithful would be brought far more easily to abandon their vices, and advance in piety and virtue, if they saw those who are set over them in the Lord, engrossed, not in the things of this world, but in the welfare of their souls, and in striving after the Kingdom of heaven. Therefore, the Council, being persuaded that the realization of this truth is the foundation of the re-establishment of ecclesiastical discipline, hereby exhorts all bishops to bear it continually in mind, so that their conduct throughout their lives, (which is as a continual sermon to those around them,) may show forth to the whole world that the purity of their actions corresponds with the eminence of their dignity. Let them take care that their habits be so regulated that all others may find in them examples of frugality, modesty, continence, and of that holy humility which makes us most agreeable in the eyes of God. This Council, then, following the example of the Council of Carthage, decrees that not only shall bishops preserve modesty and frugality in their furniture, dress, and table, but that nothing shall appear in their houses or in their whole conduct which does not breathe Christian simplicity, zeal for God, and contempt for the vanities of the world.

"The Council also emphatically forbids the employment of the revenues of the Church for the enriching of their relations or friends, as the apostolical canons forbid all bishops to bestow on others the ecclesiastical property, which belongs to God alone. If their relations should be poor, let them give to them as to other poor people, but not deprive others for the sake of enriching them. The Council exhorts them, likewise, with all the authority committed to them, to strip themselves entirely of this human affection for their brothers, nephews, or near relations, which is the source of such great scandals in the Church. And they declare at the same time that what they have laid down as regards bishops, must be equally applied to all those who possess *ecclesiastical benefices, whether seculars or regulars, each according to his position, and especially to the Cardinals of the Holy Roman Church. For as the Sovereign Pontiff takes their advice in the government of the universal Church, it would cause a still greater scandal if their lives were not so pure or so well regulated as to draw down upon them the esteem and approbation of the whole Christian world."* (Concil. Trid., Sess. 25, cap. 1, de Reform.)

CHAPTER XIV.

OF THE WISE CONDUCT AND THE REPUTATION OF THE ARCHBISHOP AMONG ALL THE PRELATES.—HIS FEELINGS, AND THOSE OF THE COUNCIL, ON EPISCOPAL GENEROSITY.

It is not necessary to dwell on the great influence acquired by the Archbishop of Braga over the minds of the fathers of the Council, both by his actions and his words. Those who were really anxious for the reform of the Church found in him a mouth-piece full of burning wisdom, zeal, and prudence, which disarmed all adversaries, and put the matter in question in the clearest light. Those who were more worldly-wise could not but admire his disinterestedness and that unalterable firmness with which he defended the cause of God, and saw Him alone in all their discussions. He was visited and consulted by all the pontiffs who, like himself, earnestly desired to further the interests of Jesus Christ. Others, who were of high birth, sought his friendship likewise; and when he saw them lukewarm in defending the cause of the Church, or the reform of the episcopacy, he would say: "If you had become soldiers, and been sent to command armies, to which your high birth would have entitled you, you would sooner have died a thousand times than do anything cowardly or unworthy of your position. And now that in your quality of bishops you are, as S. Chrysostom says, '*Generals of the army of Jesus Christ,*' you remain silent when you should speak; that is, you fly from the battle-field when you should fight. For our words are our swords, and to hold our tongues is to yield up our arms." Thus he roused the indifferent to a sense of their duty, and yet spoke with such modesty and humility, that he was beloved by all, so that the prelates in Council used to say, "*That the school of the Archbishop of Braga was the best school in the world.*"

The Cardinal of Lorraine had, ever since his arrival, testified his immense affection and veneration for this prelate, and the other French bishops did the same. Conformity of tastes and interests, and identical views as to the cause of the evils which afflicted the Church, strengthened these friendships on both sides.

We will only quote a few more words of the archbishop's on the duties of the episcopacy, as, if we were to detail all he said and did during the Council, we could fill a whole volume.

In one of their meetings, the fathers had been discussing the necessity of preventing bishops from living so much at court, where they were often engaged in affairs unworthy of their sacred profession. The Archbishop of Grenada spoke strongly on this head, and our archbishop seconded his motion in the following terms:

"This evil is the greater, because a bishop who delights in the life of a courtier must have forgotten who and what he is. If he would consider that by the unction of his consecration he is become a prince in the Kingdom of Jesus Christ, as he was made a priest by his ordination, he would think more of his real glory and honour, which is that of Jesus Christ, and would have less esteem for that of the world, which, according to holy writ, is '*but a dream and an illusion.'* They expose themselves to contempt instead of veneration by such conduct. A king does not feel himself at home, save in his own kingdom. Now the kingdom of a bishop is his diocese. He must be fallen very low if he can prefer a court to his own see; the cringing servility of a courtier to a position in which he can dispense the favours of heaven among the souls of men. Therefore we think it would be well if the Council would pronounce against this grave abuse, as it is useless for us to strive to raise the episcopal character among the faithful, if the bishops themselves, by their actions, lower their dignity in the sight of all men, and, by coming down from their thrones, prostitute their sacerdotal character, and reduce themselves to the level of ordinary worldlings."

At the conclusion of this sitting, the Council promulgated the following ordinance:

"*That the Council, having learnt with great sorrow, that some bishops, forgetting what they are, have dishonoured the episcopal dignity, and lowered themselves in an indecent manner before kings and princes, not only by yielding their proper rank, but by accepting offices about these royal persons unworthy of their sacerdotal character, hereby renews all that has been said or written in the canons and apostolic ordinances touching the behaviour of bishops; and orders all such in future to flee from these abuses: so that, having ever before their eyes the rank and dignity which God has conferred upon them, they may remember always to act as fathers and pastors of their flocks. The Council likewise orders that all royal personages and all the faithful shall show the reverence and honour due to prelates, as to fathers given to them by God Himself.*"

CHAPTER XV.

DECREE OF THE COUNCIL OF TRENT, WHEREBY ALL THE ANCIENT CANONS ARE RENEWED TOUCHING THE LIFE AND MORALS OF THE CLERGY.

Dom Bartholomew having thus laboured so energetically for the reform of the bishops of the Church, next set to work to bring about a reformation of the clergy. He said: "That in vain would bishops be found worthy of their posts if they had no one to second their efforts. That if the Council had striven, by their decrees, to improve the character of the heads of the body of Christ, which was His Church, they must now find persons who would be as hands and feet to the chief pastors. For even if a man had all the qualities in the world to make a good bishop, and was undoubtedly called thereunto by God, he would be powerless to fulfil the duties of his charge if, instead of finding helpers among his clergy, he found rather enemies, ready to destroy all that he was striving to build up. That they must therefore strive to remedy these grave evils, by amending the scandalous lives of many of the Church's ministers. That he thought the best plan would be to renew all the ancient canons on this subject, drawn up by previous holy Popes, Fathers, and Councils; so that if their exhortations failed in their effect, they should have the power to act against these violators of the Church's rules, and arrest by penalties and punishments the career of those whom the fear of God could not touch."

The fathers consequently published the following decree:

"*Nothing leads the faithful more strongly to the practice of piety and virtue, than the example of those who are set apart for the service of God, and whose daily life is like a visible lesson to them. For, having left the world to lead a higher life, all others look upon them as models whom they are bound to imitate. Therefore it is necessary that the clergy, who have been called to labour in the Lord's vineyard, should lead holy, moral, and regular lives, and that nothing in their houses or in their manners should be found to give rise to suspicions of any kind; that they should be grave and modest, whether in walking, or at home, in words, looks, or gestures, in fact, in everything about them. They should avoid the most trifling faults, remembering that they are serious ones in persons of their position. In a word, that they should be looked up to and respected by all for the purity of their acts and intentions. In order, then, that the Church of God should take care to enforce regularity and discipline in this matter, the Council decrees that, in future, all the ordinances of Popes and Councils on this head shall be strictly enforced, especially those regarding the lives, honesty, sobriety, dress, and education of the clergy, and against luxury, debauchery, dancing, games of chance, secular amusements, and all criminal actions into which they may fall. Likewise regarding their abstention from worldly affairs or trading. And the Council wills that all these ordinances, which are numerous and very useful, shall be observed, and that under the same pains and penalties as heretofore, or even more strictly, according to the sentences which may be imposed by the ordinary. And no appeal shall suspend the execution of this sentence, if it regard the correction of morals. That if the bishops discover that any of these ordinances have fallen into disuse, they shall enforce them anew, and that as speedily as possible. And let them see that they are strictly observed, notwithstanding the abuses or old customs which may have crept in to the contrary, whatever they may be, for fear that, by neglecting to reform the morals of those who are subject to their rule, they should themselves be chastised by the just vengeance of God."* (Concil. Trident., Sess. 22, de Reform, cap. 1.)

CHAPTER XVI.

THE ARCHBISHOP SPEAKS STRONGLY IN THE COUNCIL ON THE ABUSES CURRENT IN THE MATTER OF CHURCH PATRONAGE. —ORDINANCE OF THE POPE, AND CONDUCT OF S. CHARLES ON THE SUBJECT.

While they were discussing the questions of Holy Orders, one of the principal points on which the archbishop insisted was, that they should devise some means of correcting the pernicious abuses which had crept in regarding the nomination to benefices. For those who conferred them often did so to all kinds of persons, without examining into their characters or qualifications, but only thinking of the patronage given or received. One day, when the subject was under discussion, the archbishop spoke with even more vehemence than usual, as follows:

"Of what use will it be to the Church that the Council draw up excellent decrees if, after all, they should not be obeyed? If in these days a bishop should be as holy as S. Martin, or as firm as S. Ambrose, of what use will his charity and zeal be, if he be compelled to place his sheep under the care of a robber instead of a pastor, because a worldly man had given him the cure, and obtained the necessary papers from Rome? Who can hear without grief and horror that oft-repeated saying, which some people even venture to defend, 'that the Pope is the lord, and not the dispenser of benefices, and that he may give them as he likes, and to whom he likes?'

"This idea is as pernicious to souls as it is false in itself. And who would dare maintain it, unless he were equally prepared to maintain that it is of no importance whether souls are saved or damned? Is it not certain that if you were to ask a man which he would choose of two doctors, one of whom was very skilful, and the other very ignorant, he would laugh you and your question to scorn? As for me, I declare before God and before the whole Church, that if they do not speedily remedy this terrible abuse, I neither dare to, nor can govern my diocese, and that I shall be constrained to try and find some solitude '*not to see my child die of thirst*,' as Hagar said of her son Ishmael; so as not again to witness a misfortune like that which, not many months ago, happened before my very eyes. During the time that there was a vacancy in the Holy See, from the death of the Pope, I had found a worthy pastor for one of the churches in my diocese, where there are a great number of souls. A ravishing wolf, (for I can call him nothing else,) scented out the fact that the actual nomination to this benefice rests, not with me, but with the gentlemen of the conclave in Rome. He started off instantly, and travelled post haste to the Holy City, where he employed every possible means, and left no stone unturned, to obtain the cure for himself. He succeeded at last, and came back triumphant to take possession of this poor flock of Jesus Christ's, which he ravaged to such an extent that every day I weep and groan over the results.

"And let no one tell me that the glory and authority of the court of Rome will be diminished or weakened if she gave up her control over benefices. I maintain, on the contrary, that this same authority would be very much strengthened, as it is certain that when every one knows that the Pope is labouring for the salvation of souls, and that his only anxiety is to ensure this end by the best possible means, the honour of the Roman Court, both spiritual and temporal, would only be thereby increased. For if the parochial churches were provided with worthy pastors, the faithful would be strengthened in their obedience to the Holy See, and would be far less liable to fall into heresy and schism. Therefore, the best way to remedy so great an evil would be, to compel the bishops, and all those who have the right of conferring benefices, to give them only to men who have been carefully examined and proved to be worthy, as is already observed in the dioceses of Burgos and Placenzia."

The archbishop's words convinced the greater part of the prelates. But as the affair seemed to touch the jurisdiction of the Holy See, the legates represented that the question must be referred to the judgment of the Sovereign Pontiff, and await his answer. To this proposal all were agreed; and the archbishop, who felt the full importance of the decision, hastened that very hour to the Portuguese ambassador, and begged of him to write to His Holiness, and to the minister of the king, Dom Sebastian, who was then in Rome, to make them understand how much the welfare of the Church depended on this affair. He wrote also himself to Rome, believing with reason that what he had said touching this sovereign authority in the matter of nomination, would have the more effect from its being entirely in conformity with the advice which had been previously given to Paul III. For this Pope, who first convoked the Council of Trent, having chosen, in 1538, four cardinals, among whom were Contarini and Sadolet, two archbishops, one bishop, one rector, and the master of the sacred palace, to know from them the best means of reforming the crying abuses which then existed in the Church, they drew up a paper in the following terms, which paper was printed at Antwerp a year after:

"*There are certain theologians, whom we would rather call flatterers, who have dared to maintain that the Sovereign Pontiff is the lord and master over all benefices;*

from which it follows, as they pretend, that the Pope may legitimately appoint whom he pleases." And they add: *" Most Holy Father, from this source alone many abuses have arisen, and such dangerous maladies, that many think the Church in such a state as to render her cure almost desperate."*

Finally, they heard from Rome soon after, that His Holiness had ordained, *" That the nomination of the Pope would only be available if the person on whom he had conferred a benefice was approved of and found worthy by his ordinary."*

This decree having been made public, the Council ordered at the same time, that cures should only be conferred by the concurrence of many; that is, by choosing among a number who should present themselves, the one who was judged most qualified for the post. This was the more necessary then to prevent benefices being given to utterly ignorant persons, who were entirely incapable of the cure of souls. And we see in the life of S. Charles how wisely he availed himself of this ordinance:

" As to what relates to benefices," says Giussano, (liv. 8, chap. 30,) *" although S. Charles followed the decree of the Council as regards the concurrence of candidates, nevertheless, all his ecclesiastics were so submissive to his will, that no one presented himself for examination who had not previously received the order to do so from himself. For, knowing both his enlightenment and his charity, they wished in all things to depend on him, feeling that they could conscientiously undertake a charge to which he had called them; and that, on the contrary, the man who had done anything to procure a benefice for himself, deserved to be despised, and to be considered devoid of the true ecclesiastical spirit."*

CHAPTER XVII.

LETTER FROM THE ARCHBISHOP TO HIS VICAR-GENERAL, IN WHICH IS SHOWN HIS LOVE FOR RELIGIOUS POVERTY, AND THE CARE HE TOOK OF THE YOUNG CLERGY WHOM HE HAD BROUGHT UP, AND OF THE VIRGINS CONSECRATED TO GOD.

The loving zeal of the archbishop was, as we have shown, fully devoted to the affairs of the Council. And yet, whenever he had a moment's respite, his eyes turned to the beloved diocese which God had confided to him, and which he loved with a truly paternal tenderness and affection. Having founded a convent of his order in the town of Viano, a short time before his departure, he wrote several times to a Dominican Father, to whom he had entrusted the work, to hear how it was going on. We will give our readers one of these letters, to show his love of holy poverty, his minute care and charity for the virgins consecrated to God, and his indefatigable vigilance in all matters which concerned his ministry :

"My dear Father,

"*When I think of the peace you enjoy in Jesus Christ, it is some consolation to me in the midst of the multitude of affairs and anxieties around us; and I feel as if it were a rest to me to think of you. And as we are but members of one and the same body, under the same head, so you should share in our agitations as we try to share in your peace.*" (S. Aug. Ep. 81.) This feeling was expressed by S. Augustine, writing to some religious, whose words I venture to appropriate, because I feel myself in the same dispositions as regards you. I expected you would have forestalled me in writing; but you see it is I who write first, to ask for some tidings of the new monastery. I am rejoiced that it is you who have undertaken to superintend the building, not so much from your knowledge of architecture, but because you understand the practice of poverty, which will not allow of your breaking the rules, even to please the architect. For without that, I should fear, on my return, to find what our holy father S. Dominic did, who, having found his monks building a magnificent monastery at Bologna, exclaimed, with tears: *'What! even in my lifetime you begin to build palaces!'* Therefore, I entreat of you, for the love of God, to build a modest and humble building, and to take care not to follow the advice of F. John Romero, the architect of Gonzala, who is inclined, by his natural taste, to every kind of splendour and magnificence.

"Worldly men may seek such things, but we must flee from them. For as their spirit is entirely contrary to ours, they ought to hate what we love, and we to love what they hate. If we wish to build for God, do not let us offend Him by fancying to please Him. You must look after this the more narrowly, as this monastery is built with the money of the poor. The only thing which is important is, that the building should be solid and durable. If Brother Romero wishes to exceed the bounds of religious simplicity in the building, do not fear to oppose him, and to appeal to my judgment against his. For he was brought up in the magnificent convent of Victoria, where his mind has been filled with gigantic architectural proportions.

"After having said so much about the external building, you may imagine that I am even more anxious for the interior. I trust you will have special charity for the young clergy whom we are to bring up there. Try and win their hearts, so that they may listen to your advice with greater readiness. Feed them with the love of God, and train them in respect for and meditation on the Holy Scriptures, and of some holy father, like S. Bernard or S. Gregory the Great, which you should give them to read. Labour to ground them thoroughly in piety, which is far more important than learning. For the words of a wise Pagan, as quoted by S. Augustine, are very true: '*That it is very easy to impart knowledge to one who only thinks of becoming good.*' (S. Aug. Epist. 20.)

"I do not recommend our mothers and sisters of S. Anne to your care, for they are too closely united to God not to win the reverence of all those who serve them. I will only entreat of you to assist and console them with the greatest care. Be their confessor, if you can. If not, choose a confessor for them who shall be really capable. They would not be true spouses of Jesus Christ if they had other interests than His; nor true daughters of the Church if they did not feel for all the woes and anxieties of their divine mother.

"At last we have finished the question of residence. I should have wished that we could have done more in the matter; but what we have decreed will be enough for any bishop with a conscience. We are labouring now at the reformation of the morals of the clergy, and this matter marches very slowly. Recommend this affair to the prayers of the sisters, and tell them that I have great confidence in them, and that I hope that our wants, and those of the Church, will be always present to their minds. If their charity be truly Catholic and Christian, it must be as wide as the Holy Spirit, who hath put it into their hearts, and who 'filleth the whole earth.' We are fighting against the corruption of morals by our decrees; and they must fight against them by their fasts and prayers, and by the example of their holy lives. If their faith be as humble and as ardent as it should be, I shall expect from them great and powerful help, for God says in holy writ: 'That He hath regard to the prayer of the humble, and He hath not despised their petition;' and again, 'That He hath heard the voice of their weeping.' (Psalm ci., verse 118; Psalm vi., verse 9.) Give the holy mother abbess and her saintly company the blessing which I wish them, and bestow upon them with my whole heart."

CHAPTER XVIII.

THE ARCHBISHOP LEAVES TRENT TO GO TO ROME WITH THE CARDINAL OF LORRAINE.—HOW HE BEHAVED DURING HIS JOURNEY.

The archbishop had resolved not to return to Spain without having previously visited Rome, to confer with the Pope on several important matters regarding himself and his diocese. He was very anxious to make this journey during the sitting of the Council, so as not to retard his return to his diocese. While he was pondering upon this, God gave him the occasion, for there being a suspension of the sittings of the Council for two months, he resolved at once to profit by this opportunity to go to Rome.

It happened that, at the same time, the Cardinal of Lorraine had decided to go and consult the holy Father, and the great affection and esteem he had for our holy prelate made him earnestly desire that they should travel together. The archbishop, though greatly honoured by the proposal, consented to it with difficulty, because he dreaded the magnificence which would be sure to attend the journey of so great a prince.

They left Trent on the 18th of September, 1563, with three of the French bishops. This society was very agreeable to the archbishop, because they chanted the psalms and hymns of the Church as they went along. But if he were in this way consoled, he was equally annoyed at the frequent and magnificent receptions given to the cardinal, not only on account of his ecclesiastical dignity, but for the honour of his noble house, which was then one of the most powerful in France. For as he had insisted that the archbishop should sit by his side in the carriage, he naturally came in for a share of all the honours and civilities showered on the cardinal, which were insupportable to his modesty, so that on every possible occasion he tried to escape them; that is, whenever he could do so without wanting in respect to his illustrious companion.

They arrived in this way at Ferrara, where the grand duke, having come to meet the cardinal, and conduct him into the town, had taken the archbishop's place in the state carriage.

The archbishop thought this was a favourable moment, and asked them if they would allow him to go quietly to one of the monasteries of his order, which was in that same town. The grand duke would not hear of it; but the archbishop renewing his entreaties, the cardinal said to the duke, in French: "That he had better consent to let him do as he wished," to which the grand duke at last reluctantly consented.

The archbishop, jumping out of the carriage, took with him only Father Henry of Tabora, and went on foot to his monastery at Ferrara, where they came as two simple religious, who begged for hospitality. They went to the father prior, and threw themselves at his feet, according to custom, to ask for his benediction. But our holy prelate did not remain long concealed, for a religious of the same monastery, who had seen him at Trent, recognised him at once, and revealed his name and rank to the prior, greatly to his disgust.

The next morning he started very early to visit the convent of Bologna, which contains the relics of S. Dominic. He had sent on his suite the night before, so as to be unknown on the way, and to travel with greater peace and recollection. Having come into the church and adored the Most Holy Sacrament, he went and prostrated himself with the utmost humility of soul and body before the tomb of this great saint. And one of the petitions he uttered with many tears was, that, as he had chosen to be "*abject in the house of God*," as one of his humblest disciples, but had nevertheless been dragged from this position, against his will, to become a father and prince of the Church, of which he was utterly unworthy, he conjured S. Dominic to use his all-powerful intercession with God, so that he might be speedily delivered from this burden, which he felt to be more heavy and insupportable every day.

When he left the chapel, the prior and all the monks came to pay him their respects. He tried at first to persuade them that they were mistaken; but it was useless, for the Cardinal of Lorraine, who took delight in unmasking what he called the "*stratagems of the archbishop's humility*," had sent one of his officers to give notice of his arrival to the prior, adding that he was going to surprise them, and would appear *incognito* as a poor Portuguese religious, which was exactly what he intended doing.

The holy prelate, having spoken to the religious and the novices a few words full of charity and tenderness, left them, and went to Sienna, where great preparations had been made for the arrival of the cardinal, who soon after entered amidst the sound of trumpets and an immense number of guards and men on horseback. The archbishop saw it all without being himself discovered, and told him afterwards that though he had a great respect for the magnificence of the Church's ceremonies, he did not like the pomp of the century, and that seeing him so surrounded by armed men made him feel as if he were a prisoner of state, whom he had often seen led in that way from town to town under the care of the archers and the guards. The cardinal laughed; but the archbishop escaped, and hid himself in a convent of his order, where the prior received him, and made him dine in the refectory as a simple monk.

The next morning, the Cardinal of Lorraine, who suspected what had happened, came to the convent, asked for the prior, and begged to know if no religious of his order had been admitted the night before. The prior replied simply, that "no one had come save two poor monks from Spain." The cardinal burst out laughing, and told him that one of these was the renowned Archbishop of Braga, the most learned and holy prelate in the Council. He then went away, delighted at the confusion and astonishment of the poor prior, of which he made great fun afterwards with the cardinals who had received him in one of their palaces.

CHAPTER XIX.

THE ARRIVAL OF THE PRELATE AT ROME.—THE PORTUGUESE AMBASSADOR PAYS HIM GREAT HONOUR, AND OBTAINS FROM THE POPE AN ORDER THAT HE SHOULD LIVE IN HIS PALACE.

When our holy prelate arrived within sight of Rome, he persuaded the cardinal to let him leave the carriage, and taking only Father Henry of Tabora, he proceeded on foot, and hastened to enter before the rest, so as to remain unknown. Dom Alvaro de Çastro, ambassador to Rome from the King of Portugal, had received notice of the day the archbishop would leave Trent, and of the extraordinary speed with which he had performed the journey. Therefore, having minutely calculated the distances, he fancied he might arrive on that particular day, and wished much to go out to meet him, and conduct him to his palace. He sent accordingly, early in the morning, two men on horseback on the high-road to Sienna, and told them that when they met the Archbishop of Braga, one was to return post haste to let him know, and the other was to remain with the archbishop, and try to amuse and keep him back, so as to give the ambassador time to come and meet him in a magnificent equipage, suited to a person of his dignity.

The two horsemen met the archbishop, but never dreamt who he was, seeing only what appeared to be two poor monks on foot. They passed on, therefore, and having met some of the cardinal's suite, inquired eagerly after the archbishop. They replied he had gone on in front, and at last they found out that he was one of the two religious they had passed on their way. They galloped back as fast as they could; but he was already arrived in Rome, where he went straight to S. Peter's, on the Vatican Hill, to revere the relics of that great apostle. He then said his Mass, as it was yet quite early, and remained absorbed in prayer in the side chapel where he had said it, so as to be quiet and away from the crowd. He there waited for the return of a messenger whom he had sent to the prior of the Minerva Convent, begging him to prepare him a room.

In the meantime the ambassador had received his disappointed messengers, and heard from them how the archbishop had arrived secretly in Rome, and defeated his schemes. Not being able to hit upon any other method, he sent all his servants into the different streets and churches of the city to try to find him. Two of them went to S. Peter's, and there discovered him as we have described. They told him of the anxiety of their master to receive him, and of all the trouble he had already taken on his account. The archbishop was very much provoked to find himself thus discovered so soon; and excused himself from accepting the ambassador's hospitality, saying that he was determined only to lodge in a house of his order.

Finding him inexorable, they resorted to artifice, and told him that the convent of the Minerva was very far off; that it was too late to wait there for the return of his messenger; and implored him to allow them, at any rate, to conduct him to his monastery. At last he yielded to their importunity, and they led him by different streets to the ambassador's palace. When they had come to the door, they told him that they were close to the Minerva, and that one of them would go in and find out if the room had been prepared for his reception. Having accordingly warned the ambassador of the archbishop's arrival, the former ran quickly into the street, embraced the prelate, and said that he implored him to be a little more sociable with those of his own nation, who were specially grateful to him for the way he had maintained their interests at the Council. That it was not generous on his part, having done so much, to be unwilling to receive anything in return, and implored him therefore to accept his hospitality.

The archbishop, though much surprised, answered courteously, and saw that he was compelled to remain at the palace, at any rate, for that day. But the ambassador, judging by the trouble he had had to bring him, that he should have still more difficulty in retaining him, sent to the Pope, imploring His Holiness to order the archbishop to remain where he was, representing to him that any contrary course would be a great injury to the ambassador.

The Pope instantly sent his principal physician, and told the archbishop "That he was rejoiced at his arrival; that he wished to see him the next day; and that he ordered him to lodge, during his residence in Rome, either in the sacred palace, or in the palace of the ambassador of Portugal." The archbishop had nothing left for it but to thank His Holiness, and said, pleasantly, to the ambassador, "That he had no power any longer to resist his civilities, as he had clothed them, as it were, with the Pope's authority:" so that this affair was concluded entirely to the ambassador's satisfaction.

CHAPTER XX.

THE HOLY PRELATE HAS AN AUDIENCE OF THE POPE AND OF S. CHARLES, AND IS MOST FAVOURABLY RECEIVED BY BOTH.

That same day the Cardinal of Lorraine made his entry into Rome, where he met with a magnificent reception. The two cardinals, S. Charles Borromeo and Altaemps, nephews of the Pope, who had gone outside the gates to receive him, conducted him to the sacred palace, where his lodging had been prepared. As the cardinal had so great an esteem for our archbishop, he did not fail to talk of him to the Pope the very evening of his first audience. He told him that he had brought with him the Archbishop of Braga, who was known to His Holiness by the great reputation he had earned at the Council. That he was in truth a bishop of the primitive Church. That the French bishops were all agreed about him, for that no one had shown such warmth for the reform of the Church. That his zeal might be said to have gone almost beyond bounds for he had even ventured to speak of the reform of the cardinals! "A design," he added, smiling, "of which I might have complained to your Holiness, if I did not fear that Monseigneur Cardinal Borromeo, who is certainly as 'reformed' as this good prelate would wish us all to be, would take the opposite side against me."

The Pope, and S. Charles, who was also present, received this compliment with a smile, and showed great esteem and affection for the cardinal.

The next day the archbishop was summoned to his audience, and received by His Holiness with extraordinary favour, and with marks of honour widely different from those which he generally accorded to bishops. After the first few words, the Pope said: "That for a long time he had wished to make his acquaintance. That he was very much pleased at his having been the first to obey his summons to the Council, and at the way he had conducted himself there. That he could not express a wish more in conformity with the will of God than that he might find many other bishops in the Church who would resemble him. That he knew he had laboured valiantly for the reform of the bishops and the cardinals, which he had quite as much at heart as himself." Then, taking the hand of his nephew S. Charles, and putting it in the archbishop's, he said: "I place this young man in your hands; begin with him the reformation of the Church."

The holy prelate replied: "That if he had found the cardinals in the state to which God had brought Cardinal Borromeo, he would not have proposed a reform of their order to the Council. But that he would have brought them forward, on the contrary, as models for the reformation of the bishops and other ministers of Jesus Christ." But perceiving, by the expression of S. Charles' face, and by his change of colour, that this compliment was displeasing to his humility, he did not say any more.

After the Pope had questioned him on several other points regarding the Council, he dismissed him, telling him to come again after dinner. S. Charles left the audience-chamber of the Pope at the same time, and carried off the archbishop to his own rooms in the sacred palace. As soon as they were alone together, the archbishop told him "how delighted he was to be able to thank him in person for his good offices during the Council. That he had often feared that his intentions would be misinterpreted at Rome, although his heart was full of veneration for the Sovereign Pontiff and the Holy See; and that he thought he could not show this devotion more plainly than in doing his utmost to bring about the reformation of the discipline of the Church, as the depravity of morals had caused the heresies which had separated entire kingdoms from the Vicar of Jesus Christ. That he felt he owed to the good offices and wisdom of S. Charles the favourable manner in which his endeavours had been viewed by the Pope, as well as the kindness with which he had just received him, and testified his approval of his proceedings during the Council."

S. Charles replied: "That it was true that, having always had a very great respect for his person and conduct, he had been very glad to encourage the Pope in the same sentiments. That nevertheless the archbishop did not owe this esteem to his good offices, but to his own piety and zeal; being well persuaded that as the archbishop only considered the glory of God and the good of souls in his labours, he should serve our Lord best by serving him."

This holy cardinal, whom God destined hereafter to be the glory of his age, and a living image of the holy bishops who had preceded him, although he was still quite young, and had not yet attained the height of sanctity to which he afterwards arrived, was already determined to trample under foot all human and worldly considerations, to belong to God alone, and to see Him in every action he undertook.

And it was the conviction that our archbishop was filled with the same dispositions which had given him so high an esteem for his person, as will appear still more clearly in the secret conferences they held together before leaving Rome, of which more hereafter.

CHAPTER XXI.

THE CARDINALS RECEIVE THE ARCHBISHOP WITH GREAT HONOUR.—HE SHOWS THEM HIS HORROR OF LUXURY; AND SPEAKS HIS MIND PLAINLY TO THE POPE AS TO THE MAGNIFICENCE OF HIS BUILDINGS.

The Pope, who had conceived a particular affection for the archbishop, invited him constantly to dine with him, either alone or with the Cardinal of Lorraine. And his Holiness desired that he and no other should bring him his napkin before and after dinner.

One day, having gone towards evening to the castle of S. Angelo, where he knew that the Pope had dined with the Cardinal of Lorraine, he waited in the ante-chamber till they had come out. No sooner did the Pope perceive the archbishop, than he exclaimed: "Monseigneur of Braga, how is it you did not dine with us to-day?" The archbishop replied, smiling: "Because your Holiness did not invite me to the wedding." The Pope replied, with much tenderness and affection: "I will not accept your excuse, for you know very well that you are always invited to my table; and I insist henceforth that you come every day during your stay in Rome without missing a single one."

The great esteem with which he was thus honoured

by the Pope, induced all the cardinals to pay him the utmost civility. Many of them organised extraordinary fêtes in his honour, although they knew that it was he who always spoke the most strongly against their luxury, and who was doing his utmost to make them reform it.

Cardinal Alexandrin, a religious of his order, and who was afterwards made Pope under title of Pius V., conceived the greatest affection for him the first time he saw him. They were, in fact, the two greatest lights of the Order of S. Dominic. This cardinal delighted in talking to our archbishop, but as his stay in Rome was so short, (for he was only there seventeen days,) he could not have him to himself, save once, when he carried him off to dine in his own apartments in the sacred palace.

There was another cardinal who made a great fuss with him, less to show his affection than to display his riches. One day, accordingly, he invited him to a magnificent entertainment at his house. After dinner, he showed him a quantity of rare objects of art, of which his palace was full: ancient marble statues, original pictures of great merit, and a wonderful collection of rare and curious medals. And in showing off all these treasures, the cardinal described their value and history, and did his best to excite his envy and admiration.

But the holy prelate, who had been silent all the time, at last said: "If I were a Roman, and you first consul or dictator, I should say a great deal of the beautiful and magnificent things you have been good enough to show me. But being a Christian, by the grace of God, and you too, and moreover a cardinal, while I am a bishop, you must forgive my saying that any praise I could utter would be unworthy both of you and me."

He used this holy liberty wherever he went, and had great difficulty in repressing his indignation at the secular magnificence of the bishops and cardinals in Rome at that time. And when some tried to justify it by saying that gold and silver vessels cost, after all, less than others, for it was an expense only once incurred, and that after their deaths, they would serve to pay their servants or their debts, which were generally very heavy in such houses, he would reply, that he saw no excuse for such extravagance when the whole town was filled with the poor and miserable; and that, instead of spending so much money in selfish pomp, they had better put it out to interest by giving it to the poor, so as to send it before them to heaven.

But his zeal did not stop here. He even ventured to say something of the same kind to the Pope, though in a more veiled and cautious manner, befitting the profound reverence he felt towards the Holy See.

One day, the Sovereign Pontiff sent for him to consult him in a matter of grave importance. And after having passed the morning together, he insisted on his dining with him. And instead of putting the archbishop at a little table at the side, as was the custom, his Holiness made him sit by him at his own table, that he might be able to talk to him with greater ease and freedom. Their conversation turned on the government of the Church, and the Pope was delighted with all he said. Then the man of God, looking up and seeing all the magnificent plate on the sideboard, resolved to take advantage of the Pope's favourable humour to say something on the subject. So, taking up a beautiful silver gilt vase on the table, he said to the Pope: " Your Holiness must allow me to tell you that we have in Portugal vases not less beautiful than this one, though far less costly. They are made of porcelain, and come from India and China. As they are new, I believe they would be more admired than even gold and silver. The aristocracy, and even the princes and the king himself, have introduced them into their palaces in

Portugal, and use them even at their finest entertainments."

The Pope, with a smile, replied: "I understand you very well, Monseigneur of Braga. You mean that the china would do for me, and these gold vases for the poor. But to enable me to compare the two, remember, when you return to Portugal, to ask the Cardinal Infanta, your friend, from me, to send me some. For if it be as beautiful as you represent, I shall be very glad to make use of it."

The archbishop reported these words to the Portuguese ambassador, who hastened to communicate them to the Cardinal Dom Henry. And very soon after, the cardinal sent the most beautiful porcelain possible to the Pope, every one being enchanted to make an offering of this sort to the Holy Father. The Pope was delighted with it; used the vases constantly at his table, and made presents of the rest to the cardinals and princes of the Roman court.

The next day, the Pope having sent for the archbishop, took him with him to see that beautiful garden of the Sovereign Pontiffs, named the Belvedere, and showing him the works he was having executed, said, laughing: "Why don't you build a palace and garden like this at Braga?"

The archbishop replied: "That he was not in a position to build palaces. And even if he were, he should not like to build them out of other people's goods, still less of the goods of the poor."

The Pope, not being at all surprised at this answer, which he expected, added: "But still, what do you think of the new buildings I have put up?"

"Most Holy Father," replied the archbishop, "as your Holiness has deigned to show them to me, it is for me to see and admire their beauty, but not to give an opinion upon them."

"No, no," replied the Pope, "I wish for your advice in

the matter; and I assure you I shall not be displeased at anything you may say to me about them."

"If your Holiness commands me to speak," answered the archbishop, "I must say that it would be impossible for me to erect fine buildings, which time consumes, and which the Son of God will burn in the day of judgment. This palace is worthy of the architects who have planned it, and who have omitted nothing to enhance its beauty. But it is not worthy of your Holiness, who, in the exalted position in which God has placed him, is destined to offer Him living tabernacles, which will survive the conflagration of the world. And as for paintings, I own that I only care for those which recall to men's minds the images of our Lord and of His saints. Those, most Holy Father, are the treasures which I pray may possess your heart and mind."

The Pope listened with his accustomed gentleness, and then said: "But what would you have me do? Would you wish me to leave all these beautiful buildings unfinished? It is not I who began them, and I do not like incurring unnecessary expenses. But I am very glad to finish what was begun before my time."

The archbishop answered, smiling: "It is quite true, holy Father, that things which are good in themselves are better when they are completed. But the only difficulty is, to know if God will reckon these buildings among the good works you have done, when you come to die."

The Pope replied: "I see very well that you are of the same mind as Cardinal di Borromeo. He has found in you a man after his own heart. For he is just as indifferent about beautiful things as you are. And I am quite sure that the palaces he will build at Milan will be just like those you intend to erect at Braga."

CHAPTER XXII.

THE ARCHBISHOP, HAVING SEEN WITH GREAT REGRET THAT THE BISHOPS IN ROME REMAINED STANDING AND BARE-HEADED, WHILE THE CARDINALS WERE SEATED, PERSUADES THE POPE TO CHANGE THIS CUSTOM.

When the Cardinal of Lorraine and the archbishop left Trent, several matters were committed to them, on which they were requested to consult his Holiness. The Pope gave them an audience for this purpose, and afterwards fixed a day on which these points should be discussed in an assembly of cardinals and bishops.

The cardinals accordingly came into the Pope's council chamber, where each took his place. The bishops remained standing and bare-headed, according to custom.

The archbishop having been specially summoned to the meeting, and desired to give his opinion, spoke with his usual firmness and wisdom.

But he was extremely indignant to see so many bishops, whose great age and ability entitled them to the utmost respect, standing there for hours, while the cardinals sat at their ease, which appeared to him a kind of profanation of the episcopate. He was the more astonished, as this was the first meeting of the kind which he had attended in Rome.

The meeting being over, he took the Cardinal of Lorraine aside, and spoke to him on the matter. The cardinal had been as much shocked as himself, and the French bishops whom he had brought with him were furious. The archbishop therefore implored the cardinal to speak to the Pope about it. But to his surprise, he found it impossible to persuade him to do so. The cardinal did not like to compromise his interest with the Pope in a matter which he thought might be disagreeable to him, and in which he felt sure he should not succeed.

The archbishop, not being able to press him any further, went out sad and dissatisfied. After some further reflection, he sent word to the Cardinal of Lorraine, that he begged he would say nothing whatever on the subject, as he hoped to have an opportunity of speaking to the Pope himself.

He thought, however, he should first like to have the opinion of his friend, Cardinal Alexandrin. But he received still less encouragement from him than from the Cardinal of Lorraine. For all he did was to try and dissuade him from making the attempt, assuring him that it would be in vain, as it was an old-established custom, which the Pope would not change. And when the archbishop replied that he was determined to speak to His Holiness about it, he replied: *"Speak as much as you will, you will gain nothing by it."* *"Dices sed nihil proficies."*

Some days after, a fresh meeting of cardinals and bishops being called by the Pope, the archbishop received a similar summons to appear. He felt that this was the moment to put his plan into execution; and so, going very early to the Vatican, the doors of which were always open to him, he was admitted at once into the Pope's presence, and spoke to him on several important points touching the Council, especially upon the best manner of bringing it to a close, a subject on which the Pope was very anxious. The archbishop's advice was so agreeable to His Holiness, that he begged him to put it down in writing, promising him that all that he had suggested should be carried out as soon as possible. And wishing still further to show his esteem for his person, the Pope added: "That he must positively promise him to return to Rome after the Council was over, and before he went back to his diocese." The archbishop made no answer, but continued talking upon several points of reform, praising His Holiness for the zeal he had shown in redressing many grievances in the Church; and then added: "But, most Holy Father, this your work is not yet completed. For if your Holiness be so anxious to do away with scandals in the Church, how can you suffer your bishops to stand bare-headed in councils, held in your presence, for four or five hours at a time, while the cardinals are covered and comfortably seated? If it be true that bishops, as bishops, are superior to cardinals, as simple cardinals, for so it has been asserted and maintained in the Council, how can it be right or just that the cardinals, whose dignity is only a human institution, should receive such honour in the presence of your Holiness, while bishops, who have been instituted by Divine authority, even by Jesus Christ Himself, and who are the legitimate successors of the apostles, are dishonoured and trampled under foot? Most Holy Father, bishops, as bishops, are brothers of your Holiness, so that the honour of your Holiness itself demands that they should be treated with respect."

The Pope listened to the archbishop with his usual attention, and then said: "That this was an ancient custom, and that it had not been introduced by him. That the popes, his predecessors, had practised it before him, and that the bishops had not taken offence at it. How can I undertake," he added, "to change a thing which has been so long established?"

The archbishop quietly replied: "As your Holiness has been good enough to allow me to speak frankly in all matters, I think that He whom you represent upon earth commands me in this instance to do so with more than my usual freedom, because the cause for which I plead is

His alone; and if I were to be silent, I think He would hold me guilty. I repeat then, most Holy Father, with all the profound respect I owe to your Holiness, and with the zeal which I feel for the honour of the Holy See, that in this matter you should fear lest it be truly, '*Dominari in clero*,' which the apostle S. Peter, of whom you are the successor, so strongly reprehends and condemns. Banish, I entreat of you, most Holy Father,—banish far from the court of Rome those customs which may be called 'ancient,' but which are in reality abuses, for they are contrary to the laws of the Church. Your Holiness must permit me to ask, if he had presided in person at the Council, how he would have treated the bishops? and if they would not have been allowed to sit down? Therefore, if it be certain that they must have been seated in that august assembly, in the sight of the whole world, is it not more reasonable and more just that they should likewise be treated with respect in a private assembly, which is held in presence of your Holiness?"

The Pope, considering the zeal and ardour with which the archbishop spoke, and the good reasons he had set before him, was touched by his words, and said, good-humouredly: "That he could not make out how it was that he always yielded to him; that he did not believe any one else had such influence over him; but that he must come to the meeting, and then he would see how he would treat the bishops."

The archbishop hoped that his cause was gained, and with heartfelt thanks withdrew. The Cardinal of Lorraine followed him into the Pope's room, and there His Holiness began telling him what the archbishop had been saying, adding: "That he had spoken in such a manner in favour of the bishops, that he felt he could not resist him, and that he had resolved to change the old custom, and treat them henceforth with greater respect."

He asked the cardinal for his opinion, who backed up the archbishop's advice, and praised His Holiness for his courage and resolution; being all the time much surprised that an affair of which he had thought the success impossible, and which he had not himself dared to attempt, should have been so easily and happily managed by the archbishop.

After dinner, the assembly was held before His Holiness, and the cardinals and bishops having arrived, the Pope spoke to them as follows:

"Pope Adrian IV. was accustomed to say that if an emperor had formerly complained that princes were very unhappy, because they only see through the eyes and hear through the ears of other people, the Sovereign Pontiffs were not less so, because they are often misinformed, and things are hidden from them which they ought to know. For those who approach them do not often consider the truth or justice of their words, but only what will please and promote their interests. And they do not tell them that which it would be useful for them to hear, but what they fancy they would like to hear.

"I speak in this manner, because I have this morning received a very important piece of advice regarding the manner in which we have hitherto treated bishops in these assemblies. It is the Archbishop of Braga who has spoken to me on this subject, and I am very much pleased with him, because he was not hindered from speaking the truth by human respect, but consulted only justice and his own conscience. He has represented to me that this custom is an abuse, and I thought so before myself. But having been long established, I hesitated to alter it. Nevertheless, I have now been convinced, by his solid reasoning on the subject, that the same zeal which should lead us to maintain good things ought equally to inspire us to destroy bad ones. Therefore we have resolved henceforth to abolish this abuse, which has passed into a custom, and henceforth to make all bishops sit covered in our assemblies."

Having thus spoken, he made a sign to all the bishops present to sit and be covered. And thus this custom, so injurious to episcopal dignity, was abolished by the wisdom and goodness of the Pope, and the generous freedom of our holy prelate.

The meeting being over, the bishops waited for the Archbishop of Braga in the hall, and being all enchanted at the change, rushed to embrace him, and testify their gratitude. Cardinal Alexandrin having joined them, exclaimed joyfully: "Who will dare now gainsay this Archbishop of Braga, who is so all-powerful? and who will refuse to canonise him after his death, when he has worked such miracles in his lifetime?"

CHAPTER XXIII.

ST. CHARLES CONSULTS OUR PRELATE ON THE WISH HE HAD TO RETIRE INTO A MONASTERY.—THE ARCHBISHOP DISSUADES HIM; BUT HE ADVISES HIM TO REPAIR TO HIS DIOCESE AS SOON AS THE AFFAIRS OF THE CHURCH WILL ALLOW HIM.

St. Charles, who had greatly esteemed the archbishop before seeing him, had conceived a still warmer regard for him since he had made his acquaintance, and observed his solid piety, and the wisdom of his words and opinions on all subjects. Some days after his arrival in Rome, therefore, he asked him to come again to his rooms, as he wanted to consult him on a matter of grave importance. On the archbishop's arrival, he carefully shut the door of his study, and then spoke to him as follows:

"No one is here but God and ourselves, and I speak as

in His presence. For a long time I have besought Him, with prayers and tears, to enlighten me in the difficult position in which I find myself. I know that He often enlightens those who are specially His, and of whom He makes His temples. Therefore, believing that it is His will that I should open my mind to you, I am going to reveal to you the secrets of my heart." The archbishop, hearing him speak in this manner, wished to excuse himself, saying that he was incapable of rendering him the service he required. But St. Charles did not give him the time to reply, and interrupted him, saying: "Do not resist that which God demands of you. No sooner had I seen you than I loved you, and felt that it was through you that God would clear up my doubts. You see my position here. You know what it is to be the Pope's nephew, and particularly loved by him. You now know also what the court and life of Rome are. The dangers which surround me are manifold. I see many of them, and I believe there are many more which I have not yet discovered. What then ought I to do? I, being young and without experience, and having no merit but in the desire to become virtuous? Here I have plenty of flatterers, who pretend that I am necessary for the interests of the Church, through my influence with the Sovereign Pontiff. But how do I know that this is the service which God requires of me? and whether He does not wish it done by some one else? What will it profit me to gain the whole world, if I thereby lose my own soul? God has given me of late a fresh love for mortification and penance, and He has bestowed upon me likewise the grace to wish for His fear and love, and my own salvation, above everything else. I am thinking, therefore, of breaking through all these ties, and retiring into a monastery, so as to live as if there were only God and me in the world."

St. Charles having spoken in this way, the archbishop remained for some time without answering. He admired in so young a man this great contempt for everything which was most attractive, magnificent, and specious in the world, and so pure and enlightened a spirit amidst all the temptations and corruptions by which he was surrounded. And the more generous his proposal, the more difficult he found it to refute it. So that, after a few minutes, he told St. Charles that he wished for a little time to recommend this affair to God. But St. Charles rejoined, "That he should soon be deprived of his presence by his departure from Rome; that this was the only opportunity he might have of speaking to him freely; and conjured him not to defer his answer, but tell him his real opinion on the matter."

The archbishop then answered: "I cannot but praise your design, for I have myself experienced the advantages and security of the religious life. You desire to leave the world as I did. But whereas I left nothing in doing this, you, on the other hand, would leave all, and I will add, that this very thought would lead me to encourage your idea. For the higher your birth, your rank, and your dignity, the greater also the perils which threaten you. But if these general reasons would favour your design, others, drawn from the times, the state of the Church, and above all, the glory of God, which is the most important of all considerations, seem to me to demand of you a different course. If you liked the world and all that it possesses; if you felt yourself enamoured of its wealth, its honours, and its pleasures, I would advise you to leave it. For then the Gospel rule, which you have already quoted, should be followed: that we must not lose our own souls in wishing to save others. But as, by the mercy of God, your dispositions are quite the reverse, I should say that what would be dangerous and even mortal to another man, would not be so to you. You wish to choose, in your doubts, the safest way; but the important thing is, to ascertain whether it be the path which God has marked out for you. And I think that the gifts and graces He has showered down upon you until this hour, prove just the contrary. Every prelate in the Council, (at least all those who know anything of the secret working of things,) is persuaded that it is owing to you that its sittings were resumed after so many years; that you have always encouraged His Holiness to favour those bishops who have a single eye to God alone in their counsels, and that it is again you who are labouring at this moment to bring that holy assembly to a satisfactory conclusion. I praise God while praising His gifts and His works in you; and I would invite you equally to praise Him, and to humble yourself before Him, that He has deigned to make use of you as His instrument for the accomplishment of the greatest good that could be done in this world. Therefore, considering all these circumstances, and the individual qualities belonging to your person, to say nothing of the peril in which the Church would be placed if you were to abandon her when you are so necessary to her reformation, it seems to me that one can trace in you clearly the finger of God, and see evident signs of His will concerning you. And as He has already made use of your firmness and zeal for the manifest advantage of the Church, and that He has promoted you to the care of an important archbishopric, I think you should listen to His voice when He tells you to '*go up higher*,' while you choose for yourself to '*sit down in the lowest place.*' (S. Luke xiv. verse 10.) And that you may confidently trust in His goodness and mercy, that He will fill you so abundantly with His grace and Holy Spirit, that all your future life will correspond with its happy and holy commencement."

St. Charles was touched at the archbishop's words, yet made one or two other objections, which were, however, answered by our prelate. And as he had, in reality, so great an esteem for his enlightenment in divine matters, he finally told him that he would give up the idea of going out of the state where God had placed him, as the archbishop had convinced him that it was not what God demanded of him.

The biographers of St. Charles all allude to this critical moment in his life, and Ripamont speaks of it in the following terms: "*This holy cardinal, towards the close of the Council of Trent, began to lead a truly apostolic life; and then, being attracted by the sweetness of a contemplative and religious life, he made up his mind to renounce all things and to retire from the world. But the Archbishop of Braga dissuaded him; and St. Charles, having opened his whole heart to him, the archbishop showed him the powerful reasons which existed against his design, and proved to him that he could not carry it out without exposing the Church to very great dangers.*" *(Ripam., lib. 2, de Vita S. Carl., p. iii.)*

Giussano bears witness to the same thing in his Life of St. Charles: "*He thought of leaving the world, and getting rid of all his cares. But not to act according to his own judgment in a matter of such importance, he took the advice of the Archbishop of Braga, a venerable prelate of a most holy life, and an admirable example, for whom St. Charles had a particular esteem and veneration. And this archbishop strongly dissuaded him from the idea.*" *(Giuss., livr. 1, chap. 8.)*

St. Charles next said to the archbishop: "That although he had determined to follow his advice and remain in the world, he thought himself obliged to quit the court of Rome, to go and reside in his own diocese of Milan. That it was true that the Pope was particularly fond of him, and wished to keep him always about his person. That it might also be true that the part he had taken in the government of affairs had been useful to the Church. But that, being an archbishop, it was necessary he should reside near his cathedral, and that he felt he no longer belonged to himself, but to his people."

The archbishop replied: "That what he had just said was entirely in conformity with what he had himself maintained in the Council regarding the residence of bishops. But that he thought St. Charles should do nothing hastily in this matter. That he ought to consider that his uncle, the Pope, was a very old man. That if he were to retire from the management of affairs, another might take his place who might abuse the authority with which the Pope would entrust him. Therefore, he advised him to suspend this resolution for the present, though he might arrange everything to carry it into execution as soon as God gave him the opportunity, and likewise the means to prevent any bad consequences resulting from it." *(Ripamont, ibid., page 112.)*

St. Charles having warmly thanked the archbishop, rose, and said, while embracing him: "You fancied you had come to Rome about your own affairs and those of the Council, but in truth it was for me that God sent you. He has delivered me, through you, from the heavy weight which lay on my heart, and has given me the grace of discerning clearly the path in which He wishes me to walk."

CHAPTER XXIV.

OF THE HOLY PRELATE'S AVERSION FOR HUMAN AND SECULAR THINGS.—OF THE INFLUENCE HE HAD WITH THE POPE, AND THE LIBERTY WITH WHICH HE SPOKE TO HIM.

Our saint had only been ten or twelve days in Rome. He had come there for very important affairs, many of which had been already concluded. But nevertheless he was very sick of the whole thing, and made as much haste as he could to wind up all his business, having his heart in the Council only, and in his diocese.

For all that others come from so far to admire and see in Rome the magnificence of the churches and palaces, the beauty of the buildings and villas, the rare curiosities in statues and architecture, and the originals of the most famous pictures, which men's tastes have placed beyond price,—all these things appeared to him, as St. Chrysostom said, as "*an illusion and a dream.*"

The sight of those glorious buildings and luxurious interiors only made the condition of the poor and of the working classes more deplorable to him. And he used to be surprised that the remains of ancient Rome, and the wrecks of her vast empire, instead of acting as a warning to Christians of the vanity and fragility of all earthly things, only served to excite their curiosity and pleasure, and made them strive to rival the Pagans in pomp and luxury.

He watched the continual flux and reflux of persons, with their different businesses and disputes, by whom the Pope was hourly besieged, and often talked of it with St. Charles, who was as much bored with it as himself, and said: "That he saw with his own eyes with how much reason St. Bernard one day exclaimed to Pope Eugenius: '*Wake up, most Holy Father! understand the miserable slavery into which you are plunged by this multitude of affairs, and shake off with all your might the insupportable yoke imposed upon you. Do you think you are not a slave, because other men are subject to you? You are under subjection to as many masters as there are men who have recourse to you. You are for ever in the midst of noise and tumult, and wherever you go, you feel the weight of the burden which overwhelms you.*'" *(De Consid., lib. 1, cap. 3.)*

The Pope, however, treated the archbishop with the most marked consideration, and did everything to make him enjoy and prolong his stay in Rome. He treated him with extraordinary honour, and showed him a confidence which was remarked by everybody. And as the Pope was very clever himself, he saw very well that the consideration with which he treated the archbishop raised him in the opinion of all people whose judgment was worth having; while our holy prelate only made use of his influence to relieve the poor, protect the innocent, recompense virtue, and do justice to all the world.

One day, while he was with the Pope, two persons came and threw themselves at his feet, asking permission to act a certain play they had written, in the theatre of the town. The Pope had already refused this, as he considered the piece proposed was contrary to modesty and chastity. However, that day the Pope received them more kindly, and said, smiling: "That he would refer them to the Archbishop of Braga, and that if he gave them leave, he would at once confirm the permission." They returned, quite in good spirits, to their homes: but their joy was of short duration. For on inquiring at the ambassador's palace what sort of man this Archbishop of Braga was, they gave them such a description of him, that the play-writers never had the courage to speak to him on the subject, being very sure that it would be a certain way to ruin the whole affair.

The Cardinal of Lorraine, and the archbishop, having on another occasion dined together with the Pope, His Holiness asked the cardinal to go down with him and see the works he was building at the Belvedere.

The cardinal was loud in his expressions of admiration at all he saw, and did not know how to praise everything enough; while the archbishop stood by, silent and melancholy, and looking down on the ground. Then the Pope, turning to the cardinal, said: "Now just look at this inexorable man, on whose mind I can make no sort of impression. I grant everything he asks, and yet he will not yield to me in the smallest particular. He looks upon all these beautiful buildings with a severe and jaundiced eye; and I do believe, if he could, he would change them to-morrow into a hospital!"

The archbishop replied, smiling: "Most Holy Father, even if I did not venture to express such a wish, it is very certain that the poor would do so; and your Holiness must forgive me if I add, that I would sooner have their prayers and blessings, than the exaggerated praises of the Cardinal of Lorraine."

CHAPTER XXV.

THE ARCHBISHOP IMPLORES THE POPE WITH GREAT EARNESTNESS TO CONSENT THAT HE SHOULD RESIGN HIS ARCHBISHOPRIC.—THE POPE REFUSES HIM.—THE CONVERSATION BETWEEN ST. CHARLES AND THE ARCHBISHOP ON THIS SUBJECT.

The time fixed by the holy prelate for returning to the Council was at hand, and yet he had not yet propounded to the Pope one thing which he had more at heart than any other. So, one morning he went earlier to the Vatican than usual, and entering the Pope's room, said: "Until now, most holy Father, you have overwhelmed me with honours and kindness. I feel, as I ought to do, the extreme obligation under which your Holiness has laid me, by granting so many of my requests, though hitherto it is for others that I have implored your favours. Now, however, I am going boldly to ask you for something for myself, which is the height of my ambition. It was mainly with the hope that your Holiness might favourably receive my petition that I came from Portugal to Trent, and from Trent to Rome. I beseech your Holiness, therefore, to listen to my humble supplication. For though it be of the deepest importance to me, it is a very easy thing for your Holiness to grant, and depends absolutely on yourself."

The Pope listened with great attention and much surprise, not being able to imagine what would follow this preamble. The archbishop continued: "Most Holy Father, God gave me the grace to leave the world when I was very young. I passed upwards of twenty years in religion, loving above all things a quiet and retired life, and only wishing to die to the world, as the world was dead to me. But, I know not for what hidden judgment, God permitted me to be dragged from my cell to bring me into the light of day, in the quality of archbishop. This election seems to me so unjust, and so unreasonable in every way, that every time I think of it, I pity those who made it, and still more myself, who was forced to accept it. It is quite true that I resisted it as long as I could, and that it was only the fear of breaking my vow of obedience, and threats of excommunication, which induced me to do violence to my own common sense, and to blind myself voluntarily, as it were, not to see the strange disproportion which existed between what I was and what I ought to have been, if I were worthily to undertake this charge. It is certain that the first time I was dressed in my pontifical robes, and that the mitre was placed on my head, I felt myself overwhelmed with such a burden, that it was as if a mountain had fallen upon me. And the feeling I had on that day has lasted ever since, and increased rather than diminished. For the continual experience I have of my want of enlightenment and virtue, of my ignorance in all worldly affairs, and of the little fruit I reap in my diocese or elsewhere, from my poor attempts at teaching or preaching, renews this thought and this sorrow in me day by day. Therefore, I conjure your Holiness, by the bowels of mercy of Jesus Christ, and by the paternal tenderness with which you have ever honoured me, to choose some one who will worthily fill the Archbishopric of Braga, and who may repair, by his zeal and ability, the faults I have committed. I implore you to render this signal service to the Church, and at the same time to grant me this grace and justice. St. Peter, the first of Popes, was delivered from prison by an angel, who broke his chains. You, whom God has appointed his successor, do not refuse to be to me what the angel was to St. Peter. Be my liberator; break my bonds; let me return to the life of quiet and retirement I had chosen; and let me be able to repeat with thanksgiving every day of my life: '*I know now that God has sent His angel and delivered me;*' (Acts ii. verse 11,) and give me back the liberty of the children of God."

The Pope was extremely surprised at this demand, and had some difficulty in listening to him patiently to the end. But the respect he had for his virtue, and the warmth with which the archbishop had spoken, and which appeared even more in his eyes and gestures than in his voice, prevented his interrupting him. At last he stopped, and his Holiness replied: "That he only wished that all his other bishops were called in the like manner, and had as little affection for their dignity. That he was so far from thinking that he ought to be allowed to resign his diocese, that, on the contrary, if he were not already Archbishop of Braga, now that he, (the Pope,) knew him as well as he did, he would be the only man he would choose for that post, and that he was very sure that all the prelates of the Council would be of the same opinion." Then, seeing that the archbishop was preparing to renew his entreaties, the Pope added, sternly : " Monseigneur of Braga, I order you to dismiss this idea of resignation from your thoughts, and command you to consider only, for the future, how you can best fulfil the duties of your charge; and I believe in my conscience, that in thus deciding, I am rendering a great service to God, to the Church, and to yourself." Saying which, the Pope got up to close the audience, and the archbishop was constrained to take his leave.

Soon after this interview, His Holiness sent for St. Charles, telling him of the petition of the archbishop, and how he had refused it. He added: "That never had an ambitious man pleaded more eagerly for promotion, than the archbishop had to be allowed to tender his resignation." The cardinal was filled with admiration at his great humility, and on leaving the Pope, sent for the archbishop, and said to him: "I see you are sad, but it appears to me I ought to be so far more than you. I know that the Pope is the cause of it; but if you think you have reason to complain of His Holiness, I have much more reason to complain of you. What! you conjure the Pope to let you retire from the world, and at the same time you plunge me into it, when I wish to leave it. You think you cannot in conscience continue to be archbishop, and yet you advised me to be one. You are advanced in age, while I am young; you have experience and knowledge, and I have none. You have already had the government of a vast diocese, and you have lately borne, as it were, the weight of the whole Church, by labouring as you have done at its reformation in a General Council, while I have never yet left the court of Rome. And yet you wish me to accept a burden which overwhelms you, and of which you implore, at any price, to be released! What has become of your Gospel rule, to love your neighbour as yourself? Where is your tenderness as a father, your affection as a brother, your sincerity as a friend?"

The archbishop replied: "I appreciate and love your reproaches, because springing from the aversion you have to the world and its honours. You justify, even while you are accusing me. If I did not know how earnestly you wish to flee from the splendour of dignities, I would never have engaged you to remain where you are. Your salvation is not less precious to me than my own, and I make no difference between my soul and yours. But I know very well that God sees the difference, and that the way He guides you is totally different from His conduct towards me. You remember that I told you that yours was an exceptional case, and depended on circumstances peculiar to yourself. God has given you the grace to despise the world in the midst of its greatest splendours. He has preserved you from innumerable dangers where thousands of others would have been lost. He has inspired you with the wish to be all for Him and His Church, and has confirmed you in this desire, when it seemed as if everything should have deterred you from His service. You must not then be surprised if one cannot follow ordinary rules in an exceptional case, and if the counsel given you be as extraordinary as the ways in which God has led you. It requires a miracle, it is true, for any one of your age to bear so important a charge. But this miracle is not greater than those which God has already wrought in you. And we have every reason to hope that this extraordinary and miraculous guidance will be continued and remain with you to the end. So that I can only pray to God to assist us both. But I know well that there is more to fear for me than for you, and that the dangers are not equal when the merit is unequal."

Then, changing the conversation, without further alluding to himself, the archbishop added: "That his only thought now was, how soon he could get away. That he had really only come to Rome for this affair, and that now it had failed he should return as quickly as he could." St. Charles implored him to give him some information, before he went, touching his diocese: how he had managed his visitation, and other matters, on which he wished for advice before going to Milan. The archbishop told him all he wanted. And St. Charles then saying, "That he should like to know from him what were the qualities and virtues most essential in a bishop," our holy prelate told him that he had written a little book on the subject, which he had called "*Stimulus Pastorum.*" St. Charles insisted that he should leave it behind him, that he might have a copy made of it; and he afterwards made constant use of it in his diocese.

Thus these two men of God encouraged one another in the ardent desire they had to serve our Lord and His Church; and despising all that was human and striking, even in the most holy dignities, they only thought of consecrating their labours, their anxieties, and their very lives, to the glory of God, the defence of the Church, and the sanctification of their people.

CHAPTER XXVI.

THE HOLY PRELATE LEAVES ROME, AND RETURNS TO TRENT. —HE FINDS THAT CERTAIN POINTS HAD BEEN ALTERED IN WHAT HAD BEEN RESOLVED UPON BY THE COUNCIL, AND HAS THEM REINSTATED AS BEFORE.

There was nothing in Rome any longer to detain our holy prelate, so that he sought a parting audience of His Holiness to obtain his blessing. He told him that as, instead of releasing him from his charge, he had laid it upon him more stringently than before, he implored him to grant him the graces which were necessary for the fulfilment of his duties. And as he had drawn up a little memorandum of his wants, the Pope told him to read it, and was greatly touched to find in it not a syllable which regarded his own interests, but only matters which tended to the good of souls, the relief of the poor, and the liberty which was necessary to him in the government of his diocese.

The Pope granted everything he asked for with the greatest joy, and then, expressing the deep regret he felt at his leaving Rome so soon, he added that he would not say good-bye, for that he must see him again.

Having come back the next day, the Pope told him that he thought it would be better for him to wait for his friend the Cardinal of Lorraine, and to return in his company as he had come.

The archbishop, dissimulating the real reason which made him wish to go back alone, said to the Pope, smiling, that the cardinal had a mule which was as swift as a race-horse, and that his own never could keep up with him. Upon which the Pope replied: "If the cardinal's mule is as fast as a race-horse, I have one like an eagle in swiftness, and I will make a present of him to you. Therefore I wish you to wait for the cardinal."

That very evening the Pope sent the archbishop the most beautiful mule possible, being the one on which His Holiness rode himself when he went out of Rome.

The next day again the archbishop tried to take leave of His Holiness; but the Pope said he must return the next day with the Cardinal of Lorraine, as he had certain secret things to communicate to both of them. The next morning very early, the Pope left his apartments with all his court, and went to pay a visit to the Cardinal of Lorraine, in his own rooms in the sacred palace, which was a special and public honour paid by His Holiness to the cardinal. He then sent away his court, and remained a long time with him, the only other person present being the Archbishop of Braga. The Pope afterwards made the archbishop dine and spend the whole afternoon with him; after which he gave him his blessing, and wished him good-bye. Before finally doing so, however, he drew from his finger a ring of great value, and putting it on the archbishop's hand, said: "Wear this ring for love of me, and may it always remind you of the affection which God has put in my heart for you."

The next day, which was the 16th of October, after having said his Mass very early, he left Rome. And having passed through several of his own monasteries on the way, he arrived at Trent the end of the month.

He went directly to visit the cardinal legates, who received him with great demonstrations of esteem and respect, and with many expressions of gratitude for the way in which he had negotiated different matters with the Holy See, which had been pending his return to the Council. The bishops were equally delighted to see him, and were never weary of thanking him for the holy liberty with which he had spoken to the Pope in their favour, and had obtained, as we before said, the right for them to sit and be covered in his presence.

They let him know all that had been done in the Council during his absence, and told him that on the following day the different points of reformation which had been drawn up were to be read out, in order to see if anything were to be changed in the resolutions, either in the substance or the language. And one of the prelates added, laughing: "As Monseigneur of Braga has been so favoured by His Holiness, we hope he will treat us with a little more gentleness now, and not be so very anxious to reform us." To which the Bishop of Modena replied: "We shall see to-morrow what changes Rome has wrought in him, and if he is come back less of a bishop than he went."

That very night the archbishop had copies of the articles of reform brought to him, and compared them carefully with the original ones which he had kept. But he found to his great displeasure that many things had been altered and modified, and some omitted, in the new copies. The next day, all the fathers of the Council being assembled, he pointed out these discrepancies, and even proved that several things had been inserted contrary to the sense of the original resolutions, adding: "If the ordinances on which we were agreed before I went to Rome were not just and necessary, why did we approve of them? And if they were what they ought to be, by whose authority have they been altered? In drawing them up, we hoped to satisfy what we owed to God, to truth, and to the Church. What has happened since then? Has God's honour become less important? or has His truth been diminished? or is the peril of the Church lessened? St. Paul remarked that no one could accuse him of lightness or inconsistency of conduct: '*The things that I purpose, do I purpose according to the flesh, that there should be with me, It is, and It is not?*' (2 Corinth. i. verse 17.)

"If we be successors of the apostles, as we are in reality, let us likewise be their imitators in wisdom and constancy. I do not wonder that men who conduct themselves in a human manner, and who only follow the light of reason, should be guilty of inconsistency. They are like reeds shaken by the wind, who change their feelings and thoughts as they will, having no rule but their own caprice and fancy. But for us, who are acting here as priests of the Lord, and the depositors of His truth, do not let it appear as if the Church, which is the basis and foundation of this truth, were like a house built on the sand; but let us show the whole world that our decisions, having been inspired by the Spirit of God, are founded on a rock, and are consequently immoveable."

The archbishop's advice was followed by the great majority of the prelates, so that, when it came to the vote, two hundred and six were on his side. It was therefore finally concluded that not only should the resolutions be published exactly as they were before he left Trent, but that they should even add some words to make them more stringent and more favourable to the restoration of discipline.

CHAPTER XXVII.

THE WINDING UP OF THE COUNCIL OF TRENT.—DECLARATION MADE BY THE CARDINAL OF LORRAINE IN THE NAME OF ALL THE BISHOPS OF THE GALLICAN CHURCH.—THE HOLY PRELATE TAKES LEAVE OF THE CARDINAL AND THE FRENCH BISHOPS.

The twenty-fifth sitting of the Council being over, it was happily brought to a close by the care of St. Charles Borromeo, under the pontificate of his uncle Pius IV., in the month of December, 1563. Its chronology is as follows: The bull of convocation was issued by Paul III., in 1542. The Council met in 1545, and sat from December in that year, till September, 1547. Then it was suspended for four years. Re-assembled under Julius III., it sat from the month of May, 1551, to that of April, 1552. Then for ten years again it was suspended. Finally, it was once more re-assembled by Pius IV., when our saint went first to Trent, in the month of January, 1562; and it lasted till the month of December, 1563, when it was finally closed. Thus eighteen years had elapsed between the beginning and the end of this important Council. But its actual sittings only lasted five years: two years under Paul III., when ten sittings were held; one year under Julius III., when they had six sittings; and two years under Pius IV., when they sat nine times, which makes twenty-five sittings in all. Between Popes Julius III. and Pius IV., there had reigned two other Popes, Marcellus II. and Paul IV. But the Council was not resumed during their pontificate.

The archbishop, when the Council was over, went to the Cardinal of Lorraine to express his joy and his gratitude for the friendship with which he had honoured him, both during the time they had spent at Trent and on his journey to Rome. The cardinal had, a few days previously, made the following declaration in the name of the whole Gallican Church, which he had inserted in the Acts of the Council.

DECLARATION OF THE CARDINAL OF LORRAINE, MADE IN THE COUNCIL OF TRENT, IN THE NAME OF ALL THE FRENCH BISHOPS.

"Some days ago, having to give my opinion touching certain articles of reformation, I declared that what I wished for most was, the re-establishment of the ancient discipline of the Church. But nevertheless, considering the unhappy age in which we live, and that, in the face of the universal corruption of manners, it would be impossible to employ at once all the necessary remedies, I was compelled to approve of the decrees which have been passed in the Council on the subject of the reform. Not that I think they will be sufficient to heal the wounds of the Church entirely, but because I trust that after having employed milder remedies, the Church will be able to bear stronger ones, and that then our Sovereign Pontiffs, and particularly our Holy Father, Pius IV., will be led himself, by his piety and wisdom, to supply what is wanting; and that, renewing the ancient canons, (which have been allowed to fall into disuse,) and principally the decisions of the first four Œcumenical Councils, which we think should be observed as minutely as possible; or, if His Holiness sees fit, by the calling of General Councils, he may be able to heal the wounds of the Church entirely, and to re-establish her in all her ancient vigour and purity. These are my feelings; and this declaration I make in the name of all the Bishops of France: which declaration I wish inserted in the Acts of the Council."

Some days after, the archbishop came to take leave of the Cardinal of Lorraine and of the prelates who accompanied him. The cardinal gave him the warmest proofs of his affection and esteem, and having embraced him, he implored him to ask of God that he might become an imitator of his piety and virtue, so that their present friendship should become eternal, and that they should be united in heaven as closely as they were on earth.

The bishops parted with him with equal affection, telling him how glad they were to have been honoured by his acquaintance; that they only wished there had been more like him in the Council; that they should never forget the great services he had rendered in the Council to the whole Christian world, nor what he had done for the episcopate in Rome; and ended by assuring him that when they had published in France what they knew of his person and his acts, he would have as many admirers in that great kingdom as there were bishops and persons zealous for the reform of the Church of God.

The archbishop replied: "That he was happy to think that he had tried during the Council to labour for the reformation of the Church, in which, however, he had been ably seconded by them. That as it had pleased God to unite them on so important an occasion, he implored them to continue in the same kindly feelings towards him. That although they were born in different and distant countries, and were subject to different princes, they were, nevertheless, as Christians and bishops, the subjects of one great King; and that distance or space should not exclude the perfect union of those who are one in Him, who is in every place, and fills the whole world."

END OF SECOND BOOK.

THE THIRD BOOK.

CHAPTER I.

THE ARCHBISHOP RETURNING TO HIS DIOCESE FROM TRENT, LEARNS A CURIOUS PARTICULAR REGARDING THE COUNCIL.— HE GOES TO PAY HIS RESPECTS TO PHILIP II., BY WHOM HE IS VERY WELL RECEIVED.

The Council of Trent being over, the archbishop lost no time in setting off on his return to his diocese. The tender charity he felt towards the souls whom God had entrusted to him had only been suspended during the time when he thought his duty bound him to defend the doctrines and purify the errors in the universal Church. But having now fully satisfied that obligation, he only thought of giving himself entirely to his flock, with whom he was always in spirit and in heart.

Having started from Trent with his companions, he arrived at Avignon, where he was magnificently received by the Vice-legate of His Holiness, and by the governor of the town. Being with this bishop, he heard from his lips a curious fact, which redounded to the honour of the Church and of the Council.

It appeared that two bishops from this province had been seduced by the new heresy, but had resolved equally to attend the Council, and came,—wolves in sheep's clothing—in order to endeavour to defeat the designs of the true pastors of the Church, joining in all the conferences, and listening to all the deliberations, on which they gave their opinion like the rest.

This dissimulation went on for some time; but God enlightened them by those very men whom they had considered blind. For having seen how the heretics behaved themselves in their churches, and what were their principles and designs, they were struck by the great difference shown by the ministers of Jesus Christ, and those who were enemies of the truth. They saw that the rule of these men was only their own fancy; that they were *fabricators of their own dogmas;* and that their only object was to establish their own religion on the ruins of the true one; and that Catholics, on the other hand, had their foundation on the rock of sacred tradition, which had been handed down from pontiff to pontiff, since the days of the apostles until now. That they were not inventors of any new doctrine, but only the maintainers of the rule of the primitive Church; and that, striving to preserve inviolably what St. Paul calls *"the deposit of truth which had been confided to them,"* (1 Timothy vi., verse 2,) they wished to leave to their posterity what they had received from their fathers.

These two bishops openly declared the effect which had been produced upon them by the sight of the Council, and how touched they had been at the zeal of the bishops, particularly those of Spain and Portugal, among whom they named the Archbishops of Braga and Grenada,—men who had no other end in view than the glory of God and the good of souls, who weighed everything in the balance of the sanctuary, and maintained whatever they thought just and right with unshaken firmness. They added that in neither of these men was there a trace of self-seeking, or self-interest, or ambition of any kind, but only an extreme ardour for the salvation of souls, for the re-establishment of discipline, and for the reform of all the abuses of the Church.

One of these two bishops was a master of science and eloquence, and having been entirely converted by what they had witnessed at the Council, they both confounded the heretics, who did not dare to appear again before them.

The next adventure which happened to our saint on his journey was, that having arrived at a little town in Spain, the king, Dom Philip II., entered it at the same time. He was accompanied by his minister, Ruy Gomes de Silva, who was a great favourite of the king's, which honour he did not abuse. For as this prince was both wise and prudent, he knew how to make use of good and able men, and honoured them with his confidence, while he remained master of his own actions.

Ruy Gomes heard of the arrival of the archbishop, and told the king, who instantly sent for him; and Ruy Gomes, with a large suite, met the archbishop in the street, and brought him into the king's chamber. The king received him with marked respect, and asked him many questions concerning the Council, and especially as to the reputation left by the prelates of his own kingdom. The archbishop replied: "Sire, the reputation they had was worthy of your highness' choice; for as you have only raised to the episcopate worthy persons, no one can see their actions without being filled with veneration for their virtue and piety, and with admiration for your highness' selection. I do not doubt that you have been told of the proceedings of the Council, and if so, that you will likewise have heard that the Archbishop of Grenada excelled all others; and I venture to hope that as your highness rejoices in the wise decrees which the Council has drawn up, so your highness will see to their execution throughout your kingdom, and enforce them with all the weight of your royal authority. So that, being observed in the length and breadth of the land, the ancient piety and morality of the Church may be restored."

The king listened with much pleasure to this speech, and after having shown the archbishop many marks of favour, permitted him to withdraw.

Ruy Gomes having gone down-stairs to re-conduct him to his hotel, ventured to say, "That he was surprised to hear him address the king only as 'his highness,' when he should have said, 'his majesty.'"

The archbishop replied: "That the glory of a Christian prince was to yield the greatest honour to God. That in Portugal the title of 'your majesty' was given to God alone, and that of 'highness' only to kings."

The king himself, who knew the Portuguese custom, was not at all offended, and only respected the archbishop the more.

CHAPTER II.

THE ARCHBISHOP, HEARING THAT GREAT PREPARATIONS WERE BEING MADE FOR HIS ARRIVAL AT BRAGA, CHEATS THEM ALL BY SUDDENLY APPEARING IN HIS CATHEDRAL CHURCH.—THE JOY OF THE PEOPLE AT HIS RETURN.

The archbishop finally arrived on the soil of Portugal in the month of February, 1564. He was then fifty years old, having made his religious profession at sixteen, been consecrated bishop at forty-five, and having spent two and a half years in his diocese, and two and a half at Trent.

No sooner had his return been rumoured at Braga, than the whole town was filled with joy, and they prepared to give him a magnificent reception. But the archbishop hearing this, was determined to prevent them, and slipping into the town one night, he appeared the following day quite unexpectedly in his cathedral, and mounted the pulpit to speak to the people, this being the second Sunday in Lent.

His sermon was full of burning zeal and charity. He began by telling them: "That it was only his duty to the universal Church which had torn him from his flock for so long a time; that even in his absence they had been always in his thoughts; that he hoped God had received the prayers he had daily offered up for them, instead of the services he would have tried to render them; that the Council having maintained the faith against all the errors of the heretics, had made the most excellent regulations to arrest these disorders, and re-establish discipline and morality in the Church; that he trusted that as the bishops had thus laboured, the faithful would contribute, by their submission and obedience, to carry their decrees into execution." He added to this such expressions of affection and interest in his people, that many could not help praising God out loud for his happy return, and rejoicing with tears at seeing him once more. The poor especially declared, that if others were glad to welcome home their beloved pastor, they had far more reason for rejoicing, as they had in him a father who was never weary of helping them in their need.

The service being over, the archbishop left the cathedral, surrounded by an immense multitude, who, with transports and cries of joy, escorted him to his palace. No sooner was he arrived, than the town council came to pay him their respects, and spoke as follows:

"That it was not necessary for them to dwell on the happiness his return had produced, as it was shown on every face. But that they must venture to make one complaint, and that was, that he had deprived them of the means of showing their affection by the reception they had destined for him. That formerly, do what they would, they could never content the Archbishop of Braga by their display; but that as for him, they were not even at liberty to render him the most legitimate and indispensable honour. That in such a matter his modesty should have yielded to his charity, so as not to deprive his own children of the joy and satisfaction they would have had in welcoming their father home again in the best manner they could."

The archbishop, who read their joy in their faces even more than in their words, excused himself in so loving and courteous a manner, and showed them such marks of true pastoral affection, that his people were constrained to forgive him, and forget their disappointment.

CHAPTER III.

THE ARCHBISHOP FOUNDS HIS SEMINARY, ACCORDING TO ONE OF THE ORDINANCES PASSED BY THE COUNCIL.

This holy prelate resumed his episcopal functions by inquiring minutely of his vicar-general about everything that had passed in his diocese during his absence Then, having fulfilled this obligation, he took several days to implore the assistance and blessing of God, so that he might labour with fresh vigour to carry out all that the Council had ordained. And after mature consideration, as to what he should begin first, he thought he would commence by establishing a seminary. Having resolved upon this, he called his chapter together and all his clergy, and represented to them the obligation under which he lay to set the example to all the other churches in the kingdom of obedience to the decrees of the Council. That one of the most important was that by which they had ordained the foundation of seminaries in every diocese, where young men should be trained for the service of the sanctuary under the eye of the bishop. He added that he had received a special brief from the Pope on the subject, and conjured them to take part with joy in so holy and important a work, assuring them that he would set the example, and contribute all that was in his power towards the undertaking.

As it was a question of giving money, very few relished this proposal of the archbishop's, and many found great difficulties in its execution. Some excused themselves on account of the poverty of their prebendaries; others said that the subscriptions should have been begun sooner. A few who were better disposed, said they would do what they could in the future, but could not resolve to pay anything for the past, as the papal brief suggested.

The canons of the cathedral church complained more loudly than the rest, saying that besides the contributions they had to give from their prebendaries, which consisted in fruits, they would be obliged now to pay hard money from the daily offerings they received.

Great murmuring and discontent followed; but the archbishop listened to everybody's complaints with so much gentleness, and managed the grumblers with such tact and skill, that by degrees he appeased the storm which his proposal had raised.

He consented to modify the apostolic brief in two points, one of which was, that no arrears of payment for past years would be required; and the next, that those who were prebends in the cathedral church, and had no revenues but the daily offerings, should be excused from any contribution, if the Pope would allow it; and he offered to write himself to Rome to implore His Holiness to agree to his proposal. This satisfied everybody, for they knew the influence he had with the Pope, so that, by his wise moderation, the decree was carried out with the consent and approbation even of those who were at first the most offended at the idea. Having thus softened all opposition, he had no difficulty in inducing them to levy a contribution of two per cent. on the revenues of all the benefices of the archbishopric. And being anxious to encourage them by his example, he did not content himself with the proposed tax, but advanced three hundred ducats, so that the building might be begun at once. And the workmen were so diligent that his seminary was the first built either in Spain or Portugal.

In six months he had room enough to lodge sixty students, and having shown such anxiety about the building, he was not less keen as to those who were to fill it. He selected himself, out of all the youths in his diocese, those who appeared to him the most likely to be good and pious, and set over them professors whose charity and prudence equalled their ability. And he ordered them to watch over the habits and morals of the boys more carefully than over their studies, saying that science and cleverness, without piety and virtue, would be useless for his purpose, which was to train students for the service of God and the good of souls, and not men who looked upon holy orders as a means of raising themselves in station, in order to satisfy their pride,—a detestable abuse from which his diocese had already suffered too much.

From this seminary came forth many learned, virtuous, and holy men, who worthily governed many of the churches in the archbishopric of Braga; God thus rewarding the zeal and charity of our holy prelate, and letting him enjoy the fruit of his labours by witnessing the success of his undertaking.

CHAPTER IV.

THE CHAPTER CLAIMING THE RIGHT OF VISITATION IN THE TOWN, THE ARCHBISHOP DECLARES TO HIS COUNCIL THAT HE IS RESOLVED TO DISPUTE THIS RIGHT, AND VISIT HIMSELF.

The establishment of his seminary was a great joy to the archbishop. But another matter now claimed his attention, and one which he felt he could not dispense with, though he foresaw it would bring down upon him the most violent opposition.

In order to understand the subject in dispute, we must premise that the jurisdiction, both spiritual and temporal, of the archbishop, was shared by his chapter. This practice gave rise to many disputes and law-suits. Finally, it was agreed that the revenues of the see were to be divided equally between the archbishop and the chapter; and that as to jurisdiction, the temporal should be reserved to the archbishop, and the spiritual divided between them. And it was settled that the chapter should exercise this power in all the parishes and chapelries of the town, and in the churches of St. James and St. John, without the archbishop's interference; while the archbishop should have unlimited power over the rest of the churches in the archbishopric, without the interference of the chapter.

This arrangement at first seemed to settle all differences; but fresh evils arose. The chapter, in virtue of their power, appointed two visitors, who visited the churches and people in the town; so that the archbishop, though the pastor of all these souls, had his hands tied, and did not dare interfere in or take knowledge of any scandals which might arise among the clergy of the city, which became the fertile source of endless and crying disorders. For men of great wealth and infamous lives had the principal voice in the election of these visitors, whose duty should have been to arrest license and punish immorality; and so they made themselves masters of the very men who should have been their judges. The more weight they had, from their riches and dignity, the more dangerous was their example. For the humbler sort imitated the richer, and were certain of impunity in their vices, seeing that they were practised by the highest personages in the town. Even the archbishop's visitations in the country were of little use, because the guilty defended themselves by the example of those in the city, and if they were punished, they cried out against the manifest injustice of their sentence, and pretended that our holy prelate was a respecter of persons.

This reversal of all order had gone on for a long while. Many of the previous archbishops had tried to remedy it, but being discouraged by the furious opposition which was roused in the town, they gave it up, and contented themselves with the wish. Later on, brothers and sons of the king had mounted the archepiscopal throne, and relying on royal authority, had striven boldly to do away with this abuse, but all in vain. Their efforts seemed only to strengthen and confirm the authority of the chapter.

The archbishop, after informing himself very carefully of all that had passed in this matter with his predecessors, resolved to strike a blow to emancipate himself from this pernicious thraldom, and calling his council together, announced to them that he was resolved, come what might, to fulfil his duty as pastor of souls, and visit himself every parish in the city.

His council were extremely surprised, and represented to him: "That his zeal was most praiseworthy, but that what he proposed was impossible. That any attempt of the kind would change his warmest friends into bitter enemies, and his present admirers into violent persecutors. That the peace which reigned in his diocese was the fruit of his zeal and piety, and that it would be very unwise to trouble it of his own accord. That they implored him to consider what it would be to irritate and rouse against himself so large and important a chapter, who would obstinately maintain possession of that which they considered a vested right, and which old custom had sanctioned for so long. That he could not be ignorant of the futile endeavours which his predecessors had made to accomplish the like reform; and that if princes of the blood, supported by all the authority of the king, had failed to do away with this abuse, it was difficult to suppose that he could by any possibility succeed."

The archbishop replied: "That he was touched by the affection which prompted their advice, but that he could not in conscience follow it. That it was true that bishops should beware of troubling the peace of their diocese. That to them especially were these words of St. Paul addressed: '*If it be possible, as much as lieth in you, have peace with all men.*' (Romans xii. verse 18.) But the apostle says, '*If it be possible.*' Now he, (the archbishop,) considered that on him was laid the indispensable duty of looking after the souls whom God had confided to him. That he felt himself more than ever obliged to do this now, from a decree passed in the Council of Trent, ordering all bishops, not only to make a yearly visitation of their dioceses, but not to leave a single church unvisited. That if the chapter would let him fulfil this duty in peace, he should be delighted; but that if they attempted to prevent him, he should be compelled to assert his rights, and to demand his reinstatement in a power which they had unjustly assumed, and which was inviolably attached to the episcopal dignity." He added further: "That God having placed him in his present pósition, he could not permit that, in his own metropolitan city, he should have only the title of archbishop, while others usurped his functions. That it was perfectly true that peace was to be maintained if possible, and was infinitely to be preferred to contests and disputes; but that the saints had declared that in some cases *'war was worth more than peace,'* that is, when peace could only be bought by the sacrifice of justice, and by allowing impunity to crime. That even if St. Gregory had said, *'It was better to allow the birth of a scandal, than to abandon the truth,'* he would say the same: that if any one were scandalised at his proceedings, which they had no reason to be, it were better that he should suffer this evil than permit pastoral charity to be abandoned to such an extent, that it should be forbidden him to render any service to souls whose salvation ought to be dearer to him than his life. That he knew well that he had not the merit of many of his predecessors, nor the authority of the prelates of royal blood, who had in vain endeavoured to bring about this reform. But if it were for no other reason, their example would have made him use every effort to wrest so unjust an usurpation. That he was not troubled at the thought of failure or success. That it was enough for him to do what his duty demanded of him, leaving the issue to God, Who would do what was best pleasing to Himself."

His council expressed their great satisfaction at his answer. They added: "That though they foresaw, as he did, that this business would give him great annoyance, and raise him up a host of enemies, still they did not doubt that those who recognised its justice and necessity, and who appreciated the purity of his zeal and intention, would be greatly edified; and that they would consider his efforts to be allowed to perform with full liberty the duties of his office as deserving of their highest praise and consideration."

CHAPTER V.

THE ARCHBISHOP COMMENCES HIS VISITATION OF THE TOWN, DESPITE THE REMONSTRANCES OF THE CHAPTER.—LETTER OF ST. CHARLES ON THE SUBJECT.—CONCLUSION OF THE AFFAIR.

This matter having thus been resolved upon, the archbishop lost no time in putting it into execution. And having established his seminary, as we have already described, he signified to his chapter officially, that they were to abstain from appointing visitors, because he had determined to visit himself every member of his flock. That he felt himself bound to do so by the recent decrees of the Council, notwithstanding the conventions of his predecessors, for that no prelate could lawfully cede, to the prejudice of his successors, any portion of his spiritual authority. He also announced the day on which he was about to begin this visitation.

The rumour of this intention of the archbishop's having spread through the town, excited immense surprise and anger. Those who previously admired his virtue, now pretended to suspect his character, and their esteem was changed to accusations of his person. They called his boldness as presumptuous as it was indiscreet; and demanded if he thought himself holier than other prelates who had left the chapter alone? or more powerful than the princes who had attempted the like interference in vain? The principal personages of the town were more wounded even than the rest, but concealed their thoughts and dissimulated their resentment. They were accustomed to lead lives of unchecked licence and vice, and they had found, in the visitors of the chapter, men like-minded to themselves, who never troubled them in their licentious passions or pleasures. Therefore, the thought of falling into the hands of the archbishop filled them with fear and fury. They felt that a man whom they had looked upon before as a friend, would now be their judge. His dignity, his unimpeachable virtue, and his zeal for justice, seemed to them simply intolerable; and they fled, as from an enemy, from one who in reality loved them as a father.

The canons, whom the archbishop's intention had irritated to the last degree, were enchanted at the change which had been wrought in the public feeling, and they did everything they could to foster the anger against him, as being more favourable to their interests.

The day appointed by the holy prelate having arrived, he went early in the morning to his cathedral church, accompanied by all the notaries and officers of his court, and declared his resolution in presence of all the canons in chapter, who had brought a number of powerful personages to support their cause. They first requested him to abstain from visiting the town, as an interference with the jurisdiction of the chapter, and implored him not to trouble them in the possession of rights which had been theirs for centuries. Then they passed to formal protests against his proceedings, and to all such formalities as are observed on similar occasions.

The archbishop replied in a few words with great gentleness and moderation. But although so gentle in his answer, he showed the utmost firmness and constancy in adhering to the resolution he had formed. The chapter endeavoured again to defend their rights. But the archbishop would not yield in the smallest particular.

Directly after, he commenced his visitation of the different churches of the town, and informed himself of the morals and habits of all the persons in the city, whether clerical or secular. And in spite of the strenuous opposition of the chapter, he continued till he had visited every one. He answered with gentleness, and without the least alteration of his usual sweetness, all the protests which were renewed every day in each church against his interference; but pursued the work of God with an immoveable constancy to the end.

The chapter, finding their efforts to arrest his proceedings fruitless, resolved to push their cause at Rome, where it was finally to be judged. A long time was spent in these proceedings. For this affair having begun in 1564, was not ended till the year 1565. We will relate the matter in a few words, not to interrupt so important a portion of the archbishop's history.

The canons, many of whom were very rich, and understood more about law-suits than church affairs, omitted nothing which could serve their cause with the Pope and his principal ministers. They spoke of the archbishop in outrageous terms; and to strengthen their cause they enlisted in their complaints various monasteries, colleges, and military orders, who, having been visited by the archbishop in the interval, (as we shall presently see,) were furious at his discovery of their vices.

Their hope was, that if they could not altogether discredit him at Rome, their cause would be justified by the number and importance of the complainants. For general complaints, however unjust, have always a certain weight, and especially against the absent, for they induce men to believe that there must be some ground for such universal reprobation.

The archbishop, however, did not forget, on his side, to defend his cause, which he considered to be more that of God than his own. He kept His Holiness fully informed of all that had passed, but wrote with the utmost moderation. He represented to him that the sole origin of these troubles was his determination to carry out the decrees of the Council of Trent, and from the fact that men could not bear to change the scandalous lives they had so long led with impunity. He also employed the authority of the Cardinal Infanta, Dom Henry, a very pious prince, who was the Pope's legate *à latere* in Portugal. He kept him "*au courant*" of all his actions, asking his advice in every matter, and begging him to keep the Pope informed of every particular of the dispute.

Pope Pius IV. still governed the Church, and as he had known by personal experience the high character and holy intentions of the Archbishop of Braga, he was sensibly touched at the persecution endured by him, having himself been an eye-witness of his holiness and disinterestedness. So, determining to support him on so important an occasion, he made use of his nephew, St. Charles, to write him the strongest letters of approbation. We will here give one of these letters, which will abundantly show that all the efforts of the archbishop's enemies had been powerless in weakening the respect and admiration felt for him in Rome.

LETTER FROM ST. CHARLES TO THE ARCHBISHOP.

"It would be impossible for me to do otherwise than greatly to esteem your zeal for the observance of the decrees of the Council of Trent by all those whom God has placed under your pastoral authority. If any should be found who dared to resist, instead of obeying you, I feel sure that they will be obliged at last to yield to your tenderness and piety, and to recognise their own injustice. For our Holy Father is more than ever determined to enforce that which has been decreed in so august a council, under the guidance of the Holy Spirit, and which has subsequently been confirmed by His Holiness himself. So far from suffering these ordinances to be disregarded, which he looks upon as columns of the faith and of Catholic truth, he wills to confirm them daily by new and more stringent decrees. Therefore, if there be men in your diocese who forget themselves so far as to resist your wise regulations, you must, in your wisdom, employ such measures as shall force them to be regarded, in spite of the opposition of such persons, and use the authority and severity which you know are prescribed to you by the law of God. For you can do nothing which will be more agreeable to His Holiness. And I entreat of you to believe that never for one moment has the Pope suspected your faith or your innocence; or that he has ever listened to the unjust complaints of your accusers. For there is nothing of which he is more convinced, and of which he has more abundant proofs, than of your integrity, your wisdom, and your constancy in all virtue and Catholic truth. So that, even if the malice of men had raised up a thousand slanderers against you, and as many false witnesses, your character is too far above suspicion to make any man in his senses believe in their accusations, or to diminish in the smallest degree the esteem and affection which His Holiness entertains for your person. This is his message to you. But what shall I say of myself to you, who are always present in my heart and mind, and whom I have set before me as a model whom I propose with all my might to imitate? Shall I tell you what I think? I firmly believe that there is nothing in the Archbishop of Braga which is not worthy of all praise, and that he is not only Primate of the kingdom by his dignity, but still more by his virtues, and that in many other Christian kingdoms besides his own. Therefore, those who have undertaken to discredit you with the Holy See, have done nothing thereby but become their own accusers; as in the judgment of all persons here whose opinion is worth having, and especially of the Holy

Father and myself, no one can resist your advice, unless they be determined to renounce at the same time both piety and reason. But since these persons have thus unwittingly borne witness to your holiness and your prudence, I do not doubt that your wisdom will pardon their fault, and that if they repent, you will throw a veil of forgetfulness over this misunderstanding. And I hope that those to whom you show this leniency will feel themselves bound to you by still closer links of submission, respect, and friendship. However, should the differences which have arisen with your chapter be of so obstinate a nature as not to be appeased by your wisdom, (which I have great difficulty in believing,) His Holiness has written, and given full power to his serene highness, Dom Henry Infanta, cardinal and legate of the Holy See, to take cognisance of them, and settle the matter, which I feel that this wise and virtuous prince will do with his accustomed equity and prudence. I have helped Peter Tavaris with all my interest with the Holy Father; he loves and respects you very much. I will only add, which I hope you already feel, that there is nothing on earth I would not do to render you a service. I conjure you only to remember me in your prayers.

"From Rome, 3rd April, 1565."

The Pope sent at the same time a brief to his legate, Dom Henry, by which he desired him to bring about a reconciliation between the archbishop and his chapter. And if they could not agree, His Holiness appointed him as sole arbiter and judge in the cause. We transcribe the brief as follows:

"Pius IV., Pope, to Dom Henry, Cardinal Infanta of Portugal, and our well-beloved son. Grace and the apostolic benediction. The testimony you have borne to the merits of our venerable brother, the Archbishop of Braga, has had such weight with us, from the great faith we have and ought to have in your words and opinion, that if we had entertained the smallest doubt on the subject, it would have been instantly dispelled. But he gave us himself in the Council such striking proofs of probity, piety, and respect for the Holy See, that we conceived the most favourable opinion of this prelate, which no accusation or complaint can in any way alter. And the esteem we had already conceived for his virtue was very much enhanced when we heard with what zeal he was labouring to carry into effect the decrees of the Council. But as certain differences have arisen between him and his chapter, we desire that there may be found some legitimate agreement, so that he should not be troubled in the exercise of his holy charge; and if their differences cannot be appeased by gentle means, we give you full power, by these our letters to you as our legate, to take cognisance of this affair, so as to judge it, and bring it to a conclusion with equity and justice. We have written the same thing to our venerable brother, the Archbishop of Braga.

"Done at Rome, in the Church of St. Peter, 28th March, 1565, being the sixth year of our pontificate."

No sooner had Dom Henry received this brief, than he wrote to the archbishop and to the chapter, to beg them to think over some terms of agreement, and to confer with him upon the subject, so that he might assist them as a friend, and favour them with his credit with the Holy See as papal legate.

But the chapter, either because they suspected him of too great an affection for the archbishop, or because they hoped still to gain their cause, would not accept his arbitration. And in spite of all the authority given him by the Pope, he could never bring them to reason. This matter dragged on for a long while, even to the pontificate of Pius V.

At last it pleased God to put an end to so weary and obstinate a controversy. It was finally settled between the archbishop and the chapter, and enrolled in a solemn and irrevocable treaty, that the Archbishop of Braga should visit in person all the clergy of the town, and that he should likewise nominate two of the members of the chapter to make the visitation of the laymen, which visitors should be obliged to account to the archbishop for all that they found during their visitation.

Thus, without violating the pretended rights of the chapter, the archbishop carried out his principle, finding easily two men in the body of canons who had the same views as himself, and therefore being fully informed of the moral condition of all the members of his flock.

CHAPTER VI.

THE ARCHBISHOP VISITS THE CHURCHES OF THE MILITARY KNIGHTS COMMANDERS.—WITH WHAT FIRMNESS HE REPRESSES THE INSOLENCE OF COMMANDER POYAREZ, WHO WAS CONVERTED BY HEARING HIS MASS.

Whilst this affair of the chapter was still pending, the holy prelate undertook a still more difficult work, and that was the visitation of the churches of the Knights Templars, who pretended to be entirely exempt from the visits or authority of the ordinary. He spoke of it first to his council, who endeavoured to dissuade him, saying, "That he had already enough on his hands with the chapter; that he would strengthen the designs of his enemies by enlisting such powerful bodies as the commanders of the religious military orders on their side; that if he attacked the abuses he would undoubtedly find in their districts, these men would elude all judicial proceedings by sheltering themselves either on ecclesiastical rights or royal privileges, and that they would not hesitate to resort to open violence at the point of the sword, if any one were bold enough to attack them; that they implored him to pause before he embarked in such a fearful struggle with bodies so powerful as these military orders, and with the king himself, who was their leader and protector."

The archbishop replied: "I know that in undertaking this reform, I shall strengthen the canons against me. But the same reasons which forced me to contest their unjust privileges, equally compel me to act in the way I propose. The affairs of God cannot be guided solely by the rules of human prudence. The duty of my charge compels me to act as I am doing. This is enough for me. '*A wise and holy affair,*' says St. Bernard, '*can only have a good issue.*' If I succeed in what I am about to attempt, so much the better; if not, I hope God will accept my good intention; and I shall bless Him that He has relieved me of the care of a part of my diocese. I wish with all my heart to have peace with God and men. But if I cannot please God without displeasing men, I am very willing that they should complain of my conduct, if only I do the will of God."

His council, who were mostly holy and God-fearing men, could not but admire his zeal, and yield to reasons which were so purely supernatural; and the archbishop being confirmed in his resolution, resolved to execute it without delay.

He began first with the Churches of the Order of St. John of Malta, and finding that they were utterly neglected, and without anything necessary for the divine service, he seized the revenues of the commanders, and ordered that they should be applied to the repair of the fabrics, and the providing of all things necessary for Holy Mass. He announced that he had no intention thereby to injure the Knights, but to remedy the disorders he found in their churches, where he established several new curates and vicars. He did the same in the churches of the Order called of "Christ." And having thus begun his reforms, he did not leave a single church unvisited; and making a note of everything wanted, insisted on their being supplied, notwithstanding all their pretended privileges.

The fury of all these men, thus detected in simony and fraud, may be imagined. Complaints and murmurs were heard against him in every part of the kingdom. He had not only the knights as his enemies, but all their relations and friends. First they had recourse to protestations and prohibitions, which they caused to be published by the conservators of their different orders. Then they resorted to libellous pamphlets against his person and character; but he remained firm and unmoved amidst the storm, never showing the smallest anger or resentment. At last, they went so far as to fulminate censures and excommunications against him. But he only laughed at them, knowing their nullity, and all the more, as, to console the timid, he had obtained from Rome a special brief from Pius IV., absolving him from all such excommunications.

As, however, the accusations against him were so violent, he wrote to the different tribunals, to the apostolic judges, to the king's council, and to the king himself, to justify his proceedings. And as he brought forward such wise and weighty reasons for his conduct, and that what he had done was not only justified by the flagrant abuses he had discovered, but by the authority of his person, and the veneration which all good men felt for his zeal and character, his words produced the most favourable impression on men's minds. We will here relate one anecdote during this stormy visitation, which will show more than ever the admirable wisdom and magnanimity of our saint.

There was a town called Poyarez, which was the headquarters of a great body of the Knights of St. John. The archbishop had been warned that he would find the churches in this township as miserable and neglected as in that of Baroso. He resolved therefore to go there. And as the commander was what was called a bailiff of the order, and one of its great dignitaries, he wrote to Rome for special authority to deal with him. The Pope sent him full powers to act, which brief arrived at the most favourable moment, namely, just as he was approaching the gates of Poyarez.

He entered the town, visited all the churches, and found them all in the disgraceful state we have described. He made a memorandum of all the things which were necessary for the repairs and ornaments of each church, and, by the authority of the papal brief, confiscated the revenues of the commanders until the expenses of these repairs had been defrayed. All this was done with the greatest calmness and regularity possible.

The next day, being at a village close to Poyarez, he had got up very early in the morning, as was his custom, to say his office, when the commander struck terror into the hearts of every one, by arriving at the village with a large body of armed men, both horse and foot soldiers. He was a man of a certain age, but of great vigour and determination. He had a very fierce look, and his fury made his eyes seem on fire. He entered proudly into the archbishop's house, and desired him to come and speak to him. The holy prelate, being perfectly calm, and having complete command over himself, quietly replied that he must be good enough to wait till he had finished his prayers.

The commander walked up and down, his anger only increasing at the delay. After a time, he sent a second messenger to the archbishop, to tell him he was waiting. The archbishop made him the same answer. At last, having finished his office, he told his servants to let the commander come in; and seeing the fury depicted in his face, he asked him gently what he wanted of him?

The commander replied: "That he was the bailiff of Poyarez. That he begged to know by what authority he had ventured to act as he had done in his township? That if it were as Archbishop of Braga, he had known many others besides himself, and none would have ventured to take such liberties, or to treat him with such pride and contempt." And then, launching forth into complaints and menaces, he added, "That if the archbishop persisted in such conduct, he should know how to take the law into his own hands, and teach him to show some difference between a commander and the miserable curates of his diocese."

The archbishop replied with quiet dignity: "That as to his authority for the visitation, he had received it from the Council of Trent, which commanded him to visit every church in his diocese, whether exempt or not exempt; that besides, he held in his hands a brief from the Pope, ordering him expressly to visit this town of Poyarez." He added: "This I think is a sufficient answer to your complaints; but as for your menaces, Mr. Commander, I tell you plainly, that they do not intimidate me in the least; and that, although you have chosen to come with such a body of armed men to visit a solitary and defenceless bishop, I shall continue to do here all that it is my duty to do, and with the same freedom as if I were in my own palace of Braga. I know very well the distinction between persons of your position and rank, and peasants or men of the people. But I wish you knew as well the difference between a gentleman who has received his property from his father, which he can deal with as he pleases, and a commander of a religious order, who has received his revenues from the Church, and who is bound to use them according to the laws of the Church. The property of this township is not yours, but belongs to the poor. You are simply its dispenser, if you give them the portion which belongs to them. But instead of that, you dissipate their heritage, and rob them of their dues, to satisfy your own ambition and pleasures. What! the Church makes you the receiver of her goods, and you enrich yourself with her spoils, and leave her temples without furniture, her sheep without pastors, and her poor without help! Is it thus that you fulfil the vows you have made as a religious of the Order of St. John of Malta? You have sworn that you will be always ready to spill your blood for the defence of the Church, and yet you employ the arms she has given you to fight the Turks and her greatest enemies, to insult her priests and outrage her bishops. Consider, I beg of you, what you are doing, and what you ought to do. We ought all to fear death; but you are of an age which must make you think of it more seriously than others. God is not mocked. You cannot attack Him with impunity. Sooner or later we must all fall into His hands. Fear His judgments; avert His vengeance. Put yourself in a condition to deserve His grace, and do not shut the door on His mercy, while His goodness invites you to be reconciled to Him."

The holy prelate spoke with all his usual tenderness and persuasion. But the bailiff only became more furious than before, and threatened him in a way which showed that his passion had got the better of his reason, till the listeners were filled with indignation and impatience; but the archbishop was not the least troubled, and no change could be seen on his countenance. He quietly got up, and went to the church to say his Mass, and with such calmness, that when his suite, who were very angry at their master's treatment, wanted him to punish the commander on the spot, he replied: "God forbid! All that I shall do will be to recommend him earnestly to God in the Holy Sacrifice which I am about to offer Him, so that He may give him the grace to repent and confess his faults."

The bailiff, still breathing out vengeance against the archbishop, followed him to the church, and remained there during Mass. Meanwhile, the holy prelate recommended his soul to God so fervently during the Holy Sacrifice, that God heard his prayer, and opened the eyes of the commander to the sins he had committed, in spite of the passion which still blinded him. Finally, his heart was so entirely changed, that when the Mass was over, he went and threw himself at the feet of the archbishop, confessing his sins with many tears, and imploring his pardon. He did this in the sight of all the people, who could hardly believe what they saw. The archbishop raised him directly, and embraced him with as much affection and tenderness as if they had been friends all their lives. The bailiff confessed out loud that God had entirely converted him during the Mass, and had opened the eyes of his soul, so as to show him how far he had wandered from the right way. And as a proof of his true conversion, he announced that he was ready to provide all that was needful in his churches, as the archbishop had ordered, and even to adorn them with far greater magnificence, and he concluded by saying that he was ready to accept any penance the archbishop might impose upon him for his past sins.

The archbishop, recognising in this marvellous conversion a visible intervention of the Most High, gave him all the advice necessary for his thorough reconciliation with God, and rescinded the order he had given to confiscate his revenues. The commander went home full of sorrow and confusion at his treatment of so fatherly a pastor, and yet full of gratitude to God, who had shown him such signal mercy, and opened his eyes to his previous miserable condition. All those who accompanied him, and whom he had summoned to be the ministers of his vengeance, were strangely surprised to see such a sudden change in the temper of their master. He assured them that God had wrought this miracle in him during the Holy Sacrifice, owing to the piety and prayers of the archbishop; and he ever after considered him as his father, and was never weary of proclaiming his holiness and virtue throughout the country.

CHAPTER VII.

THE ARCHBISHOP GOES INTO THE WILDEST CORNER OF HIS DIOCESE.—HOW HIS SUITE ESCAPE A GREAT DANGER.—THE MANNER IN WHICH HE PROVIDED PASTORS FOR THESE ABANDONED PEASANTS.

In the archbishopric of Braga there are a great many villages high up in the mountains. But one of them, named Baroso, is so inaccessible, on account of the precipices and snow-covered mountains which surround it, that it would appear to be more a home for wild beasts than for men. Nevertheless, this district is thickly peopled, and there were even a great many churches there. The archbishop having determined to visit every portion of his diocese, decided to begin by this wild outlying country, in spite of the remonstrances of his friends, to whose representations as to the perils of the way, he only replied: "They are my sheep, therefore, wherever they may be, I must seek them; and if they are sick, I must heal them."

Arriving at the foot of the mountains, he found that his friends had not exaggerated the difficulties of the undertaking, for not only were there no roads, but the state of the people was terrible. There were hardly any traces left of Christianity, and the peasants seemed as barbarous as savages.

The rumour of the archbishop's arrival, however, spread through the mountains, and filled these poor people with ineffable joy. They came in troops to welcome him, dancing and singing, with boys dressed up as girls, and masked, chaunting the most extraordinary songs, of which one of the choruses was: "*Blessed be the Holy Trinity, sister of our Lady,*" and other similar words, showing their utter ignorance of the commonest Christian truths; yet very touching to the archbishop, who saw their wish to give him a welcome after the best fashion they could. Those who accompanied him could not help laughing; but he, though smiling sweetly in order to gain their hearts, could not help groaning internally at the profound ignorance these poor souls displayed. He asked one of the men, "How many commandments there were?" The man, stretching out his two hands, counted *ten* on his fingers; but what they were he had not an idea. The archbishop, considering himself as the father of these poor people, instantly set to work to teach them as he would little children. They were docile and gentle, and he never ceased instructing and praying with them, and encouraging them in every way in his power till he had made them understand the outlines, at least, of Christian truth.

One day, the archbishop, being in the midst of the mountains, wished to go from one spot called the "Caves of Baroso," to another point called "The Eminence," on account of its extraordinary height above the surrounding country. The only path was a very narrow, steep track through the mountains, with such fearful precipices on both sides that the very sight of them made one giddy. They went singly, one after the other, the mules first, who bore the luggage and provisions, (for there was no food in that country,) and then the servants and visitors who accompanied the prelate. He was a long way behind, with one person only, who always accompanied him. All of a sudden, one of the mules stumbled and fell, and rolling over the side, dragged down, in his fall, one after the other of his companions. A great cry arose, the men invoking the names of Jesus and Mary, as all thought their last hour was come. The archbishop heard their cry, and told his companion to go and see what he could do to help them, while he, throwing himself off his horse, and lifting up his eyes to heaven, prayed earnestly and in silence for some time. Then mounting, he said gaily to the boy who held his horse: "God be praised, that He has not allowed any one of us to perish."

In the meanwhile, those who had fallen over the precipice were able to recover themselves, and by degrees even the mules were saved, and brought back to the path again, which was nothing less than a miracle, and so considered by their drivers, who had given themselves up for lost as well as their beasts; so that, having reached the top of the mountain, they stopped, and with one accord gave thanks to God for their wonderful deliverance. But then they became anxious about the archbishop, who did not appear, and some returned down the mountain to look for him, fearing a like accident might have befallen him. But he soon came in sight, and before any one had spoken to him, he exclaimed: "My children, let us praise and thank God, who has saved you and the mules from so great a peril." At these words, they looked at one another with astonishment, knowing very well that the archbishop could not have seen what had happened with his bodily eyes, and fully recognising that they owed their safety to his all-powerful intercession with God.

On the height of this mountain, called, as we have said, "The Eminence," was a broad, flat plain, well cultivated in many parts. In spite of the elevation, fruit-trees abounded, and the plain was thickly peopled. The archbishop went straight to the first church he saw, where he met with the same reception as before. But the inhabitants were even more amazed, for the oldest amongst them had never seen anything but one poor priest, who used to be sent from time to time as visitor by the archbishops. And many years had passed since any fresh priest had been seen at all in that wild spot.

The archbishop said his Mass, preached, and afterwards administered the sacraments of baptism and confirmation. Many of the people cried for joy; others listened, holding up their hands to heaven; whilst the greater part remained on their knees. Their astonishment was at its height when they saw him in his pontifical vestments, with his mitre and crozier. After the service, he visited all the churches in the plain, the misery and neglect of which filled him with sorrow. Many had neither doors nor windows. In others, Mass had not been said for months, for no priest could be found who would venture so far. And those who would consent to live there, only did so because they were so ignorant or bad that no one would have them elsewhere. It was impossible to say Mass in most of these churches, for want of the commonest furniture. The chalices were only of lead, so that the archbishop had them melted down, and silver ones substituted. He resolved to stay among these poor souls as long as he could, and sitting among the rocks like a real shepherd, he would teach these neglected sheep with the utmost sweetness and patience, until he had communicated to them, bit by bit, the most necessary elements of the Christian Faith. Then, when he had thus broken to them the Bread of Life, he would see after their temporal wants, giving them alms and provisions, and making a list of all the clothes they wanted. He was so touched at the wild and barbarous state of this portion of his flock, that he could not forgive himself for not having come to visit them sooner. All that he could do for the moment was, to recommend them to God in prayer. And the Holy Spirit inspired him with an idea which afterwards brought forth great fruit. It was, to choose out the most intelligent of the boys, and take them with him to Braga. There he placed them under the care of competent masters, who brought them up in modesty and virtue. The archbishop lodged these poor children in his own palace, and at his expense. They had a little refectory, where they dined together; and finally, when they were old enough, if he found in them suitable dispositions, he ordained them, and having trained them in his own seminary for the care of souls, he sent them home to evangelize their own people, which they did with the happiest results.

Thus this good pastor went everywhere, seeking his lost and strayed sheep, until every corner of his vast diocese had been visited, examined, and reformed.

CHAPTER VIII.

THE EXTRAORDINARY CONVERSIONS OF THE ARCHBISHOP; AND WITH WHAT FORCE AND AUTHORITY HE REPRESSED VICE.

One of the holy Fathers of the Greek Church has said, with reason: "*That a true pastor and spiritual pilot is one who has acquired such strength and light, by the infusion of the Holy Spirit, and by his own experience in the guidance of souls, that he can drag a man, not only from the midst of storms and tempests, but from the very deepest abyss of passion and vice.*" This grace was granted by God to our holy prelate, as we shall presently relate to our readers.

One day he was told that in a neighbouring house lived a man of high birth and great riches, who had deserted his wife, and lived openly with another woman. This man was a very demon of pride, and as he feared neither God nor man, every one was afraid to go near him. When the visitors came to his house, he laughed them to scorn. And the predecessors of the archbishop had given him up as a hopeless case, and a man on whom no impression could be made.

The archbishop, having recommended the affair to God, resolved to go and speak to him with severity. And having found him at home, he represented to him in the strongest terms the scandal he gave to the whole world, the horrible nature of his crime, the shameful life he led, —one utterly unworthy of a man of his rank; and lastly, the peril he was in of eternal damnation. And being filled with holy anger, he commanded him, under pain of excommunication, to drive from his house the cause of this scandal, and to change his way of life; declaring that if he did not do this within a certain time, he would not give him absolution, or admit him to any divine office in any church in his diocese, "so that you will live and die," he added, "like a heretic or a Moor."

This gentleman was at first too much surprised at the archbishop's boldness to answer him; but then became furious, loaded the prelate with insults, and went out of the room, filled with rage and vengeance, and declaring that after such an insult he had the right to do what he pleased to repair it.

The archbishop made no answer, but lifting up his eyes to heaven, besought God to touch his heart, and save a soul for whom he had such real compassion. His prayer was heard. Soon after, the gentleman came back, filled with fear at the judgments of God, and throwing himself at the archbishop's feet, implored his pardon for his insolence and crimes. He placed himself entirely in his hands, and said he would submit to anything the archbishop would enjoin.

The prelate received him tenderly, and seeing that he was determined at once, not only to dismiss the woman who had enthralled him, but to make every amends in his power for the scandal he had given, treated him with the greatest kindness, and finally reconciled him to God. A very short time after he had accomplished his penance, he was taken dangerously ill, and having received the last sacraments with fervent devotion and many tears, he died, giving all the marks of the most sincere contrition.

Almost the same thing happened with another rich man, who was a member of the king's privy council, and had been living a most scandalous life, till, touched to the quick by the archbishop's representations, he entirely repented, and became to the end a model of holy living, and an example of the power of the grace of Jesus Christ.

Another time, during one of his visitations, he heard that the Seneschal of that town was a most licentious character, and that justice depended solely on the caprice of a miserable woman, by whom he was, as it were, possessed, and who had got such influence over him, that she literally governed the whole country.

The prelate sent for him, and when he arrived in his presence, said to him, sternly: "I hear you are a great thief." The Seneschal remained confused and stupefied, never having been addressed in such a fashion; but at last said: "That he was very much surprised at the archbishop's treatment. That he considered it was an affront to a minister of the king, and to a public officer of justice." "Well, I mean to prove to you," replied the archbishop, "that you are a thief. I know, by the depositions and the evidence of several irreproachable witnesses, that you keep a miserable woman, and that all those who seek for justice at your hands, be they good or bad, are obliged to treat with this infamous creature, and that you only do what she orders. That is what I call robbing men of justice, and being yourself a public robber." He gave him then a very severe reprimand, and warned him that his future depended on the faithful administration of his charge; for if he would not change his conduct, he should give notice to the king of his scandals, which might cost him, not only his place, but his life." The magistrate, confounded by his words, implored pardon of the prelate, and promised to obey him in everything. The archbishop ordered that that very hour this miserable woman should be driven out of the town, she being the great impediment to his salvation. The Seneschal acknowledged his fault, and entirely changed his way of life, which had the happiest effect on his subordinates, who, seeing that their superior had been compelled to yield to the archbishop, and forced to administer impartial justice, found themselves obliged to abstain from all violent or irregular measures, if not from the fear of God, at least from that of men.

One day, when the archbishop was visiting a district called "beyond the mountains," they came to tell him that the provost of the town of Chaves had violently entered the church of that place, and had dragged out a criminal who had fled for safety to this sanctuary. The fact was, that the magistrate, wishing to surprise a man whom he suspected of homicide, had come upon him as he was about to commit the act, and the would-be murderer, running away, took refuge in the church, and shut the door. The provost, filled with rage at his escape, sent for a hatchet, and seeing that none of his men dared profane so holy a place, seized the hatchet himself, broke open the doors, cut them in pieces, and finding the prisoner clinging to the altar, dragged him away, loaded him with chains, and threw him into a deep dungeon.

The archbishop, being informed of the sacrilege, went at once to the spot, and having obtained judicial evidence of the truth of the statement, assembled the clergy and religious orders of the town, and ordered a general procession, which he led himself, the crosses being covered, and the priests chanting in a sad tone the Psalm "*Quare fremuerunt gentes,*" &c. The procession made the round of the town, and then came into the church, when the holy prelate went into the pulpit, and spoke to the people, (who had assembled in great numbers,) on the sacrilege which had been committed, and the reparation he had striven to offer, ending by pronouncing a sentence of excommunication against the provost, and publicly declaring him under an interdict.

The provost, filled with compunction, came and begged

pardon of the archbishop, and released the prisoner, assuring him that it was from a zeal for justice, and from no disrespect to so holy a place, that he had been induced to commit this act of irreverence. The archbishop treated him with great kindness, and accepted his submission. But as the scandal had been so public a one, he exacted that his penance should be the same, and ordered him, the following Sunday morning, during the divine office, to remain bare-headed at the door of the church he had violated, bearing on his shoulder the hatchet which had been the instrument of his sacrilege.

CHAPTER IX.

ON THE ARCHBISHOP'S TREATMENT OF ECCLESIASTICS WHO LED IRREGULAR LIVES, AND THEIR CONVERSION.

If the archbishop was thus zealous in the reform of the laity, he was still more anxious to repress all scandals in ecclesiastics, of whom St. Gregory has written: "*That as their crimes are more heinous than those of other men, God frequently abandons them to their blindness and impenitence of heart, so that they become deaf to all advice.*" (Gregor., in 1 Reg., cap. 2.)

On Christmas Eve, the archbishop went into the sacristy of his cathedral church to put on his pontifical vestments, having the intention to offer the Holy Sacrifice on that solemn night, when he perceived one of the principal canons commencing likewise to vest, in order to serve his Mass as deacon. He went up to him, and whispered in his ear, "That he need not trouble himself to do that, as he could not allow him to officiate that night at the altar."

These words made the canon so angry, that forgetting

all prudence, he asked the archbishop out loud: "What reason he had for forbidding him to do so, and thereby making him lose the rank and privilege which was his by right?"

The archbishop, without being troubled, calmly replied: "No one knows the reason better than yourself."

Upon this, the canon began to complain even more loudly, saying that it was a public affront, that he would have redress, and would go to law about it immediately. The holy prelate quietly answered: "That he might do what he pleased, only not accompany him to the altar."

Then the canon, striving to conceal his anger, and moderating the tone of his voice, conjured the archbishop to allow him to finish vesting, as he had begun. But seeing that he was inflexible, as usual when he had decided on a course which he considered necessary for the honour and glory of God, the canon flew into a greater rage than ever, and rushed out of church, declaring that he would be avenged.

This action on the part of the archbishop was very ill-received by the chapter, even by those who were his staunchest friends. But it was perfectly right and just; for the archbishop had discovered, in his late visitation, that this canon was living a life of public vice and infamy. He had done everything to win him by gentleness and kindness, to change his habits; and out of respect to his rank and character had privately admonished him in many ways. But finding all his efforts fruitless, and that the canon still kept the woman he was living with in his house, he felt that a stronger remedy was needful, and that he could not suffer the altar of God to be profaned, (especially on so solemn an occasion,) by the sacrilegious ministry of a man so unworthy to approach the sacraments.

This wretched canon, however, determined to carry

out his revenge, cited the archbishop to appear at Lisbon, before the Seneschal of the court, to give an account of his conduct. But the holy prelate, not wishing to publish the infamies of this unhappy priest in court, as he would have been compelled to do, wrote at once to the king, telling him the whole matter, and begging his highness to send a Seneschal to Braga, who should drive out of the town the woman who was the cause of this terrible scandal.

The king at once did what he wished; and the officer he sent showed such tact and understanding in executing his commission, that dissimulating his errand, he surprised the wretched lady one morning, and conveying her out of the town to a place a great distance off, forbid her, by order of the king, and under the threat of the heaviest penalties, to set foot again in Braga.

The archbishop then wrote to his agent in Lisbon to stop the proceedings which he had been compelled to set on foot against the canon, and even to pay the expenses of the suit. This extraordinary generosity touched the miserable priest so powerfully, that he was entirely conquered. He came to implore the archbishop's forgiveness, and ever after lived a life of such holiness and penance that he hardly ever stirred from his own house. And he preserved so vivid a recollection of this benefit, that when, many years after, the archbishop had retired to Viano, he was the first to pay him his respects, and offer him his service and his goods, saying, with tears: "That if he were to give him all he had in the world, it would be nothing compared to what the archbishop had done for him, in saving his soul from eternal death."

This same canon soon after fell seriously ill. He accepted this sickness as a sign of God's mercy, who had imposed this penance upon one who had not had the courage to impose enough on himself. He recovered after a time, but with the entire loss of his sight. In spite of his blindness, he had himself carried in a litter to him whom he always styled his greatest benefactor. He used to say that his only consolation in the midst of his darkness was to have a talk with the archbishop. Our holy prelate encouraged and consoled him with the extreme charity and tenderness which were natural to him, and never ceased admiring the incomprehensible providence of God, which thus draws souls from the brink of a precipice, and knows how to find a remedy for the most incurable of maladies.

We will give another instance of the archbishop's extraordinary success in dealing with difficult and desperate cases.

There was a church on the frontiers of Portugal and Gallicia which for a long time had not been visited by any Archbishop of Braga, although it was under their jurisdiction. The rector of this church was a man as powerful and rich in worldly goods as he was poor and destitute in heavenly ones. He had always lived a profligate life, profaning in his person the priesthood of Jesus Christ, and scandalizing the whole country. He had had twelve sons, whom he considered as his body guard and protectors, although they were in reality but so many witnesses of his shame. As he was quite determined not to change his way of life, he made use of his power and riches to obtain exemption from any visitation, which he dreaded above everything. He always had spies in the neighbouring villages, and when he heard that the visitors were coming, he hired a body of soldiers from the frontiers of Gallicia, and fortified himself in his church and presbytery, with his garrison and his whole family. His sons were tall, powerful men, and worthy of the race from which they sprang.

When the visitors consequently arrived at his house,

they found him entrenched in this manner, and were too happy to be able to escape out of his hands with their lives. For this man was not to be softened by prayers or remonstrances, and laughed to scorn the censures and excommunications of the Church.

The archbishop was very much touched at the loss of this soul, and at the scandal which fell on the Church in consequence of these proceedings. Finally, he resolved to risk his life to try and convert this man, and having arrived at the nearest village, he asked how far it was to his house, and how long it would take to get there? He was told that at the first rumour of his intended visit the rector had shut himself up according to his usual custom, and was resolved to defend his church and his house against all visitors, and even against the archbishop himself. Nothing daunted, however, the holy prelate rose earlier than usual one morning, and having spent many hours in fervent prayer, heartily commending this soul to God, he ordered none of his suite to leave the place where they were, until they were warned by a signal which he was to give them. And then, taking with him only a monk of his own order, who always accompanied him in his journeys, he set out on foot on the rough and stony road which led to this man's dwelling. As he had become very weak from his rigorous fasting and penances, he suffered very much from fatigue during this long walk, but persevered, and finally reached the house, at the door of which he knocked with a little mace which he held in his hand. The sentinels instantly gave the alarm. But when the rector saw that they were only two poor religious, (as he thought,) and quite alone, he was not in the least disturbed, being persuaded that the archbishop would appear with a great train of men and horses, well armed, to attack his fortifications. So he came down himself to the door, and asked what the monks wanted.

The archbishop, when he saw the soul for whom he had so eagerly sought, filled with hope, exclaimed with a gay and smiling countenance: "Do you know, my son, why I have come here? I have come to frighten you with this little mace, and to remind you that you are a lost sheep, whose pastor is come to seek and save you." So saying, he walked into the house. And the rector was so amazed, and at the same time so confused, that he never dreamt of resistance. But it was the hour of God's grace, and after a few moments, this violent and hardened sinner was at the feet of his pastor, pouring out his repentance amidst sobs and tears. At last he said in a broken voice to the archbishop: "I have sinned against God and against you. I entreat the pardon of God with my whole heart for my enormous crimes, and promise to lead a new life." The archbishop, overjoyed, raised him, and embraced him with paternal tenderness, and assured him that if he persevered in these feelings, God, who had sent him to open his eyes, would have mercy upon him, and forgive him his sins. Then, giving the signal to his suite, they hurried, as they thought, to his assistance, and found the lion changed into a lamb, and the archbishop triumphant. He stayed a long time in this place, visiting all the people, restoring the church, which was in the last stage of neglect, and teaching the peasants, (who were sunk in the lowest ignorance,) all that was necessary for their salvation. He preached continually, baptised, confirmed, and distributed large alms among the poor. The rector submitted himself, with the most profound humility, to the archbishop's orders, and when he came to see what his past life had been, and the horrible scandal he had caused, he was filled with such despair as almost to disbelieve in God's mercy:

so that the archbishop's task was to try and console him, and to quote the words of St. Augustine: "*That the sinner should consider well the depth of his wounds, but at the same time remember the greatness of Him who had called him to repentance; for, however serious his illness might be, it could not be incurable to the All-mighty Physician who had willed to heal him.*" (St. Aug., in Psalm l.)

The rumour of this extraordinary conversion spread throughout Portugal, and rejoiced all good men, while it raised still higher the esteem and reverence in which they held their pastor, whose zeal and charity had saved the Church from the continuance of so great a scandal.

CHAPTER X.

OF THE GREAT CHARITY OF THE ARCHBISHOP DURING THE FAMINE, AND THE WAY HE EXHORTED THE RICH TO GIVE ALMS AND HELP THE POOR.

In 1567, the scarcity which had already existed for some years in the country of Portugal, increased to such an extent that a terrible famine was the result. The town of Braga was filled with poor. For the country people, who depended on their crops for the maintenance of themselves and their families, had nothing to support them when the harvests failed. Many were reduced to positive starvation. Others were constrained to sell everything they possessed, bit by bit, and to kill their cattle for food, although without their oxen the cultivation of their fields was impossible. Finally, they were reduced to begging their bread from door to door, and their only consoler was the archbishop, who seemed to multiply himself and all belonging to him, in order to feed his people. He stopped all the buildings that were going on in his monastery at Viano, and at the Jesuit College, in order to spend the money in more extensive relief works, and denied himself and his household all but the actual necessaries of life, not being able to bear to see the suffering of his flock. It seemed as if a curse had fallen on all the crops beyond the Douro. The fruit trees failed, like all the rest. Wheat bread was four ducats a loaf, and many, having sold everything they had, died of hunger by the road-side. The holy prelate, walking or riding in the streets, saw men fall before him in the last stage of exhaustion, and conveyed them to a hospital he had opened for the purpose, where every effort was made to restore them, but often in vain. The number of starving poor round the archbishop's house was upwards of three thousand, and it required all the order and regularity for which he was so noted, to be able to feed them at all. They used to ring a great bell every day at the time of the archbishop's dinner, when the poor people flocked to the gates, and were let in at a certain door, when Father John of Leyra, and one or two other priests, gave them bread, soup, or money, according to their needs, or the number of their children, of which an exact account was kept; while they received at the same time a short instruction of a very simple kind, so that they might learn the knowledge of God, and bless Him even in their poverty. The archbishop often watched the distribution himself, to see that all was done fairly and in good order; and if from his window he saw any poor fellow who had come too late for the daily meal, he would call one of his servants, and insist on something being found for him, not being able to bear the idea of any one going away from his door empty and starving. His charity did not limit itself to the poor; he also sought out those of a higher class, who often came in disguise at night to implore his aid, and to whom he would give in secret all he could, to save them and their families from death. On the first day of the week he would double the food given. And this went on till the abundant harvest of 1575 restored the people to comparative comfort.

It would have been impossible for the archbishop to meet this tremendous expense, if he had not shown as much wisdom as forethought in the matter. For, like the patriarch Joseph, he had foreseen the coming famine, and sent to all the provinces in the kingdom for supplies of wheat and other provisions, which he stored up for the hour of need. But as, in spite of this precaution, he very soon entirely exhausted his revenues, he borrowed a large sum to meet the pressing needs of his people, trusting to God for the future. Many rich men also, touched by the example and exhortations of their holy pastor, came forward liberally to help him. For he never ceased preaching against the avarice and hardness of those who, having large stores of wheat, watched the rise of the market, as St. Basil says, in order to make an exorbitant profit out of the sufferings of others, thus trafficking in the public misery, and making a harvest out of others' loss. He told the rich "that they were very much mistaken if they considered themselves such complete masters of their wealth as to be able, at such a time, to spend it in useless frivolity; that if God will demand of us an account of every idle word, still more would He exact an account of every superfluous expense and extravagance in the administration of our goods. That after having taken the share which Christian moderation required, according to the station of each, the rest belonged of right to the poor. That if luxury were at all times an evil, it became criminal in a time of famine. That if one Christian could see another fainting and dying for want of food, without being touched with pity, and helping him to the best of his power, he could not be called a Christian, but rather, as St. Basil says, '*a wild beast, as execrable as a murderer or a homicide.*' That although God had told us to love our brethren as ourselves, and that Jesus Christ had said we were to look upon and love the poor as Himself, he did not dare ask as much of the rich, but would only implore them to treat the poor as well as they did the beasts which ministered to their vanity; and that as their horses were still covered with gold and silk trappings, in spite of the public misery, they might, at least, not leave the poor of Jesus Christ to die of cold, hunger, and nudity." He added: "That those who had large fortunes were very much mistaken if they thought they were fulfilling their duty by giving a trifle only. That, according to holy writ, '*those who had much were to give much,*' and that the measure of their riches should be that of their alms. That they ought to give the more liberally, as they only possessed, in reality, that which they gave away, for that only would save their souls, and lead to their eternal salvation. That unless they made use of their riches in this way, they were infinitely more to be pitied than the poor, who only suffered in this transitory life, while the miserly rich would do so to all eternity. That it was useless to ask what would become of the rich who gave no alms, as Jesus Christ had made their damnation an article of faith, and their sentence was written in His Gospel in the most formal terms. For in shutting up their bowels of compassion to their brethren, as St. Basil says, they equally shut up those of God's mercy; and while treating Jesus Christ so cruelly in the person of His poor, they show that they would rather have Him as an avenger and an enemy, than as a friend and protector, when He comes in His glory to judge the world."

CHAPTER XI.

A PRIEST FROM BRAGA ACCUSES THE ARCHBISHOP TO THE POPE.—THE SECRET ANIMOSITY FELT BY MANY AT HIS CONDUCT.—THE CALUMNIATOR, BEING CONDEMNED, IMPLORES FORGIVENESS OF THE PRELATE.

A few years after the archbishop's return from Trent, he held a provincial council in the city of Braga, to which he summoned all his suffragan bishops, as the fathers in council had decreed. Of the acts of this synod we know little, except that Father Louis of Grenada says: *"That the archbishop then drew up many wise and useful rules for the better regulation of his diocese."*

The holy prelate drew up a copy of these, and sent it to Rome for further confirmation by His Holiness. The agent of the King of Portugal, with several of the chapter, objected strongly to several of the decrees of the synod, but they were nevertheless approved of and confirmed by Pope Pius V., in 1571. But his enemies took advantage of this council to calumniate our saint; for the matter we have previously referred to regarding the visitation had roused the anger of all the licentious persons in his diocese. Previous archbishops had, by their own luxurious lives, rather encouraged than repressed their worldliness and immorality. But the great virtue of their present pastor, and his determination to enforce discipline, while it edified the good, exasperated those who considered licence their right, and the necessity of living according to their priestly state an intolerable yoke. Many secretly grumbled at the change, but did not dare openly to complain, finding it impossible to bring home any accusation against the archbishop, which should bear even the semblance of truth. At last, the Devil inspired one man to become the instrument of the persecution which soon arose against our saint, and which only resulted in perfecting his humility and patience.

There was a priest in his diocese whose life seemed tolerably respectable, and who was therefore favourably received by the archbishop. Later on, various suspicious circumstances arose, proving that his virtue was only an outward sham, and the archbishop accordingly withdrew his favours from him. This exasperated the priest: and finding it impossible to revenge himself at Braga, where the character of the holy prelate was too well known, he betook himself to Rome, and there drew up a formal accusation against him, under different heads, of which we will only mention two: The first, that in his provincial synod he had forced the bishops to consent to his proposals by threats of violence, and had placed a body of guards at the doors; the second, that he had compelled many priests in his diocese to leave their livings against their will.

These calumnies, although clumsily fabricated, were at first believed by some people in Rome. For men are naturally disposed to believe evil of each other; and this often arises from envy, so that they are not sorry to see doubts thrown on the virtue of those who are so immeasurably their superiors.

But in this struggle the archbishop had one great advantage. For not only was the present Pope a Dominican, but his own particular friend; so that His Holiness hastened to send a draft of the accusations against him to the archbishop himself, who received them with his wonted calmness. Feeling, however, the obligation under which he lay to clear his reputation as bishop, he instantly sent a detailed reply in writing to these accusations, and gave irrefragable proofs of the entire falsehood of the charges made against him.

Those who, though just as much exasperated against the holy prelate, had yet sufficient wisdom to control their passion, did not dare take part with his accuser, knowing how impossible it would be for him to prove the facts he had alleged, or to impose upon the Pope. Therefore, the whole matter having been carefully inquired into, and the priest convicted of falsehood, and of having endeavoured to vilify before the Holy See one of the holiest bishops of the age, the Pope pronounced these words: "*Si delator est in urbe, queratur et suspendatur.*" But the unhappy man, having received timely warning of the failure of his plot, made his escape, and thus saved his neck.

His Holiness answered the archbishop's letter by a brief couched in the most affectionate terms, in which, after having consoled him for the calumnies heaped upon him, he calls him "*thrice blessed to have been persecuted for truth and justice's sake,*" and encourages him to preserve the same zeal for holy discipline, and to continue to govern his church as he had done before, concluding by an exhortation "*to fight with confidence in the cause of God; for should a thousand witnesses come to Rome to bring forward accusations against him, he would not give the smallest credit to any one of their assertions.*"

His accuser, in the meanwhile, fled to Portugal, and knowing the charity of the archbishop, hoped to receive pardon and impunity for his crime. But the affair had made so much noise in the kingdom, and especially at court, that the king, Dom Sebastian, ordered him instantly to be seized, and banished from his dominions. It seemed as if God had permitted this to show the gentleness of the archbishop; for this priest, finding himself thus forsaken by God and men, felt that he could only throw himself on the mercy of one whom he had so cruelly injured. So that, one day, in the face of all the people, he threw himself at the archbishop's feet, and implored his forgiveness. The archbishop raised him with the utmost tenderness, embraced him, and becoming his intercessor with the King and the Pope, obtained at last their pardon; thus proving himself to be one of those excellent pastors of whom St. Bernard speaks: *"Who, when they find any whom God has placed under their authority murmuring against and disobeying them, and even going the length of abusing and injuring them, do not consider themselves as their masters, but as their fathers and physicians, and taking pity on their madness, instead of wishing to punish or be revenged on them, strive only how they may best heal and cure them."* (St. Bernard, in Cant., ser. 25, num. 2.)

But at the same time the holy prelate warned him in private, that if he thought seriously of his eternal safety, he ought to consider the malediction pronounced by the Son of God, in the Gospel, against those who scandalized their brethren. He represented to him that there is no greater scandal than to blacken, by false accusations, the pastor whom he knew in his heart was doing his best to fulfil the duties of his charge, and thereby striving to ruin him in the esteem and confidence of his flock, which would destroy all his influence for good, both past and future: and that God alone could sound the depths of a wound so deep and so difficult to heal. He implored him, therefore, to strive to assuage His wrath and avert His justice, by bringing forth worthy fruits of penance, and such as might be proportioned to his fault. He bid him likewise remember that when the Church was in the full vigour of its ancient discipline, and had great saints as bishops, who were full of compassion for sinners, she yet decreed in her canons: *"That those who calumniated their brothers should do penance all their lives, and could only receive Holy Communion at the hour of their deaths."*

CHAPTER XII.

WITH WHAT MODERATION THE ARCHBISHOP BORE THE IN-
JURIES WHICH PASSIONATE PERSONS SAID OR DID PUB-
LICLY AGAINST HIM.

We have seen in the preceding chapter how God drew glory to His servant from the very insults and calumnies with which he had been assailed. But the spirit of malice and lies, finding himself foiled in the first attempt, resolved to try a second.

The archbishop, while making a visitation of his diocese, found certain persons who were in the practice of grievous sins. And as he always mingled sweetness with severity, he publicly reproved these disorders, while he pointed out to them the remedies they were to use to obtain God's forgiveness, and to be enabled to lead more Christian lives in the future. But these men were of the number of those of whom holy writ speaks as children resisting the yoke: "*who fear neither God nor men; who are rebellious to the light, and have sold themselves to work evil.*" (Job xxiv., verse 23; 2 Kings xxi., verse 20.)

One amongst them, especially, was eminent for his riches and position; and as he felt himself more wounded than the rest, on account of the rank he held, he fostered their angry passions by encouraging his own. Finally, they all conspired together to revenge the injury which they pretended the archbishop had done them.

For this purpose they waited till night-fall, and having assembled in great numbers at the door of his lodging, they first made a great noise with different instruments, to attract the attention of people, and make them come to the windows, so as to have as many witnesses as possible to the insult they wished to perpetrate on him. Then they began to abuse him in the most outrageous manner. They vented the most furious imprecations against him, some, in fact, which modesty forbids my relating, and used words worthy only of that malignant spirit who makes the mouths of men the instruments of his hatred and fury.

It was the hour when the archbishop was occupied with his chapter and other officers connected with the visitation, with whom he was discussing the best means for putting a stop to these disorders, so as to procure the greater good of souls. He heard the cries and imprecations of these madmen outside without appearing in the least troubled, or showing the smallest change of expression, but went on quietly writing, as he had begun, without so much as lifting his eyes from the paper. Those who were with him were extremely indignant at this scandalous proceeding, and could not help admiring the imperturbable peace of the archbishop, who treated this shower of abuse and ignominy as if it had been an agreeable concert of music. But the holy prelate made them a sign to be silent; and though their patience was sorely tried, nevertheless they were restrained by his authority, and by their admiration for his extraordinary moderation.

The row lasted a long time: those who were in the street went on repeating their offensive and insulting speeches, and the holy prelate bore them with the same patience. At last, seeing that no notice was taken of them, and that there was not a sound in the archbishop's house, where they hoped to have caused so much trouble and disorder, they became perfectly furious, burst forth into loud cries, and called him, in a stentorian voice, "*Heretic*," and "*Lutheran*."

At these words the humility of the archbishop was a little troubled, and looking up from the paper on which he was writing, he said: "'As for that, *no;* I am neither a heretic nor a Lutheran. May God, who gave me my faith, be for ever blessed."

Then turning towards his friends, he spoke calmly as follows: "My brethren, these people are sent by God to prove us. Though they accuse us of false crimes, there are many real faults which we have committed, and for which they might justly reproach us. But if they bring charges of heresy against me, I am bound to answer them; for the saints teach us that silence on such a point is forbidden to a Christian." Then he knelt down and prayed with great fervour for those who were insulting him. Very soon the doors and windows of the neighbouring houses were opened, and their owners having come out into the street, and heard what was being said against the archbishop, were very indignant, and declared that he was not only innocent of the charges brought against him, but that he was a great saint, and that all those who blamed him were themselves bad men, deserving exemplary punishment.

The archbishop was no more moved by the praises of these people than by the insults of the others. He rose from his knees, and said, smiling: "You see, both our friends and enemies make a mistake. For though, by the grace of God, I am neither a heretic nor a Lutheran, through my own grave fault I am not good, still less a saint." Thus he confounded the devices of the enemy of souls, who attacked him more dangerously by this second temptation than by the first; and remained as firmly rooted in humility amidst praise as he had been patient in bearing injuries.

The next day the news of the insult which had been offered to the archbishop spread like wild-fire through the town, and the people, who were full of affection for the holy prelate, were both horrified and indignant. The magistrates directly began to collect evidence on the subject, which they were obliged to do, not only from the respect due to the archbishop, but from the laws of the kingdom. The good prelate, hearing that several people had, in consequence, been put in prison, sent to the judge, and begged him to leave the affair alone. The judge replied that their punishment was richly deserved, and begged for instructions as to what should be done with those who had been arrested.

The archbishop replied: "That in the school of Jesus Christ he had learnt not to render evil for evil, but to love his enemies, and do good to those that hated and calumniated him. That, therefore, all he wished for was, that the prisoners should repent of the fault they had committed before God, so that they might obtain His pardon. That as for himself, he forgave them with all his heart, and he hoped they would treat those who had been taken up with great gentleness, and take no further steps to find the remainder, hoping that God would touch their hearts with His grace, according to his prayer for them, so that they might seek mercy from Him, and appease His justice, which was often more easily satisfied than that of men."

The judge, who was a good and wise man, and who realized the full extent of these men's iniquities, replied: "That the archbishop's words were worthy of his episcopal heart; but that, as he fulfilled his duty, so he implored him leave to perform his own as judge. That the more the archbishop showed his goodness and sweetness towards these persons, the more justice must feel indignation at their crime, and use severity towards those who had so cruelly outraged a prelate who felt towards them all a father's tenderness. That he would so far yield to his charity as not to hunt up any more of the accomplices of the criminals, but that of those who were already in the hands of justice he felt he must make an example, so as to stop a recurrence of such insolence and scandal, whereby the laws of God, the Church, and the kingdom were equally outraged."

The news of this affair spread throughout the kingdom, and the king, being informed of it, sent to the Seneschal of the province with stringent orders to inquire into the affair, and punish the guilty with the utmost severity.

The archbishop, seeing that the zeal of the young prince in this matter really proceeded from his zeal for God, and the respect he felt towards the prelacy, did not dare directly to oppose his orders; but he worked so effectively with the Seneschal, that in a very short time the whole business was hushed up. For he only wished for God as an avenger of any injuries he might receive; and he prayed that this might be effected, not by punishing the guilty, but by changing their bad dispositions into good ones, and bringing about a true conversion in their souls.

CHAPTER XIII.

THE HOLY PRELATE RETURNS TO BRAGA DURING THE PLAGUE, IN SPITE OF THE ENTREATIES OF EVERY ONE THAT HE SHOULD NOT EXPOSE HIMSELF TO THE DANGER OF INFECTION.—WITH WHAT CHARITY AND DEVOTION HE CARES FOR THE DYING AND THE DEAD.—THE CARDINAL OF PORTUGAL AND THE KING IMPLORE HIM TO LEAVE THE SCENE OF DANGER.—HE EXCUSES HIMSELF BY A LETTER.

God, who is pleased to exercise the virtues of His saints in all ways, having shown forth the charity of the archbishop during the famine, now ordained that it should be still further manifested during the plague.

For more than forty years the town of Lisbon had been exempt from this great calamity, when, in 1568, a malignant fever broke out, accompanied with erysipelas and other dangerous symptoms. At first the nature of the malady was doubtful. It was so catching, that when one person in a house was attacked, all the others took it immediately. At last, it appeared too clearly that it was the plague, and very soon the ravages it caused throughout the town were fearful. Some people declared it had been brought in some bales of merchandise from Venice; others discovered various other ingenious reasons; but scarcely any one thought of it as a judgment from God. For men who live for their senses and with little faith, often judge of the events of life more like pagans than Christians. They attribute the dealings of God's providence to chance, instead of revering the justice which chastens them; and they are like brute beasts, who attack the stone which wounds them, without thinking of the hand which directs the blow.

Our holy prelate, hearing that the plague had begun in Lisbon, felt convinced that it would speedily spread to the other towns in the kingdom. He felt also that the real cause of this great calamity was that God had determined to punish the crimes of men, so that they might recollect themselves, and return to the paths of virtue; and that the fear of the plague, which killed their bodies, might awaken in them a still more wholesome fear of the judgments prepared for the godless and impenitent.

All those who could leave the towns did so, and went into the country, where the air was purer. But in a good many the infection had already been taken, so that by this very exodus the evil was spread over the whole country. The town of Viano, being a mercantile city with a very flourishing trade, was attacked with the utmost violence. People fled right and left with the utmost precipitation.

A certain lady of high rank left the town like the rest, in a small boat, which landed her further down the river, at a little town called the Pont de Lima. But before she could reach the place, the malady seized her with such violence that she was obliged to stop on the road at a labourer's cottage. This lady was a good Christian, and her first thought was to send for a confessor. But the terror of the plague was such, that no one could be found to assist her, either in body or soul. By a strange coincidence it happened that the archbishop was making a visitation of this very town, and was in a spot not far from this cottage. The rumour of what had happened came to his ears, and filled him with sorrow, and he instantly set off to confess this poor lady. Those who were with him were horrified, and did their utmost to stop him. They represented to him the fool-hardiness of running such a risk, and at the same time the value of his life, as archbishop, with the whole diocese depending upon him.

But the more they argued, the more determined he was to go, and his only terror was lest he should be too late. To all their entreaties his reply was: "I am answerable for this soul. She needs a confessor, and no one else will go; therefore it is my business. Her eternal safety is as dear to me as my own, and far more precious than my life." At last, one of his chaplains, who had just heard of the matter, came running towards him, and throwing himself at the archbishop's feet, implored his blessing, and leave to offer himself, in his stead, to go and hear the confession of the dying lady. The archbishop, seeing his courage, and that he was well fitted for the task, at last allowed him to go, so that he might not lose the merit of such an action; saying to those around him: "That he had no objection to her being assisted by another, but that if no one had come forward, he should most certainly have gone himself, as he was the pastor of all those who had no other."

The archbishop was on his way back to Braga, when he received information that the plague had really reached that town. A terrible picture was given him of the suddenness of the deaths, the terror of the survivors, the consequent abandonment of the sick, even by their nearest relations, and the extreme risk every one ran who came near the place. This sad news filled him with sorrow, although it did not surprise him, as he had expected it all along. Praying heartily to God that good might arise to his people from this chastisement, he hastened his steps towards the stricken city. He first stopped at the monastery of St. Fructuosus, near the town, to ascertain the exact truth of the reports; but no sooner was his arrival known, than the magistrates and principal officers of the city met together, and determined to prevent his entrance into the place. The archbishop, however, stole a march upon them, and met them, walking quietly up to the gates as if nothing had happened. They implored and conjured him to turn back, saying: "That the air would be more dangerous for him than for those who had been already exposed to it. That he could show his charity quite as well by giving his orders from a distance. That he risked all in exposing his own life; and that if anything happened to him, it would not only destroy the courage of all who were striving to remedy the evil, but be the ruin of the whole diocese and country."

The archbishop thanked them for their affectionate solicitude, but added: "That he not only owed his care to his people, but a good example to all. That several of the clergy had already taken flight. If he were to do the same thing, he would justify the cowardice of the weak, and tempt the strength of the courageous. It is therefore clearly my duty," he continued, "to raise the former, and encourage the latter; and by not fearing to expose myself to danger, to become an example and a model to all. This is the obvious duty of my position. You, as magistrates and citizens, have the care of the temporal necessities of the town; but on me is laid a far more important charge, which is that of the souls whose eternal welfare is at stake. And therefore, as much as the soul is raised above the body, so much greater and more indispensable is my obligation than yours. On me, as bishop and father of all, is laid the duty of consoling and helping the sick, and administering to the dying, and you cannot imagine for a moment that I should consider my own health in comparison with the salvation of my flock. The greatest evil which this plague can do to me is, that I should dread it more than to be wanting in my duty to God and to my own people. My life is in His hands, and belongs to those whom He has given to me. If I die with them, well, then I shall die among my own flock, as a good shepherd should do. It would be the greatest grace which God could show to a bishop. And all I am afraid of at this moment is, lest my life should not be worthy of so glorious a death."

All the holy prelate's hearers were moved with joy and fear at this courageous answer, and yet could not help praising God for his generous resolve. For though, on the one hand, they feared for his life, on the other they saw as clearly as he did, (and as was proved by the sequel,) that his presence alone could keep men up to their duties amidst the universal panic; that even the courage of the most valiant might fail if the malady increased in intensity, and that then the sick and dying would be deprived of every spiritual assistance or consolation. The same generous feeling which animated the archbishop was likewise put into the heart of St.

Charles Borromeo. He acted in a similar manner, and when dissuaded from exposing his life in a moment of extreme danger from a like plague, replied that what would not be obligatory on others would be so on him, as by his episcopate he was bound to strive to arrive at perfection; and every one admiring his charity and zeal, felt there was nothing to answer to such arguments.

Dom Bartholomew, therefore, proceeded on his way to his palace, and there deliberated as to the best way of helping his stricken flock.

The first thing which he did was to prepare a large building outside the town, in a very healthy and open spot, called the " New Meadow," to receive all the plague-stricken folk. He established in this hospital the best surgeons and medical men he could find, with a large staff of assistants, and everything that was necessary for the service of the sick. He was determined that nothing should be wanting for their spiritual as well as temporal comfort, and sent a certain number of priests, to whom he specially recommended the poorest and most neglected among the sick and dying. Having arranged the hospital, he chose a clever and active man, to whom he gave a number of assistants, to go through every street of the town, and find out who were attacked by the fever, so as to separate them from their neighbours, and remove them to the hospital we have already spoken of. He also organised a body of men for the burial of the dead, which, in the panic, had been sadly neglected. These same people were also employed in purifying the houses of the sick, and disinfecting their beds and furniture. He then opened another large house for convalescents, so that they might be separated as soon as possible from the very sick, and hold no communication with them.

Every day of his life he visited both these hospitals, asking every possible question of the doctors and their assistants, as to what would be most useful for their patients, and instantly supplying their needs. He ordered a guard to watch the gates of the town, so as to prevent the ingress of fresh people. And to help to purify the air, he had large fires lit in all the public squares, where infected articles were burnt, besides insisting on the utmost cleanliness being observed in all the streets of the town. This never-ceasing vigilance, and his almost superhuman charity, had such happy effects, that the poor suffered far less than could be expected in so general a calamity; the mortality also was far less than in other towns in the kingdom; and though the greater part of the canons and dignitaries of the cathedral had taken to flight, not a single parish priest abandoned his flock: the divine office was said as usual in all the churches, and the noble example of the archbishop inspired confidence and courage in all his fellow-workers. The account of his holy generosity soon spread throughout the kingdom. At court the sensation created was very great, and the king was told that the archbishop exposed his life every day for the very poorest of his subjects. The young king was only seventeen, but as his heart was truly noble, he was delighted with all he heard of the charity of the great prelate, and wrote to him to implore him, now that he had put everything in such perfect order, to leave Braga, and take some care of his own life, which was as precious to the king as it was valuable and even necessary to the welfare of the whole kingdom.

The Cardinal Infanta Dom Henry wrote in the same sense, expressing his deep love and veneration for the archbishop, and conjuring him not to exhaust his strength any further. The archbishop answered in the following letter:

TO H. E. THE CARDINAL OF PORTUGAL.

" Eminence,

"I have received the proofs of your royal highness' kindness and friendship with a joy mingled with sorrow that I am unable in conscience to accede to the request contained in your letter. But what consoles me is the thought that, notwithstanding the kind interest your highness takes in the preservation of my life, I am perfectly confident that if you were here, and saw all that passed, and the evils my absence would occasion, not only would you approve of my conduct, but you would forbid me to stir. At the beginning of February, a few persons died without any one being aware of the real cause of their decease. But soon after, Dom Laurence Viero, a physician as Christian in his habits as he is skilful in his profession, declared that their illness was no other than the much-dreaded plague. It is impossible to describe the consternation and confusion which this announcement produced in the town. The very next day, two-thirds of its inhabitants took to flight, hoping thereby to escape a death which every one considered imminent. Hardly any people remained in the place, save the poor and the artisans, with a small number of magistrates and the parish priests, who all implored me not to enter the town. If these persons, and the large number of poor who crowd the city, saw me leave it at this moment, they would lose all courage at once, and would strive to fly like the others. All the dignitaries of the cathedral, and the greater part of the canons, fled at the first panic. And the priests that remain for the services of the Church would follow their example, if they saw me abandon my post. Therefore I feel that your Eminence, if he saw the state of things here, could not approve of my departure, as I should then leave the poor without help, and the dead and the dying without any one to administer the sacraments, or care for their salvation. As I have been very well during all this trying time, I am much more able to bear the fatigue now that the sickness is diminishing day by day, by God's mercy, and through the sanitary measures we have adopted. The plague-stricken and the convalescents are placed in two separate hospitals, where they receive every possible care and attention. If I were to leave them now, when they still so urgently need my services, I think that fear and sadness alone would cause the deaths of many, without thinking of the bad example which my flight would occasion to the other bishops and the parish priests of the province. For I have received letters from many amongst them, saying that what we have done at Braga has given them courage to suffer all that God may send, and that if the plague reaches them, they are quite determined to follow our example, and remain with their flocks, being willing to risk their lives for their salvation.

"I feel confident that your royal highness will therefore approve of my determination to remain at Braga, and that you will make my reasons acceptable to the king likewise, who has deigned to honour me with a letter in the same sense, and with the same idea,—that of withdrawing me from danger. If all his subjects are bound by their oath of allegiance to give their lives for his service, I am sure that his wisdom and piety will make him easily understand that pastors, and especially bishops, are still more bound to expose their lives for Jesus Christ, and for the souls whom He has redeemed with His Precious Blood."

The archbishop consequently remained at his post, placing all his trust in God alone, as in Him who is the sovereign master of health and sickness, life and death. He adored the sovereign justice, which had sent this scourge to strike his flock, while giving thanks to His mercy who had in so many cases afflicted the body with the sole aim of healing the soul. He had from the first taken the utmost care to have public and private prayers said in every church and convent in the diocese; and he exhorted every one to repentance, so as to appease the just anger of God, and draw down mercy on the guilty. After having spent the whole day himself in tending the sick and dying, he would employ the greater part of the night in prayer, pleading for his people. He redoubled his tears, prayers, fasts, and penances, and offered himself to God as a living holocaust for his flock.

The plague gradually ceased. It was evident that God regarded the indefatigable labours and prayers of His faithful servant, for there was far less mortality and suffering from this pestilence in Braga than in any other town of Portugal.

CHAPTER XIV.

THE ARCHBISHOP EXCOMMUNICATES THE PRESIDENT OF THE COURT OF ASSIZES, WHO USURPED THE RIGHTS OF THE CHURCH.— HE JUSTIFIES THIS ACTION ON HIS PART IN A LETTER TO THE KING, AND FINALLY OBTAINS ALL THAT HE WISHES.

The extraordinary charity of the holy prelate during the plague had won him golden opinions at court and throughout the kingdom. But now a fresh trouble arose, which threatened to disgrace him altogether with the king, in spite of the esteem which he had hitherto entertained for him.

There is an ancient custom in Portugal that the king shall send from time to time throughout the kingdom a sort of special commission of judges, to inquire into disorders, listen to the complaints of the poor, defend the weak against the strong, and do justice to every one.

The king, Dom Sebastian, accordingly appointed about this time two of these commissions of justice; one in the lands of Algarva, and the other in the provinces beyond the Douro. The president of this last was Dom Peter D'Acuyna, who was at the head of the ordnance in Lisbon, and who had five counsellors with him, all men of tried ability. The letters patent under the great seal for this commission were sent out in 1570, and authorized Dom Peter to exercise unlimited jurisdiction in all the towns and villages of the diocese of Braga, as well as in the town itself; although hitherto this diocese had been exempted by special decrees. The archbishop being warned of his arrival, inquired more particularly as to his powers, and found that Dom Peter had already begun to carry out the orders of the king in the hamlet of Dornelles, which was under the archbishop's special jurisdiction. This troubled our holy prelate a good deal, for it was entirely contrary to the laws of the kingdom, which had invested the Archbishops of Braga alone with these powers, which had never before been disputed by any King of Portugal. He felt, moreover, that Dom Peter was acting by an express order from the young king, who, although good and pious, was extremely jealous of his authority, and when once irritated, would proceed to great acts of violence.

But on the other hand, the rights of the Church were clear and indisputable. No previous archbishops had ever tolerated such an infringement of their privileges; and all previous Kings of Portugal had authorized and confirmed this independence of the Archbishops of Braga of all royal jurisdiction; so that, after mature deliberation, he decided to assert the rights of the Church, no matter what might happen.

In order not to precipitate matters, however, he sent a courteous message to the president, Dom Peter, calmly stating the case, and begging him to abstain from interference in those towns and villages which were subject to the archbishop's sole jurisdiction, as his predecessors had always done.

The president, taking no heed of his remonstrance, informed the archbishop that what he was doing was simply to act according to the orders he had received. The prelate wrote to him again, saying that he was sure that the king was too just to wish to usurp an authority which had always been vested in the archbishops who held that see; and that if he persisted in doing violence to the Church, he should be compelled to resort to ecclesiastical censures and excommunication.

The president disregarded these threats, and continued in the same course, till at length the archbishop, finding him deaf to his admonitions, pronounced against him and those who aided and abetted him the sentence of excommunication.

The president, who never dreamt that the archbishop was in earnest, was strangely surprised and offended, and wrote a furious letter to the young king, representing to him that the outrage perpetrated by the prelate reacted on his royal person, and that if such insolence and audacity were tolerated, nothing but revolt and disobedience could be expected from the rest of his subjects.

The archbishop took it for granted that the president would act in this way, and so sent Dr. Antony Francis to court, in whom he had great confidence, with the following letter to the king.

LETTER TO DOM SEBASTIAN, KING OF PORTUGAL.

"Sire,

"Knowing your royal highness' goodness and piety, I feel sure that you will allow me a favourable hearing while I explain to your highness the causes which have compelled me to act as I have done towards the president of your commission. The Archbishops of Braga, Sire, have from time immemorial possessed, not only ecclesiastical, but civil jurisdiction over the whole diocese. The kings, your predecessors, have always recognised that fact, and only reserved to the royal judges an appeal in certain criminal cases, desiring that all civil authority should rest with the archbishop. Had these kings thus acted from goodness alone, and to show their respect for the primacy, your highness' piety would naturally incline him to preserve this privilege to the see.

"But this temporal sovereignty, Sire, was not given as a mark of royal favour. It is a right acquired by the Church, to which the Kings of Portugal have always consented, and was obtained by the cession of large domains and lands to the crown. Your royal highness will see this in the formal contracts which were exchanged between the Kings of Portugal and the Archbishops of Braga, of which I take the liberty to send you a copy. Your highness will see that it was Dom Alphonsus V. who, in virtue of this exchange, confirmed the Archbishops of Braga in these rights, which all his royal successors have been scrupulous to maintain. It is a well known fact, that when Dom John III., the grandfather of your royal highness, honoured Braga with his presence, no sooner had he arrived on the frontiers of the diocese, than he commanded the royal judges who accompanied him to suspend all their functions, and even to divest themselves of the insignia of their office while they remained on the archbishop's territory, nor would he employ any other officers but those belonging to the diocese during his residence there.

"It is this example, Sire, which I venture to propose to your royal highness. I feel sure that you will be more disposed to imitate the piety of your royal ancestors, than to follow the advice of those who have violated the laws which these wise princes laid down, and who yet hope to win from your highness' goodness impunity for their proceedings. If they complain of us to your royal highness that we have had recourse to ecclesiastical censures, you must allow me to say that it is we, rather, who should accuse them, that they have compelled us, despite our continued admonitions and remonstrances, to have recourse to the last resource left to us by the Church. If these gentlemen have any fresh reason to give for their proceedings, I would implore very humbly that the affair be referred to the Archbishop of St. James in Compostella, who was named, in the apostolic briefs which confirmed our contracts with the Kings of Portugal, as the supreme arbiter and judge of any differences which might arise on this subject. But if the president and officers of justice persist in thus infringing the rights of the see, your royal highness must excuse me if I take the only course which remains open to me. I have never wished, by the grace of God, and I still less wish now that I fully know its burdens, to be a bishop; and to prove to your royal highness that I am in earnest, I send my mitre by Dr. Antony Francis, with full powers to give in my resignation, as your highness will doubtless find many more worthy of this rank than myself. But as long as I hold this charge, which was laid upon me against my will, the Church at Braga shall always maintain its ancient privileges, and it will be easier to take away my life than to force me to consent to see her stripped of rights which are legitimately hers, and which I am bound to leave intact to the archbishops who will be my successors. If your royal highness has not been duly informed of the truth of these things, and does not consider it his duty to put an end to this state of violence, I hereby declare that I am resolved to start instantly for Rome, even if I be forced to go on foot, with only a stick in my hand, to complain of the injury done to the see before the apostolical tribunal and the successor of St. Peter, who will listen to the complaints of the weak and oppressed, and will do justice to them against the mighty and the princes who abuse their power."

This letter was duly brought to the king, who read it with all the attention which it deserved. He had always had a very high opinion of the archbishop's charity and pastoral vigilance, and so, having calmly considered all the reasons he had adduced for maintaining the rights of his church against the proceedings of the royal judges, so far from being offended at the apostolic boldness with which he wrote, he conceived a still stronger affection and veneration for his person. He therefore replied at once that he approved of his conduct; that he would order the judges to leave his territory; and that he granted him with joy all that he asked, not only in consideration of his own great personal merits, but because he knew with what care and vigilance justice had been administered in the town of Braga and throughout the diocese.

The king added an order to this letter, commanding the president and the judges to leave instantly the territory of Braga, and to annul all their acts during their residence there.

The archbishop was full of thankfulness and praise to God, who had thus touched the heart of the king. But fearing that the letter might be interpreted as having been written more from affection to his person than respect for the rights of the see, he sent for two lawyers, and in their presence protested, in writing, against the recent violation of the law, annulled all that the judges had done, and further stated that what the king had now decreed, he had been obliged by his conscience to do, so as to prevent any similar infraction of the Church's rights. In fact, during the archbishop's lifetime, no similar attempt was ever made, and no judge ever entered the diocese of Braga, except at his personal request.

Hardly, however, had the holy prelate got out of this difficulty, than he was thrown into another, which obliged him for the first time to leave his diocese.

A large part of the revenue of the archbishopric consisted in a great quantity of wheat and other crops, which had been for centuries regularly paid in to the treasury. All of a sudden, certain persons refused to pay their share, and having been summoned by the ecclesiastical authorities, they declined to attend, saying that this was not an ecclesiastical, but a secular matter. Censures were unavailing, as they then referred to a crown judge appointed by the king to listen to the complaints of such of his subjects as found fault with the ecclesiastical judges. These men obtained a judgment in their favour; and the obstinacy and bitterness which these repeated trials called forth, incensed the officers of the archbishop, so as to make them forbid to the pleaders any entrance into the churches. At last, appeal was made to the king, who desired the officers to suspend all proceedings till he had spoken to the archbishop. He then wrote a letter to the prelate, in which he said he was quite willing to conform to his wishes, but that he hoped he would not persist in excommunicating those who differed from the decision of his officers.

The archbishop saw directly by this letter that the king's mind had been prejudiced against him. Therefore, although he hated leaving his own diocese, (which he had never done since the Council of Trent,) yet, seeing the grave consequences which might arise from this business, he determined to go and speak to the king in person, and for that purpose started for Coimbra, where the king was then staying.

The king showed great joy at his arrival, as he had been for a long time anxious to know personally a man who was so celebrated in his kingdom for his holiness and charity. He received him, therefore, with extraordinary honours, listened to all he had to say on the matter which had brought him to court, and promised to give him entire satisfaction on that point, as on every other.

One day, he said he very much wished to hear him preach, as he had heard so much of his sermons. The holy prelate hastened to comply with his wish, and preached in his presence before the whole court. He took the opportunity to inveigh in a special manner against the extravagance and extraordinary luxury which then prevailed in Portugal. The king was very much struck with his preaching, and it gave him the idea of trying to stop, by edicts, the excesses which were committed by his subjects on that head, and which were daily on the increase; so that the fear of human punishments might stop those who were not deterred by the warnings of the preacher, or the judgments of God.

The archbishop, after a few days at Coimbra, implored the king to wind up his business, so that he might be free to return to his diocese.

The king, though very sorry to lose him, respected his holy impatience, which was quite contrary to that of the majority of prelates, to whom a longer residence at court was generally most agreeable. He therefore gave orders to his ministers to see that the wishes of the archbishop should be carried out without delay. The prelate, after expressing his humble and hearty thanks for his kindness, took his leave of the king, and hastened to return with renewed ardour to the functions of his charge.

CHAPTER XV.

DOM SEBASTIAN, KING OF PORTUGAL, UNDERTAKES A CRUSADE IN AFRICA AGAINST THE MOORS.—THE ARCHBISHOP, AND ALL HIS COUNSELLORS, OPPOSE AND DREAD THIS EXPEDITION.

We have now recorded the principal actions of this holy prelate in the management of his diocese. His biographers have not told us everything in detail which he did, for that was not necessary to arrive at a just judgment of his character. He was not one of those who are only remarkable in great things, and neglect smaller matters. His conduct, on the contrary, was always regulated by the highest motives, and he was of the number of the wise men of whom holy Scripture writes: "*That they neglect nothing, because they fear God;*" and that "*Preparing their heart before Him, they only think of how they may best please Him.*" (Eccles. vii., verse 19.)

We come now to a great event, which was the defeat and death of Dom Sebastian, King of Portugal, to whom, as we have seen, the archbishop was under great and numerous obligations. For the holy prelate took an important part in this deplorable affair, which had grave consequences in his future life. And we will give an account of these events here, not to satisfy common curiosity, but, as St. Augustine teaches us: "*That history is useful, even to theologians themselves, when they look upon all that has happened to peoples and kingdoms as an effect of God's providence, who presides over all; so that, discovering by the eye of faith His invisible guidance, hidden, as it often is, under visible causes, and the secret order which He maintains amidst the disorders of the century, they may adore His sovereign wisdom, which reigns over the just and the unjust, and punishes or rewards them with admirable justice. And hence arises that wonderful harmony and incomparable beauty in the government of the world, for which the angels praise God without ceasing, but which is perceived by a very small number of persons."* (St. Aug. de Doct. Ch., lib. 2, cap. 28. Idem in Psalm vii.)

An Italian gentleman has described the enterprise and defeat of this prince in his "*History of the Union of the Crowns of Portugal and Castille.*" Besides the connection which this event had with the life of Dom Bartholomew, we shall thus see a true picture of the inconstancy and fragility of all human things, and how fearful and incomprehensible are the judgments of God with regard to kings and people, when He permits the result of one battle to decide the fate of a kingdom for ages upon ages.

Dom Sebastian I. began to reign in Portugal in 1557, being then only four years old. And although brought up in an atmosphere of peace and tranquillity, still, no sooner was he of an age to act for himself, than he showed the most warlike dispositions. Therefore, in 1574, being twenty years of age, he resolved, against the advice of the wisest of his council, to go into Africa, which he did with four galleys, a few other sailing ships, and a small band of soldiers. He could only reconnoitre the country at that time, as he soon found he was too weak to fight.

But he showed then his noble heart, and a courage which went to the verge of temerity, in engaging himself personally in every skirmish with the Moors. When compelled to return to Lisbon, his only dream was how he could get together a powerful army, in order to go back to Africa and redeem the Christians there. While his mind was full of these thoughts, an event occurred which gave him a favourable opportunity for carrying out his project.

Muley Mahomet, of the race of the Cherifs, having succeeded his father, Abdullah, and reigned for some years in the kingdom of Morocco, his paternal uncle laid claim to the crown, in virtue of a law that the brothers of deceased sovereigns should succeed to the throne before sons or nephews. Therefore, in spite of the small number of his followers, he resolved to conquer the kingdom, or perish in the attempt. And having in vain asked the help of Philip II., King of Spain, he entered Morocco with three thousand troops only, granted him by the Turks. Several persons joined his standard, and having attacked the king, his nephew, he gained three successive battles against him, in the last of which he defeated an army of sixty thousand cavalry and ten thousand infantry.

Thus Muley Mahomet lost the kingdom of Morocco, and Moluc, his uncle, remained in possession, having acquired an extraordinary reputation both among Christians and barbarians. The vanquished king took refuge in Portugal, where he represented to Dom Sebastian that the Moors were divided among themselves; that a strong party still remained faithful to him; and that if he would only land in Africa with a good army, he would speedily become king, and could then make his own conditions.

This idea was most agreeable to Dom Sebastian, corresponding, as it did, so exactly with his own views and wishes. And being full of exultation at the prospect of success thus held out to him, he convened his council, and proposed at once to assemble his army, and sail for Africa. The wisest of his counsellors did all they could to dissuade him, and represented to him the danger which might arise from this expedition, not only to his person but to his kingdom. But their opposition was fruitless. He was resolved on the enterprise, and only waited for means to accomplish it.

He first called out bodies of the tradesmen and middle-class in Lisbon, whom he had drilled as volunteers, sharing in their fatigues, and living himself as a common soldier. When he went hunting he would fight with the most ferocious wild beasts to test his courage; and if he were going to sea, he would always choose a time of storm and tempest, as if it were fainthearted to wait for a calm. His great anxiety was next to see Philip II., King of Spain, and get his aid in the war. The two kings met, and Philip, who was his uncle, showed him great affection, but tried with all his might to dissuade him from this undertaking, and especially from going in person, representing to him the impossibility under which he lay of assisting him. But seeing that he could not make him change his design, he told him that the Duke of Alva had assured him that no such war could be undertaken without fourteen or fifteen thousand foreign troops, not Portuguese, but Spaniards, Italians, and Germans; and that he would promise to try and raise five thousand if his affairs in Italy would enable him to spare them. Sebastian then asked for the hand of his daughter in marriage, which Philip promised him.

The King of Portugal came back from the meeting in great spirits, but was as much determined as ever to hasten his voyage to Africa. In order to meet the preliminary expenses of the war he put heavy taxes on both clergy and people, which caused great murmuring and discontent throughout the kingdom. After a long period of negotiation Philip II. informed him that, Flanders being threatened, he could not send him the help he had promised: and once more he did his utmost to dissuade Dom Sebastian from his expedition, foreseeing all the dangers to which he might be exposed. He not only wrote repeatedly in this sense himself, but he made the Duke of Alva do the same, who was the great captain of the age. As a last resource he sent the Duke of Medina Cœli to implore him to desist. But it was all in vain; and finally he determined to sail without the Spanish contingent.

The holy archbishop, and all those who were with him, were extremely grieved at the young king's resolution, and did their utmost to dissuade him. They foresaw all the present and future evils of the enterprise. But finding all counsels unavailing, they could only lift their hands to heaven, and implore our Lord to enlighten and guide one who was thus precipitating himself into unknown perils, without any regard for the consequences.

The king being thus immoveable in his resolve, he came one morning with all his troops to the cathedral in Lisbon, where, having had his standard blessed with great pomp, he gave it to his principal aide-de-camp. And instead of returning to his palace, as was expected, he went straight on board his galley, announcing his intention of submitting to no further delay. He was compelled, however, to wait for eight days in the harbour, for the embarkation of the troops and the rest of the crew.

As the young prince was very religious, and looked upon this expedition against the infidels as a holy war, and a real crusade, he took with him many pious and holy persons. Arias de Silva, Bishop of Oporto, and Emanuel de Meneses, Bishop of Coimbra, accompanied him, together with a large body of ecclesiastics and religious.

At last, on the 17th of June, 1578, the whole fleet set sail, the wind being favourable; and thus began this voyage, which was to have such fatal consequences. The king started full of joy and confidence, fancying that nothing but victories awaited him in Africa, but leaving his kingdom exhausted of men and money, and exposed to all the dangers which were the deplorable consequences of so ill-contrived and ill-conceived an expedition.

CHAPTER XVI.

DOM SEBASTIAN, IN SPITE OF THE ADVICE OF HIS OFFICERS, OFFERS BATTLE TO THE KING OF MOROCCO.—THE ARCHBISHOP OFFERS UP CONTINUAL PRAYERS FOR HIM THROUGHOUT HIS DIOCESE.—HIS DEFEAT AND DEATH. ADMIRABLE PIETY OF THOMAS OF JESUS, OF THE AUGUSTINIAN ORDER, TAKEN PRISONER IN THIS BATTLE.

When the fleet arrived on the coast of Africa, he commanded his troops to disembark at Arzilla, which was a small town in the possession of the Portuguese, where he landed his whole army. It was composed of eight thousand Portuguese, three thousand Germans, two thousand Castillians, and six hundred Italians; in fact, about thirteen thousand men in all, and fifteen hundred horses. Moluc, King of Morocco, of whom we have before spoken, having heard of his arrival, first began to treat of peace. For having both wisdom and experience, he did not wish to waste the lives of his subjects, though he felt he was much the strongest. He offered to give Sebastian the fields which surrounded the fortresses he had in Africa, to cultivate and to hold. But Sebastian replied, that having made all his preparations for war, he could not make peace without receiving three places in Africa, of which Alarache was one. The barbarian replied, that he should wait to consider this proposal, till the Portuguese had laid siege to the town of Morocco; that he had won the kingdom by gaining three battles; and that he should defend it in the same manner.

He then began in earnest his preparations for war. He was ill of a mortal disease, of which he died shortly after; but nevertheless he gave orders for everything himself. Fearing lest some of his troops should desert to his nephew, Muley Mahomet, whose crown he had usurped, he openly declared that those who would not fight voluntarily for him should stop at home or join his nephew's standard, and then sent a skirmishing party of three thousand cavalry to reconnoitre the Christian camp, and harass their flanks. He did this also in order to test his men, and separate the traitors from the rest, lest they should turn against him on the day of battle. And the Moors, seeing the generosity of the king, took this order as a proof of his confidence in their honour, and determined to justify it by their inviolable fidelity.

From the very first, the Portuguese showed their want of courage and experience. For six hundred of the Moorish cavalry having come near to reconnoitre them, they, never having before seen the enemy close at hand, fled back to their ships in great disorder. Sebastian was not disconcerted, however, at this cowardice on the part of his men, and seeing that the Moors had not taken advantage of the panic, began to despise them, and resolved to leave the fortress and lodge in the camp, to be ready to repulse the first attack.

The very next day, two thousand Moorish cavalry having appeared, the king attacked them with six hundred men, and the Moors, having no orders to fight, retired. The king pursued them more than three leagues, with far more courage than prudence. For he acted more as a private soldier than a general, and did not consider that in exposing his own person to such risks, he exposed the safety of his whole army.

Mahomet, the exiled king, who had persuaded Sebastian to come to Africa, was afraid at first that he would take possession of the country himself, instead of helping him to regain his kingdom. But having seen the utter want of discipline of his troops, he despaired of success against the reigning King of Morocco. He therefore advised Sebastian not to dream of a pitched battle, but to go coasting with his ships, and take the town of Alarache, which would be easily surprised. He added, that Dom Sebastian could then return gloriously to Portugal, leaving a garrison in the conquered towns, who would subsequently be able to induce the Moors to revolt, should anything happen to their king.

Sebastian brought this matter before his council, who strongly advised him to follow the advice given, representing to him the great advantage the enemy would have over him on land from their intimate knowledge of the country; that provisions would fail him in the interior, as he had no means of conveying supplies; that even if the Christians were infinitely braver than the Moors, they might easily be overpowered by superior numbers; that it was only a matter of prudence to moderate his ardour, to save not only his own life, but those of his troops; that the siege of Alarache was easily managed by sea; that its success could be ensured, and that such a plan would get him out of all his difficulties.

But the prince, who was bent on a pitched battle, would not even listen with patience to these counsels. Then some among his evil counsellors pretended to yield to his reasons, flattered his ambition, and endeavoured to pique him, by saying it was well he should show the King of Spain that Portugal could conquer the Moors without his assistance.

Thus all contributed to ensure the ruin of this poor prince, and many among his officers thought more of their own interest than that of their master's, and spoke to him, not according to their own judgment, but to flatter his wishes.

The king therefore gave orders that the whole army should leave the shore and take the field against the enemy. The King of Morocco, being warned of the march of the Portuguese, was delighted to see them advancing into the interior; for, knowing that his own troops were more numerous and in far better discipline, he had no apprehension as to the result of a battle. But being very prudent, his plan at first was to draw them on, and then cut off their retreat towards the sea, so as to compel them to yield, or perish for want of provisions, without losing a single man on his side. But he could not carry out his plan as completely as he wished, because he was so ill that he felt he had only a few days to live.

Therefore, he determined to fight, and appointing his brother general-in-chief of his troops, he ordered him to place his army in battle array, and to conquer or die; and that if he did the least thing unworthy of his position he would strangle him with his own hands. Then he had himself carried in a litter from rank to rank, encouraging his troops, and giving orders, as if he were in perfect health. Soon after, his scouts brought him word that the Portuguese army was drawing near, and he therefore sent a squadron of cavalry to reconnoitre. These arrived at a moment when the Portuguese were re-crossing a little river, as the king thought the stream would be a good line of division between the two armies. The Moors imagined the Christians were retreating, and wanted to follow them, but the King of Morocco, as prudent as he was brave, forbade them to stir.

The night passed without alarm, and the two armies being drawn up opposite each other, Dom Sebastian called his council, which included all his principal officers, and asked their advice. Some of them still urged a retreat towards the sea; others thought it was too late, and that they could not retreat in the very face of the enemy. Mahomet, however, knowing the courage and strength of the Moorish army, earnestly entreated the king to give up the idea of a pitched battle. But Dom Sebastian was bent on fighting, and believing that one Christian was worth five or six Moors, he insisted on going forward. He divided his army into three corps; in the first he placed the Castillians, Germans, and Italians, each commanded by their own officers; while the Portuguese formed the other two. The cavalry was placed at the two wings; the Duke of Avero commanded the right corps, where Mahomet and his Moors also fought; the king commanded the left, together with the Duke of Barcellos, the eldest son of the Duke of Braganza.

The King of Morocco also put his army in battle array. He had ten thousand infantry and forty thousand cavalry, twenty-five thousand of whom were picked troops, either Turks or renegade Christians. He placed his infantry in the shape of a crescent, with two squadrons of cavalry guarding each flank. The rest of his cavalry formed the rear guard, with orders to extend by degrees, until they had completely surrounded the little Portuguese army, so as to attack them on all sides at once. During these preparations, however, his malady made such fearful progress, that he felt himself dying, and feared he could not live through the day, for which reason he ordered his cavalry at once to encircle the Portuguese camp, so that the Christian army found itself completely surrounded and hemmed in on all sides.

The Portuguese, seized with an uncontrollable panic at this unexpected movement, threw themselves on the ground to avoid the fire of the enemy; so that Sebastian, fearing a total rout, gave the signal for battle. His advanced guard made so bold a stand against the Moorish infantry, that they fell back and were put to flight, with the loss of their standard; while the Duke of Avero with his right wing charged the cavalry, and completed their defeat. The dying Moorish King, forgetting his physical state, in his rage at this unexpected result, sprang from his litter in spite of the entreaty of his followers, and jumping on his horse, raised his sword to rally his flying soldiery. But the effort was too much for him, and he fell fainting in the arms of one of his men, who laid him back in the litter, where he instantly expired. But, according to his orders, his death was kept a profound secret, the officers pretending to come to him for orders at every moment, and so this misfortune did not hinder the ultimate success of the Moors. For the Duke of Avero, after the first brush of success, was attacked by a great squadron of cavalry, who pressed so hardly on his ranks, that he was compelled to retire, and in so doing, put all the infantry in confusion. And the same thing happened to the left wing, where the king commanded, so that the disorder of the army increased every moment. The Spaniards and Germans, however, fought with the utmost bravery, and upwards of two thousand Moors bit the dust. But they were finally overpowered by superior numbers, and were compelled to fall back. Francis of Tavora, who commanded the rear guard, bore up for a long while against the Moorish charge, but being killed by a musket shot, his soldiers were seized with a panic, and only thought of surrendering to the enemy, in spite of the presence of the king, who had galloped up to their support.

The Duke of Avero was the next victim; and all the officers being either killed or wounded, the Christians ignominiously took to flight, and the Moors with their scimitars hacked them to pieces right and left. The young king performed prodigies of valour, giving every order himself, and exposing his person almost recklessly wherever the danger was the most imminent and the fight the hottest. But his standard-bearer and his equerries being all killed, he found himself at last almost alone, and in this way was surrounded and killed by the Moors, who were disputing as to which was the leader of the Christians. His body was identified by the Portuguese prisoners among a heap of slain, and was carried on a horse into the infidel camp, stripped and naked like the rest.

Such was the deplorable end of this gallant young prince. He may be said to have been grand, both in his faults and in his virtues. He had great zeal for religion; loved and protected all persons of virtue and merit; had truly royal generosity and liberality; a heart capable of the most noble undertakings, and a magnanimity which equalled, if it did not surpass, that of his ancestors in the most illustrious of past ages. But one defect marred all these noble qualities, which was his pride of spirit, which made him inflexible in his determinations, and incapable of yielding to the counsels or opinions of any one but himself. He was only twenty-four years of age when he died, so that his fault was perhaps the more excusable, in spite of the deplorable results to his people and kingdom.

Mahomet, seeing the utter rout of the Christian army, and fearing to fall into the hands of his uncle, of whose death he was unaware, fled towards the coast. But in so doing he had to pass a river by a ford, so as to reach Arzilla, the Portuguese fortress, and the water being deeper than he expected, he was drowned.

Thus this sanguinary and ill-timed battle caused the deaths of all three kings, though in such different ways; the King of Morocco by illness, the King of Portugal in battle, after fighting for six hours with unparalelled bravery, and Mahomet by drowning, during his ignominious flight.

The Bishops of Oporto and Coimbra were likewise killed; and most of the priests and religious in the Christian army were made prisoners, and suffered much at the hands of these barbarians. There was one of these, Thomas of Jesus, of the Augustinian Order, who gave such a noble example of constancy and piety, and bore all his sufferings in so heroic and Christian a manner, that we think a short notice of his captivity is here due to the glory of God.

He was of the illustrious house of Andrada, and had been master of the novices in his order, besides prior and visitor. The king, Dom Sebastian, had been very anxious for his company on this ill-fated expedition, having great faith in his piety and prayers. Having been taken prisoner by the Moors, he suffered such tortures at their hands, as only those can imagine who have realized them. For, besides the natural hatred of these barbarians against all Christians, they redoubled their cruelty against one whom they knew to be eminent for his piety, so that they might compel him, by their tyranny, to renounce Jesus Christ.

This holy confessor, finding himself reduced to this extremity, redoubled his faith and confidence in God, so that not only did he remain immoveable in his zeal, but became the support and consoler of his brethren. He represented to them continually that, suffering as they did for the cause of Jesus Christ, Jesus Himself suffered with them, and would sustain their weakness by His all-powerful hand. He instructed and consoled them by his words and example; and one of them, Peter of Navarre, having been induced to renounce his faith, he converted and strengthened him so powerfully that he afterwards endured a horrible martyrdom for Jesus Christ, not only with courage, but with joy. The Moors, who hated him all the more when they saw he was as the head and master of the rest of the Christian captives, threw him into an awful and loathsome dungeon, where he had no light but what could come in through the cracks of the door, and left him almost to perish from hunger and thirst. In this horrible position he composed a book, entitled "*Labores Jesu*," (the Travails of Jesus,) consoling himself in all his sufferings by meditation on those of his Saviour. His sister, the Countess of Linarez, and his other relations, who were all persons of high rank, having heard of the fearful state in which he was, sent a special ambassador to Morocco to pay his ransom and rescue him. But to their despair he replied, that though he was most grateful to them for their care of him, he would rather be a slave in the dungeons o. Morocco, than free in Portugal, as he did not consider himself the prisoner of the Moors, but the captive of Jesus Christ. He begged that his ransom might be employed in liberating others who were more in danger of losing their faith through ill-usage and torture. Thus he passed the rest of his life, praising and blessing God for his sufferings without ceasing, and rendering every kind of service to the other captives, for the love of whom he had preferred slavery to freedom. After so long and terrible a trial of his charity and constancy, he died on the 17th April, 1582, after four years of this horrible captivity; and having thus been the voluntary sharer in the sufferings of Jesus Christ, he went to rejoin Him in glory.

Thus God made use of this unfortunate enterprise to sanctify the soul of His servant, and to save many others by his means, having given so admirable an example of charity and patience, both to his fellow-prisoners and to all succeeding ages.

CHAPTER XVII.

DOM HENRY, CARDINAL, REIGNS IN PORTUGAL AFTER DOM SEBASTIAN.—HIS AFFECTION FOR OUR HOLY PRELATE.—HIS CONDUCT AND DEATH.—ALL THE KINGDOM OF PORTUGAL BEING IN CONFUSION, THE ARCHBISHOP FINDS HIMSELF OBLIGED TO RETIRE FOR A TIME FROM BRAGA.

The news of the defeat and death of the king filled all Lisbon and Portugal with profound grief. There was not a family who had not a special share in the common sorrow. Women wept for their husbands, sisters their brothers, children their fathers, fathers their children, while many noble houses were extinguished that day by the death of those who were the sole representatives of their families.

The holy archbishop, whose charity felt all public calamities so keenly, had a particular reason for grieving on this occasion, for he had always had a great personal affection for the young king, who, on his side, had taken every opportunity to show his esteem and veneration for him. He took care to recommend him specially to God by Masses and prayers, and to give him all the aid which the dead can receive from the piety of the living. But as his faith was as enlightened as his charity, he could not look upon this great calamity from a purely human point of view, but adored the hand of God in His secret dispensations, looking upon them as the accomplishment of the eternal designs of His sovereign will.

Sebastian I. was succeeded by the Cardinal Dom Henry,

his uncle, brother of Dom John III., who was then in his sixty-seventh year.

Great hopes were entertained of his goodness and piety, as his well known sweetness and gentleness of character would, it was thought, ensure moderation in his counsels, and contribute to the happiness of his people. But his first acts caused universal disappointment; for having been rather badly treated by the ministers of the late king, who would allow him no share whatever in the government, he took the earliest opportunity of dismissing them all, and depriving them of their posts. Upon which an Italian author says, " That he did not imitate Louis XII. of France, who, on being urged to avenge himself on those who had ill-treated him as Duke of Orleans, replied: ' *We will let the Duke of Orleans revenge the injuries of the Duke of Orleans.*'"

Dom Henry was overwhelmed with anxiety during his reign as to who should be his successor, and showed his irresolution even in his will; so that royalty, which seems to most men the height of human felicity, only tended to destroy his peace of mind, to shorten his life, and to diminish the esteem which had been previously entertained for his person. It had been hoped that he would choose prudent and disinterested men as his ministers, and remain himself always master of the government. But, on the contrary, he let himself be governed by his servants and by unworthy persons, who, seeing his age and weakness, only thought of aggrandising themselves, and acting according to their own interests. Thus it might be said of him what was said of a certain emperor: " That whilst he was in a private position he appeared too great, but that his reputation diminished with his dignity; and that he would have been found worthy of the kingdom if he had never been king."

One thing must be said in his favour, and that was, that

he never changed in his affection or esteem for the Archbishop of Braga, who had always been his personal friend, and to whom he extended the like affection when he became king. Dom Bartholomew, therefore, obtained without difficulty everything he wished for during his reign. But, unhappily, it lasted only a year and a half, as he died at the beginning of the year 1580. The archbishop felt his death keenly, both as his king and as his friend. He performed the funeral obsequies with all the honour which was due to the last of the race of the kings, in the male line, who had reigned in Portugal for four hundred and eighty-six years. And he also organized public prayers and processions, to implore the help of God, and to avert the revolution which he feared was impending. He preached frequently, exhorting every one to be earnest in prayer that God would choose a virtuous and pious king, who should give peace to his people, and preserve the country from the evils which threatened it of civil war. In fact, the kingdom of Portugal was filled with confusion and trouble by the death of the king. The King of Spain, the Duke of Braganza, the Prince of Parma, Dom Antonio, the illegitimate son of Louis Infanta of Portugal, the Duke of Savoy, the Queen of France, Catherine de Medicis, widow of Henry II., all laid claim to the vacant throne. By some, the Pope even was supposed to have some pretensions to the crown; while the people of Portugal maintained that the race of kings in the male line being extinct, the election of his successor rested with themselves.

Thus the kingdom was divided against itself, and it was evident that the strongest would win the day. The town of Santaren declared for Dom Antonio, and several other places followed this example. But the archbishop, although he had been his tutor, as he was intended for the Church, and he had therefore everything to hope from his election, refused to take any part whatever in a matter which he considered purely human and secular, and therefore could not be persuaded to induce the town of Braga to declare in his favour. But seeing that it was impossible to persuade his flock to keep the peace, and that he was appealed to on all sides, he resolved, though with great sorrow, to leave his diocese for a time, and retire to the town of Tuy, a little place in Gallicia. His grief at leaving his flock, and at the grave dangers which threatened his country, brought on a violent fit of illness, and the fever increased to such a degree that he prepared himself for death. But his course was not yet run, and God raised him up again to merit still further in this world before receiving his crown. The bishop of the place was unwearied in his care of him, and when he began to recover a little strength, he had the joy of hearing that peace was restored to his country by the election of Philip II., King of Spain. He returned as soon as he could to Braga, where he was received with all the more joy by his people, as his absence had been the more felt, and his dangerous illness had made them apprehend that there might be a fear that they would lose him for ever.

CHAPTER XVIII.

PHILIP II. TAKES POSSESSION OF THE KINGDOM OF PORTUGAL, AND SELECTS THE ARCHBISHOP OF BRAGA TO RECEIVE HIS OATHS.

Towards the beginning of the year 1581, the archbishop received a letter from the king, Dom Philip II., saying that he had resolved to convoke the estates of the kingdom in the town of Thomar, to deliberate upon the best form of government, and that he wished him to be present, together with the other Portuguese Bishops.

The archbishop at first excused himself on the ground of his health. But his real reason was his dislike to leaving his flock, and the aversion his humility felt for the pomp and state which it would be necessary for him to assume on such an occasion.

The king then wrote a second time, and renewed his request in terms more urgent and honourable than before. He requested his presence as that of the most honourable of the estates of the kingdom, and finally said he would not pronounce his oath as king except before him.

The archbishop replied, that under these circumstances he had no alternative but to obey. But that he hoped he would forgive him for suggesting that his presence might give rise to some difficulties, for that the Church of Braga was in possession of the primacy of Spain; so that he was compelled, as archbishop of that see, and conservator of its rights, to have the primatial cross carried before the assembly. That he foresaw this might cause disturbance, and that the Archbishops of Lisbon and Evora might oppose it, so that he felt it would be better if he were not to be present, lest he should thus trouble the public joy on so solemn an occasion. The king replied, that the rights of his see would be respected, and that he need not fear that any one would interfere to prevent his doing his duty.

Accordingly, the holy prelate came to Thomar on the 2nd April, 1581. The king had arrived some days before, and was lodged in a magnificent house belonging to the Knights of the Order of Christ. The archbishop entered the town, having his primatial cross carried before him, and had a memorandum taken of the fact by the apostolic notary; and the next day he went to present himself to the king. On the 16th of the same month, which is the day when the Church of Braga celebrates the Feast of St. Fructuosa, the chambers were opened in due form. They chose for this purpose the spacious vestibule in front of the palace of the Knights of Christ, and after having hung it with rich draperies, a magnificent throne was erected, and on it the arm-chair of the king, above which was a very handsome dais. On the steps below the throne were seated the prelates and grandees of Spain, and the officers of the crown; and the rest of the vestibule was filled with seats for the deputies from all the different towns of the kingdom.

The archbishop having arrived at the assembly, was conducted to the steps of the throne, his primate's cross being carried before him. As he expected, the Archbishops of Lisbon and Evora protested loudly against this act, saying that he had no right to have it carried before him out of his own diocese, and that the question of the primacy between him and the Archbishop of Toledo had not yet been settled.

The archbishop, nevertheless, took the first place, and answered them in a few words: "That his see was in possession of the primacy, and that he was bound to preserve its rights."

Philip II. entered soon after, having the royal sceptre in his hand, and the crown on his head. The Bishop of Leyra opened the proceedings, after which the Archbishop of Braga, having on either side of him the Archbishops of Lisbon and Evora, ascended the steps of the throne where the king was sitting, to whom he presented a missal, with a cross beautifully encrusted with precious stones. The king having knelt down, took the customary oath in the hands of the holy archbishop, swearing to maintain inviolate the laws, liberties, and privileges of the kingdom. And all the estates of the realm afterwards tendered to him the oath of fidelity. The ceremony was concluded by a solemn "*Te Deum,*" which was chanted as an act of thanksgiving. The Archbishop of Braga said the prayers, and gave the apostolic benediction. And the king then entering the sacristy, deposited at the foot of the crucifix his crown and sceptre, quoting the words of David: "*Domine non est exaltatum cor meum, neque elati sunt oculi mei.*" (Psalm cxxx.)

CHAPTER XIX.

THE ARCHBISHOP OBTAINS LEAVE FROM GREGORY XIII. TO RESIGN HIS ARCHBISHOPRIC, AND RETIRE TO VIANO.

We have already seen how often our holy archbishop had laboured to obtain leave to resign his charge, and how he had asked it in vain of Pope Pius IV. When Pius V. was raised to the pontificate, he wrote to him: "That he hoped he would imitate Him of whom he was the vicar on earth, and who said in His Gospel: '*Come to Me all you that labour and are burdened, and I will refresh you.*' (Matt. xi. verse 28.) That he had always been overwhelmed with the weight of his charge, and that he expected to obtain his relief from him."

The Pope replied: "That they were both members of the same religious order; that he had no more dreamt of becoming pope than Dom Bartholomew of becoming archbishop; and that if, in spite of his weakness and exhaustion, he was compelled to bear the whole burden of the Church, still more ought the archbishop to be consoled in his minor charge; and that both must wait with patience till it pleased God to release them from their labours."

The archbishop often renewed his petition, but in vain. Pius V. had far too high an opinion of his sanctity and zeal to release him. Then Pius V. died, and the archbishop made the same request to Gregory XIII., but with the same result. At last, seeing the favourable dispositions of the new king towards him, and hoping that he would have greater weight with the Pope, he opened his heart to Philip II., representing to him that having laboured for twenty-three years in the diocese of Braga, he felt that his advanced age, and the weakness consequent on his late severe illness, incapacitated him from supporting so heavy a burden any longer; that he had always been utterly unworthy of such a charge; and he ended by entreating him to write to the Pope in his favour, so that His Holiness might consent to his resignation, and that he might appoint at the same time to that great church a person whose piety, vigilance, and charity should cover and repair the many faults he had committed during the years of his administration.

The king was very much touched at his request, and seeing that he asked for it with so much ardour, he promised him to write to the Pope, which he accordingly did. The archbishop at the same time renewed his entreaties to His Holiness, to obtain that grace.

These despatches having arrived at Rome, were presented to His Holiness, and read at the consistory, with the letter of the King of Spain, who, at the end of his epistle, conjured the Pope to give this consolation to a prelate who asked for it with such eagerness. A good many of the cardinals opposed the proposal, and one of them told the Pope that the whole world knew that the archbishop was the father of the poor, and the defender of the rights of the Church. That as for him, he did not speak from hearsay, but from his own personal knowledge; that he had been with him at the Council of Trent, where he appeared as a perfect model of sanctity, and an example to all prelates; that if his age and weakness did not enable him to perform his arduous duties as heretofore, he could easily have a coadjutor; but that it would be terrible to deprive the ecclesiastical order of so great and noble a model. Other members of the council spoke in the same strain. Nevertheless, the Pope, remembering the many importunities of the archbishop on this subject, said at last that he would, though very unwillingly, accept his resignation.

The question then arose as to his pension. When the archbishop himself was referred to on the subject, by the king, he said that fifty ducats annually would suffice him; and he would have accepted nothing, if he had not feared to be a burden on the monastery of Viano, where he was about to retire, on account of his age and many infirmities. But the Pope insisted on his accepting a pension of two thousand five hundred pounds, without which he positively refused to send the bulls for his successor, who was Dom John Alphonso, of Vasconcelos.

It is easy to imagine the despair of the people of Braga, when they heard that their beloved archbishop's resignation had actually been accepted. They saw themselves on the point of losing a pastor who, for twenty-three years, had been indefatigable in the duties of his charge; who had eschewed its pomp and state, and only delighted in its onerous duties; who had nourished them with the word of God, and was filled with extraordinary lights and wisdom; who considered the wants of the poor as his own, and looked upon the revenues of the Church as belonging to them instead of himself; who, during the famine, had saved the lives of thousands by his self-denying charity, and in the plague had exposed himself to almost certain death for the safety of his flock. Thus all wept at his loss, as their protector, consoler, father, and friend. A large number of persons went to implore him to reconsider his decision, saying how indispensable he was, not only to their happiness, but to their eternal salvation, and conjuring him not to abandon his flock. The archbishop spoke to them with great tenderness, and even wept with them, saying: "That he had always been persuaded that this dignity was very disproportioned to his insufficiency; that it was high time he should leave a charge for which he had always been unfit; that after having given twenty-three years to these duties to his neighbour, he felt he must be permitted to spend the few remaining years that were left to him in retreat, self-examination, and expiation of his faults; that if, when he was younger and stronger, he could, by hard work and application, supply in some way his want of capacity, it was different now, when old age and sickness rendered him incapable of fulfilling his functions; that he implored them to believe that he should never be separated either from his flock or his church; that he should bear both ever in his heart; that they would be the objects of his love, of his prayers, and of his tears; and that he hoped, by offering them incessantly to God, and himself with them, he would really be of greater service to them than he could have been by the imperfect performance of the functions of his ministry."

All who listened to him burst into tears, and were inconsolable at their loss, although they felt they had no right to grudge him the holy repose which God had prepared for him. His whole flock accompanied him to the Monastery of the Holy Cross at Viano, which the archbishop himself had founded, and which he had chosen for his resting-place. As soon as he had arrived, he went to adore the Blessed Sacrament in the church. And the prior and all the monks having come forward to meet him and to kiss his hand, the holy prelate threw himself into the arms of the prior, and then at his feet, asking for his blessing. Then, embracing the monks, one after the other, he said to them: "My dear brethren, I have always had an extreme desire to live amongst you. I was torn from you by force, and I return to you with joy. I ask of your charity that you would suffer me in your holy company, and that you should give me, as alms, the smallest cell in your monastery, where I may retire and die in peace. But I conjure you not to be scandalized if you see me with a very small amount of recollection and of attention to the rules. For I come here with the resolution to repair, by the grace of God, and by your good example, all that I have lost in the world of the good education I formerly received in this holy order."

After having spoken thus, he turned to those who had accompanied him, and whose grief seemed only to redouble as the moment of their separation from him drew near. He particularly conjured the ecclesiastics among them to remember that what they had hitherto done was not for a poor, weak mortal like himself, but for God, who worked in them, and would reward them for their labours. That therefore he implored them to continue the holy works they had begun, while he assured them and all the priests of his diocese, that if God deigned to regard his weakness, and did not refuse to receive his prayers, he would try, in his retreat, to imitate Moses on the mountain, and lifting continually his hands to heaven to implore the help of God, while they, like Joshua, led the army of the Lord, and fought against the enemies of His people in the plains.

CHAPTER XX.

OCCUPATIONS OF DOM BARTHOLOMEW AFTER HIS RETREAT IN THE MONASTERY.—HIS LOVE OF PRAYER AND MEDITATION ON HOLY SCRIPTURE.—HIS EXTREME CHARITY TOWARDS THE POOR.

The new archbishop lived a very short time after his elevation to the see; and the fresh choice of the Pope fell on Dom Augustus of Jesus, a religious of the Order of St. Augustine, a wise and holy man, who had a special veneration for Dom Bartholomew, and chose him as a model and a guide.

Dom Bartholomew, seeing himself at last released from his onerous duties, thought of nothing but of purifying his soul in his peaceful retreat, and striving so to die to all things in this world as to live but for God. His only object was to be the least and most abject person in the house, and he was only remarked among the monks from his extraordinary modesty and humility. He obeyed the superior as if he were the youngest novice, declaring that all should forget he had been archbishop, as he had forgotten it himself. And to prove that he had not chosen this sort of retreat from idleness, or a disinclination to labour, he would go on foot, as long as he was able, to the villages near the monastery, to teach the catechism to the poorest of the country people. He never seemed to think this work in any way beneath him, and wonderful were the fruits of his charity and zeal. But after three years his state of health compelled him to desist from the fatigue. He devoted himself then more than ever to prayer and contemplation, keeping his mind fixed on God, and living continually in His presence, so that he attained to that holy peace of which St. Gregory of Nazianzum speaks, when he writes: *"Nothing seems to me comparable to the happiness of a man who, shutting his senses to all earthly things, lives as if he were independent of the world and the flesh; who takes no part in any worldly concern, unless constrained to do so by some inevitable necessity; whose conversation is in heaven; who withdraws his mind from all visible things, and fixes it on the divine mysteries; who becomes day by day as a stainless mirror of divine perfection; who tastes already, by a lively hope, the delights of his future inheritance; and who, although he may remain still among men, yet, by the power of the Holy Spirit, lives with God and His angels." (Orat. 1, post. imit.)*

Besides his continual prayer, Dom Bartholomew was always recalling with profound humility the many mercies and blessings he had received from God. He considered himself as a man who had come back from a perilous voyage, during which he had been a hundred times in danger, either from pirates, or from rocks, or from tempests; and being filled with gratitude at the numberless graces and favours which had been showered upon him, he would exclaim with David: *"What shall I render to the Lord for all the things He hath rendered to me?"* and again: *"Come and hear, all ye that fear God, and I will tell you what great things He hath done for my soul."* (Psalm cxv. verse 12, and Psalm lxv. verse 16.)

But his principal occupation in his retreat was the devout study of Holy Scripture. He knew that the word of God is as a divine treasure, containing all spiritual riches, more precious than gold and diamonds; a source of living water, springing up into life everlasting; a celestial armour, whereby we may be able to "extinguish the darts of the wicked one," and as David says, "a lamp to lighten our paths," and guide our feet into the way of peace. So that this sacred reading was, as St. Augustine exclaims, "*the delight of his heart,*" and his whole day was as a continual intercourse with God, either by prayer or the study of His word.

The care of the poor and administering to their wants was the only pleasure he allowed himself. For as, by the decree of Pope Gregory XIII., and the injunction of the king, Philip II., he was compelled to accept the pension of his archbishopric, he distributed it among the sick and suffering with a tenderness and wisdom which doubled the value of his gifts. He would deprive himself of real necessaries in order not to refuse any who asked his assistance; of which we will give one notable example. One day, returning from church to his monastery, having been preaching in a neighbouring village, he found a great number of poor people waiting for him on the road. He distributed amongst them all he had, until a poor woman came and implored his help, to whom he replied that he was grieved to say he had not a farthing left. But she went on importuning him, saying that she was a widow with an orphan girl, and had not even a bed on which to lie. The holy man was terribly distressed at her story, and thought within himself how he could help her, seeing that he had given away all his money, and did not expect any more for a long time. At last, not wishing to lose this occasion of helping a widow and an orphan whom God had thrown in his way, he told her to come at dusk to the window of his cell, for the monastery had no enclosure, and described to her exactly how it was situated, that she might not make a mistake. And so, when evening came, he shut himself up in his cell after compline, made a packet of his bed, only keeping the bedstead, and then looked out of the window to see if the poor widow was near. To his great joy he found she was waiting, and so threw out his bedding to her, which she carried off with great delight. The holy prelate had therefore nothing left to sleep on but the bare boards; but he found rest in the thought that God had thus given him the grace and opportunity to help others. He was determined to try and preserve as long as he could this poverty of Jesus Christ, *who "had not where to lay His head,"* so that he kept himself constantly in his cell, and when any one came to see him he would go out into the passage, shutting the door behind him, so that no one should discover his loss.

But at last it pleased God to reveal the charity of His servant in an action so calculated to inflame the zeal of the other religious, and to confound the pride and hardness of the rich. The poor woman talked of her wonderful gift from the holy archbishop all over the town, and after several days it came to the ears of the prior and the monks. They could hardly believe it for some time, and then understood why it was he had let no one come into his cell of late. The prior, determining to see for himself if it were true, surprised him the next morning in his cell, and found, as he had been told, nothing but the trestles of his bedstead, without a palliasse or a mattress, or even a blanket or a counterpane. He asked him gravely, as if he had heard nothing, "What had become of his bed?" The archbishop colouring, replied: "My father, some one is using it who wants it more than I do. But I assure you I make myself very comfortable without it." The prior would not say any more for fear of vexing him; but he took care to send him a good bed that night, with an order to use it. And as the archbishop had made a vow of obedience to him, he was obliged to accept it, however contrary to his inclination, and also promised not to give it away in future.

We may judge by this action how his charity and self-denial increased instead of diminishing as he advanced in years, according to the words of Holy Scripture, which compares the old age of the saints to that of the eagle, because, as the natural man gets weaker, having in him the seeds of corruption and death, so the spiritual man becomes stronger, because the Holy Spirit which is in him is eternal.

CHAPTER XXI.

THE HOLY PRELATE FALLS ILL OF A MALADY WHICH ENDS IN HIS DEATH.—HIS EXTREME PATIENCE IN SUFFERING.—DOM AUGUSTINE, HIS SUCCESSOR IN THE ARCHBISHOPRIC OF BRAGA, COMES TO VISIT HIM.

It was nearly eight years since the holy prelate had retired to the Monastery of the Holy Cross at Viano. But the last four years were very trying to him, from the state of suffering to which he was reduced. At the end of the year 1590, he began to feel a great deal of pain, which reduced him to a state of extreme weakness. He hid it for a long time, either because he did not know the serious nature of his illness, or because he wished to suffer in silence. The monks only remarked that he got up later and went to bed earlier, that he was extremely weak, and that he looked dreadfully ill.

At last, towards the beginning of July, feeling his pains increase, he knew that his hour was at hand, and that concealment much longer was impossible. He made a supreme effort to say Mass, and visited for the last time all the holy altars. He did his best to console the poor, who never failed to come to his Mass. He then went to his cell, and passing by that of Father Andrew of the Cross, who was his particular friend, said to him with a transport of joy: "My dear father, I come to announce to you my happiness. I think God is about to grant to me what I have asked of Him for some time. Do not forget to recommend me to Him very specially at this moment, because I urgently need His assistance." He then went on to his cell, and took to his bed. The doctors were sent for, and found that his illness arose from kidney disease; that he suffered from retention of urine, which his modesty had made him unwilling to reveal, and that his patience and silence under the agony had greatly aggravated the evil. They did everything they could to relieve him, but with little or no success; for his sufferings hourly increased, as did likewise his courage. He had become so completely master of himself, that in his agony he never uttered a word of complaint, and what he suffered was only found out by his fainting away continually from the pain. His soul was always recollected in God, and he never ceased praising and blessing Him for all His mercies.

The dangerous illness of the archbishop having been made known in Viano, the people were filled with sorrow, and the bad news quickly spread through all the towns and villages of the diocese. The reigning archbishop was at Braga, and no sooner did he hear of it, than he started off on foot, and walked all night till he reached Viano. He was accompanied by a great number of the ecclesiastics and nobles of Braga. He would not wait for the customary reception, but asked directly he arrived at the monastery, "Which was the archbishop's cell?" and hastened to it at once. As soon as he came in, he went up to the bedside of the dying saint, and could not conceal his emotion at his extreme sufferings. He took his hands in his, and strove to console him by every possible expression of affection, as well as by words of piety. He spoke to him less as an archbishop to an archbishop than as a son to a much-loved father. He told him that he had come to assist him to the utmost of his power, and that he should consider himself too happy to be able to render him the smallest service. These words were followed by deeds, for he insisted upon doing everything for the sick man himself, and that with a tenderness and a devotion which brought tears to the eyes of the assistants. The dying archbishop was in such a state extreme of weakness and exhaustion, that he could not express his gratitude for his loving services, save by the expression of his face and of his eyes.

All day long a succession of magistrates and people of every class arrived at the gates of the monastery to ask for tidings of their beloved father in God, till at last the people of Viano became alarmed, and conceived the idea that the Archbishop of Braga and his followers intended to carry off the body of their beloved prelate as soon as he was dead. They came, therefore, in a body to Dom Augustine, to conjure him in the name of God not to go against the desire of the dying saint, who had expressly said that he wished to be buried in the monastery of Viano. Dom Augustine received the deputation with great kindness, and spoke to them in general terms, though with much sweetness and charity. They then went to their dying father in God, and implored his benediction for themselves and the whole town of Viano. The holy prelate strove to raise himself, and give it to them as well as he could, and they received it with sobs and tears, which none could control. No sooner had they left the monastery than they armed the inhabitants, and in a moment sentinels were placed all round the monastery and its neighbourhood, who kept guard day and night, till the holy man was buried. And the zeal and affection for him was so great, that the noblest amongst the people of the town took a pride in sharing the watch. They lit thousands of torches likewise during the night, for fear of a surprise. In fact, they were willing to risk or do anything rather than allow any one to steal from them the precious remains of one whom they already revered as a saint, and whom they considered as the most precious treasure their city could possess.

CHAPTER XXII.

HAPPY DEATH OF DOM BARTHOLOMEW.—THE TOWN OF BRAGA PLEADS FOR HIS BODY.—THE INHABITANTS OF VIANO TAKE UP ARMS TO KEEP IT.—HE IS FINALLY BURIED IN THE MONASTERY.

Dom Bartholomew had received the Holy Viaticum as soon as he was declared to be in danger, and had the happiness of communicating very often during his illness. The physicians seeing that his end was approaching, warned Dom Augustine to delay no longer to give him Extreme Unction. The archbishop consequently administered this sacrament with great fervour, and in the midst of a large number of people.

The devotion and peace with which the dying saint received it were wonderful. His weakness seemed to have left him for a time, and his mind was perfectly clear and free. He implored all the assistants, with touching humility, to help him with their prayers, so that the holy unction might produce in him the effects which Jesus Christ intended by its institution.

When they repeated the seven Penitential Psalms, he said himself the alternate verses, without making a single mistake, and the canons and the monks repeated the others. But as their tears and sorrow sometimes choked their utterance, the holy prelate frequently said their verses as well as his own, with all the calmness of a man in perfect health.

At last, having fallen again into a state of extreme exhaustion, which the very effort he had lately made probably augmented, and being actually on the point of expiring, Dom Augustine, who had never left him day or night, began the prayers for the recommendation of a soul. They were frequently interrupted by his tears and those of the assistants. About a quarter of an hour after, Dom Bartholomew lifted his eyes and hands to heaven, and without any movement or convulsion gave up his holy soul to God, on the 16th July, in the year 1590, between seven and eight o'clock in the evening, at the age of seventy-six years and two months.

The death of the holy prelate was no sooner announced by the mournful tolling of the bells, than the grief of the people burst forth without restraint. Every one felt as if they had lost what was dearest to them in the world, and as for the poor, they were inconsolable.

Dom Augustine gave orders as to the funeral, which he determined to take upon himself. And the next morning the body of the holy prelate was dressed in his pontifical vestments, and exposed in his cell to the veneration of the faithful. The people came in crowds to kiss his dress, and touch his body with their rosaries and other objects of devotion, and all wept for him as for a real father.

When they were preparing to carry him down to the church of the monastery, a great deputation of canons, nobles, and magistrates of Braga came to claim his body as that of their own archbishop, offering to give him a magnificent funeral, and to erect a lovely monument and chapel in his honour. On the other hand, the magistrates and nobles of Viano threw themselves at the feet of Dom Augustine, declaring that he had chosen the monastery of Viano as his last resting-place, and that there was not a man in Viano who would not fight to prevent their losing so precious a deposit. At last, Dom Augustine yielded to their representations, and delivered over the body to the prior, to be interred with the other religious of the monastery. It was then taken to the church, and no sooner did it appear in the street, than a tremendous cry arose from the crowd, some weeping, some praising, and some invoking him as a saint. In vain the officers tried to keep some sort of order in the funeral procession. The people broke through the ranks so as to get nearer the beloved body, and it was with the utmost difficulty that the convoy reached the church. Thousands of wax lights and torches illuminated the building, and two priests incensed the body day and night whilst it was exposed. Dom Augustine officiated pontifically, and the ceremonies were so prolonged that it was four o'clock in the evening before the Mass was over. The body was finally deposited at the foot of the altar, and subsequently a magnificent tomb was erected over it.

So great was the veneration of the people of Viano for their holy prelate, that they were not satisfied even when the body had been deposited in their church. They therefore resolved to station a guard of thirty soldiers, who should watch the tomb night and day, lest the people of Braga should come surreptitiously and carry the body away. But at last the prior and the monks persuaded them to give it up, not thinking it reasonable that the peace of the monastery should be thus troubled by a fear without any foundation.

CHAPTER XXIII.

OF THE MIRACLES WROUGHT BY THE SERVANT OF GOD DURING HIS LIFE AND AFTER HIS DEATH.

Although the perfection of the saints does not depend upon their working miracles,—for the great Precursor, who was praised by our Lord Jesus Christ as the greatest of men, never performed any, as mentioned in the Gospel, —still it is well to record some of the wonderful things which happened during the life and after the death of Dom Bartholomew, that God may be glorified by the evidence of the graces which it pleased Him to shower on His faithful servant. Among other things, his biographers state that at his birth a mark was perceived on his hand which very much puzzled his mother and those about him. It was a cross with four *flœur de lys* distinctly imprinted on it, and which remained all his life, and was seen after his death. This happened to be the arms of the Order of St. Dominic, by which it appears that God had destined him from the first to be one of the lights of that order.

On one occasion, when he was archbishop, and in the midst of one of his visitations, he came to a desert place where there was nothing whatever to be had. The people who were with him began to complain bitterly at finding nothing to eat or to drink. He calmly reproved them for their want of faith, and kneeling down, began to pray. Almost immediately appeared a number of persons from the neighbouring villages bringing with them every species of provisions; which was looked upon by those around him as a direct answer from God, and a reward of his faith.

After he had resigned his bishopric, and retired to the monastery of Viano, it was remarked several times that the wheat which he gave out of a sack to the poor visibly multiplied, and money in a like manner; and once a large sum was found in his place in the choir, which no one could account for unless by supernatural means. Although those who recorded these miracles were men worthy of belief, still, such things are only mentioned with a certain reserve: for we may not speak of saints but in a manner worthy of them. Therefore, the only extraordinary things we will here mention are those recorded by Father Louis of Grenada, the same father who refused for himself the archbishopric which he advised the Queen to confer on Dom Bartholomew, and whose authority on all spiritual matters has been always unquestioned. Of the miracles which occurred after Dom Bartholomew's death Father Louis knew nothing, as he died in 1588, that is, a year and a half before the holy prelate.

In the town of Viano, a lady who was eight months gone with child, was seized with such violent pains that she lost the power of speech. The doctors who were attending her feared it would be impossible to save both herself and her child, and after seeing her for five days in this agony, which they could not relieve, they began to despair. As this lady had the greatest veneration for the archbishop, they ran to the monastery, and asking for Father John of the Cross, implored him to give them something that had been worn by the holy prelate. He did so, and no sooner had his clothes touched the lady, than she spoke, and said that her pains had ceased, and she felt quite well. The cure was complete, and at the end of nine months she was confined of a fine boy without any difficulty. The news of this cure having been spread through the town, a poor woman who had been three days in labour, had recourse to the same remedy, and with a like happy result. A man had a very bad attack of quinsey throat, which threatened to choke him. His parents asked for a girdle which the prelate generally used, and had no sooner put it round his throat, than the quinsey burst, and he was soon quite well.

A little child in Lisbon had his face completely eaten away by a cancer. His mother took him to the archbishop to get his blessing, and ask for his prayers. And the third time she did so, the child was perfectly cured.

A gentleman of Viano being in danger of losing his sight, went to find the holy prelate after Mass, and implored him to read the Gospel over him. He did this for nine days in succession, and each time he felt the sight improving. On the ninth day he recovered his eyesight completely.

A ship laden with wheat was coming into port, when a furious tempest arose, and the vessel was on the point of being driven on some rocks on which two other ships had lately been wrecked. Every one rushed to the shore, striving in vain to help, and crying out that she must inevitably go to pieces. Dom Bartholomew was told of it, and throwing himself on his knees, prayed with the greatest fervour for a few moments, when, to the amazement of the lookers-on, the tempest suddenly ceased, and the vessel rode into the harbour in safety.

When the holy archbishop took to his bed in his last illness, several little children from the town came up to kiss his hand, sent by their mothers to get his blessing. One of these children had a nasty ulcer in his arm, which caused him great pain. One day, this boy having kissed the prelate's hand, asked him if he would touch his bad arm. The moment he did so, the child felt such relief that he ran home joyfully to his mother, saying he was cured. The mother turned up the sleeve of his shirt to look at the wound, and found it entirely healed, and what was still more extraordinary, without any mark of where the ulcer had been.

Since the death of Dom Bartholomew, a Religious of the Monastery of St. Anne of Viano, of the Order of St. Benedict, called Mary of Nazareth, was paralysed on one side, and her arm was, as it were, quite dead. One day the mitre of the holy prelate was brought to the convent for a sick person who had asked for it. The poor paralysed nun felt all of a sudden a strong inspiration that if she could touch this mitre she too should be cured. She entreated her superior to let her try: the mitre was brought and laid upon her paralysed arm, when a sort of electric shock seemed to pass through her, and she felt that a divine virtue had gone out of it. Her paralysed arm became directly soft and flexible, so that she could bend and stretch it out, and she was, in fact, completely cured from that hour.

Dr. Manuel Pinto de Rocha, Seneschal of the town of Viano, was seized with cholera, and suffered such agonies that death was thought imminent. He sent in all haste to the monastery for a confessor, and also begged for the archbishop's mitre. No sooner had they placed it on the part affected, than the violent pain he had been suffering from entirely ceased, and, to the amazement of the medical men, he was soon quite well.

Those who have compiled biographies of Dom Bartholomew, have recorded that during his retreat at Viano he received constant entreaties to pray for persons and ships in great peril, and that in all cases they had been saved; and that almost every day the sick came, or were carried up to the church of the monastery, to hear his Mass and get his blessing, after which they almost invariably found themselves cured of their diseases. But what we have already mentioned, from the authority of Father Louis of Grenada and other persons, is sufficient to show us how God manifested the holiness of His servant by extraordinary instances of His power and mercy, and how precious in His sight is the death of His saints.

CHAPTER XXIV.

HOW THE BODY OF THE VENERABLE PRELATE WAS TAKEN UP NINETEEN YEARS AFTER HIS DEATH, AND PUT IN A RICH TOMB.

About nineteen years after the death of the venerable archbishop, it pleased our Lord still further to honour his memory by the translation of his holy body.

The spot where it had been deposited was extremely damp, not only from its natural situation, but because it was not raised enough above ground; so that many complained that sufficient honour had not been done to their beloved and saint-like prelate. All the priors who had succeeded one another in the monastery wished very much to effect this removal, seeing the wonders which God wrought day by day through the merits of the holy prelate, and the great crowd of persons who came to recommend themselves to his prayers. But the monastery was too poor to undertake the expense.

At last, Father Bartholomew of Pinto resolved to carry out the plan in which his predecessors had failed to succeed. He spoke to Dom Augustine, the reigning Archbishop of Braga, who warmly encouraged him in the idea, and promised him one hundred ducats towards the expenses. Dom Christopher di Mora, who had been viceroy in Portugal, and the particular friend of Philip II., obtained from Philip III. permission to erect this monument, and also a grant of one hundred ducats towards the outlay. A great number of bishops and pious persons likewise hastened to contribute to so pious a work. The monument was at last completed, and having been brought from Lisbon to Viano, notice was given that the translation of the body would be made the first Sunday in October, in the year 1607. But several accidents having occurred, it had to be postponed to the 24th of May, 1609, which happened to be the day of the Translation of the relics of St. Dominic. The Bishop of Fez officiated on this occasion, instead of the Archbishop of Braga, who, to his great mortification, was unable to attend from serious illness. All the chapter and the dignitaries of Braga assisted, with an infinity of other persons and ecclesiastics of every rank.

When the solemn opening of the sepulchre was made, the body of the saint was found entire. The head was thinner, but all the other parts of the flesh were as solid and fresh as if he had been embalmed, or had only died the day before. And although nineteen years had elapsed since he had been buried in this damp place, not only was there no disagreeable smell, but a sort of aromatic perfume arose from the body, which was patent to every one. The head especially exhaled this delicious and extraordinary odour.

The body having been laid in the choir, and the veil lifted from the face, the prior of the convent said in a loud voice: "That he swore, as before God, that the body before them was that of the illustrious Archbishop of Braga, Dom Bartholomew of the Martyrs." The Bishop of Fez made a profound bow, and embraced the body with much reverence, as did the prior and all those who were present.

The church had been closed all this time, but now the

crowd besieged the doors, which were no sooner opened than an incredible number of people entered, and that with such eagerness, that the soldiers who were on guard, and the monks themselves, were unable to prevent their crowding round the body, and touching it with their rosaries, &c. The delicious odour it exhaled, and the freshness of its appearance, were considered equally miraculous by all.

After the ceremonies were concluded, the holy body of the saint was deposited in the new and beautiful tomb prepared for its reception, by the provincial and the prior of the convent. And all the principal people of Viano considered it an honour to assist in placing the great stone which closed the tomb, and which they sealed in various places with the seals and the armorial bearings of the town.

END OF THE THIRD BOOK.

FOURTH BOOK.

CHAPTER I.

THE INTENTION OF THIS BOOK IS TO POURTRAY THE FEELINGS OF DOM BARTHOLOMEW BY HIS OWN WORDS, AND TO MAKE REFLECTIONS ON HIS LIFE.—THAT THE INSTRUCTIONS IT CONTAINS WILL BE USEFUL TO ALL THE FAITHFUL.

Having in the preceding pages described the admirable actions of this holy prelate, we might naturally think there was nothing left to add to the history of his life. But as the writings of the holy Fathers are not considered less important than their biographies, as they speak *"out of the abundance of their heart,"* the same thing may be said of the book of this great bishop, wherein he teaches those doctrines which are, as it were, the source of his actions, and communicates them to others after his death.

He compiled this book in Latin, at the beginning of his episcopate. It treats of the duties and virtues of priests, and is entitled *"Stimulus Pastorum."* He did not intend the manuscript to see the light, as he composed it for his own use. But he took it with him to the Council of Trent, where, as we have said, St. Charles Borromeo opened his heart to him, and according to his advice, decided to reside henceforth at the seat of his archbishopric, which was at Milan. This holy cardinal, wishing to know how Dom Bartholomew conducted himself in his diocese on different occasions, the archbishop lent him this book, written by his own hand, so that he might see the holy rules which he followed, and his feelings on the duties of the episcopate.

St. Charles had the greatest veneration for this book, and had it printed in Italian, after which he sent a copy to Father Louis of Grenada, begging him to have it printed likewise in Lisbon.

This book consists of two parts. In the first, the archbishop expresses the sentiments of the Fathers on the episcopate, and gives long extracts from their works. St. Gregory the Great, St. Bernard, St. Augustine, St. Gregory of Nazianzum, and St. Chrysostom, were his principal authorities, but especially the holy Pope St. Gregory.

In the second part he speaks himself of the duties of the pastoral charge, and of the virtues required of those to whom they are entrusted.

We will add to this summary of his writings, the opinions of St. Charles, he being so closely united to Dom Bartholomew in mutual affection, and in their love of God: and conclude by some other actions in his life which had been omitted in his history, so as to give additional interest to his instructions.

Some of these relate solely to the pastoral charge. But many are useful to all the faithful, for the faith, hope, and charity which formed the basis of his teaching are equally binding upon all. Thus St. Augustine writes: *"If a man chooses to act as the head of his family in a truly Christian spirit, he fulfils, as it were, the duties of a bishop."* (Aug. de Sanct., Ser. 51.)

Thus, if there be a close connection, according to this holy doctor, between the duties of persons living in the world and those of the pastors of the Church, it is easy to see that what is written for one applies to the other. We have, however, confined ourselves to such reflections as regard charity, love of the poor, prayer, confidence in God, and similar virtues; so that the reading of this book should edify persons of all classes.

CHAPTER II.

DOM BARTHOLOMEW PROPOSES ST. GREGORY'S PASTORAL AS A RULE FOR ALL PRELATES.—THE QUALITIES WHICH THAT GREAT POPE REQUIRED FOR THE EPISCOPATE ARE SPECIALLY FOUND IN OUR HOLY ARCHBISHOP.

Dom Bartholomew began his meditations on the duties of bishops by the words of St. Gregory the Great, who considered that we should judge of the virtues required of a bishop by the importance of his ministry. *"To be raised to a bishopric,"* writes this holy Pope, *"is to be chosen to become the chief and guide of the people of God; to be an example of all virtue, and a perfect model of evangelical perfection, according to the words of St. Paul: 'That it behoveth a bishop to be blameless.'"* (1 Tim. iii. verse 2.) (St. Greg. Past., pag. 1, cap. 7 and 8.)

And the same saint continues, in the beginning of his pastoral: *"There is no human art which a man attempts to teach, if he have not first applied himself with care and study to learn it thoroughly himself. What then can be said of the presumption and temerity of those who dare to embark in the pastoral charge without any knowledge of its duties, since the art of guiding souls is the art of arts, and the most important of all sciences? Who does not know that it is infinitely easier to cure the wounds of the body than those of the soul? Yet, while a man would never dare practice as a doctor without a knowledge of medicine, people are found who are not afraid of undertaking the office of physician of souls, without the smallest knowledge of the rules or remedies required in this divine science.*" (Greg. Past., pag. 1, cap. 1.) And he then quotes the words of the prophet against those who thus force themselves unworthily into pastoral functions, and of whom God complains: "*They have reigned, but not by Me; they have been princes, and I knew them not.*" (Oseo viii. verse 4.)

The first of those whom this holy Pope considers as unworthy of the episcopate are those who, as he writes: "*Become masters in the Church more through their own intrigues than by the call of Him who is its Chief and its Spouse; who have none of the virtues incumbent on their position; and not having any real vocation, but prompted by their own ambition, usurp and steal this supreme dignity rather than receive it, and raise themselves by pride to this ministry of humility.*" (Greg. Past., cap. 1.)

Secondly, the Pope teaches us that God rejects as His ministers those who may be gifted and clever, but who are not really virtuous, nor grounded in humility. "*For this reason,*" he says, "*that when God sent the prophet Samuel to choose among the children of Isai the man who was to be king of Israel, (which was a type of the future election of bishops,) He rejected the eldest son, whom Samuel fancied from his height and noble presence, He would have selected. And God said to him: 'Look not on his countenance, nor on the height of his stature, because I have rejected him; nor do I judge according to the look of man, for man seeth those things that appear, but the Lord beholdeth the heart.*' (1 Kings xvi. verse 7.) *This eldest son,*" continues St. Gregory, "*is the type of those learned men who are eaten up with pride. His great height denotes their vast knowledge; his noble presence, the charm of their exterior actions and manner. When, therefore, God rejects him, as we have read, it is as if He said: 'Men are prone to estimate highly those who excel in learning and exterior advantages, but I think little either of science or works, unless there be first a real foundation of piety and humility.'"*

In the third place, St. Gregory objects to the appointment to the episcopate of those who are only distinguished by human and secular learning. "*Holy Church,*" he writes, "*does not choose as a guide of souls a man who, instead of devoting himself to heavenly studies, labours to prove himself clever and intelligent in worldly affairs; but selects rather one who is beloved of God from his interior and spiritual life. For a true pastor does not care to feed his flock with perishable and terrestrial goods, but with such as are heavenly and eternal.*" (Idem., v. 8.)

Fourthly, the Pope teaches us that he does not mean that those are to be promoted to the government of the Church who have no knowledge, "*but those whose humility is enlightened by the gift of wisdom; who can do what God commands, because they are humble; and who can command others, because they are wise.*" (Ibid., v. 9.)

If we think over the life and character of Dom Bartholomew when he was chosen bishop, we shall see in him all the qualities which that great Pope requires of those who are to be raised to this supreme dignity. For, nearly thirty years before, he had left everything on earth to embrace the religious life; he had devoted himself, not only to prayer, but to the study of the Holy Scriptures and of the Fathers of the Church, and had thus learnt that wisdom which God impresses on the heart, by the light of His word, and the unction of His Holy Spirit; while he was thoroughly grounded in humility, that great foundation of all virtue.

It is remarkable also that those who determined to raise him to that dignity, for the edification of the whole Church, followed exactly St. Gregory's rules in their selection. For the holy Pope, speaking again of the consecration of David, by the prophet Samuel, to be king over Israel, (which kingdom was a type of the royal priesthood of Jesus Christ,) and of the words of the Lord, "*Thou shalt anoint him whom I shall show to thee,*" says: "*This proves that although men may consecrate bishops, it is God who elects them; and that when, through respect of the world and the flesh, people are selected who are devoid of virtue and merit, the choice falls upon those who are not pointed out by God. Therefore, God says to His prophet: 'Thou shalt anoint him whom I shall show to thee;' so that no one shall be anointed bishop in the Church unless he be found worthy of so great an honour by the testimony of the word of God. For thus our Lord speaks to us still. It is in the Holy Scriptures that we learn how holy and perfect those should be who aspire to be pastors of the flock of Christ. And thus we choose one whom God has pointed out when we select a bishop who in all things comes up to the character of a bishop as pourtrayed in the Bible.*"

We see how the Queen of Portugal acted in this manner in the election of Dom Bartholomew, having no regard to flesh and blood, or to human respect, but acting exactly according to the rules of the holy Pope, in her choice of a bishop, so that she verified in her person the words of Pope Leo: "*That he who has an upright heart, tending sincerely to God, finds in his own conscience the rule of conduct which is prescribed to us by the authority of the apostles and the ordinances of the holy canons.*" (S. Leo, Epist. 92.)

CHAPTER III.

THAT THE REPUGNANCE FELT BY DOM BARTHOLOMEW TO HIS ELECTION AS BISHOP, ARISING FROM HIS EXTREME HUMILITY, WAS EXACTLY IN ACCORDANCE WITH THE RULES LAID DOWN BY ST. GREGORY.

We will now recall what were the dispositions of Dom Bartholomew himself at this grave moment of his life, and shall find that they are exactly conformable to the feelings of the holiest doctors of the Church. For he followed the two rules which St. Gregory prescribed in his pastoral: one, to fly from all dignities, in imitation of Jesus Christ, who fled when they wished to make Him a king; and the second, to yield when that dignity was forced upon him by obedience, as Moses accepted at last the charge laid upon him by God, although he had resisted and refused it at first. The holy pontiff writes: "*Let him whose virtue is too weak to bear the pastoral dignity, beware lest he accept it, for fear that, wishing to raise himself above others, he should lead his flock over the precipice. It is recorded in the Gospel that Jesus made His escape when they wanted to make Him a king, and yet, who could have reigned more justly than He, who was the Sovereign Master and Creator of all men? But He made Himself man, not only to redeem us by His sufferings, but also to instruct us by every action of His life; and therefore He would not be made king, and He would be crucified. He rejected the supreme honour that was offered to Him, and gave Himself up to a shameful death,* so that those who were to be His members and His imitators should learn by so glorious an example to fly from honours and dignities, and love humiliations and abasement." (St. Greg. Past., pag. 1, cap. 3.)

"And yet," continues this great Pope, "a man must not be obstinate in his refusal, when it seems clear that the call is from God. This is shown us in the conduct of Moses, who at first refused the leadership of the people of Israel, and then accepted it from a spirit of obedience. For as he would have shown pride had he embarked without hesitation in so difficult a task, it would have been equal presumption on his part to refuse when God called upon him to obey. So that he showed humility and submission, both by his refusal and his acceptance. Let those, therefore, who are so rash as not only not to fear, but even to wish to command others, consider how great a risk they run, as even the greatest saints trembled at being chosen to lead the people of God, even when directly commanded to do so by Him. Yet, to-day, the weakest and least virtuous amongst us sigh after such a charge! They are, in reality, sinking under the weight of their own sins, and yet are enchanted if the burdens of others are laid upon them. They cannot answer for their own souls, and they choose to make themselves responsible for those of a whole people!"

But our holy prelate did not merely resemble Moses by the manner in which he first refused, and then accepted this important pastoral charge. He was also like him in the way in which he left a life of retirement and obscurity, to become the light of the whole Church; so that, amidst the grandeur and high functions to which his dignity called him, he always maintained, like the great prophet, that profound humility and humble opinion of himself which had led to his first refusal. Passing from a cell to a palace, from poverty to riches, from solitude to all the bustle of the great world, he yet remained unchanged in himself, and his virtue not only was unimpaired by the dangers which surrounded him, but shone the more brightly from the courage with which he surmounted them. That is what the authors of Dom Bartholomew's life remark very judiciously, that it is easy to judge what he was as a monk, by considering what he was as archbishop; wherein he formed a notable contrast to some who appear models of virtue in their monastery, and then, when promoted to be bishops, give themselves up to vanity and worldly pleasures, and are intoxicated by the honours and riches of the world. So St. Chrysostom remarks: "*Supposing a man had lived a very holy life in religion, still I would not elect him as bishop unless I were persuaded that he possessed likewise extraordinary prudence and the spirit of perseverance; because I have known many who had passed all their lives in the practice of fasting and mortification, who had always served God with zeal, and had shown every example of virtue as long as they were solitaries or religious, when they were brought forward in a public position, and had to guide and correct others, have proved themselves incapable of the charge, and by giving up their habits of austerity, have been losers themselves without benefitting any one else.*" (St. Chrysostom de Sacerd., lib. 3, cap. 7.)

St. Augustine teaches us the same thing when he shows the merit of bishops and priests who keep themselves pure in the midst of the world, while compelled to guide those who are entangled in the occupations and engagements of the age. "*I know many bishops, priests, and other administrators of the divine mysteries, who are most holy men, and whose virtue seems to me the more admirable, because it is so difficult to preserve it amidst constant intercourse with men, and amid the troubles and distractions of common life. For they have not merely the guidance of holy souls, but of sick souls which must be healed. They must bear patiently with the sins of their people, and tolerate evil, so as to be able to cure it. On such occasions it is very difficult to remain firmly in a holy life, and to preserve peace and calmness of spirit. For there is this great difference between religious and ecclesiastics: that the former are amidst those who are all striving after perfection; whereas ecclesiastics are amongst those who must be taught how to live aright.*" (August. de Mor. Eccle., cap. 32.)

Dom Bartholomew was fully convinced of these truths, and hence, as we have seen, his fright at being made bishop, dreading lest he should lose his own soul without saving those of others. And although he felt himself exempt from worldly ambition and self-interest, and only desired to serve God, yet he always feared lest there might be in the depths of his soul a secret self-complacency which might lead him to take pleasure in the dignity thrust upon him. Therefore, being extremely humble, he applied to himself those words of St. Gregory in his pastoral: "*Those who desire dignities in the Church generally fancy they do so with the view of serving God. And although ambition may have prompted them, they only think of the good works they will accomplish, and the great good they fancy they will do. And thus hiding from themselves their secret motives and intentions, they dwell on their pretended wish to do good, which is only on the surface. For the spirit of a man often seduces him, and disguises him from himself. He pretends to love souls, while he is really indifferent to them; and to despise the glories of this world, which in reality he loves. Whilst passionately desiring this dignity, he is timid in seeking it, and only brave when he has obtained it, for the fear of not getting it makes him timid; while, when he has obtained it, he considers it is due to his merit. And when, in this purely human manner, he begins to carry out the duties of his charge, he easily forgets all his fine plans for good, which he before fancied were his sole motive in desiring it. Lest, therefore, we should fall into such an illusion of mind, let us look back on the way in which we have previously lived. Let each consider what he did as a private person, and he will soon find out if he is capable of doing the good which he proposes to himself in the guidance of others. He who was proud in a low and humble state cannot become humble when he finds himself raised above all others. He who has loved praise when he could not obtain it, is not likely to despise it when it is tendered to him. He who has not been able to bear poverty when he was in an inferior position, will find it hard to conquer avarice when he becomes the depositor of wealth, which he is to employ for the relief of many. Let each one judge, by the actions of his past life, what he will be fit for in the future, for fear that, in the eager wish to possess some great position, he should deceive himself with false views, and delude himself with imaginary good resolutions."* (St. Greg. Past., pag. 1, cap. 9.)

Dom Bartholomew quoted these words when they wished to drag him from his cell, to prove that the imperfections of his past life rendered him incapable of being made a bishop. For thus the humble apply to themselves what is written for the proud, while the proud never take home what is written for them; because the humble do not see their own merits, while the proud fancy they have virtues which do not exist. And the pure and holy life which Dom Bartholomew had led in his monastery was the best pledge of the great things which he was to accomplish in his episcopate.

CHAPTER IV.

DOM BARTHOLOMEW SHOWS, BY THE TEACHING OF THE FATHERS, HOW PASTORS SHOULD DEVOTE THEMSELVES TO PRAYER AND TO MEDITATION ON HOLY THINGS.—THAT THIS ADVICE IS USEFUL TO ALL THE FAITHFUL, AND HOW THEY ARE TO PRACTISE IT.

To show what the archbishop was during his episcopate, we will quote the character of a perfect bishop, from the words of St. Gregory, which Dom Bartholomew gave as a model for all prelates; and we shall thereby see how the life of this holy man was in accordance with the picture drawn of a true pontiff of Jesus Christ.

"*There should be,*" writes St. Gregory, "*as much difference between the virtue of a bishop and that of his people, as there is between a shepherd, who is a man, and his sheep, who are unreasoning animals. Therefore, let him who has the care of souls consider well to what purity and what perfection he must attain, and to which his ministerial charge obliges him, inasmuch as his people must be looked upon in the same light as a shepherd does his sheep. When, then, there is a question of choosing a prelate whose holy life must be the rule and example of his flock, he must be a man who, being dead to all the passions of the flesh, lives a divine and supernatural life; who tramples under foot the goods of this world; who fears no temporal evil, and only desires celestial riches; who, far from coveting what he has not got, is always ready to give what he has; who is ever inclined to pardon and indulgence, because he has bowels of compassion and tenderness, and yet who is not weakly indulgent, but inflexible in matters of justice and equity; who does not fall into sin, but deplores the sins of others, as if he himself had committed them; who sympathises with the infirmities of the weak, and rejoices over the advancement of his brethren, as if it were his own; whose actions are a model of imitation to all those who are under his authority; who is never guilty of any action which could cause scandal or shame; who, while striving after personal holiness, does not neglect the instruction of others; who waters the dry ground of their souls by the stream of celestial doctrines; who is so given to prayer that he knows by experience that he shall obtain from God all that he asks, being one of those to whom the word of God to the prophet is addressed: 'Thou shalt no sooner open thy mouth in prayer than I will say, Here I am.' For if some one came to ask us to intercede for him with some mighty person whom he had offended, but who was unknown to us, we should reply at once, that not having access to this personage, we could not plead for him. If, then, a man would blush to present himself before another mortal when he does not think he is in sufficient favour with him to venture to intercede for one who has offended him, how can a man who knows, by the actions of his past life, that he has not deserved that God should extend His friendship and divine familiarity towards him, dare to take upon himself the office of mediator and intercessor for souls? How should he have the courage to plead for mercy for his brethren, when he does not know if he has received it himself? For it is to be feared that he whom we employ to appease the just indignation of God towards the guilty would irritate Him still more by his own sins; as it would happen with regard to a powerful person whom we wished to appease, when he who speaks to him in favour of the offender is himself disagreeable to him."* (St. Greg. Past., page 2, cap. 1., and page 1, cap. 10, 11.)

We will pause a moment to consider one of the characteristics of a good pastor, on which St. Gregory lays the greatest stress, namely, that a bishop should be a man of prayer; one who, by the progress he has already made in the spiritual life, is in a position to obtain from God what he asks of Him for the salvation of his people. On this subject Dom Bartholomew writes: "Woe to you! O pontiff of God! if the source of piety and devotion be dried up in you. For sincere and interior piety is really that fountain of living water which sanctifies all our actions, and without which we remain dry and barren branches. This is the celestial wine which fills our hearts with divine joy; this is the balm which heals the wounds of our souls. *It is the language in which we speak to God,* writes St. Bernard, *and without which our souls remain dumb.* (In Cant. serm. 45, num. 7.) It is this spirit of prayer which brings down upon us the manna from heaven, and which, sustaining our hearts with celestial food, enables us to work in the Lord's vineyard, and to bear the burden and heat of the day, amidst the continual anxieties, cares, and toils of the pastoral charge."

For this reason St. Gregory wills: "*That while the pastor lowers himself towards his inferiors with the tenderest compassion, he must at the same time be raised above them by the sublimity of his prayers, lest his wish to live in constant communion with God should make him fail in care of, and compassion towards, the weak ones of his flock; or that, being absorbed by the tenderness of his charity towards them, he should cease to raise his heart continually to God by holy aspirations.*" (St. Greg. Pastor., part 2, cap. 5.)

Dom Bartholomew shows still more clearly that unless exterior occupations, however holy, are not sustained and, as it were, "*seasoned by prayer,*" according to the words of St. Basil, they easily make us lose the taste which the soul may have previously conceived for speaking with God.

To prove this, he again quotes the words of St. Gregory: "*Very often, when a man is engaged in the pastoral charge, his heart becomes agitated, and torn in pieces, as it were, by the multitude of occupations and cares which overwhelm him on all sides, and he becomes the less capable of doing any one thing really well, because his mind is so troubled and confused by the multiplicity of affairs which are brought before him at the same time. 'My son,' says the Wise man, 'meddle not with many matters;' for it is not easy to be recollected in spirit, and to apply oneself diligently to any particular business, while one's mind is distracted amongst so many. A soul which in that way pours itself out in exterior matters, easily loses the interior fear of God, which is its only real strength. Continual exterior distractions make a man forget what is within him, and he thinks of everything except his own soul. He is so engrossed by the toils of the way that he forgets the final object towards which he should tend. Thus, ceasing to seek only for God, (which was the end he had first proposed to himself,) he has no time for reflection, and is heedless of the graces he loses or the faults he commits. In this way Ezechias did not think he was sinning when he showed all his treasures and perfumed chambers to the King of Babylon.* (Isaiah xxxix. verse 2.) *And yet God made him see, by the slavery to which He condemned his children, that an action he had thought allowable was, in reality, a very grave fault.*" (Greg. Pastor, p. 1, cap. 4.)

This holy Pope, having thus shown how dangerous is this spirit of distraction, proposes the following remedies, quoted by Dom Bartholomew in his book: "*To enable a pastor to fulfil all his various functions without hurting his own soul, he must, being filled with the fear and love of God, apply himself every day to meditation on the Holy*

Scriptures, and strive to find, by the salutary warnings of God's word, a renewal of holy desires, interior vigilance, and that wise circumspection which must regulate our whole lives. For it is not believable how quickly our minds become dissipated by constant intercourse with men. Therefore, as we are thus continually weighted and drawn downwards by these exterior occupations, we must labour continually to raise ourselves by the study and meditation of holy things." (Stim. Past., cap. 4. Greg. Past., part 2, cap. 11.)

St. Augustine teaches us the same thing in a celebrated passage, which we will here give in its entirety, because Dom Bartholomew wished all pastors to weigh it well, as it shows us clearly that, whether in solitude or amidst the arduous duties of the pastoral charge, we must apply ourselves to meditation on the word of God by a spirit of piety and prayer. This great saint writes:

" There are three modes of life among Christians: those who are at rest; those who are in action; and the third, which is a mixture of the two. We must not live so quiet and retired a life as to prevent our thinking of serving our neighbour, nor give ourselves up so entirely to active duties as to omit to nourish ourselves with the word of God. All wish to know the truth, the contemplation of which is the portion of those who lead a tranquil life. But one cannot wish to be raised to an important charge in the Church, although such charges are necessary for the guidance of the people of God; and even when one may guide them aright, it is not a thing to be desired. Thus, the love we have for the truth would lead us to seek a holy repose, but the necessity laid upon us by charity obliges us sometimes to receive such a charge. If such a burden be not laid upon us, we should occupy ourselves entirely with searching for truth; but if it be laid upon us, we should bear it as a necessary obligation imposed upon us by charity. But even then we must beware lest we deprive ourselves

altogether of the sweetness which we experience by meditation on the word of God, for fear that, not being sustained by this celestial food, we should sink under the weight of our labours." (St. August. de Civ. Dei, lib. 19, cap. 19.)

"We ought continually to raise our hearts to God," adds Dom Bartholomew, "and expose them to the rays of His light, so that our prayer should kindle a fire in our souls, from whence a heat may come forth which will spread over all our actions. We must strive to procure this peace by every possible effort, and ask it of God with many sighs, so that amidst this crowd of affairs and continual distractions, our minds may remain always quiet and calm, and preserve their liberty and vigour. That is why St. Paul in the Acts, exhorting bishops, says, '*Attendite vobis et universo gregi*' (Acts xx. verse 28); that is, first watch over yourselves, and then you will be able to watch over the whole flock. Woe to you, O pastor of the Church, if, leaving off prayer by degrees, and then the knowledge of yourself and of your duties, you begin to be indifferent to your faults, and to have less and less scruple about certain things, which in reality you ought to have. Instead of this, you should continually be asking pardon of God for your negligences, and imploring His light to avoid them in future. Perhaps the cause of David's fall was that he had relaxed, little by little, in self-examination and the practices of piety." (Stimul. Pastor., cap. 4.)

St. Bernard was so afraid that Pope Eugenius, being overwhelmed with exterior business, should forget the care of his own soul, that he wrote to him as follows:

"*It is not long ago that you enjoyed with God the delights of His Holy Spirit. You cannot so soon have forgotten them, and I feel sure that you still feel their loss. A recent wound always gives pain. I should fear nothing so much for you as that kind of indifference and false peace which sometimes* arises after a deprivation of some great good. When a wound has been neglected, it often becomes incurable, and therefore insensible, for great pain cannot last. It must necessarily diminish, either by being cured, or because by long habit one ceases to feel it. The dissipation and distractions of your present position were at first insupportable to you. But, little by little, you get accustomed to them; the yoke becomes less heavy; then it feels light; very soon it does not weigh upon you at all; till at last you begin to like and find pleasure in it. Thus, by an insensible progress, one falls into hardness of heart, and from that abyss to a feeling of disgust for, and aversion to holy things. Therefore, I have always feared, and I still fear for you, that, postponing to find a remedy for these distractions, and no longer feeling them to be a burden, you should be plunged into an indifference from which it may be impossible to draw you out. I repeat what I have said: I very much fear that amidst this crowd of worldly occupations, which are, as I know, forced upon you, and as you see no way out of them, your soul may become accustomed to the turmoil, and so hardened to it that you may lose, little by little, the feeling of wholesome fear and sorrow. It would, of course, be more prudent of you to withdraw yourself from it all for a time, rather than suffer yourself to be dragged into a state which is the very last you would desire to be in. You ask me, in what state? I reply, that of hardness of heart. Do not go on asking me what that hardness means. For if the very thought of it does not fill you with fear, you are already arrived at that state. It is only a hardened heart which has no horror of itself, because it is dead to all feeling. A man thus hardened is never saved, unless God, by a miracle of mercy, does to him what the prophet speaks of in Ezechiel xi. verse 9: 'I will take away the stony heart out of their flesh, and will give them a heart of flesh.' What, then, is this stony heart? It is a heart which is never *touched by compunction; which is never softened by feelings of piety; which is never moved by prayers; which will not yield to threats; which will not correct itself; but, on the contrary, is all the more hardened under the rod of chastisement. He is ungrateful towards God for all the benefits he has received; disobedient to all the counsels given; and deaf to all reprimands or judgments. He is without shame in dishonest things; without fear in danger. He is inhuman in human things, and rash in divine ones. He forgets the past, neglects the present, and does not foresee the future. He only remembers in the past the injuries he has received; he thinks of the present time only to lose it; he only looks to the future to avenge himself. And to sum up, in one word, all that can be said of so terrible a misfortune, a hardened heart is one that fears neither God nor men. This is the abyss into which your unhappy occupations will drag you at last, if you continue as you have begun, to give yourself up entirely to them, neglecting those safeguards which are necessary to the salvation of your own soul."* (St. Bernard de Consid., lib. 1, cap. 42.)

St. Bernard goes on to exhort the Pope to apply himself diligently to prayer, and to meditation on the word of God. He reminds him: "*That he must work hard to know himself. That he must consider before God what he is according to nature, according to the exalted rank he held in the Church, and according to his way of life; so as to draw down upon his soul the grace of God, and to make his piety as remarkable as his dignity.*" (*Bernard de Considera.*, lib. 2, c. iv.)

It is easy to see that these instructions, though applied by the holy fathers to ecclesiastics and pastors, are equally valuable to all the faithful. For if pastors are to dread "*hardness of heart,*" even in the midst of the holiest functions, how much greater must be the danger of ordinary people amidst the distractions of secular business, unless they guard themselves by prayer, exercises of piety, and meditation on the word of God, as far as their occupations and worldly engagements will permit? If there be no affairs so urgent as to prevent their taking daily what is necessary for the support of their bodies, how much stronger a reason is there to obtain from God what is equally needful for the life of their souls? And this can easily be done, not by interrupting their occupations, if they be good and Christian, but by sanctifying them. For if they are careful to offer them to God, remembering His presence, with the intention of pleasing Him, and offering up their hearts to Him by short ejaculatory prayers, (thus following the advice of St. Paul: "*Whether you eat or drink, or whatsoever else you do, do all to the glory of God,*" 1 Cor. x. verse 31,) all their exterior occupations not only will not turn them away from God, but will help them to hold converse with Him, and so far from hindering their petitions, their whole lives will become one prayer.

Thus St. Augustine taught his flock: "*My brethren,*" he says, "*David assures us in the Psalms that he praised God all the day long. But you will say, How can we do this? And I answer, That you can if you will. Whatever you do, do it well, and you will thus always praise God. When you chant the Psalms in the church, you praise God; not because His praises are in your mouth, but because they are in your heart. When you have left the church, if you go to your meals, be temperate, and then you will still be praising God. If you go to your usual business, each one according to his state of life, deceive no one, and you will praise God. If you have fields or grounds, do no wrong, and have no lawsuits with any one, and so again will you praise God. Thus, by acting in a just and Christian manner throughout the day, you will praise God during the whole day.*" (St. Augustine, in Psalm xxxiv., in fine.)

We have remarked in the life of our holy archbishop with how much exactitude and zeal he gave himself to prayer and to meditation on the word of God, according to the advice of these great saints. And as he felt that this spiritual and interior life as bishop and pastor was the source of all his strength, we will now see what he taught about the manner of instructing his people.

CHAPTER V.

OF THE OBLIGATION LAID UPON PASTORS TO INSTRUCT THEIR PEOPLE, AND PREACH TO THEM THE WORD OF GOD.

St. Gregory the Great, describing a perfect bishop, says, not only that he should be raised above all others, by his love of meditation and his spirit of prayer, but also that he should devote himself specially to the instruction of his people. According to this holy Pope, prayer and the preaching of the word are inseparable: one brings down light from heaven, while the other communicates it. For the pastor can only give what he has himself received, and he ought to receive abundantly, so that out of the plenitude of his graces he may be able to enrich others without impoverishing himself. Thus Dom Bartholomew says: "It is needful that a bishop, according to the word of St. Chrysostom, should be entirely filled with the fire which Jesus Christ came to kindle in the earth, and which the Holy Spirit has brought from heaven. He must be as the light and the sun of his diocese, which illumines all and warms all. He must be occupied incessantly in gaining souls for God, preaching continually both by word and example. Thus the Apostle teaches us in his Epistle to Timothy: *'Attend unto reading, to exhortation, and to doctrine;'* and again: *'Take heed to thyself and to doctrine; be earnest in them. For in doing this thou shalt both save thyself and them that hear thee.'* (1 Tim. iv. verses 13 and 16.) We see also that it is written in the Psalms: '*I am appointed king by Him over Sion, His holy mountain, preaching His commandment.*' (Psalm ii. verse 6.)

"What do you say to this, cowardly and idle pastors, who have shown so much zeal in raising yourselves to the dignity of preachers of the Gospel, and yet so much lukewarmness and negligence in fulfilling this duty? Jesus Christ said that He had come to preach, and you say that you cannot fulfil the other duties of your position and prepare sermons. Yet the holy doctors, who are our spiritual fathers,—St. Gregory (Pope), St. Ambrose, St. Augustine, and the rest,—found no difficulty in combining both duties. They governed their dioceses, and yet found time to instruct their people. Moreover, they managed to enrich the whole Church with their marvellous writings. If you really be too much occupied to attend to everything, give up part of your business to others, but reserve to yourself the preaching to and instructing of your people. For so you are ordered to do by the Fourth Council of Carthage, where St. Augustine himself was present, when it is said: '*That the bishop should not take care himself of the widows, and orphans, and strangers, but give them in charge to his archdeacon or deacon; and that he should not occupy himself with his temporal affairs, but give all his time to prayer and preaching the word of God.*' (Concil. Carthag. 4, cap. 17, canon. 20.) The Fathers of the Council here teach us a great truth, which they had themselves learned from the apostles, when they say in the Acts, regarding the distribution of the alms of the Church: '*It is not reason that we should leave the word of God and serve tables. Wherefore, look ye out among you seven men of good reputation, full of the Holy Ghost and wisdom, whom we may appoint over the business. But we will give ourselves continually to prayer and to the ministry of the word.'* (Acts vi., verses 2, 3, 4.) Therefore, if the apostles preferred prayer and preaching to the care of the poor, the widows, and orphans, how much more would they have preferred them to lawsuits and worldly occupations? What is more unworthy of a bishop, than to be absorbed in secular business, and to be unable to give any time to prayer or meditation on the word of God, so as to enable himself to instruct his people? 'But,' they say, 'we give them preachers, who do this duty far better than we could.' That is not the opinion of the Fathers, who showed clearly how much they preferred a bishop's preaching to that of a simple priest, when they say, in the Second Council of Seville, held in 1692, *'It is not allowable for a priest to teach or exhort the people in presence of his bishop.'* (Council Hispal. 2, can. 7.) And even if it should happen that a bishop should have less knowledge and science, and more difficulty in expressing himself, it is still an undoubted fact that the word of a chief pastor has a force and a power of conviction which no other can have; just as a mother's milk is better for her child than that of a nurse, although it may be less good in quality." (Stim. Pastor.)

It appears by these words of Dom Bartholomew that when he uses the term "preaching," he does not mean merely set sermons, but all the instructions he may give to his people, whether in the pulpit, or in a more familiar, short, and simple way, which is often more useful and more proportioned to the intelligence of the lower orders. Therefore he considered that no bishops could be excused from this duty owing to any natural defect, such as want of voice, memory, or strength of body, because they can imitate St. Leo, or St. Peter Chrysologus, or St. Bernard, and many others of the Fathers, whose exhortations often did not last a quarter of an hour, or even less; and call to mind that St. Gregory the Great, when very old and infirm, still did not think himself dispensed from instructing his people: while St. Augustine in his old age, after having spoken for about ten minutes, concluded with these words: "*Be faithful, my children, in practising the few duties I have mentioned to you. For an old man should preserve not only gravity but brevity in his discourses.*" (Aug. Dom. 1, post. Oct. Epiph., serm 1.) The Council of Trent likewise orders pastors "*to instruct their flocks briefly and clearly.*" *Cum brevitate et facilitate.* (Concil. Trid., Sess. 5, cap. 2, de reform.)

Therefore the archbishop considered, (according to his own practice,) that a bishop ought to perform no principal functions of his charge without some little exhortation, however short and simple it might be. For a few words from a bishop who loves his flock, and who speaks out of the abundance of his heart, being strengthened by his dignity and his example, would unquestionably have more effect than a long sermon preached by any one else.

Thus it was said of Dom Bartholomew himself, that his words were words of fire, that they penetrated the very hearts of his hearers, and that when he had discovered the reigning faults or abuses of any particular place or congregation, he showed such an insight into the evil and its remedy, and so diversified his instructions according to the characters and qualities of his hearers, that each one believed that the prelate could see what was passing at the bottom of his heart, and fancied that the archbishop was preaching only for him; thus verifying the words of St. Chrysostom, that the only way to guide souls is by preaching, which is the real remedy for all evils. He writes: "*Those who treat the human body have many and various remedies: they have many different instruments; they have a kind of food on purpose for invalids;*

while often change of air alone will restore a man to health; and sometimes a wholesome sleep will remove all difficulty from the case. But this variety of remedies does not exist with us. After the example given by our actions, the art of treating and curing souls consists but in one point, and that is, to know how to apply instruction by the word. This powerful weapon takes the place of medicines and all other remedies. It is thus that we can raise the soul of one who is depressed; that we can confound the proud; that we can retrench what is superfluous; that we can supply what is wanting; and that we can touch upon all the other points which contribute to the cure of the soul." (Stim. Past., p. 93. St. Chrys. de Sacerd., lib. 4, c. 3.)

For this same reason St. Gregory compares "*a church without a bishop to a barren field which, having no one to water it, remains dry and sterile.*" (Greg., lib. 4, epistle 37.) "*But,*" he adds, "*when a bishop has been appointed, it is like a stream which, spreading on all sides, gives fertility to the ground, and brings forth fruits and flowers in human souls, through the celestial source from which flows the preaching of the word.*"

"You will perhaps say," (writes our holy prelate,) "that you have been diligent in instructing your flock, but that you see little or no result. St. Bernard will answer your objection, as he did Pope Eugenius: '*You think that you cannot be useful to your people, but yet they are your charge, and you cannot hide their wounds. You think it is labour lost, and are persuaded that they are incurable. But do not be discouraged; God requires you to treat this sick man, but He does not say that you will cure him. 'Take care of him,' says the Gospel. St. Paul also says, 'I have laboured more abundantly than all'* (1 Cor. xv. verse 10); *but he does not say, 'I have brought forth more fruit,'—only 'I have laboured more.' And the same apostle tells us that we shall be rewarded, not according to our success, but to our work: 'And every man shall receive his own reward, according to his own labour.'* (1 Corinth. iii. verse 8.) *Think only of doing your best, and what depends upon you, and do not trouble about the rest. God will be very well able to do without you what depends on Him alone. Take care to plant, to water, to cultivate, to watch, and you will have fulfilled your duty. As for giving the increase, that is God's affair, and not yours, and He will give it when it pleaseth Him. So that if He does not vouchsafe it, you will lose nothing thereby. Your reward is assured, for it is written in Holy Scripture, that God 'renders to the just the wages of their labours.'* (Wisdom x. verse 17.) *Dispense, then, the bread of heaven without negligence. Recollect that you will only have to give account for the one talent which has been entrusted to you. If you have received much, give freely; if you have received little, give of that little. For he who is not faithful in little things, will not be so in great ones. Give all you have, because it will be required of you, even to the uttermost farthing. Believe me, that your duty and peace of conscience depend on the fidelity with which you have fulfilled these two obligations: to dispense the word of God, and to give a good example. Nevertheless, if you are wise, you will add a third, which is, love of prayer. These three things are necessary to a pastor—preaching, action, and prayer; but the greatest of all is prayer. For, as action bears out the word, so prayer draws down the grace which forms and animates both.*" (St. Bern., epistle 201.)

St. Gregory again speaks of the advantage of the bishop's preaching, in these words: "*The tongue of the bishop is the remedy which cures the good, and the dart which pierces the wicked. It should reprove the proud, appease those who are angry, excite the negligent, kindle fresh love in the lukewarm, strengthen the weak, soften those whose souls are filled with bitterness, and console all who are disposed to give way to distrust and discouragement.*"

This same truth, which Dom Bartholomew so earnestly recommended, was equally insisted upon and diligently practised by St. Charles. They had both learnt it, not only from the Fathers and from tradition, but also from the Council of Trent, which expressly says, in two different places, that *"preaching is the principal function of a bishop."*

It is remarked in the life of St. Charles, that when very young, and employed by his uncle, the Pope, in the government of the whole Church, he always practised preaching, though he had a slight difficulty in speaking, and continually tried to induce all the cardinals who were bishops to do the same. And it is mentioned, that having gone to take possession of his cathedral at Milan, during the life-time of Pius IV., and having preached in the middle of Mass, the Pope expressed great joy at his having done so, and said before every one: "*That he was himself obliged to preach in his quality of Sovereign Pontiff, and that all the cardinals and bishops who had the care of souls were compelled to nourish them with the word of God.*"

CHAPTER VI.

HOW DOM BARTHOLOMEW LABOURED TO SHOW THE NECESSITY OF BISHOPS RESIDING IN THEIR DIOCESES. — THAT HIS OPINIONS WERE IN EXACT CONFORMITY WITH THOSE OF ST. CHARLES.

Although preaching the word of God is one of the principal functions of a bishop, its utility depends on several other things, and specially on the fact that a bishop should reside in his diocese. We have seen how Dom Bartholomew laboured to bring about a decision to this effect at the Council of Trent, and how he succeeded, in spite of the most strenuous opposition on the part of the non-residents. He was, in fact, so convinced of the necessity of this principle, that, in writing his book, he presupposes that the bishop shall be resident in his diocese, unless he were obliged to leave it for a time for the benefit of the whole Church, or some other urgent reason. Therefore, among the shortcomings of bishops he does not allude to such as are absentees from their dioceses, and who, abandoning the flocks entrusted to them by God, take pleasure in worldly business or amusements, because he considered it was not worth while to represent the duties of the episcopacy to men who, as he said, "*seem to have forgotten that they are bishops at all.*" (Stim. Past., p. 15.)

But here again we must draw our reader's attention to the great conformity which exists between his feelings on the subject and those of St. Charles. For he left the government of the whole Church, in which he had been employed by his uncle the Pope, in order to go and reside in his diocese. And it is recorded in the cardinal's life, that having once in his absence sent his vicar-general, Ormanetto, to Milan, that wise and experienced priest wrote him word: "*That what he had given him to do exceeded his strength, and that it seemed to him impossible that a church should be well governed without the presence of its proper pastor, for this grace was reserved to the bishop;*" which gave St. Charles a still greater zeal for residence.

He showed the same admirable sentiments when Pope Pius V., at the commencement of his pontificate, wanted to insist on his remaining with him to help him in the government of the Church. For St. Charles publicly declared: "*That if the Pope forced him to remain in Rome, he should renounce his cardinalate, as he considered that the salvation of souls was infinitely preferable to all the honours and dignities of this world.*" (Giussano, lib. 2, chap. 2.)

In the same way, whenever he met any bishops who were habitually absent from their sees, he wrote to the Pope to compel them to reside; and one day, when he was exhorting a cardinal, who was a bishop, to return to his church, and this cardinal replying, "That his bishopric was a very small one, and easily administered by his vicar-general, St. Charles answered: *"That if there were but one soul in his diocese, that soul needed the presence of its pastor."* (Giussano, lib. 8, chap. 13.)

CHAPTER VII.

HOW PASTORS SHOULD SET A GOOD EXAMPLE BY THE REGULATION OF THEIR HOUSEHOLD AND SERVANTS.—OPINIONS OF DOM BARTHOLOMEW AS TO THE VISITATION OF BISHOPS.

The first thing incumbent on a bishop who finds himself called by God to the government of His Church is, according to Dom Bartholomew, to regulate his person, his household, and all that surrounds him, so that his house should be a model of virtue, and that people should see in his actions what he preaches in his words. Our archbishop copied his rules from St. Gregory, who speaks in these terms: *"A bishop should excel all others in the practice of virtue, so that his holy life should be as a living voice, teaching men how they should love and serve God, and that his flock should be led as much by his personal character as by his words. As he is bound to show to men the most perfect way, so must he equally be to them a model of evangelical perfection. For words have far more weight when they are borne out by deeds, and it is far easier to obey when men see you practise yourself what you preach."* (Greg. Past., pag. 2, cap. 3.) But as the interior life of a bishop is better known to God than to men, he ought to show his mind by the regulation of his household, and of all those who are connected with him.

Dom Bartholomew lays great stress upon this, and quotes the important advice given by St. Bernard to Pope Eugenius, in the following words: *"You must not have any one about your person whose habits and morals are unknown to you, lest you should be the last to hear of the scandals going on in your house, which I have known to happen to many good people. You must leave to others particular offices and employments, but you are bound to watch yourself over the discipline of your house, and not leave it to others, or trust to any one but yourself. If you observe any insolence in word or deed among your servants, correct it at once, for impunity is the mother of boldness in wrong-doing, and leads to every kind of excess. The ornaments of a bishop's house should be holiness, modesty, and honesty. The discipline established in it is the guardian of those virtues. If the priests who are ranked among your upper servants are not more wise, recollected, and holy than the rest, they will become the laughing-stock of the whole world. Do not suffer for a moment that anything in the countenance, manner, or dress of those about you should shock modesty or respectability. Being a bishop as you are, teach the other bishops not to have in their court those smart little pages of noble birth, all frizzed and dressed up, because it is not fitting to see such marks of worldly vanity in persons who are about the pontiffs of Jesus Christ."* (Bern. de Consider. lib. 4, c. 4.)

But with the necessary care which a bishop should take of his house and servants, a grave defect sometimes arises, which makes this virtue degenerate into a vice. For some, under the pretext of having an eye to everything in their households, instead of choosing a man of confidence, to whom they can entrust all minor matters, are always interfering themselves, and thus, being absorbed in a multitude of petty details, have no time for really serious duties.

Dom Bartholomew in this matter also follows the advice of St. Bernard to Pope Eugenius: "*Appoint a man in your household who shall order everything, and let every one be accountable to him alone. Choose him with care and discretion, and then trust in his fidelity, and give yourself entirely to the care of your own soul and of the Church of God. If you have some trouble in finding a man who is at once clever and faithful, give the preference to the one who is faithful. Even if you cannot find a very able man, I should advise you to bear with him rather than embark in this labyrinth of secular bothers. Recollect, our Lord had Judas for His procurator. What is more disgraceful in a bishop than to see him anxious about his furniture and all the little details of his house, spying into everything, suspicious of every one, and who is angry and put out if the least thing should be broken or missing? I know of some, (to their shame be it spoken,) who every day of their lives go into the smallest expense incurred in their household, and register everything, and insist upon all accounts being laid before them, down to the smallest farthing. It was not thus that the Egyptian Pharao behaved, when he left the whole care of his house to Joseph, not even knowing what he had. Let a Christian blush not to trust a Christian. Here is a pagan who trusted implicitly in the honesty of his slave, and although he was a stranger, he entrusted all his goods to him. It is a strange thing that bishops think they have only too many people fit to be entrusted with the care of souls, and yet that they can find no one to whom they like to confide their temporal goods. Verily, they show discernment and wisdom in this, that they esteem little things so much, and great ones so little. And this shows us clearly that we care for our own losses far more than for those of Jesus Christ. We give ourselves no end of trouble to weigh each day's expenses, and are indifferent to the evils which afflict the flock of Jesus Christ. We dispute and reason with our steward on the number of loaves which he has bought, and the price of meat; and we have rarely any time left to speak to our priests about the disorders and sins of the people. If our horse falls, we raise him instantly; but when a soul falls, no one gives himself the trouble to pick him up. I am not surprised that we take so little care of others, as we do not take any heed of our own falls, although they are continual. About all these wretched little questions of household expenditure we are troubled and worried, and cannot help showing how they affect us. But would it not be more reasonable to be anxious about the loss of our souls? Why do you not rather suffer yourself to be defrauded, as St. Paul says? I conjure you, therefore,—you who are to teach others,—to instruct yourself, and to learn, if you have not already done so, to esteem more what you are than what you possess. Let all these transitory matters, which you cannot retain if you would, pass outside. The stream by its constant flow makes a deep hollow in the earth; in the same way the worry of temporal business undermines the soul which is absorbed by it. Therefore I advise you to wash your hands altogether of these sort of worries. Make up your mind to ignore many things, to dissimulate others, and to forget a good many."* (St. Bern. de Consid., lib. 4, cap. 6.)

If we compare this passage with the one we have before quoted, we shall see that the saint knew how to steer between these two extremes: one of which would be, if a bishop gave up the care of his house and all that he had to his servants, without troubling whether they were good or bad, and without watching over their morals and conduct, which would be a great fault; and the other, if he occupied himself so much with all those petty cares as to neglect his own soul and the souls of others, which would be a still more serious evil.

Dom Bartholomew steered clear of both these vices; for,

as we have seen, he appointed Father John of Leyra, a religious of his own order, whose wisdom and virtue he had long known, to be the steward of his household and the administrator of all his worldly affairs, so that he freed himself of all that sort of business. But at the same time he watched over his servants, striving that they should be irreproachable in conduct, and that his household might be a model and an example to all others. So that one of the authors of his life says: "That he visited first his own house, then his own city, and then the whole diocese."

Having dwelt on the obligation laid upon bishops to regulate their own households, the holy prelate next insists on the necessity of a regular visitation of their dioceses. This is the way in which he speaks: "Among the duties of a bishop, there is none greater than that of visitation. It is like the soul of his episcopal character, for by it the bishop communicates his presence and his charity to all the body of his diocese, and pours out the graces and blessings of heaven on all those who form its members. As the sun in its course fills the earth with a light and heat which vivify every living thing, so a bishop in his visitation enlightens and animates all by his exhortations, his tenderness, and his remonstrances. He thus finds out for himself the real character and conduct of his priests; he strengthens the good; rouses the negligent; corrects the bad; perfects what is praiseworthy; stops disorders and scandals; appeases divisions; consoles the afflicted; relieves the poor; and in fact, in a thousand different ways comes to the assistance of the Church, which is his spouse, and that with a tenderness, a vigilance, and an authority, which no other visitor whom he might delegate could possibly have, and which can only emanate from a person of his character and position." (Stim. Past., cap. 1.)

It was in these earnest terms that Dom Bartholomew recommended to all prelates this important episcopal function. His own conduct in this respect has been fully reported in this biography: and everywhere we see his invincible courage; the zeal and devotion with which he entered into every circumstance connected with each mission; his prudence in dealing with difficult cases, and in selecting worthy pastors for the most neglected districts; above all, the admirable mixture in him of firmness and decision, with that sweetness and wisdom which are the most powerful auxiliaries in the task of winning souls.

CHAPTER VIII.

THE HOLY PRELATE PROVES HOW PASTORS SHOULD FOLLOW THE RULES OF JESUS CHRIST, AND OF THE APOSTLES AND SAINTS, WITHOUT LISTENING TO THE JUDGMENTS OR LAX SPIRIT OF THE AGE.

St. Gregory of Nazianzum said that he had drawn down great evils and great persecutions upon himself "*because in all things he had thought of God alone.*" This disposition, which is not merely a merit, but the source of all virtue, was strikingly exemplified in the life of the holy bishop of whom we are writing. He adopted himself, and gave to others, the rule of following God according to the example of Jesus Christ and His saints, and not to trouble oneself with the opinions and judgments of men. This is how he speaks on that subject in his book: "St. Bernard teaches us that the purity of intention of a pastor consists in seeking only the glory of God and the salvation of his people. It is a small matter if we are considered good in the judgment of men, especially in such miserable times as these; but what we must seek after is to be holy in the sight of God. Remember this true saying, that what is true and just is ordinarily approved of by very few people, while the greater number praise what is bad and false. All the Jews cried out, '*Not this Man, but Barabbas;*' that is, Barabbas was worth more than Jesus Christ. The holy Precursor at the same time said of the Saviour, '*Behold the Lamb of God.*' In whom, then, are we to believe? In one man, or in the many? Therefore, let us not follow the opinions of the majority of mankind, but rather those who differ from them entirely, and who often appear eccentric or paradoxes. We must judge of things as they are in themselves, and not according to the abuses and the false maxims of the age in which we live. That is what made St. Thomas say: '*That if we listen to what men say, we shall never do anything good. The Wise man says: 'He that observeth the wind shall not sow; and he that considereth the clouds shall never reap.'* (Eccles. xi. verse 4. St. Thom., super Matt. xi.) The only model which can keep us from corruption must be Himself incorruptible, namely, Jesus Christ. Therefore, in the actions which belong specially to a bishop who wishes to live according to the Gospel, he must consult no one. *Super actionibus quæ manifestè pertinent ad Evangelicum Episcopum, non oportes considere quemquam.* If any one advises you to the contrary, believe that he has lost his wits. *Insanire puta, si quis aliud consulerit.* Those who do not see this truth are infatuated by intercourse with, and love of the world. God has honoured you," he continues, "with the episcopal dignity, so that you might fight manfully against the immorality, the depravity, and the bad habits which the age has sanctioned and tries to make lawful, but which David calls, '*Vanities and lying follies.*' (Psalm xxxix. verse 5.) You cannot exterminate these follies from the earth except by maintaining strongly the examples and instructions of the apostles. You ought to be very glad to pass as extravagant in the eyes of men, so as to be able to say with St. Paul, '*We are fools ; or*

Christ's sake, but you are wise in Christ.' (1 Corinth. iv. verse 10.) The Church has ordered, in the Fourth Council of Carthage, that bishops ought to have nothing at their table which speaks of the magnificence and luxury of the age, and that the same rule should apply to their furniture, and their whole house. But now-a-days, bishops declare, on the contrary, that all this outward pomp and show are necessary, in order that they may have that authority over the people which is needful to the performance of their charge. So that the ministers of Jesus Christ wish to be wiser and more prudent than Jesus Christ Himself. The Saviour sent men filled with His Spirit, but who were poor and humble like Him, to conquer the world; and yet now people fancy they should use the magnificence of the world, and conform themselves to its spirit, in order to triumph over it. But as David did not need Saul's armour to conquer Goliath, so, if we are true disciples of Jesus Christ, we shall not need worldly arms to overcome the world." *(Stim. Pastor., cap. 5 and 6.)*

Dom Bartholomew goes on to answer another objection: "Some people say, 'Beware of going to extremes: it is safer to walk in the common road.' Certainly, if the saints and those great bishops of antiquity had not done things which savoured of excess, and if their zeal had not led them into some extremes and apostolic singularities, they would never have been saints, nor would their names be in such honour, nor their memory in benediction throughout the whole Church. Far from us, then, be all customs and practices which are not conformable with the spirit and doctrine of the Gospel, and with the examples of the saints, for the words of Jesus Christ are immutable: *Every plant which My Heavenly Father hath not planted shall be rooted up.'* (Matt. xv. verse 13.) If some bishops who live in this manner appear singular and eccentric when compared with other bishops in this century, their conduct nevertheless should not be condemned either as singular or presumptuous. But those, on the contrary, who are bold enough to go against the maxims and examples of the saints, fall themselves into a criminal singularity, and into grave sins of pride. And what is more insupportable is, that they dare to say, that 'one must accommodate oneself to the age;' as if the spirit of Jesus Christ and the rules of the Gospel were to change with the times, and be subservient to the feelings and follies of men. Whereas, we ought to labour, on the contrary, to make all times conformable to the ordinances of the Church, and to reform all that may be defective in them by the immutable laws of the Holy Spirit. For it is flesh and blood, and not the Spirit of God, that has made our age incapable of the pure and holy virtue of the ancient Fathers. It is the human will, which is always striving to satisfy its desires, and thus finds a thousand defenders, and endless apparently good reasons to cloak and excuse itself. But the word of God and the rules of the saints remain firm and inviolable. They have not been established to change with the times, but to be immutable throughout all ages, and to submit and subject all things to them." *(Stim. Past., p. 26.)*

Dom Bartholomew here quotes the words of St. Gregory on the same subject: "*The high priest had twelve precious stones in his breast-plate, on which the names of the twelve patriarchs were inscribed. What is this a symbol of, but that the names of the saints should be always, as it were, written in our hearts, so that we may go over and over again in our memories their holy words and actions? For a prelate would be irreproachable in his conduct if he continually bore in mind the examples of the Fathers who have preceded him, striving always to follow in their steps, and to walk in the traces of those great saints.*" (Greg. Pastor., p. 2, cap. 2.)

Our archbishop was faithful in practising the rules laid down by this holy Pope. For no sooner had he entered his archepiscopal palace, than he called to remembrance the many holy bishops who had governed the church before him, and invoked their aid, imploring them to cast their eyes on him, and to obtain for him the grace to revive in his own person their holy conduct in the Church, that he might become the successor of their piety as well as of their see.

Father Louis of Grenada, speaking of this, writes: "Knowing the exact account which God would demand of him for the government of his diocese, he only thought of how he could best fulfil this arduous charge. Therefore, shutting his eyes to the abuses of the age, he looked back to the example of those holy bishops who had preceded him, and whose apostolic zeal shone in their lives, and by their miracles after their death. From these great lights he drew up the rules for his own conduct. He made the most minute researches in the libraries of Braga, to discover all the manuscripts which treated of the lives of his holy predecessors. And he composed a book, with long extracts drawn from St. Gregory, St. Bernard, and other Fathers of the Church, touching the virtues and duties of bishops, which he called '*Stimulus Pastorum.*'"

This disposition was equally engraved in the heart of his friend, the great St. Charles, who had no sooner arrived at Milan, than he took the great St. Ambrose, his predecessor, as his model. "And having laboured at the election of Gregory XIII. to the Chair of St. Peter, as being the most worthy of that dignity, the new Pope desired to have his advice respecting his administration; and St. Charles gave him at once St. Gregory's Pastoral and St. Bernard's Letters to Pope Eugenius, so that he might follow their teaching and example in the government of the whole Church. Later on, the plague broke out in Milan, and as he found that the priests were doubting whether or not to expose their lives to help the sick, St.

Charles collected all the extracts he could find from the Fathers of the Church on this subject, and among the rest, the Epistle of St. Denis of Alexandria, as reported by Eusebius; two letters of St. Cyprian, (one on the plague, and one on alms;) two homilies of St. Gregory of Nyssa; and the admirable Epistle of St. Augustine to Honoratus, on the 'Obligation of Pastors not to abandon their flocks;' and having had all these translated in the vulgar tongue, and afterwards printed, he placed them in the hands of every one, so that all might study those lessons of charity which each should have for his brethren, according to the old rules of the Church and of her greatest saints." *(Giussano, liv. 2, chap. 30.)*

Dom Bartholomew being filled with the same spirit, used to say that "if one could not imitate the saints in everything, it was, at any rate, most useful to set them before us continually as examples, either to excite us to doing more than we usually do, or to humble us by making us feel how immeasurably we fall short of their standard, even when men praise us as doing more than many others. St. Gregory writes: *"Bad prelates, instead of following the example of true pastors, in comparison of whom they would feel their own nothingness, turn their eyes, on the contrary, towards those who are worse than themselves, and so they imagine they are something good after all."* "But as for you," continues Dom Bartholomew, "do not cease striving to grow daily in virtue, until you become like unto St. Martin, St. Ambrose, and the other holy bishops of the Church of God." *(Stimul. Past., cap. 5.)*

This truth was so engraved in his heart and mind that even in his holiest actions he always thought he did much less than he ought, and was persuaded that on a similar occasion those great saints would have acted quite differently. Therefore, when some one complained that during the famine he retrenched the expenses of his household too much, so as to relieve a greater number of poor, he replied: "God forbid that I should be so blind as not to be convinced that if St. Martin, or St. Ambrose, or any of those holy bishops of old times, were to see my table to-day, whilst my people were dying of hunger, they would judge that I was doing far less than I ought." This was the judgment of this humble imitator of the saints on himself. But others held a widely different opinion. Father Louis of Grenada mentions that Dom Fernando Martinez, ambassador of the King of Portugal at the Council of Trent, used to say: "I do not know what St. Augustine, St. John Chrysostom, and other great bishops did in old times, but it seems to me impossible that their virtue should be more exemplary and christian than that of the Archbishop of Braga."

CHAPTER IX.

OF THE ZEAL WHICH PASTORS SHOULD SHOW IN OPPOSING THE SCANDALS AND DISORDERS OF THE AGE, AND IN LABOURING FOR THE CONVERSION OF SINNERS.

The spiritual zeal which inflames the hearts of God's true ministers makes them undertake the most difficult tasks, and remain firm and unshaken amidst all human opposition, when it is a question of rendering what is due to our Lord, and satisfying the obligations of duty.

Dom Bartholomew quoted the words of St. Gregory on this point: "*There are some pastors, not guided by the spirit of prudence, who, fearing to lose the good will of men, hesitate about speaking the truth. In that way they do not guard their flocks like shepherds, (as Jesus Christ teaches them,) but as mercenaries who, when they see the wolf coming, hide themselves and remain silent. When God complained of the* scandals of His people by the mouth of the prophet Jeremiah, He said: '*Thy prophets have seen false and foolish things for thee, and they have not laid open thy iniquity to excite thee to penance.*' (Lamentations ii. verse 14.) The pastors of the Church are frequently called prophets in holy writ, because they teach us that all present things are fleeting and transitory, and promise and prophesy to us future good. And God accuses them of false visions when they do not make sinners feel a horror of their lives, and when, by flattering instead of reproving them, they lure them into a false peace." (Greg. Past., p. 2, cap. 4.) Dom Bartholomew speaks strongly in the same sense: "It is necessary that he who wishes to save sinners should speak to them frankly words of truth and wisdom. Therefore, at the consecration of a bishop, when giving him the crozier, the Church says: '*Receive the pastoral staff, that you may employ it in correcting vices with charitable severity.*' And speaking of the duties of bishops, she adds: '*We order expressly all bishops to apply themselves to correcting the disorders of those who are subject to them, and particularly clerks, and to watch with care and prudence over the reformation of their habits, for fear that they should be accountable for the blood of souls; so that they may be able to say with St. Paul: 'That they are clear from the blood of all men.*' (Acts xx. verse 26.) St. Augustine writes: '*The gentleness which overlooks and fosters sin, not daring to reprove it, for fear of saddening those who commit it, is like the weakness of one who will not take a knife away from a child for fear he should cry, without considering that he may wound or kill himself with it. We rouse the lethargic by waking them, and exasperate madmen by binding them, and yet we love both. We only torment them because we care for them, and by giving them pain effect a cure.*' (Aug. in Psal. xxxiv. verse 23.) Ask then of God, O pastors of souls," continues Dom Bartholomew, "to give you the grace, so that it may be said of you what the prophet Micheas said of himself: '*I am filled with the strength of the Spirit of the Lord, with judgment and power, to declare unto Jacob his wickedness, and to Israel his sin.*' (Mich. iii. verse 8.) This was the disposition of St. Chrysostom, as recorded in his life, who, having lifted up his voice with episcopal courage against the scandals which existed among his clergy, condemning them by his own example, reproving them by his words, and striving to stop them in their downward course by just and legitimate punishments, drew down upon himself their hatred and aversion; and being overcome by persecution, after having suffered extreme cruelties, he actually lost his life in an exile brought upon him by his zeal for the reformation of the Church. It is of pastors such as these that the Son of God speaks: '*You shall be hated of all men for My name's sake.*'" (Matt. x. verse 22.)

Those who have written Dom Bartholomew's life relate that "when it was a question of reproving public or scandalous vices, he had no respect of persons. The great and the little were alike to him on this point. He looked upon them all as children of the Church, and considered that the same remedies should be applied to the same wounds, in the same way as doctors make no difference in their treatment of patients suffering from the same disease, whether they be princes or subjects. Even he was often heard to say that it was principally against the great people in this world that, according to the laws of God and the Church, the vigour of episcopal authority should make itself felt." And so that confessors should be filled with the same spirit, he wrote: "We order and exhort all confessors to act with perfect disinterestedness and an incorruptible liberty as regards their penitents: let them beware lest they spare them out of regard to their position or to any human consideration, and let them seek for nothing but their eternal salvation. They are as private preachers, who dispense to each the divine word, and who may gain many souls to God if they think only of their real spiritual welfare, and know how to acquit themselves worthily of their important ministry. We never ought," he continues, " to act with over-indulgence towards sinners, as St. Ambrose recommends to us in his commentary on those words of the Psalm: 'Have mercy on me according to Thy word' (Psalm cxviii. verse 58) : *'Though it be very necessary in the Church to have bowels of mercy, we must nevertheless be very careful to observe the laws of justice, lest those who by their sins have been deprived of the participation in the divine mysteries, should obtain, through the easy-going character of the priest, by a few tears, or a passing contrition, a communion which they should ask and labour for for a long time before it be granted to them. For when you treat an unworthy person with too great indulgence, you become an occasion of fall and ruin to many. For too great facility in the reconciliation of sinners becomes an occasion of fresh sin.'"*

CHAPTER X.

DOM BARTHOLOMEW SHOWS, BY THE EXAMPLE OF ST. GREGORY, WITH WHAT FIRMNESS BISHOPS SHOULD DEFEND THE CHURCH, AND MAINTAIN TRUTH AND JUSTICE.

One of the most important functions of the episcopate is the firmness with which prelates should maintain justice and truth as before God, without being carried away by promises, or allowing themselves to be intimidated by the threats of men. On this subject the holy prelate spoke in these terms: "Bishops often abandon the duties of their charge from weakness and indecision, and seeing that their relations and friends complain that they expose themselves

to the displeasure of the great in this world, they yield to
base and interested motives. But as for you, ask of God a
brave and constant heart, and one which will be immutably
fixed on all that He will require of you. Do not believe
those who try to persuade you of the contrary. Despise
their solicitations, however urgent they may be. You
have nothing either to lose or to hope for in this life; and
when it is a question of doing your duty, there is no man
on this earth of whom you should be afraid. For this
reason be firm and courageous, and at the same time wise
and circumspect, and think only of how you can best please
God and Him alone. For, as the prophet says: '*God hath
scattered the bones of those that please men.*' (Psalm lii.
verse 6.) St. Gregory the Great speaks also in these
terms: '*God reproaches pastors for their timidity by the
voice of His prophets, when He says:* '*They are dumb dogs,
not able to bark*' (Isaiah lvi. verse 10) ; *and again:* '*You
have not gone up to face the enemy, nor have you set up a
wall for the house of Israel, to stand in battle in the day of
the Lord.*' (Ezechiel xiii. verse 5.) *That is, you have not
resisted the powers of this world, or spoken up for the defence
of the Church. Going before the enemies of the Lord is, to
oppose the efforts of the wicked by zeal and the love of justice.*' (Greg. Past. 2, cap. 4.) '*The Holy Spirit teaches us
by the mouth of David:* '*They have trembled for fear when
there was no fear.*' (Psalm xiii. verse 5.) *For you will
often see a man who will make up his mind at first to defend
the truth courageously: but then, when he comes to think it
over, he recollects that he will thus irritate some person in
power; and so, shrinking from the anger of a man, he forgets that he will thus fall under the wrath of God Himself,
who is the Sovereign Truth.*' (Greg. Moral., lib. 7, cap. 11.)
'*It sometimes happens,*' continues that great Pope, '*that a
man will mistake his fear for humility, and that when fearing some temporal evil, he does not dare speak in defence of*

charity, and remains silent, he flatters himself that he is only following God's ordinance, by remaining subject to those who are above him.' (Greg. Moral., lib. 32, cap. 17.) For this reason St. Thomas remarks: '*That between the two extremes of timidity and boldness, it is more necessary to overcome the first than the second. For it is more difficult to repress timidity than to moderate boldness, because the dangers which result from the latter are sufficient to prevent its excess, whereas they only feed timidity by the thought of the serious evils which threaten it.*'" (St. Thomas 2, qu. 123, art. 6.) Dom Bartholomew excites bishops to arm themselves with courage and fortitude, by these words of the Wise man: "*Seek not to be made a judge,*" (that is, a head over the people of God,) "*unless thou have strength enough to extirpate iniquities; lest thou fear the person of the powerful, and lay a stumbling-block for thy integrity.*" (Eccle. vii. verse 6.)

Thus it was recorded of our holy prelate, that when certain great personages pressed him to grant them something which was contrary to right and justice, or what he considered his duty to God, he treated them always very civilly, but was inflexible in his refusal to do what they wished. And speaking of the firmness with which he was compelled to act in such matters, he said: "*He who does not listen to the words of truth and justice, which come from God, does not deserve to be listened to himself.*" St. Gregory exclaims: "*The just is bold as a lion, and remains as courageous and firm. The lion does not fear any other beast that may attack him, for he knows he is the strongest. In the same way, when the just sees himself attacked by men, he looks into his own heart, and remains firm in his own conscience, feeling sure to conquer in the end, for he only loves Him Whom no one can take from him, and in Whom alone is his confidence and strength. To despise all that is transitory, and to desire eternal goods alone, is the foundation of all true generosity. Thus the soul, which is lifted up above the earth, and whose treasure is in heaven, is, as it were, inaccessible and out of the reach of her enemies.*" (Greg. Moral., lib. 31, cap. 14.) The Pope continues: "*Sometimes we are left in peace if we do not give ourselves the trouble to oppose the injustice and violence of the bad. But if our souls are touched by a sincere wish of eternal good, if we look to the true light, if we burn with the flames of divine love, we ought, as far as our rank in the Church will permit, and the business in question demand, go before those who commit injustice, even when they do not seek us, to oppose their excesses and neutralise their efforts. For when they unjustly oppress those whom we love, they wound us ourselves, whatever veneration and respect they may show us.*" (St. Greg. Moral. lib. 31, cap. 14.)

We have seen in this history how this generosity of soul was manifested in our holy archbishop, not only during the council and his journey to Rome, but in the whole administration of his diocese, so that it was true of him what St. Gregory of Nazianzum said: "*That the true servant of God feared one thing only, and that was lest he should fear anything more than God.*" (St. Gregor. Nazianz., orat. 12.) Especially was this virtue shown in his struggle with the young king, Dom Sebastian, regarding the rights and liberty of his Church, in which he conquered by his courage and firmness. So true is it that nothing is more powerful in the minds of princes than a wise magnanimity in a great bishop; so that it was well said on another occasion: "*That when bishops were Ambroses, kings would become like Theodosius.*" For a prince will easily bear the opposition of a bishop in defence of his church, when his wisdom and consistency show that he is only actuated in his resistance by pure and disinterested zeal for God, with the sole fear of being found wanting in the obligations laid upon him by his pastoral charge. Another proof of this was given by his friend, St. Charles Borromeo. Some years after the death of this saint, Pope Clement VIII. having given the archbishopric of Milan to Cardinal Frederick Borromeo, his relation, the ministers of King Philip II. advised him to oppose the nomination, saying, that as the cardinal had been brought up in the school of St. Charles, he might in the same way interfere with the royal prerogatives in Milan. But that wise prince replied: *"Let him only be as holy as St. Charles, and I shall entirely approve of his maintaining as much as he wills the rights of his church."*

CHAPTER XI.

OF THE ZEAL WHICH BISHOPS SHOULD HAVE IN ADMITTING TO HOLY ORDERS, AND TO BENEFICES IN THE CHURCH, THOSE ONLY WHO WERE WORTHY OF SERVING HER.

If Dom Bartholomew was firm and inflexible in maintaining the rights of his church, he was not less so to procure worthy ministers for her service, and to drive away those whose only calls to the sanctuary were ambition and self-interest. St. Chrysostom teaches us that zeal for the beauty of God's house, and the banishing of those who can only dishonour and shame His service, are among the chief episcopal duties. *"If a bishop,"* he writes, *"prefers pleasing certain persons, (by admitting into the clerical body men who do not deserve it,) to saving his own soul, he will have God for an enemy instead of men, which would be the greatest of all misfortunes. But what is more, when once these men become priests, they cause endless scandals in the Church, and nothing but disorders and shipwrecks are the result. As then a bishop must bear the brunt of so much opposition, and do such unpopular acts for the public good, what ought to be the qualities of his soul? He must be grave, without being proud; he must be feared, and yet be moderate; he ought to have the authority of a man who commands, and yet be civil and amenable; he must be humble, and yet not weak; he must be strong and vigorous, and yet gentle. He ought to have all these virtues, so that he may remain master in the strife, and especially that he may with perfect liberty, and in spite of all opposition, only admit among the clergy worthy persons, and reject all those whom he considers unfit, even if the whole world were to conspire to constrain him to receive them. In a word, he must have for his only end and aim the glory of God and the edification of the Church, and act in all such matters neither by likes nor dislikes, neither by interest nor by favour."* (Chrysostom de Sacerd., lib. 3, c. 7.)

Those who have written the life of our holy archbishop have mentioned a curious incident connected with this subject. There were several persons of rank in his diocese who had church patronage. They used to name the curates, and present them to the archbishop, who was bound to receive them if they were found capable. But very often the last thing these patrons thought of in their choice was virtue or merit. They made use of their interest to reward those who were in their service, by giving these cures to some of their relations. They insisted that their nomination should suffice, and that the bishop must accept any one they presented. This abuse had gone on for many years, because their high rank gave them boldness, and that previous bishops were too timid to oppose their wishes. But no sooner was Dom Bartholomew promoted to the archbishopric, than the whole face of things was changed. He began by refusing every man who had been nominated, as he found they were entirely incapable and unworthy. He represented to these patrons that "as they had altogether mistaken the character of the men required, it was his duty to reform their choice. That their eternal welfare and nothing less was at stake. That there was no greater crime than to introduce a mercenary into the flock of Jesus Christ, and a murderer of souls in the place of a true pastor. That if in this matter they acted according to the maxims of this world, without regarding the judgments of God, it was his duty to behave as a bishop, and to fear the terrible account which would be required of him at the last day." At first this proceeding on his part was considered intolerable. The patrons were furious, and accused him of refusing to give the livings to their protégés that he might bestow them on his own. But after a time, seeing that when they presented really worthy subjects to him, he received them with joy, they became convinced that his firmness in this matter arose neither from bad temper nor self-interest, but solely from the sincerity of his zeal. And so their anger and unjust complaints were changed by degrees into respect and admiration for his virtue.

Here is what he wrote in his book on this subject: "The first duty of a bishop is to give good pastors to his church. He ought to have continually before him these words of the apostle: '*Impose not hands lightly upon any man; neither be partaker of other men's sins.*' (1 Tim. v. verse 22.) Therefore, when a cure falls vacant, say to God with the apostles: '*Thou, Lord, who knowest the hearts of all men, show whether of those two Thou hast chosen.*' Thou knowest, O my God, that in this election I wish to have no respect for flesh and blood, but that my only wish is to choose a priest who shall be faithful to Thee, and a physician who may heal the souls whom Thou hast purchased with Thy Blood. Remember what is written in the Gospel, that our Lord passed all the night in prayer before He chose His twelve apostles. O, how deplorable is the negligence of the pontiffs of Jesus Christ, if, when they see whole flocks in their diocese abandoned to the wolves, that is, to carnal and ignorant pastors, more fit to destroy souls than to heal them, they do not weep and sigh at so grave a scandal, even if they cannot remedy it. Should we not do our very utmost to prevent so great an evil? But alas! *'how great is our blindness and insensibility,'* as St. Augustine exclaims, *'that we are only shocked at what we consider extraordinary things; and that for common and ordinary abuses, not only we feel no horror for them, but we often give them up, though in so doing we commit grave crimes.'* (Aug. in Epist. ad Gal., cap. 4. verse 11.) Thus, we often see benefices given to men who are utterly unworthy of them, for no other reason but because it is the custom, and we have the habit of seeing it done. And yet is it not true that the pastor is for the Church, and not the Church for the pastor? For no one should give a living to a man to enrich him, but the cure should be given to one who can be of service to his flock. Just as when one chooses a doctor for the sick, one has their cure at heart, —not the advantage of the medical man. This is the source of endless evils and scandals, and especially where the distribution of benefices falls into many hands. St. Gregory the Great shows us in his letters with what care he sought for worthy pastors to fill up vacant churches. For having heard that there was at Syracuse a pastor of singular holiness, he wrote at once to the bishop to know *' if he were really what he was reported to be? and if so, if he would send him at once to Rome, so that he might appoint him bishop.'"* (Greg., lib. 2, epist. 26, 29, 30.)

Dom Bartholomew was so careful in this matter that, as we have seen in his visitations, he made a note of all the priests, and added a memorandum of the good or bad qualities of each, so that he might choose which amongst them were the most worthy to fill up the vacant churches.

CHAPTER XII.

THAT A BISHOP SHOULD CONDUCT HIMSELF IN A SPIRIT OF GENTLENESS, WITHOUT USING HIS AUTHORITY IN AN IMPERIOUS MANNER.—OF THE TENDERNESS AND CHARITY SHOWN BY DOM BARTHOLOMEW TO WIN SOULS.

It is a great thing for a bishop to have zeal against sin, courage in danger, and a disinterested vigilance never to admit an unworthy subject into the ranks of the clergy. But these qualities must be tempered by two others, namely, compassion and sweetness, without which they would degenerate into an excessive and immoderate severity. Dom Bartholomew shows this by again quoting the words of St. Gregory, who compares the soul of a bishop to the ark of alliance: "*The heart of a bishop*," he writes, "*is like the ark of the new alliance; and as formerly there was contained in the ark the tables of the law, the rod of Moses, and the pot of manna, so the bishop should bear in his heart the intelligence of the law, and the uprightness of justice, with the manna of sweetness, tenderness, and charity.*" (St. Greg. Past., part 2, cap. 6.)

Our archbishop further shows, by the same holy Pope, how this sweetness and gentleness are founded on the authority of the word of God, and on the example of the apostles themselves: "*There is naturally*," he says, "*an equality among men. But as vice or virtue makes them unequal, sin is the cause why the one should be subject to the other. And the providence of God, making use of this difference between them, has ordained that, not being able to* guide themselves, one should command, and the other obey. Those, then, who are appointed to govern, should not consider the superiority of their charge so much as their common human nature, and ought to rejoice, not that they are superiors, but that their government may be of use to others. We read in the Scriptures that God told Noah after the deluge that he was to make himself feared by all animals. He did not say that one man was to make himself feared by another, but only by animals, because it would be a pride contrary to nature if we wish to make ourselves formidable to one who is our equal. It is, however, necessary that those who command should be, to a certain degree, feared by those who obey; but this is only when they do not fear God, so that those who are not turned away from sin by fear of the judgments of God should be deterred at least by that of men. And when those who are in authority are thus feared by the bad, one may say that they do not impose fear on men so much as on animals, as they are only dreaded by those who, by their scandalous lives, have passed, as it were, from the nature of men to that of beasts. But if man easily becomes proud, even if there should be nothing in him to boast of, how much more easily will he become so when he sees himself in a position of authority and honour? To enable him, therefore, to use this power as he ought, he must, while exercising the duties of his charge, fight at the same time against this pride which his position inspires, so that, while considering all men as his equals, he should only raise himself above them by greater zeal against sin and the vices of the age.'" (Stim. Past., page 10. St. Greg. Past., part 2, cap. 6.) He then shows us an admirable example of the sweetness with which souls should be governed, in the conduct of the first apostles, St. Peter and St. Paul, "This union of gentleness and strength is admirably shown in the conduct of the first pastors. For St. Peter, to whom God had given the supremacy over the whole Church, seeing (as we read in the Acts), that Cornelius was a good man, and one who feared God, when he threw himself humbly at his feet, refused this mark of excessive respect, and said, lifting him up: 'Arise, I myself also am a man.' (Acts x. verse 20.) But when Ananias and Saphira fell into sin, he showed at once how his charge raised him above the rest. For having seen into the bottom of their hearts by the light of the Holy Spirit, he killed them by one or two words. Thus he showed that he possessed supreme authority in the Church, when it was necessary to avenge crime; although he considered himself one with his brethren who were good, and refused the honour they wished to pay him. In the same way, St. Paul, speaking to those who feared God, seemed to ignore that he was set over them, when he says: 'Not because we exercise dominion over your faith, but we are helpers of your joy, for in faith you stand.' (2 Corinth. i. verse 23.) As if he had said: 'We do not exercise dominion over your faith, for that is firm, and in that point we are alike.' He even seems to ignore that he was raised above his brethren, when he says to them: 'We became little ones in the midst of you.' (1 Thess. ii. verse 7.) And again : 'We are ourselves your servants, through Jesus Christ.' (2 Cor. iv. verse 5.) But when he finds a scandal to be redressed, he remembers that he is one in authority, and shows it by saying: 'What will you? Shall I come to you with a rod? or in charity and in the spirit of meekness?' (1 Cor. iv. verse 21.) Thus a man conducts himself wisely in a position of authority, when he governs in such a manner that his dominion is over vices rather than over his brethren. Even when he is compelled to resort to chastisement against the sinner, he should always temper it with charity, and his conduct should be so wise and moderate that the severity of a father should be mingled with the tenderness of a mother. He ought to make himself so loving and accessible to those under him, that they should not blush to disclose to him their most secret faults, so that when they are tempted, and find themselves agitated and troubled, they may have recourse to their pastor as a little child would throw himself on the bosom of his mother." (Greg. Past., ibid.)

Dom Bartholomew further wrote: "That he wished all pastors would imitate St. Bernard's charity, ' *Who, having reproved some one for a grave sin, and seeing that he did not amend, was overcome with sorrow and grief. And do not tell me,*' continues the holy doctor, '*that I ought to console myself because I have done all I could for that soul. It is just that which so greatly grieves me; because I see my son dead before my eyes, without having had it in my power to help him. For I did not think of saving my own soul by fulfilling my duty in this particular, but of saving his by bringing him back to God. And where is the mother who, seeing her son die after having done her utmost to save his life, thinks she ought to stop her tears because she could do no more to save him? If, then, a mother be inconsolable at the loss of one who has only passed through a temporal death, how can I console myself at seeing one whom I love as a son incurring voluntarily an eternal death, although I have striven so hard to procure eternal riches for him?*'" (St. Bernard, in Cantic., serm. 4, number 5.)

Those who have written the life of our holy prelate speak continually of the marvellous instances of his tenderness and charity towards sinners. On one occasion, finding himself in the house of a person who, he found, was leading a scandalous life, and who seemed quite hardened in his sin, he not only threw himself at his feet, but with his face bathed in tears, he took before him a severe discipline, to show him that he would bear the punishment of his sins upon himself, as if they were his own, and do penance for them: which proceeding touched this man so much that he threw himself in his turn at the archbishop's feet, saying he would submit to anything he ordered him to do, having realized the infinite obligation he was under to Jesus Christ who died for him, by the conduct of His faithful servant who, in imitation of his Lord, took upon himself voluntarily the suffering which his crimes had deserved.

Dom Bartholomew likewise thought that this gentleness and tenderness ought to lead pastors to take pleasure in explaining the reasons of their actions to those under them, either when they order them to do something, or when they think their conduct might give scruples to the weak. St. Gregory, whom he quotes again on this head, says: *" We are all brothers, and we have all the same King, who created us by His power, and has redeemed us by His Blood. Therefore we ought never to despise our brethren, however poor and humble they may be. St. Peter had received the keys of the kingdom of heaven, by which all that he bound or loosed was to be bound or loosed in heaven. He had walked on the sea; his shadow cured the sick; a word from him could kill sinners; his prayers brought the dead to life: and yet, when by a special revelation of the Holy Ghost, he went to Cornelius, the Gentile, and the faithful afterwards inquired of him why he had gone into a Gentile house, why he had eaten with them, and why he had baptized them, we see that this great saint, although he was first among the apostles, so full of grace, and so renowned by miracles, did not answer the faithful by alleging his power and right to do what he pleased, but goes carefully into all his reasons for so acting. He tells them all that happened to him: how he saw the mysterious sheet let down from heaven; how the Holy Spirit had commanded him to go with these Gentiles; and how the Paraclete had Himself descended upon them, even before he had baptized them; and thus he explained the whole matter to them. Now if, when his proceedings were called in question by the faithful, he had only considered his rank, and position, and authority in the Church, he might have answered them in such a way that his flock would not have dared to question him any more. But then certainly he would not have been a master of gentleness and humility. As it was, he satisfied them completely by his meek conduct; and to defend himself from their reproaches, he even cited witnesses of his acts, saying: 'And these six brethren went with me also.'* (Acts xi. verse 12.) *If, then, the prince of the apostles did not disdain to give an account of all he had done to the faithful, lest they should be troubled with doubts or scruples, how much more should we, miserable sinners, when we find ourselves found fault with for something, labour to appease those who have misunderstood us by explanations full of sweetness and humility."* (Greg., lib. 9, Epist. 39.)

Dom Bartholomew was so impressed with this apostolic moderation, that it was said of him that he rather did things beneath his dignity. And although he was very learned in all episcopal matters, he frequently consulted the members of his council. He gave them the reasons for what he was about to do, and never hesitated to follow their advice instead of his own ideas, if he were convinced that they had more justice and reason on their side. And not only was he not offended when they appealed against his judgment to a superior tribunal, but he even exhorted them to do it, and to use perfect liberty in this respect, saying that he was always glad to profit by the integrity and superior wisdom of other judges in the reformation of his own errors, and the discharge of his conscience. On this point of episcopal charity he would quote the following words from St. Bernard: *"Charity is patient and gentle. She is patient when she dissimulates, tolerates, and waits for the sinner. She is gentle when she attracts, draws, and persuades him to turn from his evil way. Charity is gentle and sweet, because she loves, and loves warmly, those she tolerates; she weeps sometimes, but from the wish to serve God and souls; she weeps with those who weep, not because she is sad, but because she loves. O! motherly bowels of charity! for whether she bears the weak, or helps the more advanced;*

whether she reproves those who have gone astray, adapting to each different malady a separate treatment, she still loves all as her own children. She is sweet when she reproves, simple when she caresses, tender and sympathising when she is touched, humble and patient even in her anger. When she is offended, she only complains that it may be acknowledged; when she is despised or estranged, she tries to recall those who fly from her. True pastors," (he adds,) *"do not think of their dignity, but of fulfilling their duties. And when a soul, by a movement of frenzy, rises up against them, and even goes to the length of reproaches and injuries, they are still meek and gentle, considering that they are not the dominators over, but the physicians of men, and so do not trouble themselves to avenge themselves, but to heal them."* (Stim. Past., cap. 2. Bern. Serm. fer. 4, Hebd. Sanct., et in Cant., serm. 25, n. 2.) And again: *" Let prelates understand this, those who think little of saving souls, and whose only idea is to make themselves feared. Learn your duty, you who are appointed as judges of the earth. Learn that you should be as mothers of men, and not their masters, with dominion over their souls. Labour rather to make yourselves loved than feared. And if on rare occasions, severity be necessary, let it be the severity of a father, and not of a tyrant. Show that you are mothers of souls by consoling and loving them, and fathers when forced to reprove. Cease to be proud, and cruel, and hard, and become gentle and kind. Leave aside the rod and punishments. Tender your breasts to your children. Have an abundance of sweetness and milk for them, and not hard pride and luxury. Why do you make your yoke insupportable to those whom you ought, on the contrary, to relieve by bearing their burdens? Why does the weak soul, which has been bitten by a serpent, fly before her pastor, and dread lest he should know it; when, instead, she should run into his arms as to the bosom of a mother? If you be really spiritual, as the apostle says, 'instruct such a one in the spirit of meekness, considering thyself lest thou also be tempted.*' (Gal. vi. verse 1.) *Otherwise, as the prophet says, 'The wicked man shall die in his iniquity: but I will require his blood at thy hands, saith the Lord.'*" (Ezechiel iii. verse 18. Bern. in Cant., serm. 23, numb. 3.)

It seems that Dom Bartholomew had taken this idea, not only from St. Gregory and St. Bernard, but also from St. Augustine, who, in one of his letters, written when a simple priest, to Aurelius, Archbishop of Carthage, speaks as follows: "*One does not cure evils, as far as I can judge, by harsh and severe conduct, or by treating men in a rough or imperious manner: but it should be done by instructing, and not ordering; by exhorting, and not threatening. And when we have to deal with guilty souls, we should do so with grief, representing to them the vengeance with which holy writ threatens the impenitent, so that it may not be ourselves who are dreaded from our power, but God, who makes Himself feared by His word.*" (St. Aug., epist. 64.)

CHAPTER XIII.

OF THE PRUDENCE NECESSARY TO A BISHOP.—THAT ACCORDING TO ST. GREGORY IT SHOULD BE SHOWN PRINCIPALLY IN NOT ANTICIPATING JUDGMENT, AND BY USING GREAT RESERVE IN ECCLESIASTICAL DECISIONS.

The holy prelate having dwelt at great length on the charity and moderation of bishops, next gives us extracts from the Fathers to show the urgent necessity of prudence and circumspection in all their actions. He establishes this truth likewise by the Fourth Council of Carthage, held in the year 398, which, after describing the qualities incumbent on those who are destined for the episcopate, orders: "*That a careful examination should be made before-*

hand, as to whether he is naturally prudent, moderate, humble, gentle and affable, tender and compassionate."

Dom Bartholomew next shows, by the words of St. Bernard, that this virtue has an extensive signification, and is connected with all others. *"Prudence and discretion,"* writes that saint, *"is not so much a special virtue as the directress of all virtues, the moderator of all affections, the rule and the mistress of the whole life. Without it, virtue degenerates into vice, and natural affections change themselves into passions which destroy nature itself."* (In Cant., serm. 49.) This same saint likewise proves that if virtues are vain without charity, so even charity is lost without prudence and discretion. *"The order and regulation of charity,"* he writes, *"are absolutely necessary. For zeal without knowledge is insupportable. And thus, the more zealous a man is, the more he will need discretion to order and temper his charity. For unwise zeal is not only less useful, but becomes often pernicious, as is proved by experience. The more ardent the zeal, therefore, the more prompt the spirit, the more active the charity, the more discretion is needful to temper the zeal, moderate the spirit, and regulate and guide the charity."* (Cant., serm. 23, number 10.) St. Bernard further shows the necessity of the alliance of these virtues. *"Discretion languishes if not animated by the fire of charity, and charity becomes imprudent and hasty if not tempered by discretion. He who is really praiseworthy unites in himself both virtues, and as his prudence is kindled by charity, so his charity is guided by prudence."*

"Among all the vices opposed to this episcopal prudence," remarks Dom Bartholomew in the eleventh chapter of his *Stimul. Pastor.*, "there are none which are more contrary to it than the facility to believe the evil said of others on false reports. For this reason St. Bernard gives this advice to Pope Eugenius in the most express terms: *"There is one defect, Most Holy Father, of which, if you feel yourself guiltless, you will be the only person I know deserving of that praise among all those who are now seated on the thrones of the Church. This fault is a too great credulity, which is so subtle and dangerous an evil, that I have never met any among the great in my day who are vigilant and circumspect enough to be free from it. Hence arises the fact that they very often fly into passions for nothing; that they abandon the cause of the innocent; and that they are prejudiced and set against those who, being absent, cannot justify themselves."* (Bern. de Consid., lib. 2, cap. 14.) For this reason a Pope spoke this important word, which has been inserted in the canonical rules: *" We must not believe the evil which is said of persons until we have been given positive proofs of the truth of what is alleged." " Nos mala contra aliquem dicta, nolumus priùs credere, quàm probare."* St. Gregory writes in the same sense: *" The prophet says to the chiefs of the Jewish synagogue: ' Seek judgment, relieve the oppressed.'* (Isaiah i. verse 17.) *And the blessed Job, speaking of the life he had led before his afflictions, says of himself: ' I was the father of the poor, and the cause which I knew not I searched out most diligently.'* (Job xxix. verse 16.) *We ought to learn by these words not to be precipitate in our judgments; not to judge rashly in matters which have not yet been thoroughly examined; not to let ourselves be surprised the moment we hear something bad said of our neighbour: and not to be always ready to believe accusations against others which are not proved. And lest we should not fear enough falling into this fault, we have only to consider what is said in holy writ of the conduct of God Himself. For although to Him all things are open, and that nothing is so dark and hidden as to be unseen by the light of His eyes, nevertheless, in order to deter men from hasty judgments, He would not content Himself with what He had heard, before punishing the men of Sodom for their abominable crimes, but said, before pronouncing judgment: ' The cry of Sodom and*

Gomorrha is multiplied, and their sin is become exceedingly grievous. I will go down, and see whether they have done according to the cry that is come to Me, or whether it be not so, that I may know.' (Gen. xviii. verse 20.) Why did God, who knows all, and can do everything, represent Himself as if He doubted of a thing until its truth was clearly demonstrated, except to withdraw us, by His great example, from our indiscreet and hasty judgments, and to teach us never to believe evil of our neighbour unless we have certain proofs of its truth?" (Gregor. Moral., lib. 9, cap. 14.) Again, St. Gregory, writing to a bishop, says: "*I warn you, as I have often done before, to take great care never to do things hastily when it is a question of ecclesiastical censures. Therefore, I order you to remit the sentence you have pronounced against that priest, and to treat him with as much gentleness as you have previously done with severity.*" "*When an affair is so serious that it can only be settled by an ecclesiastical judgment, you must reflect and weigh well everything with the utmost care and exactness, so that, having no regard for any power, the matter should be decided by equity and justice.*" (Stim. Past., cap. 11.)

We have seen how carefully these instructions were followed by our holy prelate, and in his book he quotes the words of St. Augustine to a nobleman of his day on the same point: "*It is an inclination common to human nature, and against which few people are sufficiently on their guard, that when certain appearances make a thing likely, we choose to take our suspicions and our conjectures for certainties, without considering that very often the falsest things seem probable, and true ones improbable.*" (Aug. Maced., epist. 54.)

Dom Bartholomew's biographer writes on this subject: "As he had such great love of souls, he felt an extreme repugnance to fulminate excommunications, unless in extraordinary cases. For this reason he would not even make use of them against those to whom he had been compelled to forbid, for a time, their entrance into the churches, on account of their crimes, until their lives were changed. He used to say that it seemed to him too hard to cut off from the flock of Jesus Christ, without an extreme and visible necessity, sheep whom He had redeemed with His own Blood, and for whom a true pastor should even give his. That as they were exposed to extreme danger when thus cut off from the holy flock, a bishop ought to make superhuman efforts to keep them in it, just as he is obliged, when they voluntarily leave it, to attempt everything to make them come back. So, to avoid this melancholy necessity, he employed all the ingenuity of his charity to try and gain sinners, and make them leave the error of their ways." Our archbishop had not only learned this duty from St. Gregory, but also, (as we have seen,) from St. Augustine. And he quotes another letter which this great saint wrote to a young bishop, severely remonstrating with him, "*because he had pronounced a sentence of excommunication against a whole family without having properly examined if they had deserved so horrible a punishment. Do not fancy, I beg of you,*" (he continues,) "*that because we are bishops we are incapable of falling into any unjust animosity. But remember, on the contrary, that being surrounded on all sides by the snares of the tempter, we are always here below in extreme danger as men.*" (Aug. epist. 75.)

In this matter Dom Bartholomew conducted himself according to the decree of the Second Council of Seville, where we read the following important instruction to prelates, which should be of the greater weight, because St. Isidore himself presided at this council: " *We reinstate Frugitanus, priest of the Church of Cordova, who has been unjustly deposed by his bishop, and condemned to exile, although innocent. And what is more, we order, against this presumption recently introduced into the Church, that no bishop in future should be so bold as to depose a priest or deacon of any sort, without having previously examined his affair in a council. For there are many who, without proper information or knowledge of the facts, condemn persons, not by the authority of the holy canons, but by a tyrannical exercise of power. Just as they promote men without reason, because it pleases them to favour them, so they degrade others without reason, from motives of hatred and envy, without taking the trouble to prove the things of which they are accused. A bishop may consecrate priests and deacons alone, but he cannot alone take away from them the dignity he has conferred on them. Therefore we ordain, for the future, that priests and deacons cannot be condemned or deprived of the advantages attached to their ministry by the judgment of a single bishop, but that they shall be brought before the bishops assembled in council, so that they may be judged according to the canons."* (Concil. Hispal. 2, canon. 6, anno 619.)

Although councils are not generally held in these days, as they were formerly, and that this rule cannot therefore be practised in the same way, nevertheless Dom Bartholomew considered that the Church should retain the same spirit, and would not allow a bishop to depose a priest without appealing to several other persons' judgment as well as his own. And he believed that the reasons for this conduct were founded on the obligation which was laid on all pastors to obey Jesus Christ, who orders them in the Gospel, *" to be faithful and prudent, and to do justice to every one;" " which rules,"* writes St. Bernard, *" always subsist, and are as immutable as God Himself."* (Bern. de Precept. Disp., cap. 3.)

This moderation and equity were prescribed by several of the canons of the Church to all ecclesiastical judges, and we see in the general councils how they were practised by the bishops; for when they had to defend the faith of the

Church against the most obstinate heretics, they still invited them to give all their reasons in their defence, and weighed and examined each with perfect equity, as the Fathers in the Council of Nice did with regard to the Arians. And when they found them so confirmed in their errors as to be utterly incurable, and that they were, in consequence, compelled to pronounce against them the sentence of excommunication, they did so "*with extreme grief and shedding tears,*" as is expressly stated in the Council of Ephesus, when the Fathers pronounced sentence against Nestorius: "*Lacrymis perfusi ad lugubrem hanc contra eum sententiam necessariò venimus.*" (Concil. Ephes. part 1, act. 1.) And again, the same thing is related in the second act of the Council of Chalcedon, when the bishops condemned Dioscorus. For being both judges and fathers, though the punishment of these heresiarchs was very just, and that they had previously tried in vain every means to bring them to a sense of their error by condescension and gentleness, they could not make up their minds to this final step without profound sorrow. And they felt it as a man would do who is forced to submit to cutting off a member of his body to save the rest, and who was compelled to cut off his left hand with his right.

CHAPTER XIV.

HOW PASTORS SHOULD LOVE AND HELP THE POOR; AND HOW DOM BARTHOLOMEW EXCELLED IN THAT VIRTUE.

Love of the poor is a virtue inseparable from charity, and necessary to all the faithful. But as a bishop is raised by his dignity above his flock, so he ought to possess this quality in an eminent degree. We will here quote the words of Dom Bartholomew on this subject: "The hand of the bishop should be always open to the poor. He should be the refuge and helper of all who suffer. He ought to consider the poverty of his neighbour as his own. And if he has not these feelings, it is in vain he bears the name of bishop. St. Gregory, writing one day to a priest, who had not reminded him to send him what he was accustomed to do every year for the maintenance of a monastery, (he having refrained from doing so from a feeling of modesty,) says: '*That the friendship he had for him ought not to have allowed him to be so scrupulous; that he ought to consider that the alms he was bound to send him were not his own, but the property of the poor; and therefore,*' (he added,) '*I have great cause to complain of your delicacy in this matter, which made you abstain from asking for your poor, of one that loves you, the alms which in reality belong to them, and of which I am only the dispenser.*' Think over these words," (continues Dom Bartholomew,) "O pastors of men. You do not give what is your own, but what belongs to the poor. Who then will be surprised to see the poor daily at the door of the bishop's palace, as it is the house of him who is the dispenser of the wealth which God has reserved for them?" (Stimul. Pastor., cap. 3.)

He goes on to prove that St. Ambrose taught the same lesson when he was blamed for an excess of charity, having on one occasion melted down the church plate to relieve the captives and the poor. "*It is better,*" he writes, "*to have to defend the merciful actions one has performed, and to bear reproach for so doing, than to show hardness towards the poor. We have ourselves been blamed by some because we melted the sacred vessels to redeem captives. As it was not without reason that we did this, we explained it to the people. We confessed it openly, and proved to them that it was more useful to preserve souls for God than gold. For He sent the apostles without gold into the world, and without money assembled all the Church in one Body. The*

Church does not keep treasures to accumulate, but to employ them in relieving the necessities of the poor. Of what benefit is it to keep useless gold? Will not our Lord say to us: 'How is it you have allowed so many poor to die with hunger? Had you no money with which you could relieve them? How could you bear to see so many captives dying under the hands of their enemies, when you could have redeemed them when they were exposed for sale?' One could not answer such a reproach from Jesus Christ. For what could we say? 'I was afraid that the gold vessels would be wanted to adorn the temple.' Would He not reply: 'The divine mysteries and sacraments do not need gold. As they are not bought with gold, they are not reverenced the less on account of the want of it.' The redemption of captives is the real ornament of the mysteries; and the vessels with which we can redeem souls from death are what are really precious. That is the real treasure of the Lord which does what He has done with His own Blood. I never realize so strongly that the chalice is meant to contain the Blood of the Saviour, as when I see that same chalice serve for the redemption of men, and when a vessel redeems from the power of the infidels the men whom that precious Blood has redeemed from the slavery of sin. What is more beautiful, what is happier, than to be able to say, when one sees a group of captives redeemed by the Church, 'These men are redeemed by Jesus Christ?' That is truly making a good use of gold—the gold of our Lord which delivers from death; which redeems modesty; which preserves chastity. I have preferred to free all these poor people than to keep the gold and silver. This was the treasure which the martyr, St. Lawrence, reserved for God, when the judge asked him where were the treasures of the Church? And he promised to show them to him. And having a day or two later brought a great body of poor, he presented them to the judge, saying: 'These are the Church's treasures.'

And this was true, for Jesus Christ was there, and the faith in Jesus Christ. Who are the treasures of Jesus Christ but those of whom He said: 'I was hungry and you gave Me to eat;...as long as you did it to one of these My least brethren you did it to Me'? (Matt. xxv., verses 35-40.) *No one ever said to St. Lawrence, 'You ought not to have distributed these treasures of the Church among the poor, or sold the vessels which served for the administration of the sacraments.' But this distribution must be made with an earnest faith, and with a clear and circumspect wisdom. For it would be a sin for priests or bishops to apply the vessels of the Church to their own use or profit. But it is a work of mercy to distribute their value for the relief of the poor and the redemption of captives. Who can say: Why is it necessary that this poor man should live? Who can complain that the captives are set free? Who can reproach you if you have built a church for the worship of God? or bought a site to increase the Christian cemetery? It is allowable on those occasions to melt and sell even consecrated vessels. It is better first to use those which have never served for the divine mysteries, if there be any such. But if there are none I think the others may be legitimately and holily converted into money for these uses."* (St. Ambrose, 2 offic., cap. 22.)

Dom Bartholomew was so persuaded, like St. Gregory, that he was only the dispenser of the Church's revenues, that he often said: "That he considered himself as a stranger in his episcopal palace, and that he looked upon the poor as its masters and lords." The following passages were extracted by him on this subject from the life of St. Gregory: "*This holy Pope was careful to distribute to the poor, the first days of each month, the same things he himself received from his ecclesiastical property. Thus, according to the seasons of the year, he gave them wheat, wine, poultry, fish and oil, &c.*" Dom Bartholomew followed precisely the same rule. (Joan. diac., lib. 2, num. 26.)

"*St. Gregory sent persons every day through the streets of Rome, carrying soup and meat to the sick and infirm, or to those who from any accident were lame and unable to earn their bread.*" (Joan. diac., lib. 2.)

Dom Bartholomew not only did that, but appointed a doctor, whose sole business was to attend the poor, and report to him on their state.

"*St. Gregory, having blessed the food before dinner, sent a portion of each dish at table to such poor of a better class as were too timid and well born to ask an alms.*" (Ibid.)

Dom Bartholomew had so great a respect for this holy custom, that he did the same all his life. No sooner had he sat down at table, than he cut off a portion of what was set before him, to feed the shame-faced poor. He used to do this with such pleasure that he never would eat anything until he had fulfilled that duty. One day, having been invited to a magnificent feast at a friend's house, it was observed that he seemed pre-occupied, and remained without touching anything. At last he said to the host: "You are my friend, and I am the friend of the poor. If you are troubled because I do not eat, how much more unhappy should I be when I think that everything is wanting to the friends and brethren of Jesus Christ? Allow me then to begin as I always do at home, by sending them something, so that their share may sanctify ours. For however excellent may be your dishes, I own I do not find them good unless seasoned by charity."

It is recorded of St. Gregory: "*That one day a poor man having been found dead, he was so grieved because he thought he had died for want of help, that he abstained for several days from offering the Holy Sacrifice of the Mass, feeling as if he were guilty of his death.*" (Ibid. num. 29.)

We have seen in the life of Dom Bartholomew how entirely he entered into the holy Pope's feelings in this matter, and how, during the famine and the plague, he multiplied himself to supply the needs of all.

In the same way he considered hospitality as one of the great duties of bishops. He practised perfectly the advice of St. Jerome, which the Council of Aix la Chapelle, in the year 816, adopted as one of its ordinances: "*The bishop's house should be a common home where hospitality is exercised towards every one. If a layman receives two or three people in his house he performs all the duty required of him. But if a bishop does not keep open house, he is hard and inhuman.*" (Concil. Aquis. Gran., lib. 1, cap. 10.)

Dom Bartholomew conducted himself in this matter in the prudent way which was praised in St. Chrysostom, who would not open his house continually to rich noblemen and courtiers, as other Archbishops of Constantinople had done; but he exercised hospitality principally towards ecclesiastics and religious. His palace at Braga was always open to them, and as we have seen, he had a set of rooms nicely furnished for them, where the priests in his diocese came and were welcomed, and almost compelled to remain during all the time that their affairs obliged them to stop in the town.

CHAPTER XV.

WITH WHAT CARE DOM BARTHOLOMEW EXHORTED HIS PEOPLE TO GIVE ALMS, FOLLOWING IN THIS MATTER THE SPIRIT OF THE FATHERS OF THE CHURCH.

As Dom Bartholomew considered love of the poor one of the chief duties of pastors, so he was equally anxious to impress this duty on laymen, and on all the faithful. We will here give, under separate heads, the points most insisted upon by this holy prelate, who was justly called "*the father of the poor*," and which he supported by copious extracts from the works of the Fathers of the Church.

FIRST POINT.

OF THE STRICT OBLIGATION UNDER WHICH ALL CHRISTIANS LIE TO GIVE ALMS.

"*It is not enough,*" says St. Gregory, "*not to take away other people's goods; we must give of that which is our own. All men spring from the dust of the earth: the earth, then, is our common mother, and ought to produce what is necessary to feed all. In vain, then, do those consider themselves innocent who appropriate to themselves alone the goods which God has made common. For by not giving to others what they have received they become murderers and homicides; because, by keeping to themselves the wealth which would have supported the poor, who were perishing in their misery, one may say that they kill every day as many as they might have kept alive. When, then, we give the means of subsistence to those who are in want, we do not give what is our own, but what is really theirs. It is not then so much a work of mercy which we perform, as a debt which we pay. For that reason, when Jesus Christ wishes to teach us the way in which we should give alms, He says: 'Take heed that you do not your justice before men, to be seen by them.'* (St. Matt. vi. verse 1.) *He calls the mercy we show to the poor 'justice'; and David speaks in the same sense when he writes: 'He hath distributed, He hath given to the poor, and his justice remaineth for ever and ever.'* (Psalm cxi. verse 9.) *He preferred calling alms justice to mercy, because it is only just that those who have received what they possess from Him who is the Father and Lord of all, should employ it for the good of all. These persons say sometimes: 'We only use what God has given us; we do not wish for other people's goods; and if we do not do many good works deserving reward, at least we do not do bad ones.'*

These are their thoughts, but they would not dare think so if they were not deaf to the word of God. For it is not said of the rich man in the Gospel, 'who was clothed in purple and fine linen, and feasted sumptuously every day,' that he had taken other people's goods, but simply that he had not used his own in good works. And he was cast into hell after his death, not for having committed any dishonest or illicit act, but because he had given himself up to the enjoyment of the goods things of this life, which were permitted to him, without sharing them with others, or using that moderation in their use which God commands. Therefore, you must represent to people, who are thus attached to their possessions, this terrible word of St. John: 'Every tree that doth not yield good fruit shall be cut down and cast into the fire.' (Matt. iii. verse 10.) *Do not, therefore, let them fancy themselves innocent because they do not bear bad fruit, because, by neglecting to bring forth good fruit by the practice of good works, they will be cut down as trees without foliage, and which are dry even to the roots."* (Greg. Past., part 3, admon. 22.)

St. Augustine likewise teaches us that in our character of Christians and faithful, the obligation of alms-giving is necessarily included. These are his words: *"The apostle St. John says to us: 'He that hath the substance of this world, and shall see his brother in need, and shall shut up his bowels from him, how doth the charity of God abide in him? My little children, let us not love in word, nor in tongue, but in deed and in truth.'* (1 St. John iii. verses 17, 18.) *Your brother has nothing to eat; he is in the utmost misery, and perhaps overwhelmed with debts, and driven to the last extremity by his creditors; he has nothing left, and you have. He is your brother. You have been bought by the same price, and Jesus Christ has shed His Blood for him as much as for you. Reflect then a little, and see if you have any charity towards him. You will say perhaps: 'Why am I to trouble myself about this man? Why am I to go and* give my money to prevent his suffering some evil? If this thought be in your heart, the love of the Father is not in you. You are not born anew in God. Why then do you glory in the name of Christian? You bear the name, but you do not do the works. If you had the works as well as the name, when any one took you for a pagan, you would show by your deeds that you were a Christian. But if you do not act as a Christian should, of what use is it that all the world calls you a Christian, or that you bear the name, when you are not one in spirit or in truth?" (St. Aug., in epist. 1.)

Dom Bartholomew often said that we ought the more gladly to be induced to give alms when we considered it as a positive gain and a lucrative traffic, because the poor are like rich bankers, who transmit to heaven what we give them here below. St. Augustine says on this point: "*God forbids our lending money to men at usurious interest, but He orders us to lend this interest to Himself. 'He that hath mercy on the poor, lendeth to the Lord, and He will repay him.'* (Proverbs xix. verse 17.) *God does not need your money, but the poor does. You give it to the poor, and God receives it. The poor would gladly return what you lend him, but he has nothing to give. He can only show you his gratitude by praying for you; and when he does this, it is as if he said to God: 'Lord, I have been lent this money, be responsible for me.' God says to you in holy writ: 'Give to this man who has nothing,—give freely. It is I who will be responsible for him.'*" (St. Aug., serm. 146, de temp.) Again, the same saint writes: "*You are rich, you say; you have plenty of gold and silver. O! would to God you could realize how poor you are! Look at this beggar who is asking bread of you. What he is should teach you what you are. For whatever goods you may possess, however rich you may be, you are still a beggar before God. If you doubt this, consider what you do in prayer. You ask. How then can you say you are not poor, when you beg as the poor do? I*

*say more: you beg for bread. For do you not say to God,
'Give me this day my daily bread?' Is it not true, then,
that you are poor, as you are reduced each day to asking for
bread? And yet God honours you by saying: 'Give to Me
a portion of that which I have given to you. What did you
bring into this world when you came into it? I created you,
and you have only found in it the other things which I
created. You brought nothing into the world, and it is
certain you will carry nothing out. All that you have is
Mine. Why then do you not give Me some of it? You have
too much, and the poor has nothing at all. Give him of your
abundance. I ask of you for him what is in reality Mine.
Give it to him, and I will repay you. I am your creditor.
I wish to be your debtor. I wish you to be My creditor, and
that you should lend Me at interest. Give Me a little, and I
will repay you doubly. Give Me a portion of your perishable
and terrestrial goods, and I will repay you with celestial and
eternal ones.'"* (August., serm. 41, de Verb. Dom.)

SECOND POINT.

THAT CHARITY SHOULD ONLY BE GIVEN OUT OF PROPERTY LEGITIMATELY ACQUIRED.

St. Gregory writes: "*There are some men who are ready
to give in charity what they have acquired by violence. But
there is a wide difference between redeeming sins by alms,
and committing sins in order afterwards to do good works.
The bitter root of violence and rapine cannot produce the
sweet fruits of charity. Thus our Lord, speaking by the
mouth of His prophet, says: 'For I am the Lord that loves
judgment, and hates robbery in a holocaust.'* (Isaiah lxi.
verse 8.) And again: '*The sacrifices of the wicked are
abominable, because they are offered of wickedness.*' (Proverbs xxi. verse 27.) *Sometimes these persons rob the poor*

to offer something to God. But in holy writ it is said that He rejects such gifts with horror: 'He that offereth sacrifices of the goods of the poor is as one that sacrificeth the son in the presence of his father.' (Eccle. xxxiv. verse 24.) What more horrible for a father than to see with his own eyes the death of his son? And yet it is with this eye of indignation and anger that God beholds the sacrifices offered Him of the blood of the poor. But these persons deceive themselves, for they think so much of what they give, that they hide from themselves what they have taken. They turn away their eyes from their injustice and sin, and even flatter themselves that they shall obtain the reward of the just." (St. Greg. Past., part 3, admon. 22.) And again: "On the judgment day Jesus Christ will condemn to eternal flames those who are not accused of rapine or violence, but who have only abstained from giving Him to eat and drink in the person of His poor. How much more guilty therefore would those be who rob others of their goods, when it is so great a crime not to give of one's own substance to the poor? What will become of the violent and unjust, if we be condemned for a simple want of charity?"

St. Gregory does not mean that persons of this sort are not to give alms, but he wishes to show us that they ought to do like Zacheus, who thought first of making restitution of all that he had unjustly acquired, and then gave the poor what remained. And we do not think this holy Pope would think it wrong for a person who might not be able to restore everything he had taken to give alms to the poor, so as to acquit his obligation towards God. But he teaches us by these words that he would not have such persons turn away their eyes "*from their past iniquities,*" but consider their alms as a restitution, for which they should blush before God, however much they might be praised by men.

THIRD POINT.

THAT IN GIVING ALMS WE SHOULD STRIVE TO ATONE FOR AND FREE OURSELVES FROM SIN.

Dom Bartholomew, in his extreme charity for the souls which had been committed to him, taught them to look upon the alms-giving to which he so frequently exhorted them "*as a means whereby they should obtain from God the sanctification and conversion of their own souls.*" (Stim. Past., cap. 11.) "*Let those,*" writes St. Gregory, "*who already give largely to the poor remember that while striving to redeem their sins by alms, they must be very careful not to commit fresh ones. Otherwise it would be treating God as if His justice was for sale, and as if, by giving money after having offended Him, they could buy impunity for their crimes. He who gives food and clothes to the poor, and at the same time soils his own body and soul by sin, cruelly abuses that which is without comparison the most precious thing he has. For while he sacrifices his property to God, he sacrifices himself to the Devil. Sua Deo dedit et se Diabolo.*" (Greg. Past., part 3, admon. 21.)

The holy Pope further teaches us that while we are helping the poor we should ask of God not to disdain to receive our offerings, although we know ourselves to be utterly unworthy to present them. Holy writ says: "*Shut up alms in the heart of the poor, and it shall obtain help for thee against all evil.*" (Eccles. xxix. verse 15.) And the poor will pray for us, so that God may soften the hardness of our hearts, and break the chains which bind us to our sins. For sometimes persons will obtain the grace of perfect conversion after giving large alms, and especially when they had not sufficient strength of mind to break through the violence of their passions, although they wished to do so beforehand. God verifies in these souls the words of the angel Raphael to Tobias: "*For alms delivereth from death, and the same is that which purgeth away sins, and maketh to find mercy and life everlasting.*" (Tobias xii. verse 9.)

St. Chrysostom represents as strongly the advantages held out to us by redeeming our sins with alms: "*Think,*" he writes, "*how a man would wish to be able to redeem his sins after baptism if God had not granted him alms to wash them out. How many would exclaim: 'Would to God we might by our alms save ourselves from evil to come.' And now, when they can do so, they are cold and insensible. Weep for your sins,*" he continues; "*do penance in this world, lest you should weep for your torments in hell. Try and soften your Judge before appearing before Him. Those who desire the favour of an earthly judge do not wait to try and obtain it until they appear before him. They do it beforehand, through friends or counsel pleading for them. We must do the same towards God. We must try and soften Him before He ascends His tribunal. For when once He is seated there as our Judge, His justice is inexorable. One may gain Him by money, but it must pass through the hands of the poor. Repentance without alms-giving is dead. It has no wings; it cannot rise on high. It served as wings to the centurion. 'Your alms and your prayers,' said the angel to Cornelius, 'have gone up as a memorial before God.'*" (St. Chrysostom, hom. 78 and 55, tom. 1.)

FOURTH POINT.

THAT WE SHOULD GIVE LIBERALLY, AND IN PROPORTION TO OUR WEALTH.

The archbishop showed his people, by his actions even more than by his words, with what liberality we should bestow our alms, for he imitated the ardent zeal of the first Christians, of whom St. Paul said that they assisted their brethren "*according to their power, and (I bear them witness) beyond their power.*" (2 Cor. viii. verse 3.) So that his instructions had great weight, when he quoted the words of Tobias: "*According to thy ability be merciful. If thou have much, give abundantly; if thou have little, take care even so to bestow willingly a little.*" (Tobias iv. verses 8 and 9.) St. Gregory's rule on this point was: "*That one must not content oneself with giving a little, when one ought to give a good deal.*" And St. Augustine says: "*Jesus Christ has declared, 'that unless your justice abound more than that of the Scribes and Pharisees, you shall not enter into the kingdom of heaven.'* (St. Matt. v. verse 20.) *And yet the charity of Christians in the present day is much less than that of the Pharisees, for they gave the tenth of all they possessed. You who glorify yourselves with the name of Christians, think to do a great deal if you give a hundredth part of your goods. You think of what others do, not of what God expects of you. You think yourself good because you are better than the bad, instead of feeling you are to blame for not obeying Him who is infinite goodness. It does not follow that you do much because you do more than the man who does nothing. You are so barren of good works that the least thing seems to you magnificent. You deceive yourselves, and lean with a false confidence on those little grains of alms which you* gather up with great care, while you forget the huge heap of sins which you have amassed. You have perhaps given some little thing which another could not or would not give. Why do you look back to see what this one has or has not done, instead of only looking at what is expected of you by God? This is not the way you go on with earthly matters in these days. You are not content with having a good deal more than many others. You want to be as rich as the richest around you. Your eyes rest on those who precede you, without thinking of the numberless poor who are behind you. You put no limit to your passion for riches; but when it is a question of giving alms, you draw in at once. You say to yourself at once: 'How many there are who give less than I do.' And you do not say at the same time: 'How many there are who are not as rich as I am.' Why do you not follow the example of Zacheus, who gave the half of his goods to the poor? And why do you constrain us to wish that if you cannot imitate that good man, you would at least follow the example of the Pharisee, who gave the tenth of all he possessed?" (St. August. de decem. chordis, cap. 12.)

St. Chrysostom likewise teaches us that it is not enough to give alms, if we do not give as much as we possibly can. "Let us labour," he says, "for generosity; let us retrench all superfluities, and only think of distributing all we can to the poor. But you will say, 'I have given to them now and then.' That is not giving alms. If you do not give in proportion to your means, you have not done your duty. The foolish virgins had lamps and oil, only they had not enough. If you had created your own wealth even, you ought not to be so careful of it. But as all you have comes from God, and He has only made you its dispenser, why are you so stingy in your distribution of it to the poor? Do you wish me to tell you the cause of this inhumanity? It is because those who are misers in heaping up wealth are cold and indifferent when it is a question of giving alms. Those who *think only of making money, do not know how to spend it. Listen to this precept of Scripture: 'Let not mercy and truth leave thee.'* (Proverbs iii. verse 3.) *It does not say, 'Give alms once or twice;' but 'never give it up.' Whereby it proves that it is we who need it, and not charity which needs us; so that we should do all we could to preserve and encourage it.*" (St. Chrysostom, hom. 76.)

Following this principle, it was remarked of Dom Bartholomew that he never would look over his household accounts, saying that he had confided that duty to trustworthy and faithful people; but he insisted on seeing all that had been spent on alms, for he feared that his servants, having less confidence than himself in the providence of God, and dreading lest he should be straitened in his own house, should diminish the excessive expenditure which he indulged in in charity, and cut off any of the money which he had ordered should always be employed for the relief of the poor.

But some men make use of a specious pretext to escape giving alms, by saying, "I have children, and I must make money and save it for them." St. Augustine answers this argument as follows: "*You will say, 'Is it not one of the first duties of charity for a man to labour to amass a fortune for his own children?' And I answer you, 'Is it not great folly to labour so hard to heap up wealth for those who must die like himself?' Have you two children?*" (he continues,) "*then take Jesus Christ as the third. Place Him among your children. Let our Lord enter into your family. What more glorious than to adopt one who represents Jesus Christ, and be a father to him, and for your children to be his brothers?*" (St. Aug., serm. 43, de divers., cap. 11.) The same saint adds: "*I have said that I would not refuse legacies and offerings for the Church, provided they were just. But should I accept a succession which a father has left me on his death-bed, simply because he was in a rage with his son, and so altered his will when he was dying? If he were still alive, would it not be my duty to soften the father, and reconcile him to his son, so that he might not lose his inheritance? But if a man, having one son, took Jesus for his second son; or if, having ten, he put our Lord in the place of the eleventh, and gave Him in that way His share of his substance by leaving it to the Church, I should accept it."* (Idem., serm. 49 de divers., cap. 3.) St. Basil teaches this still more distinctly: *"You say, 'I want this property for my children.' This is a very plausible excuse. You cover your avarice under the plea of your children, and thus satisfy the secret inclinations of your heart. I do not accuse your son, who is innocent. But tell me, when you asked God to allow you to be a father, did you say to Him, 'Lord, give me children, so that I may not obey the precepts of Your Gospel? Give me children, so that I may not enter into the kingdom of heaven?' More than this, who can answer for their minds and conduct? and who will assure you that they will spend the money you leave them rightly? How many are there to whom riches are the first step in their downfall? The Wise man says: 'There is also another grievous evil which I have seen under the sun: riches kept to the hurt of the owner.'* (Ecclesiastes v. verse 12.) *And again: 'I hated all my application wherewith I had earnestly laboured under the sun, being like to have an heir after me, whom I know not whether he will be a wise man or a fool.'* (Ecclesiastes ii. verses 18 and 19.) *Take care, therefore, lest after having amassed riches with great toil and trouble, you only leave to your children a heritage of sin and scandal, and lest you should yourself be doubly punished, both for the good you have left undone, and because of the sins of your children, of which you have been, in one sense, the author. Your own soul, is it not nearer to you than even your children? It is to save your own soul that you should reserve a portion of your goods, and after that, you should distribute the remainder to your children. For it often happens that* when children do not succeed to the whole of their father's inheritance, they exert themselves to found a fresh establishment by their own labour. But if you neglect and abandon your own soul, who will have compassion upon her?" (St. Basil, homil. in divites.)

FIFTH POINT.

THAT WE MUST GIVE WITH DISCRETION, ACCORDING TO THE DIVERSITY OF TIMES, SEASONS, AND PERSONS.

Dom Bartholomew recommends with great care in his book that prudence should accompany alms-giving. For this reason the Christians of old days generally placed in the hands of their pastors the money they destined for the poor, because, being assured of their charity and prudence, and knowing that they were better acquainted than themselves with the condition of the poor, they thought their charity would be more acceptable to God if given according to rule and order.

St. Basil teaches us this in the following words: "*We see in the Acts, that when the early Christians had sold their possessions, they put the price at the feet of the apostles, who distributed it afterwards according as each one had need. For it needs great discernment and experience to find out those who are really poor from those who make a trade and an art of begging. He who relieves the really poor and afflicted gives to God, and will be rewarded by God; but he who gives to professional mendicants and vagabonds only helps to foster idleness and imposture. It is best to give very little to such persons in order to get rid of them, and to avert their maledictions and murmurs. But, on the other hand, charity should be bestowed with real liberality on those who are truly sufferers, and who have learned to bear with patience and equanimity the misery and want which surround them."*

Dom Bartholomew, sharing in these feelings, used the greatest discernment in the distribution of his alms. He specially devoted himself to helping those who were anxious to work but could not find any employment, and who would rather die than be reduced to asking for alms. He encouraged rich people, in times of public distress, to set about relief works, whereby hundreds were honestly employed; and often contrived to anticipate the wages due to these labourers, so as to relieve them more quickly. Whilst doing his utmost to relieve the poverty of the poor, he was very careful not to encourage them in idleness, according to St. Augustine's rule: *"Ad supplendam necessitatem non ad pascendum pigritiam."* So strongly did Dom Bartholomew dread idleness and its consequences, that he even did his utmost to persuade his younger clergy to learn a trade, as recommended in the ancient canons, so as never to have recourse to the charity of others for actual subsistence. (Concil. Carthage 4, can. 51, 52, and 53.) There is another important thing, and that is, the choice to be made of the persons entrusted with the distribution of alms, and of the kind of persons most worthy to receive them. We have seen that our holy archbishop always assisted with peculiar zeal those who had consecrated themselves to God's service in His Church, following in this matter the rule of St. Augustine, who would not wait till such persons asked for help, which they often would not do, but who went before them and anticipated their wants. *"You ought to seek out,"* he writes, *" and see if these servants of God do not need your help. Do not say: 'I will give if they ask me.' You wait till a minister of Jesus Christ pleads with you; would you treat Him as you would the passing beggar? If the priests of Jesus Christ are reduced to the condition of being obliged to ask an alms of you, beware lest they judge you beforehand.* 'How am I to find out about them?' you will ask. Inquire as much as you please as to the means of each one; no one will blame you for this. Do you fancy that all the ministers of the Church are rich? I know many who have not even daily bread. Scripture says: 'Blessed is he that understandeth concerning the needy and poor.' (Psalm xl. verse 2.) There are, then, poor people whom one must know and discern for ourselves without waiting till they ask us. It is written of ordinary poor: 'Give to all that ask of you.' But it is said of those who do not ask: 'Sudet eleemosyna tua in manu tuâ, donec invenias justum cui des illam.' Let others beg of you as much as they will, but anticipate the wants of those who do not ask. Give to the beggar; but give rather to the servant of God. The one asks, and in his voice you can detect at once what he is. But the other is silent, and for that very reason you should watch and anticipate his needs. For very probably he will ask you nothing, however great may be his distress; and his suffering will one day be your condemnation. Be then charitably curious, as I have said, and you will find out the misery of many of God's servants. Be sincere and earnest in your search, and you will discover how great is their need. But because you are very glad to make ignorance your excuse, you do not find it out. This, my brethren, is what I had to say to you on this subject. You know us well enough, as the apostle says to the faithful, not to fancy that we exhort you thus to come forward in aid of the servants of Jesus Christ from any secret views of our own." (St. Aug. on Psalm ciii. verse 14, and cxlvi. verse 8.)

We must also consider, in giving alms, the circumstances and time of more or less distress. For it is certain that in a famine, for instance, one must give more. "*You are poor,*" exclaims St. Basil, "*but there are many far poorer than yourself. You have enough wheat for ten days; and* he has only enough for to-day. If you are really charitable share equally what you have left with him who has nothing. Do not shrink from giving because you have little, lest you should prefer your own interest to the common danger of many. For if you had but one loaf, and a poor man were to ask you for a bit of it, do not refuse it to him." (St. Basil, hom. in divites.)

SIXTH POINT.

THAT WE MUST AVOID VANITY IN GIVING ALMS, AND ACCOMPANY THEM WITH HUMILITY.

One of the conditions laid down by Dom Bartholomew, (according to the advice of St. Gregory,) was, that almsgiving should be done with humility, that is, to be careful when doing it to free ourselves from that subtle poison of vanity, which spoils our best actions. He quoted on this point a letter from that great Pope to a certain bishop, whom he praised for his love of the poor, but added: *"That he had learnt with sorrow that he had spoken himself to several persons of the great alms he had given, 'from which it appears,' he adds, 'that you care for the praise of men more than that of God.' And he exhorts him to watch over himself with great circumspection, lest the worm of vanity should glide into his heart, and should spoil and corrupt all the fruit of his good works."* (Greg., lib. 2, epistl. 4.)

The same saint teaches us that in order not to seek for vain praises in our charitable actions, we should continually bear in mind this word of our Lord: *"When thou dost alms, let not thy left hand know what thy right hand doth, that thine alms may be in secret; and thy Father, who seeth in secret, will repay thee."* (Matt. vi. verses 8 and 9.)

St. Augustine comments on this passage as follows: *" Let not your left hand know what your right doth. The left hand signifies the pleasure we take in the praises of men; and the right, the pure intention to do everything which God commends. If this longing for praise glides into the heart of him who gives alms, and mixes itself up in his actions, the left hand knows very well what the right does. Therefore, Jesus Christ, in saying these words, meant: 'When you try to obey the command of God by giving alms, do not let the thought of human praise mix itself up with your good work, so that your alms may be done in secret, that is, remain at the bottom of your heart which is hidden from the sight of men. Some do this by good will alone, when they have nothing they can give to the poor. Others, on the contrary, do it to appear charitable, or to acquire some temporal advantage. The right hand alone acts in the first case, and the left only in the second. Others take, as it were, a middle course, because they give alms with the real intention of pleasing God; but yet, in their good will, a secret desire of praise slips in, or of some other temporal advantage, and so purity of intention is spoiled."* (Aug., serm. Dom. in monte, lib. 2, cap. 2.)

Although the holy prelate's position in the Church compelled him in many cases to give alms publicly, and especially as the example of his charity induced many to imitate him, nevertheless, he did as much as he could besides, privately, and especially towards those who blushed to make their wants known. He often exhorted his people to fly from vain-glory in these matters, and disapproved of the custom, when anything was given to God for the ornament of the temple, that the arms or names of the donors should be painted up, or engraved on their gifts, which custom sometimes extended even to the altar and the vessels used in the holy mysteries. He used to praise the humility and zeal of St. Charles in this matter, who, though of such noble birth, and Cardinal-Archbishop of Milan, yet insisted on effacing the arms of his house, which had been painted both on his cathedral and other places, desiring that the magnificent offerings he had given to God should be only written in heaven and in the book of life. Nevertheless, Dom Bartholomew remarks that though we are not to do our good works to be seen of men, still we must not refrain from doing them because men see and praise them. These are his words: "When the Son of Man said, 'Take care not to do your good works before men,' He adds directly, '*to be seen of them;*' that is, we must not seek our reward in the praise of men, or feed our vanity by human approval. But when He adds: '*Let your light shine before men,*' He teaches us that we may well let men see our good works, not for our own sakes, but to glorify our Heavenly Father, who has given us the grace to do them for Him, and has converted us from our sins. In this way our light will shine before men, because charity alone shines in our actions, without any form of vanity being mixed up with it. He who acts thus does not wish to be seen by men, but he wishes that God should be glorified as the sole author of all the good which is in man. So that he who admires the good done by another may imitate it, and by praise become himself praiseworthy. St. Augustine teaches us this likewise. "*My brethren, look to God in everything. Examine your conscience to know with what intention you act. If your heart does not accuse you of doing a good work from motives of vanity, remain in peace. Do not be afraid of being seen by any one when you give an alms. Fear to give it with a view to human praise: but do not fear lest another should see it and therefrom praise God. If you hide it altogether from the eyes of men, you hide from them also what they ought to imitate. In such an occasion there are two alms to give, and two poor to help. One hungers for material bread and the other for justice, as the Son of God has said: 'Blessed are they that hunger and thirst after justice.*' (Matt. v. verse 6.)

He who gives alms often finds himself between the two. If, then, he has true charity, he will have compassion on both, and try to relieve both. One seeks what he can eat, and the other what he can imitate. You give bread to the one and good example to the other. Both receive an alms, and both are greatly indebted to you. One has found what will appease his hunger, and the other what will excite his charity." (Aug., epist. Joan., tract. 8.)

Dom Bartholomew was not only anxious to guard his flock against vanity in alms-giving, but also to ground them in humility. He quotes St. Gregory again on this head: "*There are some people,*" (he writes,) "*who, before relieving a poor person, will say harsh things to him, and treat him with little or no respect. They do not seem to consider that charity and humility are inseparable, and that as charity gives us tenderness to find out the wants of our brother who is in need, humility should teach us to respect him. Although the poor may not be as rich as ourselves, are they not men and Christians as we are? When a man dares to show such pride to the poor, he renders himself more worthy of punishment by despising him, than of reward for assisting him. He becomes himself more naked inwardly than the poor is outwardly, for it is an infinitely greater misery to be without humility than without clothes. To avoid so great an evil, then, when we see the poor, pale and disfigured, covered with wounds, and with nothing but rags to clothe them, we ought to remember that their bodies are images of our souls, and that with greater truth, as our sores are inward and hidden. Therefore, when we give alms, we should always bear in mind those words of our Lord: 'Make unto you friends of the mammon of iniquity, that when you shall fail, they may receive you into everlasting dwellings.'* ' (St. Luke xvi. verse 9. *For we learn by this saying, that those who now seem so poor and miserable, will some day be infinitely rich: as, on the contrary, some who now seem rich, and* who do not employ their wealth in charity, will hereafter be infinitely poor. As then Jesus Christ advises us to make friends of the poor, so that when they become kings in heaven, they may help us to procure an eternal dwelling-place, we must not consider what we give them now as alms, but as presents which we offer to our benefactors and the patrons of our souls. If we were fully convinced of this truth, we should never dare set ourselves above them. We ought to keep in mind continually that the day will come when they will give us infinitely more than they have received from us, and that they are truly the rich, and we the real poor." (Greg. Moral, lib. 21. cap. 14.)

SEVENTH POINT.

THAT WE SHOULD GIVE WITH JOY, AND HAVE THE UTMOST TENDERNESS AND COMPASSION TOWARDS THE POOR.

Our archbishop loved the poor too well not to have immense pleasure in assisting them. He loved to see the courtyard of his palace quite full of them; and his joy knew no bounds when by his charity he was able to save so many people during the famine. He always taught others what he himself practised, that if men wish you to give willingly, God exacts it still more. "*In every gift show a cheerful countenance,*" writes the Wise man, "*and sanctify thy tithes with joy.*" (Ecclesiasticus xxxv. verse 11.) And again, St. Paul tells us to give "*Every one as he hath determined in his heart, not with sadness or of necessity, for God loveth a cheerful giver.*" (2 Corinth. ix. verse 7.) St Chrysostom shows us also with what joy we should give alms, in the following words: "*Alms-giving is only a virtue when you give willingly, gaily, liberally, and abundantly; when you are persuaded that in giving it is not you who give, but who receive, as instead of losing anything by this gift, you receive a great grace and an eternal gain. He who relieves the needs of another, ought to be gay and happy, and not sad and morose. Would you not shock reason and good taste if, when you were relieving the affliction of another, you were yourself miserable and cast down? It would be much better that you should not give at all than give with this spirit. But why are you depressed? Do you fear that your income will be diminished? If you have that idea in your mind, you had better give nothing at all. If you have not confidence that your money will be multiplied in heaven, do not give it. But perhaps you were wishing to receive the interest here below? How can you think this? Let alms be alms, and charity charity, and not a commercial and terrestrial traffic. I do not say that it has not sometimes happened that people receive their reward in this life. But that is not because they are more advanced in virtue and merit than others who do not gather the fruits of their charity in this world. On the contrary, God often treats in this way those who are weak and little inclined to give alms merely through the expectation of spiritual blessings in a future life."* (Chrysostom hom. in 2nd Epist. nd Corinth., chap. 8.)

St. Augustine writes in the same sense: *" When you fast,"* he says, *" give alms to the poor, and be very thankful that, by abstaining from your dinner, you can relieve the hunger of your brother. For if you give your bread to the poor with a good will, God will accomplish in your favour what He says in holy writ: 'Then thou shalt call and the Lord shall hear; thou shalt cry, and He shall say, Here I am.'* (Isaiah lviii. verse 9.) *There are some persons who murmur at giving charity, and only do so to rid themselves of the importunity of the petitioners, not because they have a real wish to relieve their misery. But, as the apostle says, God loves those 'who show mercy with cheerfulness.' If you give bread unwillingly to the poor, you lose both your bread and your merit."* (St. Aug. in Psal. 42 in fine. Rom. xii. verse 8.)

This joy springs from its only true source, which is love. A mother feels for the sufferings of her son, and in her grief she rejoices to be able to assist him, because she loves him. This loving tenderness of character was so remarkable in our archbishop, that Father Louis of Grenada remarks: "He was as much grieved at the misery of his people during the famine as if he suffered it himself. He never looked upon the poor as poor, but as the images of Jesus Christ, whom they represented. Therefore he was sensibly touched at their troubles, and never thought their demands ill-timed or importunate. Some persons of high rank having arrived one day to dine with the archbishop during the famine, nothing was served at table but a simple piece of beef and mutton. And seeing that they were surprised and rather discomposed, he said to them, smiling frankly: 'Those who are good enough to do me the honour of dining with me just now, must make up their minds to put up with a very poor repast. For I wish that my table should bear the marks of the suffering and privations of my flock. I do not blush at this economy, because I consider it a duty. And it seems to me that a bishop who thinks himself justified in living sumptuously when his people are dying of hunger, has forgotten that the misery of his flock should be his own, and that his wealth is the property of the poor.'"

He had followed in this matter likewise the example of St. Gregory who, preaching on the words of Job: "I wept over him that was afflicted, and my soul was tender and compassionate towards the poor," spoke as follows: *" When we give of our property, we give what is outside of us, but when we bestow our sympathy and our tears, we give a part of our hearts, and that which is most precious in us. Therefore, the compassion which accompanies alms-giving is a greater gift than the alms itself, because he who has that tenderness of heart will never fail to give his neighbour all he can, and will think nothing of everything that he does for him.*" The same saint, representing Magdalene as a figure of the whole Church, says: "*That she not only wiped the Saviour's feet, but kissed and watered them with her tears. From which we learn that it is not enough to assist the poor, who are as the feet of Jesus Christ, by giving them of our superfluity, but that we must besides show them real love and compassion.*" (Gregor. Homil. 33 in Evang.) And St. Augustine adds: "*That the poor are frequently merciful and charitable by the sympathy and compassion they have for one another; so that if the poor have this compassion, and the rich little or none of it, the poor, before God, are more charitable, although they may have scarcely anything to give, (like the widow's mite in the Gospel,) than the rich who give much.*" (Aug. in Psalm lxxxv.)

There was another branch of charity in which our saint excelled, and on which we must lightly touch, and that was his great consideration and kindness towards all those who were under him in the civil order, such as farmers and tenants on the episcopal property. He had the love of a father for them all; and no sooner had he taken possession of his see, than he gave the most stringent orders to his agents never to use any vexatious or rigorous proceedings towards them to exact what they owed him, and to remit their rents wholly or in part should any unforeseen loss or misfortune occur to them. For the same reason he would never raise the rents of the archepiscopal farms or lands, in spite of his great wish to have more money for his alms-giving, lest by practising greater charity on the one hand, he should wound it on the other. And he detested the conduct of those who, under pretence of claiming their rights, showed extreme harshness towards persons who were dependent on them, and treated them with a severity which dishonoured piety, and caused grave scandals. He spoke strongly in his book, (Stim. Past., cap. 11,) against those who are thus inexorable when anything of their own is concerned, and who will not yield a farthing of anything which belongs to them. And he would not allow their excuse, "That they were not to blame, because they only defended their rights, and demanded what was just," saying, "That they did not consider that in that very way they wounded Christian and evangelical justice, by not choosing to yield their rights, and prefering their private interest to the exercise of charity, to the relief of poor and neglected persons, and to the edification which they might give to the whole Church."

CHAPTER XVI.

WITH WHAT CARE BISHOPS SHOULD ABSTAIN FROM LUXURY, AND EMPLOY CONSCIENTIOUSLY THE PROPERTY OF THE CHURCH.—OF HOW THIS RULE SHOULD BE APPLIED TO THEIR RELATIONS.

To abstain from the luxury and display of seculars has been recommended to all bishops by the ancient councils, and especially by the Council of Trent. Dom Bartholomew spoke strongly on this point in the sixth chapter of his book, saying: "That this virtue was inseparable from the love of the poor, as it was impossible to love and assist them as he ought, and to spend in vain luxuries the Church's revenues, which have been called by the saints, '*the vows of the faithful,*' the '*goods of the poor,*' and the '*patrimony of Jesus Christ.*'" Dom Bartholomew quoted the words of St. Bernard on this subject: "*Listen, O pastors of the Church, to what famine and extreme misery drive the poor to say of you.* '*What object have you,*' (they say,) 'in making use of the property of the Church to feed your ambition? What you waste on luxuries is ours, and you rob us cruelly when you spend it in vanities. We are, like you, God's creatures; like you we have been bought by the blood of Jesus Christ. If then we are your brethren, with what possible justice can you take that which ought to feed us, to excite the curiosity of men by the sight of your magnificence, and to employ in superfluous luxuries that which is a necessity to us poor? You rob our indigence of all that you spend on your luxury, so that your vanity and love of display create two great evils, for they lose you by possessing you, and they kill us by stripping us of our due. You cover your horses and your mules with gold and silk trappings, and you leave your brothers in hunger and nakedness. And what is the more deplorable is, that the goods you thus waste are not yours. You have not earned them by your toil, although you may say in your hearts: ' Let us possess the sanctuary of God for an inheritance.'' (Psalm lxxxii. verse 13.) These," (adds the saint,) "are the thoughts of the poor, and what they are saying before God, who understands the language of the heart. For they do not dare complain of you in public, as they are obliged to implore your help in order to keep the life in their bodies. But there will come a day when they will rise with terrible strength against those who have afflicted and abandoned them in this life, for they will have for their protector and avenger one who is called in Scripture, 'the Father of the orphans and the Judge of the widows;' and then He will say to those who have failed to help them: 'Amen, I say to you, as long as you did it not to one of these least, neither did you do it to Me.'" (Matt. xxv. verse 45. Bern. de Moribus, et offic. Epis., cap. 2.)

We remember, in Dom Bartholomew's life, how strongly he expressed himself in this sense to Father Louis of Grenada, and lest it should be imagined that he held these views merely because he was a religious, he took great pains to explain that it was not as a monk, but because he was a bishop, that he had taken such care to banish all pomp and luxury from his house, following in this matter the example of the saints and the orders of the Councils.

We saw with what zeal, at the Council of Trent and in Rome, our holy prelate spoke against the luxury of the cardinals, and how the high esteem in which he was held by Pius IV. made that Pope accept his advice when he told him how much more worthy it was of a Sovereign Pontiff to build hospitals rather than palaces, and to give to the poor what belonged to them, instead of employing it in erecting sumptuous edifices which must one day perish.

St. Charles followed the same rule as Dom Bartholomew, for though the dignity and high birth of this saint might have led him to adopt the magnificence which was common to cardinals in those days, he began by retrenching, as Dom Bartholomew had done, all the useless gentlemen and seculars of his palace. He only retained one or two for lower offices which would be unfit for priests, and the rest of his household was composed entirely of ecclesiastics. He insisted upon their maintaining in everything a modesty and simplicity which should serve as an example to worldlings: and he forbid their wearing silk, which he also refused to wear himself. And though he was compelled by his dignity to appear in public in decent clothes, yet when he was alone he had such a love of humility and poverty, that he would wear such shabby attire as even the poor would have been ashamed to do. So much so, that it is related in his life that one day one of his servants gave a poor man a dressing-gown he had just left off, and the beggar thought it so disgraceful a garment, that he fancied it was given him as an insult, and came himself to St. Charles to show it, and complain of the way he had been mocked, which astonished the saint so much, that though he tried to keep a grave countenance, he could not help laughing. For the same reason he would not allow himself to be called Cardinal "*B rromeo*," after his noble house, but Cardinal of St. Praxedius, which was his title as cardinal. And instead of engraving his own arms on his seal, he had the figures of St. Ambrose and of the martyrs SS. Gervasius and Protasius engraved instead, as the protectors of the Church of Milan, with the words, "*Tales ambio defensores.*"

In the same way St. Charles believed, like Dom Bartholomew, that bishops were only dispensers and not proprietors of the Church's revenues. And God had so impressed this truth upon his heart, that when he was only fifteen or sixteen, having an abbey given him which had been resigned by his uncle, he told his father that the revenues of this ecclesiastical property could not be used for the house, as it was the patrimony of Jesus Christ, of which he was only the administrator. And after he had been made Cardinal and Archbishop of Milan, he went one day to another archbishop's house, who received him with great magnificence, and had him waited upon at table by men of high rank. But St. Charles, wishing to show how much he hated all this luxury and magnificence, determined to leave directly after dinner, although it was pouring with rain. And on his host entreating him to remain, he still insisted on departing, after having said these words: "*If I were to stay here to supper, you would give me another grand feast, as you have done at dinner, and the poor would be the losers; for the property of a bishop, when he has taken what is necessary for his house, belongs entirely to them.*" (Giussano, liv. 7 and 8, chap. 2 and 5.) In the same way, when a bishop was speaking to him one day of the magnificence of the Farnese palace, he replied in the same way as our archbishop did to the Pope at Rome: "*That it was only necessary to build eternal man-*

sions." Another cardinal having pointed out to him the beauties of his garden, St. Charles remained silent with a displeased look, and at last said: *"You would have done better if you had spent all the money that you have lavished here in building a monastery of religious."* And when some one said to him that he ought to have a garden attached to his archepiscopal palace, as other bishops had, in order to rest himself and take a little fresh air, he replied: *"A bishop's garden is the Holy Bible."* (Giussano, lib. 8, chap. 27.)

When Dom Bartholomew first came into his diocese, he was told that the Archbishops of Braga were accustomed to send every year to the Queen a certain fish which was very delicate and rare. He inquired what it cost; and finding it was very dear, he gave that amount to the poor, and wrote to the Queen as follows: "That if the property of the archbishopric had been his own, he would have been too happy to make this present to her highness. But that as it belonged to the poor, he thought he had fulfilled her intention by giving to them what it had been the custom to give to her, as he felt it was more worthy of her grandeur and of her truly royal charity to give to Jesus Christ Himself, in the person of His poor, than to rob them of the least of their goods."

This action may appear little in the sight of men, but it was great in its principles and its results, as St. Augustine said on a similar occasion: *"Quod minimum est, minimum est; sed in minimo fidelem esse magnum est."* (Aug., de Doct. Christ., lib. 4. cap. 18.)

On another occasion a great friend of our holy prelate's, and a man of high rank, but who still could not resist that natural inclination of people in his position for beautiful things, tried to persuade him to make some improvements in his palace, as his predecessors had done. The archbishop made his usual answer: "That the revenues of the

Church belonged to the poor;" but finding that he insisted, he added: "*You will forgive me if I say that what you want to induce me to do is worse than what the Devil proposed to Jesus Christ. For he counselled Him to change the stones into bread, which might have fed the poor; whereas you are trying to tempt me to change the bread of the poor into stones.*"

One of the greatest temptations which besets bishops and all those who enjoy great ecclesiastical properties, is their unregulated affection for their relations, which makes them bestow on them preferment which would be more worthily given to others. Dom Bartholomew spoke strongly against this abuse, especially in a letter which he wrote at the Council of Trent to Father John of Leyra, his vicar-general: " Act always with fear and trembling," he wrote, " as regards your relations. Self-love is a seducer who is always spreading snares for us. It tries to persuade us that we are doing for God what we are only doing for ourselves. Remember those words of St. Thomas: '*That the more a man has good natural qualities, and is inclined to mercy, the more he should watch over himself; for fear that by not acting with sufficient light and discernment, he should wound charity under the pretence of practising it.*'"

In this matter Father Louis of Grenada writes of our holy archbishop: "All those who needed help were received with great affection in his palace: and he used to say that he was the only stranger in the house, the poor being the masters, and that all he had was theirs. He looked upon them as his only relations, saving a sister he had in the Monastery of the Rosary at Lisbon, to whom he gave simply every year what was necessary for her own maintenance, so that she might not be a burden to her community, who were poor. Some one having exclaimed against what they called his excessive hardness and strictness in this matter, he replied: "If my relations complain that I am stingy with regard to them, let them remember that they were born poor. I think I do enough if I maintain them as I do the poor of my flock, and to whom I owe more as their pastor and bishop than I do to my own relations and friends. But as for enriching them, and advancing them at the expense of the Church, that will I never do as long as God gives me grace. I must be devoid of sense and faith if I were to wish to buy a temporary advantage for my relations at the cost of their damnation and mine. I may dispose as I like of the heritage of my father, and divide it among my relations; but I know no theology which would advise or permit me to enrich my parents with money which has been consecrated to God and given to the Church for the relief of the poor." He proposed to himself the example of Pope Clement IV. who, being a native of France, and having married and been a minister of the king, St. Louis, became eventually bishop and cardinal, and was elected Pope in 1264. He is praised by all writers of his life as a man of eminent virtue, given to prayer, fasting, and good works. One of his sayings was, "*A pope has no relations.*" Having had two daughters by his marriage, and one of them having become a nun, he gave her only thirty ducats, although he was naturally very liberal; and the other having married a man of some position, he only gave her three hundred ducats. And seeing that she was extravagant, and running into extraordinary expenses, he declared to her that she must make up her mind that she would never receive anything more from him as long as he lived. The following is a letter from that holy Pope on this subject, as reported by the authors of his life.

LETTER OF POPE CLEMENT IV. TO ONE OF HIS NEAREST RELATIONS.

"*Many are rejoiced at our promotion, but as for me, I only feel the weight which overwhelms me. What rejoices others fills me with sadness and fear. And if you wish to know how you ought to behave when this news reaches you, we declare to you that you must only be more humble in future. For what humbles us ought not to be a subject of exaltation to those nearest to us, for the honour of this world passes in a moment. We do not wish you or any of our relations to come to see us unless you are expressly sent for. If any one of you were to arrive with the intention of obtaining something from us, that person will have to return with shame. If my sister marries, do not strive to choose for her a person of higher rank than her own on my account. For if you do so, you will only offend me, and you must remember that you must expect nothing from me. If you marry her simply, and give her to that soldier's son, I will give you three hundred pounds for her dowry. But if you seek a great alliance for her, you must not expect a penny from me. For I declare solemnly that I will not allow any of my relations to profit in any way by the dignity to which it has pleased God to raise me: and that I wish my nearest relations should marry the same persons they would have done if I had remained a humble priest. Warn them not to leave their homes; to behave with the utmost modesty; to refuse all the presents that may be offered to them; and never to be so bold as to venture to speak to me in favour of any person whatsoever. For if they do so, it will not help in any way those they may recommend to me, and they will only do harm to themselves.*"

CHAPTER XVII.

OF THE PATIENCE PASTORS SHOULD SHOW IN THE PERSECUTIONS AND TROUBLES OF THIS LIFE.—WHAT THE VIRTUE OF THE ARCHBISHOP WAS ON THIS POINT.

We can say nothing more useful touching the patience which bishops should show amidst persecutions and contradictions than what Dom Bartholomew wrote on this subject, in the eighth chapter of his book. "Consider," he writes, "you who are bishops in the Church of God, who are those whom He sends you to instruct and govern. He teaches it to you Himself in holy writ, when He says to Ezechiel: '*Son of man, I send thee to the children of Israel, to a rebellious people that hath revolted from Me, they and their fathers, and that have transgressed My covenant even unto this day. And they to whom I send thee are children of a hard face and of an obstinate heart*,' '*a provoking house*,' '*unbelievers*,' '*destroyers*,' '*scorpions*' rather than men. (Ezechiel ii. verses 3, 4, 5, 6.) And this word of Job's is applicable to bishops: '*I was the brother of dragons, and companion of ostriches.*' (Job xxx. verse 29.) Prepare yourself, then, with a good stock of patience and gentleness. It is for this reason that St. Augustine, explaining those words of the Psalm: '*My days are vanished like smoke, and my bones are grown dry like fuel for the fire,*' (Psalm ci. verse 4,) says: '*The wicked are the fire which burn the good. The more they love them, the more they are burnt, because the loss of the bad is the greater sorrow to them, the more zeal they have for their salvation.*' The same Father, considering the continual lament of a bishop who does not see the fruit which he wishes of his labours, applies to him these words of the Psalmist: '*Have mercy on me, O Lord, for I am afflicted; my eye is troubled with wrath.*' (Psalm xxx. verse 10.) '*If you are afflicted,*' continues St. Augustine, '*Why are you at the same time wrathful? It is because you are angry at the sins of others. For who would not feel angry at seeing men renounce the vices of the age in words only and not in deeds, who confess God with their lips, and renounce Him by their habits? Who would not be moved to wrath at seeing Christians laying snares for other Christians, who are their brothers, and who betray that kiss of peace which they give one another in the Holy Mysteries?*' Amidst the perils in which you find yourself, remember the words of St. Gregory: '*That the glory of Job was to have been good amongst the bad. He who does not suffer patiently the evil of others, shows by his impatience that he is still far removed from perfection. If you do not choose to be tried by the malice of Cain, you will not become an Abel. Grains of wheat in the ear are mixed with straw. The first man had two sons; one was elected, the other a reprobate. Noah had three sons in the ark; the two first were humble, and the third by his pride insulted his father. Isaac had two children; the one preserved his humility, the other was reproved even before his birth. Jacob had twelve children; of whom one was sold because he was good, and the others sold him because they were wicked. Jesus Christ in the same way chose twelve apostles, and a traitor was amongst them to prove the rest. Thus the good and bad are always mingled in this world. The good are thus purified amongst the bad, as gold in a furnace, and they grow as lilies among thorns.*'" (Greg. Moral., lib. 20, cap. 29.)

"Whenever then we are crossed in our holiest wishes, and in our best undertakings, do not let us lose courage. We ought to hope on, and to console ourselves in Him who has said to us: '*Because he hoped in Me I will deliver him. I will protect him because he hath known My name. He shall cry to Me, and I will hear him. I am with him in tribulation, I will deliver him, I will glorify him.*' (Psalm xc. verses 14, 15.) For, as St. Gregory says: '*The opposition which is raised against our best plans is only to prove and exercise our virtue, and not a sign that God rejects us.*' (Greg., lib. 7, epist. 27.) How can a bishop be cast down or troubled when he sees himself decried by carnal and secular men, if he has engraved in his heart these words of Jesus Christ: '*Blessed are ye when they shall revile you, and persecute you, and speak all that is evil against you untruly for My sake. Be glad and rejoice, for your reward is very great in heaven. For so they persecuted the prophets that were before you*'? (St. Matt. v. verses 11 and 12.) Think also of these words in the Book of Wisdom: '*Let us lie in wait for the just, because he is not for our turn, and he is contrary to our doings, and upbraideth us with transgressions of the law, and divulgeth against us the sins of our way of life. He boasteth that he hath the knowledge of God, and calleth himself the son of God. He is become a censurer of our thoughts. He is grievous unto us even to behold; for his life is not like other men's, and his ways are very different. We are esteemed by him as triflers, and he abstaineth from our ways as from filthiness, and he preferreth the latter end of the just, and glorieth that he hath God for his Father.*' (Wisdom ii. verses 12, 13, 14, 15, 16.) Apply to yourselves, O· pontiffs of Jesus Christ, those burning words of the great martyr St. Ignatius: '*I am the wheat of Jesus Christ, which must be bruised and ground by the teeth of beasts,*' (that is, of carnal men,) '*that I may become pure bread.*' Do you fancy that you can live without afflictions and worries in the midst of a worldly and secular people? Moses cried out to God: '*I am

not able alone to bear all this people, because it is too heavy
for me. I beseech Thee to kill me, that I be not afflicted
with so great evils.' (Numbers xi. verses 14 and 15.)
Jeremiah found himself so overwhelmed with his charge
that he exclaimed, ' Cursed be the day wherein I was born.'
(Jeremiah xx. verse 14.) St. Paul cried: ' Who is weak
and I am not weak? Who is scandalized and I am not
on fire?' (2 Cor. xi. verse 29.) All saints have suffered
in this way. And you fancy you can live among the
wicked without any trouble, and in the midst of a world
where sin reigns supreme, and where the flame of unholy
and earthly desires consumes everything. St. Augustine
said in his time: *If a man commits some sin, and a
bishop reproves or blames him, people say: ' See what a
bad bishop we have!' If he do not reprove, but praise
him, they exclaim: ' There is a good bishop!' But when
he remains firm and constant in reproving what is wrong,
they seek for false accusations against him, so that his
conduct may appear suspicious. Or they say of him that
he does not practice what he preaches; or blame him for
doing things which he has never done.'* When, then, you
find yourself attacked by the malice and persecutions
of the wicked, call to mind those words St. Bernard:
*' I know no medicine so good to cure the wounds of my
soul as reproaches and injuries.'* (Bern., epist. 280, ad
Eugen.) And again, the same saint writes: *' That a man
is not really brave unless he feels his courage grow under
the difficulties and obstacles he meets with. But as for me,
I think that a man who has faith should never be so full
of confidence and strength as when God chastises him with
affliction.'* (Epist. 32.) *'For, as in the saints and elect
afflictions produce patience, and patience experience, and
experience hope, and hope salvation; so in those who are
lost and whom God reproves, affliction produces, on the contrary, weakness and discouragement; discouragement trouble,*

and trouble despair; and despair perdition and death.' To defend yourself from so dangerous a snare, remember the consolation which the Holy Spirit gives you in the person of His Spouse, according to the same St. Bernard: '*When, being blamed by some of the daughters of Jerusalem, who are marked by the thorns which pricked the lilies, those who are good and simple consoled their mother, and in her person all holy souls, by saying:* '*Recti diligunt te,*' i.e., *those who are right-minded love you.* '*Do not trouble,*' *they say,* '*to see yourself unjustly blamed by calumnious tongues, for it is certain that you are loved by those who go straight to God.*' *And that is, doubtless, a very solid consolation, that when, by striving to live aright, evil is said of us, those who have good and simple hearts love us. For it is certain that to defend us against those who unjustly accuse and run us down, it is enough that we have the affection of those who are really good, with the testimony of our own conscience. For this reason the Church, figured by the spouse, says:* '*I am black but beautiful;*' *that is, I am black from the calumnies with which they have blackened me: but I am beautiful and innocent in the eyes of God, who looks to the bottom of my heart. This blackness comes from persecution, which is the richest ornament of the spouse of Jesus Christ, if it be borne for truth and justice.*' (Bernard, in Cant., serm. 58, numbers 11 and 12.) '*Therefore, it is said in the Acts:* '*And they went from the presence of the council rejoicing that they were accounted worthy to suffer reproach for the name of Jesus.*' (Acts v. verse 41.) '*The Saviour taught us the same truth when He said: Blessed are they that suffer persecution for justice's sake.*' (Matt. v. verse 10.) '*I think that it is principally in this that the Church glorifies herself, in that she sees thus accomplished in her the words of her Spouse:* '*If they have persecuted Me they will also persecute you.*' (St. John xv. verse 20.) *For thus she says in the person of His spouse:* '*Do not consider me that I am brown, because the sun hath altered my colour.'* (Cant. i. verse 5.) *As if she said: Do not accuse me, or think I am become deformed, because in the persecution that has been stirred up against me I have lost the glory and reputation which shine in the world. Why do you reproach me for that exterior blackness, as it does not arise from an ill-regulated life, but from the ardent passion of those that persecute me?'*"

The authors of the different biographies of Dom Bartholomew remark that, especially after the Council of Trent, when he laboured so hard to re-establish discipline and the reformation of morals among his flock, he saw almost every one turn against him, and labour to destroy the esteem and reputation which his virtue had acquired in the mind of his people. We have seen in the Third Book (fifth chap.) how he suffered from his own chapter, and from the rich, whose vices he strove to repress; in the twelfth chapter how he was stigmatised as "*a Lutheran and a Heretic;*" in the sixth chapter how he suffered even personal violence; and in the eleventh chapter how he was accused at Rome by his own priests. In all these painful persecutions, which lasted during the whole of the twenty-four years while he exercised episcopal functions, he was sustained by the consolations which he gave to others in his book, and which he drew from holy writ, and from the words of the great saints. He would often quote the letter of St. Gregory to Bishop Columbus, who complained of the number of his enemies: " *You ought to be persuaded, my dear brother, that the good will be always hated and persecuted by the wicked, and that it is enough to act according to God to be tormented in this world, and torn to pieces by the calumnies of men. St. Paul said: 'All that will live godly in Christ Jesus shall suffer persecution.'* (2 Tim. iii. verse 12.) *If then you are not persecuted, it is a sign that you have less piety than you ought to have. The same apostle says to the Thessalonians: 'Yourselves know, brethren,*

that our entrance in unto you was not in vain. But having suffered many things before, and been shamefully treated (as you know) at Philippi, we had confidence in our God.' (1 Thess. ii. verses 1 and 2.) Do you not admire how this great apostle speaks, as if he should have thought his entrance useless if it had not been accompanied by afflictions and outrages? For as wheat during the winter, being covered with ice and snow, is strengthened within, and grows up afterwards more vigorously; so when charity finds itself, as it were, overwhelmed by an immense number of evils, she unites herself the more closely to God, and is led to greater zeal in holy works. I consider all these envenomed tongues, who blacken you with their slanders, like a great tempest which has been raised up against you; and your soul, being agitated by it, is like a ship in the midst of the waves. But remember that the Holy Spirit tells us, by the mouth of the prophet-king, 'Thou hast regarded my humility; Thou hast saved my soul out of distresses.' (Psalm xxx. verse 8.) For if you remain firm in the position which God demands of you amidst all these obstacles and contradictions, you will show that you are really acting as a faithful servant. Remember what the Son of God said to His well-beloved disciples: 'Amen, I say unto you, that you shall lament and weep, but the world shall rejoice.' (St. John xvi. verse 20.) Affliction not only does not discourage, but sustains and fortifies a faithful soul. A Christian, and still more a bishop, becomes stronger the more he is opposed, and more and more courageous in adversity, and he then acts with greater resolution and vigour, because, being founded, like the Church, on the immoveable stone, which is Jesus Christ, he is not shaken either by the violence of the winds and tempests, nor by the overflowing of the waters."
(St. Greg. lib. 6, epist. 2. Ibid., lib. 7. ep. 3. Ibid., lib. 7, epist. 25.) Our holy prelate was so impressed with this truth, that when he was so atrociously calumniated at Rome, he replied to his friends that, "Though he was

very sorry for the injury done to the Church and to the episcopate; yet that calumnies and persecutions were always the bishop's portion; that they inherited those as they did the apostolic dignity; and that they need not think themselves more holy than their Master, who, being holiness itself, did not fail to be accused and dishonoured as a seditious person and a villain."

The holy prelate wished likewise to fortify bishops against all the evils which might befall them, and among the rest, those of illness and bodily suffering. "Let the bishops whom God tries by sufferings," (he writes,) "remember the innumerable number of trials to which St. Gregory was exposed, and of which he gives us a sad picture in many of his letters. *'For more than twenty-seven years,'* (he writes,) *' we are living amidst the swords and violence of the Lombards, who lay the most heavy taxes upon us, and make us pay dearly for the lives which they have spared us still. All Europe is groaning under the yoke of these barbarians. The towns are destroyed; our armies defeated; whole' provinces pillaged; and the land remains barren for want of labourers to cultivate it. I find myself overwhelmed with cares, and loaded with the charge of all the bishops, priests, monasteries, and poor; in fact, of the whole population. And I am obliged at the same time to watch against the ambushes and snares laid for us by our enemies, and to be continually on my guard, not to allow myself to be surprised by the treachery and deceit of their officers. For I think that the want of humanity of men who kill us when they can is more bearable than the avarice of the judges and magistrates, who keep us in continual trouble and misery, and from whose harshness, extortions, and rapine we find it most difficult to defend ourselves."* (Greg., lib. 4, epist. 35.) Then as to his bodily health, he writes: "*For the last two years I have been constantly confined to my bed, and tormented with gout. Occasionally the pain is so violent that I can hardly keep up *for three hours on feast days to celebrate the Holy Sacrifice of the Mass; and I am obliged to go to bed directly afterwards from the agony I endure. Every day I am on the point of death, and yet I cannot die; for being so great a sinner, God wishes me to suffer a long time in this painful earthly prison-house. Therefore I address many earnest cries to Him for mercy, saying with David: Educ de custodia animam meam.'* And to a bishop he wrote again: *'Pray to our Lord for me, so that He may loose the bonds of my sins, and relieve me from the heavy burden of this mortal body. For even if the sweetness and inexpressible beauty of the celestial country which God has promised us did not attract us for itself, the multitude of afflictions which overwhelm us in this life make us run after it with still more eagerness, and in that way I find extreme pleasure in the pains which I suffer, as they do not permit me to have the least enjoyment of anything in this world."*

CHAPTER XVIII.

WHAT OUGHT TO BE THE HUMILITY OF BISHOPS, AND WHAT WAS THAT OF THE HOLY PRELATE.

"*If humility,*" as St. Bernard writes, "*is the greatest ornament of a Sovereign Pontiff,*" (Bern. de Consid., lib. 2, c. 6,) it is equally necessary in a bishop. Dom Bartholomew prefaces his chapter on that subject with the words: "*He that saith he abideth in Jesus Christ, ought himself also to walk as He walked.*" (1 John ii. verse 6.) "What other model, then, ought you to propose to yourselves, O pastors of the Church, than that of Jesus Christ? Do you think that the oracle is abolished when He spoke these words: '*The kings of the Gentiles lord it over them.* ………*But you not so; but he that is the greater among you,* let him become as the younger; and he that is the leader as he that serveth.' (St. Luke xxii. verse 25.) There is no custom, or change of time or place, which can annihilate the truth of these words of Jesus Christ: ' *Quod hominibus altum est, abominatio est ante Deum.*'" (St. Luke xvi. verse 15.) He then goes on to quote the words of St. Gregory, to show how bishops are exposed to the temptations of pride: "*Very often, a bishop, finding himself raised by his position above others, is exalted in his own thoughts, and swells with pride. For as he sees that everything is under his authority; that he has no sooner ordered anything than that his commands are executed; that if he does anything good, all those who are about and subject to him are loud in his praises; that if he does anything wrong, no one can take the liberty of contradicting or finding fault with him; and that very often others esteem in him what they ought to blame and reprove, his mind is seduced by the applause of his inferiors, and he begins to think well of himself. The high esteem which people have of his virtue makes him lose both its spirit and its truth. He forgets what he really is, by dwelling on what others fancy him to be, and instead of examining himself and recognising what he is at the bottom of his heart, he imagines that he is all that people say of him, who can only judge by the outside. He despises those who are subject to him. He does not consider the equality which the same nature and the same origin has placed between us, and he thinks he is as much above them by the eminence of his virtue, as he is by his position. Thus, lifting himself up to a pitch of pride, and despising, from this imaginary height, those whom he ought to consider his equals, he imitates those of whom it is written:* 'he beholdeth every high thing; he is king over all the children of pride.' (Job xli. verse 25.) For the first angel, esteeming very little the condition and glory which was common to all, affected empire and dominion over all the rest when he said: 'I will ascend above the heights of the clouds;

I will be like the Most High.' (Isaiah xiv. verse 14.) But when he said he would lift himself up to the very summit of greatness, he found himself, by the fearful judgment of God, precipitated into the very depths of the abyss of hell. Thus man becomes like the apostate angel, when he forgets that he is a man, and disdains to appear like others. We see in holy writ how Saul was lost in the same manner. Having first appeared humble, he became proud when he was made king, and lost by his pride the crown which his humility had obtained. This is the reproach which God made to him: *' When thou wast a little one in thine own eyes, wast thou not made the head of the tribes of Israel?'* (1 Kings xv. verse 17.) He thought himself little at first, but seeing himself raised to a great dignity, he began to think himself great. He preferred himself to all those under him, and thought himself the first in merit as well as in power and dignity. Thus he was great before God as long as he remained little in his own sight; but when he became great in his own esteem, he became little and despicable before God. Let those, then, who are employed in the government of the Church, labour to humble themselves interiorly in proportion to the grandeur and dignity they have to assume before the world. Let them beware, lest the love of power should take possession of their hearts; and do not let them give way to this passion, lest they should become its slaves, and find pleasure in having every one under their orders. The Wise man teaches us this when he says: *' Have they made thee a ruler? be not lifted up; be among them as one of them.'* (Ecclesiasticus xxxii. verse 1.) And St. Peter teaches us the same thing when he says: *' Neither as lording it over the clergy, but being made a pattern of the flock from the heart.'* (1 St. Peter v. verse 3.) And the Saviour Himself tells us what torment is reserved for the servant who takes advantage of the authority given him above the rest, when He says in the Gospel: *' But if that servant shall say in his heart, My lord is long in coming, and shall begin to strike the men-servants and maid-servants, and to eat and to drink, and be drunk, the lord of that servant will come in the day that he hopeth not, and at the hour that he knoweth not, and shall separate him, and shall appoint him his portion with unbelievers.*' (St. Luke xii. verses 45, 46.) *For it is just that he should be placed in the rank of hypocrites who, under pretext of keeping up discipline, changes the ministry of the Church (which should be a government of charity,) into one of domination and empire.*" (Greg. Pastor., part 2, cap. 6.) "*For this reason,*" continues St. Gregory, "*a chief pastor is the more bound to humble and accuse himself before God, because when he commits a fault he is not reproved by men; as, on the contrary, those who are under his guidance will be less exposed to the rigour of God's judgments, because they have a pastor to correct them when they have done wrong.*" And St. Bernard, speaking of the difficulties of government, says: "*Pauci, qui utiliter; pauciores, qui humiliter præsint.*" (Bern. in Cantic., serm. 23, number 10.)

St. Augustine, in a letter he wrote to Aurelius, Bishop of Carthage, spoke strongly on the same subject as follows: "*It is a great thing not to rejoice at being honoured and praised by men; to cut off all exterior pomp and luxury, and to seek, in what one necessarily retains, only the salvation and interest of those who esteem us. David said, with great reason:* 'God hath scattered the bones of them that please men.' (Psalm lii. verse 6.) *What is weaker or more despicable than for a man to be cast down and afflicted because people speak disparagingly of him, although he knows that what they say is false? For the vexation at being thus unjustly decried would not go to his heart so much if the love of human praise had not previously 'scattered his bones;' that is, destroyed his strength of mind. I know how solid your virtue is; and therefore I do not say this to you but to myself. I think, nevertheless, that you will agree with me how hard and difficult a thing it is to conquer the wish to be praised. And we do not realize the strength of this enemy till we have declared war against him; for although it is easy to say that we do not care for praise when we do not get it, it is very difficult not to feel pleased when we do. And yet our hearts ought to be so raised above the earth, and united to God alone, that, when we can, we ought to check those who praise us, for fear they should attribute merits to us which we do not possess, or which should belong to God; or that they should praise us for things which do exist in us, but which are not worthy of praise, like natural gifts which we share with the bad or with the beasts. If people praise us with good reason we should rejoice, not that we have pleased men, but that we have done what God expected of us, to whom should be attributed all that they esteem in us, as He is the author and principle of all that is worthy of praise. I say this to myself every day, or rather God puts it in my heart, as it is to Him we owe all the salutary warnings of holy writ, and all the holy thoughts with which He inspires us, and nevertheless, though I fight so strongly against this dangerous enemy, I am often wounded, for although I do not seek for human praise, I cannot help feeling pleased when I obtain it.*" (Aug., epist. 64, ad Aurel.) This same saint thought this passion for human approbation so dangerous that he says, in his Confessions: "*That it is one of the principal causes why God is so little feared and loved;*" "*Hinc sit vel maxim non amare té, nec castè timere te.*" And he says to God, in the same book: "*Thou knowest how many sighs my heart has breathed to Thee on this subject, and how my eyes have shed torrents of tears.*" "*Tu nosti de hâc re ad te gemitum cordis mei et flumina occulorum meorum.*" (Aug. Confess., lib. 10, cap. 36 and 37.) St. Gregory makes the following commentary on the words of Job, "*Si vidi solem cùm fulgeret:*" "*The sun marks the good works of which the Son of God has said: 'Let your light so shine before men, that they may see your good works, and glorify your Father who is in heaven.'* (St. Matt. v. verse 16.) But to see the sun in his splendour is to think over what one has done right, and to attribute the glory to oneself instead of to God alone. For there are some people who rest on the little good they have done, and forget all their sins. And yet if they considered the light and the rigour of the just Judge, they would have more fear of the evil which is still in them, than joy at the good which they have so imperfectly done. And they would be more anxious at what they owe to divine justice, than satisfied because they have paid a very small portion of their debt. For a man is not free from his creditor till he has paid all he owes. He who runs a race does not win the prize till he has come to the end of the course. And in vain will he have started if he does not persevere to the end. This life is our course, and heaven is our goal. We ought, then, to be like wise travellers, who do not look back so much on the distance they have traversed as on the road which remains for them to go. We ought, in the same way, to be more attentive to what is wanting in us than pleased at what we are, and to what we have got to do rather than to what we have done. For it is natural to weak human nature to like better to dwell on pleasant rather than unpleasant things. As we are sick in mind and heart, and we feel that reflection on our faults will be painful to us, we try to think on something more agreeable, and on which we can rest as in a soft bed. We think over all our good works, and do not meditate on the number of graces we have lost from having neglected to do a great many things which we ought to have done. Even the saints and the elect of God have been tempted in this way. But if they are really saints they turn away their eyes from this self-pleasing. They stifle the joy their virtues might afford them, and conceive a holy sadness for their negligences and defects. They look upon themselves as vile and miserable sinners; and although their lives may be most pure and exemplary, they are the only persons who do not see their own merits, which others admire and revere. For this reason St. Paul, wishing to humble himself in the midst of the miracles which he constantly wrought, recalls his past sins, saying: 'Jesus Christ hath counted me faithful, putting me in the ministry, who before was a blasphemer and a persecutor, and contumelious." (1 Tim. i. verse 13.) 'And when he thinks himself obliged to record the great graces God has bestowed upon him, he adds directly: 'For myself I will glory in nothing but in my infirmities.' (2 Corinth. xii. verse 5.) If, then, he spoke advantageously of himself, it was only for the instruction of his disciples; but that he might preserve his humility, he shows at the same time that he never allowed himself to dwell on these supernatural graces, but only on his weakness and suffering.'" (Greg. Moral., lib. 22, cap. 5.)

We have seen in the first book how entirely the archbishop acted up to these principles during his whole life, living with his priests as if they were his own brothers, and frequently saying, "That they were the coadjutors whom God had given him, that they might bear with him the weight of his heavy charge, and thus enable him the better to fulfil his duties." He had learnt this moderation and episcopal humility, not only from his own virtue, but from the canons of the Fourth Council of Carthage, which he quoted in his book as follows: "*Let the bishop, wherever he may be, never suffer a priest to remain standing in his presence, while he is sitting.*" (4, canon 34.) And again in the thirty-fifth canon: "*When the bishop is in church, or in a council of his priests, let him sit in a higher place than the rest; but when he is in his own house, let him remember what he is, and let him act as being the colleague of his priests.*" Thus we see that in the writings of the ancient bishops, when they address a priest or deacon, they put the title "*Compresbytero,*" or "*Condiacono,*" "so that they might forget, in some measure, their episcopal dignity, *which placed them above their clergy*, (according to the expression of St. Gregory,) *to remember that of priest or deacon, which was common to them both."*

What made the humility of our holy prelate so admirable was, that it seemed to increase in proportion to the great reputation which he acquired, and to the honours showered upon him, not only in the Council, where the cardinals declared him the *"first bishop in Christendom,"* but by the Sovereign Pontiffs, who all loved him, and by the Kings of Spain and Portugal, in treating with whom he showed all the courage and episcopal generosity which were the glory of the bishops in the first centuries.

St. Gregory points out this truth by an excellent comparison: *"Praises and a high reputation among men injure virtue, either in its birth, or in its progress, or in its perfection. When virtue perishes in its birth by proud thoughts, it is like a tree, which being planted in the earth, rots at once. When it perishes in its progress at the sight of its good works, it is like a tree which, having been carefully planted and grown well, is spoiled by some sudden accident, and is dried up at the roots. But when it has attained maturity, and perishes through the praises it receives, it is like a tree which, having put forth fine branches and being loaded with fruit, is thrown down and uprooted by a whirlwind. Thus the praises and applause of men are like winds which blow violently, and form a tempest of glory and reputation, which knock down the greatest souls.* St. Gregory calls the calumnies of evil tongues, 'a tempest,' '*tempestas male dicentiæ.*' And now he calls the loud praises given to the saints a tempest, '*tempestas famæ.*' Thus the life of a bishop is always full of dangers. For if he be persecuted, he has to struggle against impatience and discouragement; and if he be praised, he is tempted to vanity and complacency. And this last tempest is so much more dangerous than the former, because it can upset the soul *without its being perceived, and because it comes in a moment of great calm, when it seems as if everything were in favour of the holy intentions of good people. Therefore St. Gregory says again: 'That God often permits His servants to be dishonoured by the calumnies and evil tongues of the bad, lest they should be weakened and corrupted by the praises and applause of the good.'"* (Greg., in Job, lib. 22, cap. 5.)

CHAPTER XIX.

OF THE RESIGNATION OF THE HOLY PRELATE.—SIX REASONS WHY A BISHOP MAY LEAVE HIS BISHOPRIC.

What we have said in the last chapter regarding the humility of the archbishop brings us to the reasons why he resigned his bishopric. For it appears extraordinary that a man of such piety should not have thought it his duty to serve God all his life in the functions of his ministry. But in order to understand this matter better, we will see what are the rules laid down by the Church for those who desire to resign their bishoprics.

It is difficult to put the matter more clearly than it has been done by Pope Innocent III., in his letter to the Archbishop of Cagliari, which for this reason has been put in the Decretals. He says there are six cases in which a bishop may be allowed to resign.

1. If he be guilty of some great crime.
2. If he be too feeble in body.
3. If he be wanting in knowledge.
4. If his people are too bad.
5. If he be the cause of some great scandal.
6. If he have fallen into some irregularity. (Decret., lib. 1, de Renunt. tit. 9, cap. 10, nisi cum pridem.)

As to the first, "*A bishop,*" he writes, "*cannot ask to leave his bishopric for any faults of which his conscience may accuse him. But the sin must be so great as to prevent his fulfilling the functions of his charge, even after he has fulfilled the penance exacted for it.*" St. Chrysostom says on this subject: "*As for me, I think one ought to look upon the episcopate with a feeling of respect and reserve, which would lead us to fly at first from so difficult a position; and that if one be engaged in it, one should not wait for the verdict of men to resign it, if we commit any fault which renders us unworthy of the charge, in which case one should prevent their judgment by resigning oneself. That is the best way of drawing down the mercy of God. For if one wishes to retain a bishopric unjustly, one cannot expect or deserve indulgence and pardon, and one commits a second offence greater than the first. But ambition reigns so supremely in these days that no one can be found capable of such a resolution.*" (Chrys. de Sacerd., lib. 3, cap. 4.)

On this point there is a curious letter of St. Augustine's to Pope Celestine, of which we will here give an extract, with the circumstances which led to it. Having converted a great number of Donatists, in a town called Fusali, about forty miles from Hippo, which had always formed part of his diocese, St. Augustine was afraid that he should be unable to take all the necessary care of this people, and resolved to establish a new bishopric, and choose a man who should be bishop. He cast his eyes for this purpose on a very holy priest whom he judged worthy of this dignity; and having entreated the Primate of Numidia to come to Hippo, he presented to him this man, begging him to consecrate him. But the priest absolutely refused this dignity, and it was impossible to overcome his scruples. St. Augustine being extremely surprised at this unexpected difficulty, and seeing that the whole Church was waiting for the election, while he did not dare to send back so venerable a prelate as the primate without doing anything, after he had come so far to oblige him, chose a young man named Antony, whom he had brought up in his seminary ever since he was a child, but who was only a lector. The people of Fusali received very readily one who had been selected by St. Augustine himself, and very soon after he was consecrated. But this young bishop turned out very ill; and was accused by the leading men in his diocese of exercising a most insupportable tyranny over them by rapine, violence, and vexations of all sorts, which at last compelled St. Augustine and the other bishops to deprive him of his jurisdiction, and exempt his flock from their obedience, although he still retained the title of bishop. But Antony refused to submit to their sentence, declaring that they could not deprive him of his rights or functions. And having obtained a decree from Rome in his favour, he threatened to call out the troops and to re-enter his diocese by force. St. Augustine, who was deeply grieved, both for the sake of the people of Fusali, who were as his children, and for that of the young bishop, whom he had brought up as a son, represented the whole matter to Pope Celestine, and concluded his letter in these words: "*As far as I am myself concerned, I own to your Holiness, that in this extreme peril on both sides, of souls who are equally dear to me, I feel so overwhelmed with fear and sadness, that, if I see (which God forbid) that the Church is ravaged by one who has become bishop through my imprudence, and that in losing himself he is destroying them, I am resolved to resign my functions, and to leave my bishopric. For remembering those words of the apostle, 'If we judge ourselves we shall not be judged of the Lord,' I will thus judge myself so as to obtain pardon from Him who will come to judge the quick and dead.*" (Aug., epist. 261, ad Celest.)

We see also in the canons of the Church that there is

another reason for resigning a bishopric, which is included in the first, namely, what this Pope calls "*conscientia criminis.*" That is, when there has been something criminal in the acceptance of the charge; as, if it had been simonaical, or in any other way illegitimate and contrary to God's ordinance.

2. "*A bishop may resign his charge on account of the weakness which old age or his maladies may cause; but this must be only understood if they be such as really to incapacitate him from his functions. For otherwise the apostle would not say that 'he gloried in his infirmities and his weaknesses.' For if the languor which old age entails seems to justify a man in giving up his charge, on the other hand the wisdom, experience, and authority, which are its accompaniments, ought to lead him to remain. So the apostle says he is the stronger for his very weakness. And sometimes the soul is strengthened all the more as the body becomes enfeebled.*"

3. "*A bishop may ask to resign his bishopric if he has not enough knowledge. For, as light and knowledge are very necessary for all the spiritual functions of a bishop, and even for temporal ones, if he should feel that these qualities are wanting in him, he does well to leave his bishopric, as he has not the science necessary for its government.*" (Innoc. III. epist., ad Ep. Calan.)

St. Chrysostom speaks as follows as to a want of knowledge: "*If it be better to be cast into the sea with a millstone about one's neck, rather than to scandalize one of the least of the faithful; and if those who wound the consciences of their brothers sin against Jesus Christ Himself, how will those be treated who have not been the cause of one or two, or three persons being lost, but a whole people? Will they be excused from ignorance, or want of experience? These excuses would not be accepted. Such a defence might be made by one of the people to obtain pardon for his faults, but not by a prelate who is responsible for the sins of others. He who has been placed in a position where he is to correct the ignorance of those under him cannot plead as an excuse his own ignorance, or say, 'I have not seen the sword coming, I have not sounded the trumpet,' because it is he who, (as Ezechiel says,) is to sound it. And the prophet goes on to say: 'If the watchman see the sword coming, and sound not the trumpet, and the people look not to themselves, and the sword come and cut off a soul from among them, he indeed is taken away in his iniquity; but I will require his blood at the hand of the watchman.'"* (Ezechiel xxxiii. verse 6. Chrys. de Sacerd., lib. 6, cap. 1.) But Innocent III. adds very well: "*That although it may be very desirable that a pastor should be eminent in science, yet the perfection of his charity may supply the imperfection of his knowledge.*" (Innoc. III., in eadem. epist.) For if he really loves the Church, he will make use of the light of those who know its spirit and its rules, as if it were his own. For those who really love God may look upon all divine truths as belonging to them, according as St. Augustine teaches. And when they are enlightened by others, "*they do not receive it as a strange thing, but as something belonging to them, and which was already in their hearts by an inspiration of charity. On the contrary, he who speaks well of God, and lives wrongly, 'steals the Lord's words,' as the prophet complains, and usurps what is not his* (Jeremias xxiii. verse 30); *because he wishes to appear the friend of God when he is His enemy, and he destroys by his actions what he would seem to establish by his words.*" (August. de Doctrin. Christ., lib. 4, cap. 29.)

4. "*A bishop may give up his charge and abandon his flock when he sees them so hardened in evil that all his exhortations and care are thrown away and entirely useless.*" For thus God speaks to Ezechiel: "*I will make thy tongue stick fast to the roof of thy mouth, and thou shalt be dumb,*

and not as a man that reproveth, because they are a provoking house.' (Ezechiel iii. verse 26.) And the apostles said the same to the Jews: *'Because you reject the word of God, and judge yourselves unworthy of eternal life, behold we turn to the Gentiles.'"* (Acts xiii. verse 46. Innoc. III., in Eadem. Epist.)

There is a remarkable example of this in the life of St. Martyrius, Bishop of Antioch. For, finding his people utterly unmanageable, and the whole town of Antioch full of trouble and sedition, he left his bishopric, after having said out loud in the church: *"I renounce a disobedient clergy and a rebellious people, and a disordered and corrupt church; although at the same time I reserve to myself the episcopal dignity. (Ego clero immorigero; et populo rebelli; et ecclesiæ contaminatæ renuntio; servata interim mihi sacerdotii dignitate.")* (Baron. ann. Chr. 471, num. 5, 11.) *"A bishop, however, should not abandon his flock for every kind of disorder, but only when his sheep are turned into wolves; and when those who ought to submit themselves humbly to his orders raise themselves up proudly against him, without a hope of being able to induce them to return to their duty."* As St. Augustine also writes: *"We ought not to give up the good because of the misconduct of the bad; but we ought, on the contrary, to try and bear with the wicked, so as to be able to be of use to the good. (Non propter malos deserendi sunt boni; sed propter bonos tolerandi sunt mali.)"*

5. *"A bishop may give up his bishopric when he finds that so great a scandal has been stirred up about him that he can only appease it by his resignation. For otherwise he would seem to love temporal honour more than his eternal salvation. And he ought then to remember the words of the apostle: 'Wherefore, if meat scandalize my brother, I will never eat flesh.'* (1 Cor. viii. verse 13.) *But there is a wide difference between two kinds of scandal, which the Son of God Himself*

teaches. There is that which one gives in inducing others to do wrong, of whom Jesus Christ has said: 'he that shall scandalize one of these little ones that believe in Me, it were better for him that a millstone were hanged about his neck, and that he should be drowned in the depths of the sea.' (Matt. xviii. verse 6.) *But there is another kind of scandal which men take upon themselves when they are scandalized at that which is good, as the Pharisees were scandalized at the words of Jesus Christ. And our Saviour teaches us to despise this sort of scandal, as He did that of the Jews, saying to the apostles:* 'Let them alone; they are blind and leaders of the blind.'" (Matt. xv. verse 14.) In the same sense St. Gregory spoke that famous word, which St. Bernard has made use of since: "*It is better that a scandal should happen than that truth should be abandoned.*" *(Melius est ut scandalum oriatur, quàm ut veritas relinquatur.)* (Greg. in Ezechiel, hom. 7, and Bern., epist. 78, num. 10. Innocent III., ibid.)

We see an example of this manner of leaving a bishopric in St. Gregory of Nazianzum, who, having been chosen by the Fathers of the Second Œcumenical Council to be Bishop of Constantinople, which he had governed for a long while with marvellous wisdom and charity, seeing that a dispute had arisen among the bishops on the subject of his election, resigned his charge in presence of the whole episcopate there assembled, saying with the prophet Jonas: "*Si propter me orta est hæc tempestas, mittite me in mare.*"

In a letter which St. Augustine wrote (No. 238) to Castorius, there is an example of the same virtue. Castorius and his brother Maximian were converted Donatists, and Maximian had been made a bishop. But a great fuss having been made about his election, Maximian resolved to resign his bishopric, so as to give peace to the Church. St. Augustine praises him warmly for this act, and writes as follows to his brother: "*It is far more glorious of a man to leave the episcopal charge to preserve the Church from the perils which threaten her, than to receive it in order to fulfil its duties usefully. For such a man shows that he was worthy to receive this honour if the peace of the Church would have allowed him, as he would do nothing unworthy to retain it. Thus God has chosen your brother to show the enemies of the Church, by his noble example, that she contains in her bosom persons who do not seek their own interests, but those of Jesus Christ alone. For when he left the holy ministry which made him the dispenser of the mysteries of God, he did not abandon it from any human reason or passion, but from a love of peace, and from the charity he had for his brethren, lest, by retaining his office, the members of Jesus Christ should have been troubled by shameful and dangerous dissensions which might even have caused serious evils. May God give him that eternal peace which is promised to the Church, to reward him for the sacrifice he has made for the peace of the Church."* He then exhorts Castorius to receive the bishopric which Maximian had resigned: *"ut fratri tuo non ignominiosè cadenti, sed gloriosè cedenti succedas. Ministerium non desidiâ, aut aliqua seculali cupiditate, sed pacificâ charitate deposuit.'"* (August., epist. 238.)

6. *"A bishop may leave his bishopric if he be irregular in himself: as if he had married a second wife; or if he had only married one, if she were a widow; or if he was not born of a legitimate marriage; which are hindrances which he should not have held his tongue about when he received the bishopric."*

These are the six causes, according to Pope Innocent III., which may lead a bishop to resign his bishopric legitimately. He remarks, however, in this letter, that there are some who wish to rid themselves of episcopal functions to escape from the distractions and cares which are inseparable from the charge, and to find, in the tranquillity and repose of private life, more time to think of

God and their own salvation. But this Pope does not consider these to be sufficient reasons for relinquishing a post where God has placed us. "*Though you may feel,*" (he writes,) "*a great desire to retire into solitude, and may say with David, 'Who will give me wings like a dove? and I will fly and be at rest,'* (Psalm liv. verse 7,) *you ought nevertheless to consider that you are bound by your employment, and that you cannot free yourself and give it all up in that manner. You have a Spouse; you have no right to abandon her. For this reason I exhort you not to quit the labours of the pastoral charge; for fear that, refusing to serve Jesus Christ in His members, according to the duty of Martha, to which He has called you, He should reject you from before Him when you choose of yourself to sit with Mary at His feet.*" (Innocent III., in Eadem Epist.)

CHAPTER XX.

THAT THE HUMILITY OF THE ARCHBISHOP WAS THE REAL CAUSE OF HIS RESIGNATION.—EXAMPLE OF SEVERAL SAINTS WHO HAVE DONE THE SAME.—WISDOM OF PHILIP II. IN HIS CHOICE OF BISHOPS.

Among these six reasons given by Innocent III. there are two which Dom Bartholomew might plead when he left his diocese to retire into the monastery. The first, the weakness of his body; the second, the disorders in his flock. As to the first, there is no doubt that after his long and dangerous illness his health was much broken, and that, being sixty-seven years old, the weaknesses of age, and his continual austerities, added to his great labours, had rendered him less capable to perform the onerous functions of his charge. Yet, if we consider the spirit of Pope Innocent, it does not appear that his infirmities were such as to justify his resignation. For if his age had diminished his strength, it had likewise given him longer experience and greater authority, so that he might have followed the custom of the Church, and taken a coadjutor, as several of the cardinals entreated the Pope to insist upon, saying, "*That he ought not to be permitted to leave his bishopric, nor to deprive the episcopal order of so great an example.*" We have seen (in the third book, chap. xix.) how he implored Pius IV. to grant him leave to resign his post long before age had weakened his system, and how he had entreated Philip II. to intercede with the Pope for him to obtain this favour, basing his petition, not only on his increasing infirmities, but "*on his unworthiness of the office.*"

As to the disorders among his flock, the authors of his life remark that, seeing the blindness and hardness of heart of his people, and such obstacles raised to all his plans on their behalf, he would cry and groan before God at his powerlessness to touch their hearts, which he so ardently desired. Yet we must allow that the impression made upon his mind was not that which it would have made on that of others. For while any one else would have blamed the people, he, on the contrary, thought it was his own incapacity which was the cause of their errors, and attributed to his own want of knowledge and charity his failure in healing their souls. Therefore it was in reality his extreme humility which made him so earnest in his desire to resign his office. Certainly it was not from any shrinking from toil; for, as we read in his book, he expressly exhorts all prelates to give themselves to their labours with joy, and not to believe that the distractions of their daily life need hinder their growth in personal holiness. "Why do you complain," he writes, "as if the pastoral charge were an obstacle to devotion? On the contrary, it is a continual exercise of the highest virtues, charity, justice, and mercy. Can anything increase our love more than to have our hearts continually raised to God, and at the same time to run everywhere seeking the salvation of many souls? If you feel the affection of a spouse and a pastor, how useful should such labours be to you, and how sweet to one who loves!" (Stim. Pastor., cap. 5.)

The truth was, that having so high an idea of the importance of the episcopate, and at the same time so humble an opinion of himself, he considered that the following words of St. Bernard applied to himself: "*That it is a monstrous thing to see the highest degree of honour allied to a base mind, and a supreme dignity to a despicable life.*" (St. Bernard, de Consid., lib. 2, cap. 7.)

He had always present to his mind what he called the extreme disproportion between his charge and his virtue, and thought that God demanded of him that he should do all in his power to be relieved from his burden, which he felt to be, (as he himself said to Pope Pius IV.,) "*like a mountain which overwhelmed him.*" On this subject Father Louis of Grenada writes: "When he was settled in his diocese, and had a nearer view of the obligations of his charge, he was filled with such sorrow and discouragement that he spent whole days and nights in imploring the mercy of God, and entreating to be rescued from such great danger. He had always before his eyes the exact account he should have to give to God of the millions of souls who were under his jurisdiction. He trembled at the thought of that judgment, and the sufferings he would have to endure in the next world, which seemed to be as vividly before his mind as if he had seen them with his own eyes. A few months after he had been settled at Braga, I went to see him, and purposely turned the conversation to this point, as I wanted to find out if he still felt the extreme grief and fear which he had experienced when first compelled to accept the charge. The holy prelate spoke with such vehemence on the subject that at

last he exclaimed: 'I must not lose hope, nor take away my life, for God forbids both one and the other; but I assure you that I feel reduced to such an extremity, that those who have a halter round their necks, and are on the point of being hung, do not suffer a keener pain than I feel at this moment, and while their torture is quickly ended, mine is continual, and weighs upon me day and night.'"
We have seen, in the twentieth chapter of the first book, how he reproached Father Louis of Grenada for having made use of him "as of a shield to save his own head," and how, both after the Council of Trent, and during the pontificates of Pius IV. and Pius V., he continually renewed his entreaties to be allowed to resign his post, though always in vain. When the Queen of Portugal, who had elected him archbishop during her regency, retired from court on her son's taking the reins of government into his own hands, the holy prelate wrote her the following letter.

"Madam,

"God having given me a great affection for your highness' soul, I venture to take the liberty of expressing to you how rejoiced I am to see that you prefer a holy retreat to the vain occupations of the world. And I feel your real happiness in this matter the more as I am myself always in danger and amidst the storms and tempests to which the choice of your highness has exposed me for many years. But as it has pleased God, madam, to place your highness in a position of tranquillity, it is just that among the acts you may have to regret, you should mourn over the unworthy labourers whom you have sent into the Lord's vineyard, of whom I am the chief, and ask pardon of God, both for the error you committed in your selection, and for the faults they have fallen into since their appointment to the government of the Church. I hope, madam, for this favour from your highness, just as I feel myself bound to pray earnestly to our Lord, so that He may forgive the fault you were guilty of in naming me to this bishopric, knowing that your intention in this matter was pure and upright. I entreat your highness to be very fearful lest you should not acknowledge with sufficient gratitude the grace God has given you by not taking you away from this world during your regency, as He has thus granted you the time to weep over the faults you may have committed during that period. The more sins you discover in yourself, the more you must believe that you are enlightened by the Spirit of God. And do not flatter yourself by saying, '*I have done what I could;*' for that is all St. Paul could exclaim when he had laboured more than all the rest. We are living in an age which is the enemy of all virtue and justice, and sovereigns are incessantly importuned by interested persons, who press them, not to do justice, but to violate all laws and all rules in order to satisfy their cupidity or their passions. Finally, madam, I again conjure your highness to render continual acts of thankfulness to God that He has deigned to give you some little time before your death to think of your own salvation. It is the grace I ask daily for myself, while I beseech Him with all my heart to fill your highness with His true riches."

This letter proves how the thought of his unworthiness, instead of diminishing as time went on, increased more and more. Finally, the way in which Philip II. had treated him on his accession to the crown of Portugal, gave him courage to renew his entreaties for the king's intercession on his behalf with Pope Gregory XIII., so that he might obtain permission to resign his bishopric, which, as we have seen, was at last granted to him.

The same feeling of repugnance towards his promotion was shown by St. Chrysostom, when he was chosen, though very young, for the episcopate. *"Since the day,"* he writes, *"that you warned me that I had been thought of for the episcopate I have felt as if my soul would separate itself from my body, so violent has been my grief and fear. When I considered, on the one hand, the beauty and holiness of the Spouse of Jesus Christ, and on the other my own vices and faults, I continually bewailed and deplored my misfortune and hers. I sighed without ceasing, saying to myself: 'Who could have been the first to make such a proposal? What great offence has the Church committed against God? By what fault has she so embittered our Lord against her that He should dishonour her by entrusting her guidance into my hands?' I could not bear the thought of the greatness of my unworthiness. I was struck with astonishment, and lost the use of sight and hearing. At last I burst into tears; and the extreme distress and fear I was in really made me beside myself."* (St. Chrysostom, de Sacerd., lib. 6, cap. 6.)

The Pope St. Gregory frequently deplored, in the same way, the condition in which God had placed him, and wrote as follows: *"I am no longer the man I was. My soul is plunged in grief and bitterness. If I am grown great outwardly, within I feel I am fallen very low. I am of the number of those of whom it is written: 'When they were lifted up Thou hast cast them down.'* (Psalm lxxii. verse 18.) *For a man has fallen, who, while increasing in dignity, decreases in merit, and loses the virtue he had acquired in obscurity. I wished to follow the spirit of Jesus Christ as our Master and model, desiring to be, as it is said of Him, the outcast of men, and one despised by the people. But now I find myself overwhelmed by the weight of this dignity which has been imposed upon me. A host of affairs surround me on all sides; and when I try to recollect myself in God I find myself distracted by a thousand cares, like so many waves of the sea, or iron points which pierce my soul. I have lost all peace and tranquillity of mind. My heart is cast down, and sinks under the weight of base and terrestrial occupations. I can no longer find the wings of which David speaks, to raise myself to the contemplation of divine things. I had a favourable wind, and my bark sailed happily when I lived in the retreat of my monastery. But the sea became irritated all of a sudden; the floods rose, and a horrible tempest drove me far out of my course."* (Greg., lib. 1, epist. 5.)

This holy Pope, in his "Morals," again depicts in vivid colours the aversion felt by the just for worldly honours. He quotes the words of Job: "*Quare misero data est lux?*" "*Light,*" (he writes,) "*is given to the miserable when those who recognise, by the knowledge they have of eternal truths, that they are miserable in this life, see themselves raised against their will to the passing dignities and grandeur of the world. Their grief is redoubled at the sight, because, besides the regret they feel at seeing themselves banished from their home for a longer period, they are constrained besides to bear the weight of the honours and dignities imposed upon them. Then these persons, who are happy according to the ideas of the age, are all the more agitated and troubled. They dread lest their labours should have no other reward than that which they have received in this life, and that God, having discovered some secret sin in them, should overwhelm them with exterior grandeur, and deprive them of interior graces. But even if at the bottom of their hearts they feel that they are only seeking to please God, and do not take pleasure in all this outside show, although they are less afraid of the secret judgments of God, they do not cease to feel alarmed at their position, knowing that all that is pleasant and agreeable according to human ideas is capable of insensibly cooling the ardour of their zeal. For this reason the saints fear more to be honoured here below than to be despised, and adversity appears to them preferable to prosperity.* For *the former, weighing upon us from without, makes us look into ourselves, and increases our ardour for true riches; while the latter flatters and fills our minds, and makes our souls tepid and lukewarm, spending them on vain and exterior objects. This is the feeling of the saints with regard to worldly honours. And yet, though they fly from them with such care, God permits, by a secret judgment, that the government of others should be thrust upon them."* (Greg, Moral., lib. 5, cap. 1 and 2.)

The conviction of Dom Bartholomew that he was unworthy of the episcopate made so vivid an impression upon his mind that, considering the rule of St. Gregory, *"That he who has the necessary virtues for an ecclesiastical charge should yield when constrained to accept it, but that he who does not possess them ought not to undertake such a charge, even when pressed to do so,"* (Greg. Past., lib. 1, cap. 9,) he was persuaded that he was in the last category, and consequently ought to have resisted the appointment at all risks. Yet, as long as he was compelled to retain his position, that is, for twenty-four years, he laboured with all his might to fulfil his duties, and showed as much devotion and charity as if he thought God willed nothing of him but that he should live and die a bishop. Father Louis of Grenada, speaking of this, writes: "Though our holy prelate had such an extreme desire to be released from his dignity, yet he performed every duty of his ministry with the most exact and ardent zeal. He excited himself to labour, invoking the Holy Spirit, so that he might be filled with His grace, and obtain strength to fulfil the arduous duties laid upon him. One day, during a visitation of his diocese, those who were with him were obliged to sleep in the same room with him, the lodging being so insufficient, and when he fancied they were all asleep, one of them perceived that he rose in the night, and bursting into tears, knelt down and implored of God with deep sighs that it might please Him to assist him with His grace, so that he might faithfully perform all that his charge demanded of him." It was, therefore, not from fear of labour or a love of ease that he resigned his bishopric, but from the conviction that he was incapable and ought never to have accepted it. Some one having complained to him one day, when he had retired to his monastery, that the Archbishopric of Braga was not so well governed as when he was there, he answered: "God forbid that I should have so much presumption as not to be convinced that he who is now Archbishop acquits himself of his functions infinitely better than I could have done."

Another proof that it was not to escape from work that he had sought for solitude lies in the fact that during the first three years of his retirement, that is, as long as his strength permitted, he went on foot day by day preaching to, and catechising, all the poor people in the neighbouring villages. And just as he dreaded the functions of the episcopate as being above him, so he loved giving these humble instructions, for the lower they appeared, humanly speaking, the more he found them great in the sight of God, and in conformity with the humble opinion he always entertained of himself.

No sooner did he obtain leave to resign his bishopric than he wrote to St. Charles, with whom he was united in a true Christian friendship. St. Charles having received the news, answered him in these words: "I could not read without a secret envy what you wrote to me, that you have resigned, with the Holy Father's permission, the government of the Church of Braga, and that you have retired into a monastery of your order to prepare yourself for death. For I felt directly what security and rest of mind there is in labouring only at that work which Jesus Christ calls, '*the one thing necessary.*' The greater, then, is your present security at anchor in the port, the more I hope that you will offer your prayers to Jesus Christ for him of whom you know the infirmities and sorrows," &c.

We will here mention the examples of several other holy prelates who have left their bishoprics before their deaths.

St. Just, Archbishop of Lyons, having given up to the people a man who, after having committed a murder, had taken refuge in the church, on the promise that he should be spared, finding that in spite of the promise they had put him to death, thought himself obliged, for this sole reason, to give up his bishopric, as if he had been guilty of this homicide, although he had done his utmost to prevent it. And with the wish to do penance he left Lyons, and went as an unknown pilgrim to the Holy Land; on which occasion the author of his life writes: "*That having been illustrious for his virtue in the episcopate, he became still more so by the voluntary exile to which he condemned himself.*" (Surius. tom. v., 2 Sept.; Baron. an. Chr. 381, num. 82, 84.)

St. John the Silent having been forcibly consecrated bishop against his entreaties, made his escape, and went in disguise to the Monastery of St. Sabas. This holy solitary, admiring his great virtue, presented him to the Patriarch of Jerusalem that he might receive priest's orders, of which he judged him worthy. This compelled St. John to reveal to the patriarch that he was already a bishop. (Surius. tom. iii., 13 Maii.)

St. Peter, Archbishop of Tarantaise, of the Cistercian Order, having disguised himself, escaped to Germany, and concealed himself in a monastery of the same order. (Surius. tom. iii., 8 Maii.)

St. Amandus, Bishop of Liége, seeing that he could not manage his priests, wrote to Pope Martin I., imploring his permission to resign his bishopric. This the Pope refused, but St. Amandus still believed that God required it of him, and soon after left his bishopric. (Baron. an. Chr. 649, num. 37, et seq.)

St. Viron, a Scotch bishop, having been elected, in spite of his entreaties, by the people, and consecrated by the Pope himself, yet left his bishopric and retired to France. (Surius. tom. iii., 8 May.)

St. Theodore, Bishop of Anastasiople, not being able to endure the ill-treatment of his farmers by his officers, and finding himself powerless to prevent their cruelty and hardness, left his bishopric by the advice of St. Antiochus, a celebrated hermit. (Surius. tom. ii., April 22.)

St. Peter Damian, having for a long time entreated leave to resign his bishopric of Ostia, and Pope Nicolas II. having always refused him, at last obtained the permission, though with great trouble, from Pope Alexander II. (Baron. tom. xi., Ann. 1061, num. 28, 38.)

We might cite many other similar instances, as that of St. Wulfran, Archbishop of Sens; of St. Arnoul, Bishop of Metz; of St. Magloire, Bishop of Dol, &c. But these are enough to show that Dom Bartholomew in his retirement only followed the example and humility of a great number of other bishops who were eminent for their virtue and holiness. (Surius. 20 Mart., 16 August., 24 Oct.)

There is one other circumstance to be mentioned. When a man resigns his bishopric, he is bound at the same time to find a worthy person to replace him. Dom Bartholomew did all he could in this matter, conjuring Philip II. to select one "who should repair, by his wisdom and virtue, the many faults he had committed." The excessive care and circumspection shown by this prince in the choice of prelates gave every hope that Dom Bartholomew's wishes would be fulfilled. But it must be owned that his first successor at Braga was not a good one. However, he died shortly after, and the king then appointed a Religious of the Augustinian Order, who was a man eminent for both learning and virtue.

Those who have written the life of Philip II. speak in the following terms of his conduct in this matter: "This prince always behaved (in selecting bishops) with admirable carefulness, knowing that these elections are often very dangerous to those who make them. He took no notice whatever of the solicitations of his courtiers, or of any human recommendations, and he made it a point to consider holiness before high birth. It often happened that, rejecting persons of rank, though of powerful families, and backed up by court influence, he sought out some simple unknown priests, and bestowed the bishoprics upon them. And some among these, as eminent in humility as in all other virtues, absolutely refused to accept this dignity. He followed the old rule of the Church: *'to exclude from the episcopate those who sought it, and to bestow it, on the contrary, on those who refused it.'* For this reason, having one day decided to promote a priest whom he thought devoid of ambition, when he heard that he had followed the court in hopes of obtaining something, instantly tore up the brief which he was going to send him, and appointed another man. Another time, having chosen a religious of great virtue for a bishopric, and finding that he absolutely refused it, after having made every effort to overcome his resistance, he gave him the brief in blank, and told him to fill it up with any name he pleased, saying: *'That he was convinced he would choose an excellent bishop, as he himself was so worthy of the dignity, and therefore he would clear his own conscience by throwing on him the burden of selection.'* Although it may be very difficult for a king to ascertain the merits of individuals, as very often he can only know them through the reports of others, yet this prince, by his vigilance and wisdom, generally found out the truth;

for he used to say: "*That he looked upon that man as a traitor and an enemy who should fail to tell him simply and faithfully the exact truth in all matters, and that he should think him the more guilty if he should have received special evidence of his regard and esteem.*" On this account some of the first grandees of Spain fell into disgrace, and nearly forfeited all place in his counsels, because they had dissimulated and not told him the exact truth in certain matters." (Cabrera, pages 890, 891, 974.)

It is remarkable that not only the Spanish historians have given this praise to Philip II. touching his Christian manner of selecting prelates, but Pope Clement VIII., in the funeral oration he pronounced over his remains, bears the same witness by these words: "*There never was a prince who showed more wisdom and disinterestedness in his selection of bishops for his kingdom. For, realizing of what importance it is for the service of God and the Church that those who are called to such a heavy charge should be really worthy, he showed no regard whatever to the solicitations he received, nor to any human or temporal considerations, but selected only such as were eminent for their merits and virtue.*" (Cabrera, page 895.)

CHAPTER XXI.

OF THE MISTRUST, SCRUPLES, AND ANXIETIES, WHICH FREQUENTLY PREVENT PIOUS SOULS FROM MAKING PROGRESS IN THE WAYS OF GOD.

Although the humility of our holy prelate was so great, still his virtue was not timid and anxious, but full of faith and confidence. For this reason he devoted a whole chapter of his book to arguments against pusillanimity, vain scruples, and dangerous sadnesses, which trouble sometimes the best of pastors, and still more those of weak minds. "This life," he wrote, "is full of evils; but we should never lose hope. We should be courageous amidst all our afflictions and sorrows, and preserve a firm confidence at the bottom of our hearts." (Stimul. Pastor. cap. 10.) In speaking of this virtue, he supposes that he is addressing those who are really pious and fear to offend God. For there are some men who, though they only think how they may best follow their passions, and seem to have forgotten that they are Christians, still hope to be saved. And this hope is as presumptuous as it is vain. Such is the foolish confidence of those who, living amidst the greatest vices, are yet perfectly secure, and fancy that they shall find in the mercy of God impunity for all their crimes. This kind of confidence, as the saints say, comes from the devil. It is he who gives and maintains it in these persons; he takes care to stifle the remorse of conscience which might awaken them from the profound sleep in which they are plunged, so that nothing should trouble the peaceable and sovereign dominion he has over them. But just as the spirit of malice makes sure of those who are his by the proud confidence with which he inspires them, so does he continually trouble by distrust and discouragement those who are really the servants of God; hoping that by destroying, little by little, the confidence they have in His grace, which is their only strength, they may fall back on themselves, where they will find nothing but powerlessness and weakness.

The best remedy against this temptation is to consider that hope is not less necessary than faith. St. Bernard teaches us this admirably in the following words: "*There is a very close connection between faith and hope, for he who believes by faith in a future happiness expects by hope to enjoy it some day. For this reason the apostle says:*

'*Faith is the substance of things to be hoped for, the evidence of things that appear not.*' (Hebrews xi. verse 1.) *For hope is based on faith, as the painter makes use of the canvas on which to draw his picture. Thus faith says in our hearts: 'God hath prepared good things, which are incomprehensible to us, for those who remain faithful to Him.' And hope says: 'It is for me that these good things are reserved.' And charity says: 'I run with all my strength towards God to obtain them from Him.'*" (St. Bernard, in Psalm xc., Serm. 10, num. 1.)

We learn from these words that these three virtues, which embrace the whole Christian state, are bound together, and are born from one another. God, out of His pure mercy, gives us faith, which makes us believe all that He has done for the salvation of souls, and what He has promised to those that love Him. This faith we share with the devils; for St. James says: "*The devils also believe and tremble:*" (St. James ii. verse 19.) But what distinguishes us from these unhappy spirits is hope. To believe without hope is to believe like a devil. To believe in hope is to believe as a Christian. For as the demons believe that Jesus Christ is come "*to destroy them*" (Luke iv. verse 34); so we, on the contrary, believe, as He has said Himself, that He is come to save us. "*For God sent not His Son into the world to judge the world, but that the world may be saved by Him.*" (St. John iii. verse 17.) And as their belief is always accompanied by despair, ours, on the contrary, should be always full of hope. It happens, nevertheless, that Christian souls, who would feel the greatest scruple to have the least doubt against faith, are not afraid of not only weakening, but almost destroying hope in themselves, without considering that faith without hope is useless, that these two virtues are inseparable, and that all that is done against the one reacts on the other.

In the natural and civil life, which is an image of the soul, a man believes by a human faith, as St. Augustine says, that such a one is his father. This belief is such that if his father be a person of rank, he expects from him not only subsistence, but also all human and worldly advantages. And after that, he would be considered bad and ungrateful if he did not obey, both with respect and love, him from whom he has received and expects everything. In the same way faith makes a man believe that God has promised great things to those who are faithful to Him. Hope applies these promises to himself, so that he expects, through the mercy of God, that he will become worthy to serve Him, and thus enjoy Him eternally. And this strong faith, animated by hope, produces in us love or charity; for who would not feel himself constrained to love Him from whom he expects eternal riches?

"Thus," as our holy prelate teaches us, "the great merit of confidence is, that a man acts as a true child of God, and throws himself on His mercy and goodness, hoping that He will cause him to grow in grace by that same mercy through which it has been originally bestowed on him." *(Stim. Past., cap. 10.)*

Those who are of a contrary disposition think that it is a kind of pride to keep themselves in this sort of holy repose. St. Bernard describes perfectly the condition of these souls. "*There are some people,*" he writes, "*who hope in God, but uselessly, because they trust so much to His mercy, that they never cease offending Him. This hope only confounds and deceives, because it is without love. There are others, on the contrary, who lose hope, and who, dwelling continually on their own weaknesses are, as it were, overwhelmed in an abyss of discouragement and cowardice. These persons live in themselves; they are continually occupied with their own illnesses and languors, and always ready to make great histories of what happens to them, and of what they suffer.*

They are anxious day and night; they torment themselves as much about the evils they feel as about those they dread. They are not satisfied with the Gospel rule, that to each day its own evil suffices, but they are overwhelmed by the dread of things which perhaps will never happen. Is there a greater torment than this? or a more insupportable hell? For they are continually tormented with anxiety, and do not nourish themselves with the bread of heaven. Thus, the first hope fruitlessly: the second have no hope at all. The first live in their pride; the second in their mistrust and anxieties. Those only, therefore, abide in the strength of the Most High who desire nothing so much as to obtain it; who fear nothing but to lose it; and who devote themselves to keeping it with all the vigilance of their minds and hearts, in which consists properly true piety and the interior and spiritual adoration of God. Who can injure the man who lives under the shadow and protection of the God of heaven? and how can he fall into negligence who continually looks to God and remembers constantly that God seeth him?" (St. Bernard, in Psalm xc. serm. 1, num. 2, and serm. 2, num. 3.) To this David exhorts us when he says: "*Cast thy care upon the Lord, and He shall sustain thee*" (Psalm liv. verse 23) as a father nurtures his child. And our holy prelato remarks that the Psalmist adds: "*He shall not suffer the just to waver for ever.*" "*This life is a sea,*" writes St. Augustine; "*our souls are as ships tossed by the waves. But God is a port against these tempests, and hope is the firm and certain anchor of which St. Paul speaks*: '*Quam sicut anchoram habemus animæ tutam et firmam.*' (Heb. vi. verse 19.) As therefore the anchor cast on the shore keeps the vessel firmly amidst all the agitation of the waves and storms, in the same way the soul, which is already fixed on heaven, and lives on this earth by hope, dwells in God as in its proper port and harbour of refuge, and finds a kind of immobility even amidst the different movements and temptations of this life.

For this reason St. Paul said to the Colossians: '*He hath reconciled you in the body of His flesh through death, to present you holy and unspotted and blameless before Him; if so ye continue in the faith, grounded and settled, and immoveable from hope.*'" (Coloss. i. verse 23. August., Psalm liv. verse 23.) The archbishop speaks at the same time of the way in which these scruples and troubles of soul are opposed to that peace of conscience which all true Christians should have; and this subject we will treat of more particularly in the following chapter.

CHAPTER XXII.

THAT PEACE AND JOY SHOULD FIND THEMSELVES IN THE TRULY FAITHFUL.—THAT HUMAN SADNESS AND DISQUIET COME FROM THE TEMPTATIONS OF THE DEVIL; AND OF THE BAD EFFECTS THEY CREATE.

Dom Bartholomew writes *(Stim. Past., cap. 16)* : "The Devil, seeing that he cannot drag the fear of God from the heart of man, tries to trouble him by vain fears and imaginary dangers, so that he might not enjoy the peace of a good conscience." It is with reason that the holy prelate assures us that it is the Devil who tries to take away this peace from us. For the Son of God says in the Gospel: "*Peace I leave with you; My peace I give unto you. Not as the world giveth do I give unto you.*" (John xiv. verse 27.) And yet a state of trouble and disquiet is entirely incompatible with this peace. As then this disposition is so contrary to that which Jesus Christ desires to form in us, it must necessarily come from His enemy, who, being condemned to eternal sadness, tries to communicate some of it to souls whom he envies the happiness of being freed from his slavery, and belonging to Jesus Christ, and strives, by the immeasurable troubles with which he agitates them, to make them taste "*a beginning of hell*," as St. Bernard says; whereas Jesus Christ, by the presence and joy of His Holy Spirit, wishes to form in them a beginning of paradise.

This artifice of the Devil's is easy to detect if we remember that St. Paul thought peace of soul so essential to a Christian, that he begins all his epistles by these words, of which are composed the apostolic benediction given by him to all the faithful: "*Grace to you, and peace from God our Father, and from the Lord Jesus Christ.*" (Rom. i. verse 7.) And wishing specially to mark in what the Christian religion consists, which he calls the kingdom of God, he explains it in these words: "*For the kingdom of God is not meat and drink; but justice, peace, and joy in the Holy Ghost.*" (Rom. xiv. verse 17.) This justice, as St. Paul again says, is that "*faith that worketh by charity*" (Gal. v. verse 6); or, according to St. Augustine, *humility*, which is inseparable from love. For thus he explains those words of Jesus Christ: "*Decet nos implere omnem justitiam, id est, omnem humilitatem.*" A Christian, then, however weak he may be, if he believes, if he hopes, and if he loves God, at least in some degree, and if he be humble in this love, ought to have this peace and joy in the Holy Ghost. "*And the more he grows in grace and in virtue*," writes St. Bernard, "*the more he is strengthened in confidence.*" "*Quantùm crescis in gratia, tantùm et in fiducia dilataris.*" (Bern., in Cant., serm. 3, num. 5.)

This disposition of heart produces joy, and our holy archbishop recommends it to us by those words which Esdras speaks to the Jews in Holy Scripture: "*Nolite contristari; gaudium enim Domini est fortitudo nostra.*" (2 Esdras iii. verse 10.) This St. Paul represents to us in even stronger language: "*Rejoice in the Lord always, and again I say, rejoice."* (Philip iv. verse 4.) These words are said to all men and for all time. And although in the beginning of the Church there were a great many strong and courageous souls, there were also some weaker and more imperfect, who had their troubles and anxieties, as we have to-day, and who were tempted and exposed as we are, and a great deal more than we are, for then persecution raged, and a cruel and bloody death was almost inevitable if a man professed the Christian Faith. So that the feeble-hearted found themselves in danger of losing both faith and salvation unless they received from God the grace of martyrdom, which is the greatest He can bestow even on the most perfect. And yet, though they were exposed to such great evils, St. Paul will not allow them to remain in fear and anxiety, but in peace and joy.

This joy is sometimes sensible, and then it is a gift of God which passes away, and which He gives generally at the beginning of a conversion. This gift we ought to receive with great humility, without setting our affections upon it, for God often withdraws it very soon, and it is better for us that it should not last. But it often happens that this joy is hidden in the depths of our hearts in good will; and it is nevertheless very true and effective, as it serves to keep us inseparably attached to God, and we prefer it to all human and perishable joys.

St. Bernard represents this truth in these words to his religious: *"'Rejoice in God,' says the prophet, 'and He will give you your heart's desire.' But how is it, O holy prophet, that you exhort us thus to rejoice in the Lord, as if this joy were always in our own power? We know that we feel joy and pleasure in eating and drinking, in sleeping and resting, and many other things in this world. But what is this pleasure which is to be found in God, and which enables us to rejoice in Him? My brethren, men of the world may ask this question, but not you. For who amongst you has not often felt the peace and joy of a good conscience? Which amongst you has not often tasted the pleasure which is found in chastity, humility, and charity? This is not the kind of pleasure which is found in eating and drinking, or similar indulgences, and nevertheless it is a pleasure, and a much greater one than what is found in all other things. For these are from the flesh, and this one is from God, and when we find our joy in it, we rejoice in God. But there are many who complain that they rarely feel this sensible affection, or this pleasure which is sweeter than the most excellent honey, as the Scripture says. They do not consider that it comes from the fact that God tries them by various temptations and battles, and that they show much more firmness and courage when they practice virtue, not from the pleasure which they derive from it, but for the virtue itself, and from the sole desire of pleasing God, giving to it their whole minds, though not with sensible satisfaction. And it is indubitable that he who acts thus perfectly obeys this salutary advice of the prophet, 'Rejoice in the Lord,' because he does not speak of that sensible joy which is born of affection, but of that effective joy which produces action. For this affection belongs, properly speaking, to that beatitude which we hope for in heaven, and action belongs to the virtue which we should practice in this life."* (Bern., Serm. 5, in Quadrag, num. 6, 7.)

If we have joy of this sort, it is evident that it must always exist within us, and that often it is in the heart of those who love God when they imagine they have it not. For being compelled to allow that God preserves in them a great horror of evil, and a strong desire to remain constant in well-doing, they must own that they experience in themselves that interior pleasure "*which,*" as St. Bernard says, "*consists in chastity, humility, and all other virtues, and that they have this effective joy which produces action,*" although it may not be sensible to them: as they try to do nothing but what God commands; as they prefer His fear to all other things; and "*that it is absolutely necessary,*" as St. Augustine says, "*that we should find some pleasure in what we do, as our will is always to act according as it shall be most pleasing to Him.*"

"We ought to be very careful to preserve this joy in us," writes Dom Bartholomew, "so as to banish that sadness of heart which is a hindrance to all good. *Tristitia omnis boni impedimentum est.*" (Stimul. Past., cap. 10.) So writes also the Wise man: "*That sadness of heart is every plague. Omnis plaga tristitia cordis est.*" (Eccl. xxv. verse 17.) And he strives to turn every one away from it by these excellent words: "Give not up thy heart to sadness, but drive it from thee;" and again: "*Give not up thy soul to sadness, and afflict not thyself in thine own counsel. The joyfulness of the heart is the life of a man, and a never-failing treasure of holiness. Have pity on thy own soul, pleasing God. Gather up thy heart in His holiness, and drive away sadness far from thee. For sadness hath killed many, and there is no profit in it.*" (Eccles. xxx. verses 22, 23, 24, 25.) On this passage Dom Bartholomew writes: "That we ought to labour to banish all sorrows and anxieties from our minds, because sweetness of devotion, which surpasses all this world's pleasures, cannot subsist with this bitterness and anxiety. We ought to watch carefully over ourselves to prevent any entrance in our hearts of anxious and unmeasured cares, which produce sadness and despondency. We ought to throw ourselves continually in the bosom of God, so as to put away from our hearts all that may cause us trouble, and preserve them always in peace and confidence." In the same way St. Paul says: "*The sorrow that is according to God worketh penance, steadfast unto salvation; but the sorrow of the world worketh death.*" (2 Corinth. vii. verse 10.) And in this manner St. Chrysostom reconciles the words of Jesus

Christ, "*Blessed are they that mourn,*" with those of St. Paul, "*Rejoice always.*" "*For the tears we shed for God,*" writes this saint, "*produce the joy that we taste in God.*" And the Saviour having said, "*Blessed are they that mourn,*" adds directly, "*For they shall be comforted.*"

In this sense the author of the "Treatise on True and False Penitence," (attributed to St. Augustine,) insists that penitence itself should always be accompanied with joy. "*Penitens semper doleat, et de dolore gaudeat.*" He ought to feel keen sorrow because he has offended One who deserves to be infinitely loved; but he ought also to rejoice, because he finds in his tears, if they be sincere, a pledge of the mercy of God, and a sure hope of salvation. And if this be true of great crimes, still more is it true of daily faults, which St. Augustine calls, "*the sins of the just.*" God allows them to fall into them for their good, so that they may learn by experience, and by their very falls themselves, how weak they are, and that to remain firm they must keep themselves always close to God, as children in the arms of their mother. He who has this feeling raises himself peacefully when he has fallen, and is not wounded in falling, according to the words of the Psalmist: "*When he shall fall, he shall not be bruised, for the Lord putteth His hand under him.*" (Psalm xxxvi. verse 24.) "*The just falls on the hand of God,*" writes St. Bernard, "*and it happens, by a strange wonder, that the very sin into which he has fallen serves to make him more just. For, as St. Paul says, 'We know that to them that love God, all things work together unto good.'* (Romans viii. verse 28.) *Do not our faults even contribute to our good when they make us more humble and more careful? And does not God bear up him who falls when he is sustained by humility? The Psalmist says: 'Being pushed, I was overturned, that I might fall; but the Lord supported me.*"

(Psalm cxvii. verse 13. Bern., in Psalm xc., Serm. 2, num. 2.)

Dom Bartholomew considered "that those persons who are continually agitated by scruples and anxieties do great injustice to the infinite goodness of God, representing Him to themselves as a severe Judge, whose attributes are severity and justice, who is inexorable for the smallest faults, and who only seeks occasion to lose the souls of men."

For if St. Augustine was not afraid to say, that the temples of the idols having been upset in this world, Christians sometimes created an idol in their hearts when they represented God contrary to what He is, one may likewise say that such persons ought to fear extremely lest they should fall into this mistake without thinking of it. On this point St. Bernard writes: "*All those who will not be converted to God, and who cannot believe in His mercy, do not know Him. For they only remain in this distrust because they represent God to themselves as harsh and severe, whereas He is goodness itself; as hard and inexorable, while He is full of mercy; as cruel and terrible, instead of which He is infinitely sweet and amiable. Thus 'iniquity,' as it is said in holy writ, 'lies to itself,' and forms to itself an idol which is not God.*" (Bern., in Cant., Ser. 28, num. 2.) *("Format sibi idolum pro Deo.")* The same saint adds: "*That this mistrust is the greatest obstacle we can place in the way of our salvation.*" And exhorting holy souls to confidence, he says: "*Have you so little faith that you dare not hope that Jesus Christ will forgive you your sins,—He who has attached them to His cross by the same nails with which He has deigned to allow His hands to be pierced?*"

"The sovereign remedy against scruples," writes the holy prelate, "is to submit them humbly to a wise man. For God Himself has instituted this remedy, so that he who cannot quiet his troubles by his own lights should be delivered of them by those of another. And even should it happen that the person who directs them should make a mistake, (as scrupulous souls often imagine that they are not understood, or that they are not sufficiently known,) nevertheless it would be very useful in all cases to submit their judgments to him to whom God Himself has submitted them." (Stimul. Pastor. cap. 10.) This advice is all the more necessary, as if they begin to reason with themselves they only distress themselves more; for their thoughts only serve to exaggerate their faults and imperfections, and to make them believe that their malady is unique and singular; that what does for others is useless to them; and that they will never be cured. When they are in this state they imagine that not even the obligation under which all Christians lie to believe in the mercy of God ought to induce them to have confidence, because they fancy that their lukewarmness and negligence has made them unworthy of it. Yet, "*if God were only just,*" as St. Augustine says, "*He would not show mercy to any one, and all the guilty would perish.*" "*If the abyss of our misery,*" writes St. Bernard, "*did not find in God an abyss of mercy*" there would have been nothing left to David or St. Peter, after their falls, but despair; but because they had boundless confidence in the mercy of God, they threw themselves on His breast, and there found a refuge from His justice. "*If God,*" writes St. Augustine, "*has forgiven you great crimes, will He let you perish for the daily faults you commit?*" ("*Qui justificavit impium, deseret pium?*") (Aug. in Psalm xcvi.. verse 10.)

The holy prelate remarks very wisely, that there is generally in such scrupulous persons a mixture of self-love and secret pride, which hides itself under an appearance of humility. But, as St. Teresa says, "True humility is always peaceable and tranquil, but that of these restless souls only tends to discourage and depress them." More than this: ingratitude being a species of pride, according to St. Augustine, this disposition makes souls both proud and ungrateful. For it is certain that those who are full of scruples are also full of themselves. They live among their own troubles, and being entirely occupied with past, present, or future evils, they do not think of God's benefits. Far from feeling or praising Him for them, they do not even think of them. For "*gratitude for graces,*" as St. Bernard writes, "*presupposes the knowledge of them;*" and we do not trouble ourselves to return thanks for what we do not realize to have received. Thus the devil gains a good deal when he fills souls with scruples, because he represents God to them as a hard and severe master, and prevents their recognizing and loving His goodness, while, by making them apprehend imaginary woes, he induces them to forget the many blessings with which they have been prevented by God's mercy, so that they become at the same time ungrateful and incredulous.

St. Augustine, writing to a nobleman who had praised him very warmly, says: "*If there be anything in me which deserves praise, I have not got it of myself, but received it from Him who is the only true Wisdom. And as I feel a humble joy that He has deigned to begin His work in me, I wait also with faith and hope that He will be pleased to accomplish it; so that I may be neither ungrateful by not recognizing what He has already bestowed, nor incredulous in not hoping for that which He has not yet given me.*" (Aug. Epist. 52, ad Macedon.)

What very often deceives people is, that they imagine, because the fear of God is constantly referred to in holy writ, they do right to keep up this fear in their souls. But they ought to consider that although God wishes us to fear Him, He equally commands us in a thousand places to rejoice in Him. As, therefore, the commandments of God cannot contradict each other, and that the anxious fear in which they live is incompatible with the joy and confidence which He commands, it follows necessarily that they ought to fight against these scruples, as enemies to the disposition in which God wishes them to be, and only feel that respectful fear which is always accompanied with peace and joy. For faith leads to fear, fear to confidence, and confidence to joy. According to these words of the wise man: "*Qui timetis Dominum sperate in illum: et in oblectationem veniet vobis misericordia.*" (Eccl. ii., verse 19.) If we do not feel this grace we ought to ask it of God. For, as He commands us to have it, when He says by the mouth of David: "*Delectare in Domino et dabit tibi petitiones cordis tui*" (Psalm xxxvi., verse 4); He shows us also that it is He who gives it to us, when the same prophet says: "*Lætifica animam servi tui, quoniam ad te, Domine, animam meam levavi.*" (Psalm lxxxv., verse 4.) And in the same psalm He shows us again how fear can be allied with joy: "*Lætetur cor meum ut timeat nomen tuum.*" (Psalm lxxxv., verse 11.) St. Bernard spoke in the same sense to his own religious: "*Rejoice, but with fear and trembling. I wish you to be in a state of joy, but not of over-confidence. 'Rejoice in the Holy Ghost, but tremble lest at the same time you should fall again into sin.'*" (St. Bern. in Psalm xc., Serm. 3, num. 4.)

This is the disposition so recommended in holy Writ, which sustains the weak, and is the strength of the strong. For as mistrust makes the soul timid, and deprives it of all vigour; so hope gives it confidence amidst all dangers, so that it remains unshaken even in the midst of the greatest tribulations. "*Spe gaudentes,*" says the apostle, "*in tribulatione patientes.*" (Romans xii., verse 12.) "*He has put hope before suffering,*" writes St. Augustine, "*for how can we preserve patience amidst evils if we have not joy in the hope of good things to come?"

"Even when we find ourselves overwhelmed with sorrows and afflictions," says the holy prelate, "we ought to try and march on with confidence and joy of heart. For otherwise where would be the liberty of the children of God?—and the spirit of which the apostle says: '*You have not received the spirit of bondage again in fear, but you have received the spirit of adoption of sons of God*'? (Rom. viii., verse 15.) St. Augustine points out this truth in these words of the psalm: '*Domine ut scuto bonæ voluntatis tuæ coronasti nos.*' (Aug. in Psalm v., verse 13.) '*For we say to ourselves these words of St. Paul:* '*Who shall accuse against the elect of God? If God be for us, who is against us? He that spared not even His own Son, but delivered Him up for us all, how hath He not also, with Him, given us all things?*' (Romans viii., verse 33.) *If, then, when we were enemies of God, Jesus Christ died for us, with much stronger reason, now that we are reconciled, we shall be saved by Him from the anger and pains we have deserved. These are the arms which give us the victory over our enemy. This is the invincible shield with which we repulse the attacks of the devil, when he tries to throw us into mistrust and discouragement, and into despair of our salvation in the midst of the afflictions, temptations, and sins which surround us.*' For this reason we should always have before our eyes these words of St. Paul, which prove that we are only Christians in proportion as we advance and strengthen ourselves continually in confidence and joy: '*Domus Dei sumus nos.*' (Hebrews iii., verse 6.) That is, we are the temple and the children of God. But this is the condition attached to it: '*Si fiduciam et gloriam spei usque ad finem firmam retineamus.*'"

CHAPTER XXIII.

WHAT AN AMOUNT OF LEARNING DOM BARTHOLOMEW POSSESSED.—HIS AFFECTION FOR HOLY SCRIPTURE, AND FOR THE DOCTRINE OF THE FATHERS, AND FOR A SPIRITUAL COMPREHENSION OF THE PSALMS.

We have already seen, in this history, how Dom Bartholomew drew from holy Scripture that *science of the saints* which is so necessary for those who are called to the guidance of souls. Even when very young he excelled in the theology of the schools. The authors of his life remark that in the public disputes which are held by theologians, while people admired his science and ability, they were equally struck by his modesty and humility. And whereas superior knowledge generally inflates men with pride, in his case it seemed only to make him more humble. We have also seen how he added to this knowledge a love of prayer, meditation on holy Scripture, and a diligent study of the fathers. He spent twenty years in this way before he became bishop, and afterwards drew up all the rules for his conduct from these sources of light and grace. In this matter he followed the advice of St. Gregory: "*In order that a prelate may wisely instruct the souls which are committed to him, he must draw his teaching from the examples of the saints, from the maxims contained in holy Scripture, and from the interior and secret lights he has received in meditation and prayer. For as it is by the infusion of the Holy Ghost that the Scriptures were written, it is also through the same grace that we extract the fruit and* the use of them which God demands. He, therefore, that wishes to acquit himself perfectly of the duties of preacher and bishop ought to be humble, so as to follow the example of the holy Fathers. He ought to be learned and instruct himself continually in holy writ. And, at the same time, he must labour to purify his heart, so that he may learn from God Himself in prayer what He wishes him to do in each circumstance or difficulty. In order to teach men aright he must himself be first Christ's disciple. And yet he must not presume upon what God will teach him in prayer if he should neglect to seek the instruction of the Holy Spirit in the Scriptures, or if he disdain to follow the example of the true servants of God. And as to what regards the revelations and lights he may receive in meditation, he must believe that those only come from God which are conformable to the authority of holy Scripture and the conduct of the greatest saints." (Greg. in 1 Kings, cap. vii., verse 16.)

When Dom Bartholomew was engaged in his episcopal functions, although he was in one sense overwhelmed with a multitude of cares and duties, he always reserved the last hours of the day and a great part of the night to asking of God, by prayer and meditation on His word, for that celestial unction and joy which he looked upon as the only strength of his soul amidst his arduous labours. He never allowed himself to be interrupted at that time, and used to say: "That it was very reasonable that, after having given so many hours of the day to others, he should devote the little that remained to God Himself."

Thus he maintained himself in a frame of mind worthy of a true pastor, according to the words of St. Bernard, which he quoted in his book:

"When God rouses His spouse from her sleep, and tells her to hasten and rise, it is indubitably that she may draw souls to His service. For it is a sure sign that we are applying ourselves heartily to meditation on divine truths, when our *souls are so filled with divine love and holy zeal, and the wish to induce others to love God as we do, that we are glad to leave the rest of meditation to employ ourselves in the preaching of the Word; and that then, having thus satisfied our desire, we return to our contemplation with the more ardour, as we feel we have interrupted it with some fruit. And then, having again tasted the sweetness of God in meditation, we return with glad promptitude to win more souls. The soul is sometimes agitated in these vicissitudes. She is troubled and anxious, because she fears lest she should have let herself act according to the inclinations of her heart, lest she should sin in one way or the other, and not accomplish exactly what God demands of her. This is perhaps what Job means when he speaks those mysterious words: 'If I lie down to sleep I shall say: When shall I arise? And again I shall look for the evening, and shall be filled with sorrow and darkness.'* (Job vii., verse 4.) *As if he had said: 'In repose I accuse myself of having neglected my work; and in my work I am troubled at having interrupted my repose.' Thus a holy soul finds herself constantly agitated, and, as it were, divided between the fruit she draws from her labours, and the rest she tastes in meditation, and although what she does is always good, she is, nevertheless, continually regretting and repenting, as if she were doing wrong; and she sighs towards God every moment, imploring Him to make known His will to her. For there is no other remedy on such occasions than to have recourse to prayer and groanings before God, so that He may deign to show us Himself what He wishes us to do, and that He may point out to us the time and measure of each action.*" (Bern. in Cant., Serm. 37, num. 9, 10, cap. 1.)

Our holy prelate, amidst all the books of holy writ, had a particular veneration for the Psalms of David. After he had resigned his bishopric, he employed the greater part of his time in this kind of reading, feeling with St. Augustine: "*That they are a source of life and salvation, a common treasure which the Holy Spirit has given to His Church, wherein are contained remedies for all our passions, and spiritual riches to adorn the purest souls.*" (Aug., prolog. in Psalmos.)

The archbishop, in his retreat, as we have said, spent the greater part of his time in reading and meditating on the Psalms. And as he was so continually fed on these holy truths, he drew up an excellent commentary upon them, drawing out the spiritual sweetness he found therein as a rule for his own guidance. "*For one can only understand the Scripture,*" writes St. Athanasius, "*in proportion as one acts up to what it commands.*" And St. Jerome remarks that David said to God, "*A mandatis tuis intellexi,*" "*to show us that we cannot comprehend what God tells us in His word unless we do His will.*" Our holy prelate almost always took about with him his "*Treatise on the Psalms,*" and when the religious met after dinner, according to the custom of the order, he would read little bits of it out loud to them, which the monks listened to with as much pleasure as admiration. Referring to the study of holy writ, Dom Bartholomew used to quote the following words from St. Gregory: "*We find in the word of God a thorough knowledge of the truth, provided we seek for it with assiduity, simplicity, and humility. For as, when an unknown person presents himself to us we do not know his mind, only his face; but if we live a long time together, habit and familiarity make us penetrate into his thoughts: so, when we only look to the historical letter of Holy Scripture we see but the outside, but if we go on reading, and it becomes familiar to us, we enter into its meaning, and penetrate its hidden sweetness.*" And he adds: "*The more a man stops at the letter of the word, and only thinks of its surface meaning, the more he is incapable of understanding it.*" (Gregor. Moral., lib. 4, cap. 1.) And then, having quoted the words of Job regarding certain persons "*who only nibbled the bark of trees,*" he adds: "*That these words refer to those who only love and respect the literal sense of Holy Scripture, without giving themselves the trouble to penetrate into its interior spirit and meaning, which leads to the love of God and of our neighbour. Holy Scripture is like a lamp. The literal sense is the vase, the spiritual sense is its light; and the love which is in the heart of him who reads is like the oil which keeps it alive, and makes it burn.*" (Greg., in 1 Kings, cap. 14, verse 50.) Dom Bartholomew, following the spirit of this holy Pope, read Holy Scripture with a spirit of love and prayer. And keeping his heart fixed on God, "*legendo et inhiando,*" as St. Augustine says, he acquired such an insight into divine truths, and became so worthy a disciple of the Fathers of the Church, whom he had chosen as his masters, that he fulfilled the duties of the high dignity to which God had called him with wonderful wisdom and strength, being really mighty in deed and word. So that all the bishops at the Œcumenical Council said of him, as we have before mentioned, "*That there was no school in the world equal to that of the Archbishop of Braga.*"

CHAPTER XXIV.

HOW THE HOLY ARCHBISHOP LOVED PRAYER.—HOW HE PRACTISED AND RECOMMENDED IT TO OTHERS.

The grace of God creates saints, and prayer obtains this grace. Dom Bartholomew practised to the letter this advice of St. Paul, "*Sine intermissione orate.*" (1 Thess. v. verse 17.) For, being full of God, and desiring nothing but Himself, he found himself continually in this disposition of David: "*Lord, all my desire is before Thee, and my groaning is not hid from Thee.*" (Psalm xxxvii. verse

10.) He experienced in himself the truth of these words of St. Augustine: "*How can we pray continually? Must we be always on our knees? or remain prostrate on the earth? or raising our hands continually to heaven? There is another more interior mode of prayer, which is never interrupted, and this prayer is the desire of God. Whatever you may do, if you desire the rest of God, and this eternal and celestial Sabbath, you pray continually. If your heart loves God it will speak to Him continually. If you wish to pray without ceasing, desire without ceasing. A constant desire is a constant voice. Your heart will always speak to God if it always loves. It only ceases to speak when ceasing to love. When charity burns, the heart cries: when charity grows cold, the heart is dumb.*" "*Frigus charitatis, silentium cordis est; flagrantia charitatis, clamor cordis est.*" (Aug., in Psalm xxxvii. verse 14.)

When the archbishop went through the country during his visitations, he liked to walk alone, so as to be able to pray with more recollection and devotion. He often said that he considered this time the happiest in his life, because he was then entirely occupied with God. Besides the hours he devoted specially to this holy exercise, he often passed whole nights in prayer, especially when he was going to preach the next day, so as to learn from God what he was to teach to his people. He said sometimes that he wished God would raise up some great persecution against him, if he had not brought it on himself by his own fault, that he might be condemned to live in a cell as in a prison, and might thus be free to pray without ceasing, and to converse only with God. One day, going up-stairs, he walked so slowly, that a friend of his who was going up with him, could not help asking him the reason. The archbishop answered: "I was thinking of the different degrees of humility of which St. Benedict and the holy Fathers have written, and by which our souls are raised, little by little, to God; and I was thinking how much time it took to mount a single one, how easy it was to go down again, and to let oneself slip on to the sloping precipice of pride, and how difficult it is not to weary while mounting, step by step, up this mountain of humility."

On another occasion, when some of his party were complaining of the bitterly cold wind, as they were crossing a bit of rough country, he replied: "My children, prayer is an excellent remedy against cold. There is no hotter brazier than this celestial fire." He often said, when he saw himself so overwhelmed with business, that he could not sufficiently admire the spirit and piety of David, who, while governing so great a kingdom, and so often making war in person, yet found time to compose and sing such divine and elevating psalms, and he added: "That he could not help envying the disposition of this holy prophet, nor blushing for Christians who have so often his words in their mouths, without troubling to have, like him, God in their hearts." The love that he had for this holy exercise made him earnestly recommend it to others. He often said: "That our hearts were like water, and that as water, which is cold by itself, is only warmed by fire, that the nearer it is to the flame the quicker it gets hot, and that if moved a little away from it, it gets cold directly; so our hearts are by themselves nothing but cold, hard ice, which are only softened and warmed by drawing near to God, who is a vivifying and purifying flame. That if we remain united to Him by continual prayer and holy desires, we shall always preserve that heat which is our life. But that if we omit this holy exercise, and let ourselves go to wild thoughts and imaginations, we shall become languid and cold."

On this subject St. Augustine writes: "*We enlarge our hearts by desiring incessantly heavenly riches. For we shall receive God's promises in greater abundance if we have be-*

lieved in them with greater certainty, hoped for them with greater firmness, and desired them with greater ardour. By keeping continually alive in our hearts these holy desires, we shall pray with stronger faith, hope, and charity. It is well, however, that we should address God by vocal prayers at certain times and hours, so that being touched by the truths contained in these exterior signs, we should know how much we have advanced in these desires, and that we may encourage ourselves to grow in them more and more. For our prayers will be all the more efficacious if they spring from more ardent affection. When the apostle exhorts us to 'pray without ceasing,' it is as if he said: 'Wish without ceasing for a happy life, that is, an eternal one, and ask for it continually from Him who alone can give it you.' Thus, if we continually desire and ask this of God, we shall 'pray without ceasing.' But as amidst the cares and distractions of exterior occupations this holy desire loses its warmth by little and little, and becomes lukewarm, we fix upon certain hours of prayer, so as to recall our wandering minds, and to warn ourselves to be more attentive to the supreme good which we desire, for fear that this desire, which already begins to relax, should become quite cold and go out altogether, unless we are careful to relight it very often." (Aug., Epist. 121, ad Probam., cap. 9.)

Dom Bartholomew had so entered into the spirit of St. Augustine that he used to say: "That if our heart lives on that faith which is the source of prayer and holy desires, it ought not to be like those furnaces where the fire burns for a time and is then extinguished, but like those in which glass is made, that are kept up day and night, by continually being fed with fresh wood or coke, so that they may never go out." He used to sigh heavily when he prayed, and often shed torrents of tears, again following in this the teaching of St. Augustine, who writes: "*We pray for a long time, when our hearts, being fixed on God with respectful and humble attention, knock a long while at the door of His mercy, so that it may be opened. For generally true prayer is expressed more by sighs than words, and by tears rather than by long speeches. The life of a Christian,"* he adds, *" is the continuation of a holy desire. Tota vita Christiani sanctum desiderium est. And the more this desire burns in a holy soul, the more does she shed tears in prayer. Quantò quisque est sanctior, et desiderii sancti plenior, tantò est ejus in orando fletus uberior."* (Aug. de Civ. Dei, lib. 20, cap. 17.) We have also seen in his life how much stress he laid on the use of *ejaculatory prayers,* which St. Augustine speaks of when he says: *" It is written that the Egyptian solitaries were accustomed to make very frequent prayers, but which were very short, like arrows which their hearts shot up to God in a moment; and that they did this lest, if their prayers were longer, that that attention and vigilance of mind which are so necessary in one who prays should be by degrees weakened or relaxed."* (Aug., Epist. 121, cap. 9.) Thus Dom Bartholomew prayed without effort or affectation, believing that prayer is one of God's greatest gifts, as we obtain all through that channel, and that He has promised to give it to us when He spoke by the mouth of His prophet: *" Effundam super domum David spiritum gratiæ et precum."* (Zachar. xii. verse 10.) And again St. Paul writes: *" We know not what we should pray for as we ought, but the Spirit Himself asketh for us with unspeakable groanings."* (Romans viii. verse 26.) And in another epistle: *" Because you are sons, God hath sent the spirit of His Son into your hearts, crying, Abba, Father."* (Gal. iv. verse 6.) By which he teaches us that it is the Spirit of God who puts real prayer into our hearts; that it does not come from human learning, but from divine inspiration; and that in our prayers we should not seek for great lights, but to realize *" the profound abyss of poverty, corruption, and weakness which is in us,*" as St. Augustine says, and to have a hunger and thirst after justice, which is God Himself; "*casting all your care upon Him, for He hath care of you,*" (1 St. Peter v. verse 7,) with a faith full of confidence and love. He who thus addresses himself to God with a true feeling of his own unworthiness, with sorrow for his frequent offences against Him, and with an earnest desire to be all His, will be accepted of Him, according to the words of the Psalmist: "*Iste pauper clamavit et Dominus exaudivit eum.*" On which St. Augustine remarks: "*Wilt thou be heard? be poor. Do not ask coldly and carelessly, but cry to God out of the depths of your sorrow. Vis exaudiri? pauper esto. Dolor de te clamet non fastidium.*" (August., in Psalm xxxiii. verse 7.)

Dom Bartholomew had also great veneration for the public and general prayers of the Church. He recited or sung his office with an extraordinary devotion and attention, so that one saw that he praised God more by his heart than by his mouth. He used to take great pains, as St. Bernard advises, "*to chant the words of the Holy Spirit with a loud and energetic voice. Virili sonitu et affectu.*" And if he observed that any one said his office carelessly, he would not suffer it, for he had an ardent zeal for the worship of God, and for that public and continual homage which the Church renders Him throughout the world. When he chanted the words "Gloria Patri" after the Psalms, his fervour was so great that it was perceived even in the intonation of his voice. He thought that all the faithful, and especially those consecrated to God, ought to have a particular respect and devotion for this general prayer and for those sacred canticles, which St. Augustine calls, "the voice of the whole Church." "*Totius Ecclesiæ vox una.*" "*For as the Church,*" as St. Ambrose says, "*does nothing separately, but prays in common, acts in common, and suffers in common,*" we ought to believe that the prayers in which she unites all her children to ask mercy of God should be the most perfect and efficacious of all. "*If,*" as St. Ignatius, martyr, writes, "*the prayer of one or two persons be so strong and powerful, how much more so ought that of the whole Church to be?*" (St. Ignat., Epist. ad Ephes.) It is of this united prayer that an ancient Father has said: "*We are all united in one faith, in one discipline, and by the link of one hope. We meet together and unite together, so as to form one army corps to win God through our prayers by a holy violence, and this violence is agreeable to Him.*" "*Coïmus in cœtum, quasi manu facta Deum precationibus ambiamus. Hæc vis Deo grata est.*" (Tertull. Apol., cap. 39.) This thought ought to console imperfect souls, who complain sometimes that they cannot pray in private, as they can do it in the most perfect manner possible by uniting themselves to the public prayers of all the faithful. "*And they should love them all the more,*" writes St. Chrysostom, "*that they can supplement by these public prayers the imperfection of their own. For they must hope that their own prayers, which might be too weak to reach heaven, may ascend there when united with those of the whole Church, as a small quantity of water, which being alone would dry up immediately, is preserved if thrown into a great stream, and flows to the sea with all the rest of the waters.*"

The holy prelate, being fully persuaded of this truth, tried to inspire this devotion to all his people, and frequently recommended the religious of his order to love and respect the divine office; to celebrate it with great respect; to be affectionately exact in all its ceremonies; and to chant the sacred Canticles of the Church with faith and wisdom; "*not seeking therein,*" as St. Augustine says, "*the satisfaction of the ears, but the light and nourishment of the heart.*" "*Non quærentes sonum auris, sed lumen cordis.*" (Aug., in Psalm xlvi. verse 8.)

CHAPTER XXV.

THAT A RECOGNITION OF GOD'S BENEFITS IS NECESSARY TO AN ADVANCE IN PIETY.—WHAT THE VIRTUE OF THE ARCHBISHOP WAS ON THAT POINT.

Thankfulness is inseparable from prayer, and, according to the saints, it should begin, continue, and end it. Our holy archbishop excelled in this virtue, and had an extreme gratitude for the blessings bestowed on him by God. He had learnt this devotion from St. Paul, who always adds acts of thanksgiving to prayer. "*Sine intermissione orate, in omnibus gratias agite.*" (1 Thess. v. verse 12.) And again: "*Orationi instate, vigilantes in eā in gratiarum actione.*" (Coloss. iv. verse 2.) St. Bernard, whom Dom Bartholomew had proposed as a model for his own devotion, recommends this to the whole Church. "*Every soul who seeks God must recognise that God has prevented him, and has sought him first; for fear that by his ingratitude he should change a great happiness into a great misery. For in this way the greatest evils may arise from the greatest good, when, having become rich in our Saviour's gifts, we use them as if we had not received them, and neglect to render the glory to Him. Those who appear the greatest by the graces they have received, become the least before God, because they are not sufficiently careful to recognise His mercies, and to give Him thanks. I wished to spare you in not exposing my meaning in all its force. But I ought to say, that from being very good, they become very bad. For it is an indubitable truth that he who is good becomes bad by that alone, that he attributes to himself the grace which renders him good. This presumption is the greatest of all evils. For if some one say to me: 'I detest this pride; I acknowledge that I am only what I am by the grace of God;' but at the same time he is full of self-complacency, and very glad to receive praise for the graces he has received, what is he but a thief and a robber? And will not God say to him: 'Out of thine own mouth will I judge thee, thou wicked servant.' For can a servant commit a greater sin than to usurp the glory of his master, and take it for himself?" (Bern. in Cant., ser. 34, num. 2.) "We see many," he says elsewhere, "who ask with great eagerness for what they want. But we know very few who take care to render acts of thanksgiving to God proportioned to the greatness of His gifts. It is not that we do wrong in being so eager to ask for what we need, but we do not obtain it because we are so ungrateful. And perhaps it is a grace that we are refused, when in this state, what we ask for, lest if it were granted we should become the more guilty, as the greatness of the blessings received would make our ingratitude the greater. Therefore it is well to say on such occasions: 'That God is merciful to us in this very matter, that He does not show us mercy.' It is of no use, therefore, for sinners, that the Son of God should have cured them, like those nine lepers in the Gospel, from the visible and shameful leprosy of a criminal life, if they be infected with the plague of ingratitude, which is the more dangerous, as it is the more interior and hidden. Happy the Samaritan who knew and acknowledged that he had nothing but what he had received. He faithfully kept the deposit which had been confided to him, and came back to throw himself at the feet of Jesus Christ, rendering Him humble acts of thanksgiving. Happy is he who, on receiving each grace or blessing, turns to the Saviour, who is the plenitude of all graces. For by thus showing Him that we are not ungrateful for His gifts, we put ourselves in a position to receive fresh ones continually. It is certain that if we do not advance in virtue, it is only our ingratitude which is the cause, for He who bestows all gifts looks upon what He gives to an ingrate as lost, and therefore gives no more, for fear of losing the more graces, as He has bestowed them on one who only repays Him by ingratitude and indifference. Happy, then, he who, considering himself always as a stranger, like the good Samaritan, shows the greatest gratitude for the least benefits, feeling that what is given to one as unknown and unworthy as himself is purely a voluntary and gratuitous favour."* (Bern. de divers. serm. 27, num. 6, 7.) *"Learn,"* he continues, *"not to be slow or idle in showing gratitude. Learn to offer to God acts of thanksgiving for every separate gift. 'Take great care,' says the Wise man, 'to consider earnestly all that is presented to you at the table of the Lord.' As if he had said that we ought to thank God specially for each mercy we receive, for the greatest, the smaller, and the least. And it is commanded in the Gospels, after the multiplication of the loaves, to gather up all the fragments lest any be lost; that is to say, not to forget the smallest of God's benefits. What is more lost than what is given to one who is ungrateful? Ingratitude is the enemy of the soul, the annihilation of all merit, the dissipation of all virtue, the plague and ruin of all benefits. Ingratitude is as a burning wind, which dries up of itself the source of the goodness of God, the dew of His mercy, and the streams of His grace."* (Bern., in Cant., ser. 51, num. 7.)

When our holy archbishop had left his bishopric, and retired to the Monastery of Viano, he used to occupy himself by returning continual thanks to God for His benefits, and particularly that He had relieved him from the heavy yoke with which he had always felt himself overwhelmed. He would say to our Lord with deep feeling very often: *"Dirupisti vincula mea, tibi sacrificabo hostiam laudis."* ("You have broken my bonds, I will offer You a sacrifice of praise.") With this feeling he wrote these words on the leaf of a book which he used every day: "*The iron chains of Braga were fastened upon me on the 8th of August, 1558, and were taken away from me on the 20th February, 1582, so that I wore them for twenty-three years and a half.*"

St. Bernard said that as souls do not think enough of the daily mercies they receive, he would make a list of them in this manner:

1. "*My brethren, if you consult your own experience, is it not true that when God inspired you with that faith which conquers the world, and that by this victory you came out of a lake of misery, and an abyss of dirt and mud, you sang a new canticle to the praise of our Lord, who has shown in you the marvels of His power?*

2. "*When He established you on the rock, and led your steps in the narrow way of His precepts, I do not doubt that in the beginning of your new life He put in your mouth a canticle to give glory to the Lord.*

3. "*But when He had filled you with a spirit of true penitence, He not only forgave you your sins, but promised you also His great rewards; and did not the joy you felt in this hope of future bliss make you sing with greater ardour in the way of the Lord: " How great is the glory of God!"*

4. "*When it happens that a truth of holy Writ, which had been obscure to you, is suddenly made clear to your soul, after having received this celestial food ought you not to utter cries of joy and hymns of praise, and acts of thanksgiving to the glory of God?*

5. "*Again, in those struggles to which those are exposed without ceasing, who strive to live godly in Christ Jesus, and in the constant war they wage against the flesh, the world, and the devil, do you not feel in yourselves that you owe to God as many acts of gratitude as you have won advantages and victories over your enemies?*

6. "*Every time that you overcome a temptation, or that you resist a vice, or that you discover a secret snare which the enemy had laid for you, or that an old passion should be foun! completely cured, or that a virtue long desired and prayed for be granted you by the mercy of God, what ought you to do but to raise your voice, at each fresh benefit received in canticles of praise and acts of thanksgiving, so that God should be blessed and glorified in all His gifts? For if not, when the just Judge comes and examines all your works, he will be condemned as an ingrate who has not said to God with the prophet: 'Thy mercies were the subject of my song in the place of my pilgrimage.'* (Psalm cxviii. verse 54.) *We see also that David calls many of his psalms 'degrees,' to teach us that in proportion as we advance in virtue, and that we mount the steps which are formed in each one of us, we ought to sing at each fresh step a new canticle to the glory of Him who draws and attracts us more and more up to Him. For if not, how shall we verify in ourselves these words: 'The voice of rejoicing and of salvation is in the tabernacles of the just?'* (Psalm cxvii., verse 15.) *Or how should we obey this wholesome and excellent advice of St. Paul: 'Speaking to yourselves in psalms, and hymns, and spiritual canticles, singing and making melody in your hearts to the Lord!'*" (Ephes. v., verse 19; St. Bernard, in Cant., serm. 1, num. 6, 7.)

We have here pointed out the great conformity between our holy prelate's disposition and that of St. Bernard, from whom he drew so many of his principles of piety. For the virtue of thankfulness, being binding on all, it is very useful to show its importance and bearings; as it may be said of gratitude what the saints have said of humility, (of which it is a necessary consequence,) that with this single virtue one may obtain everything of God when one has nothing; and that, if that quality be wanting in us, one may lose all, even if one had all.

CHAPTER XXVI.

OF THE SPECIAL DEVOTION OF THE HOLY PRELATE TOWARDS THE PASSION OF OUR LORD.—OF THE LABOURS AND AUSTERITY OF HIS LIFE.

The labours and sufferings of Jesus Christ are an object of adoration and love which the Church proposes to the piety of all her children. But, with Dom Bartholomew, the love and devotion he felt towards the mysteries of the Passion were extraordinary. At the end of each hour in the Office he used to make five pious ejaculations, in honour of the five wounds of Jesus Christ, and said them with such earnestness that it seemed as if he were in spirit at the foot of the cross, receiving the drops of blood which should cure the wounds of his soul. In his "*Abridgment of the Spiritual Life,*" he gives copious extracts of St. Bernard's Sermons on the Canticles, which he calls "*words of fire,*" and "*the most delicious nourishment of souls.*" And it is in these same sermons that this saint exhorts all the world to meditation on the sufferings of Jesus Christ, and that in the most touching manner.

St. Bernard, explaining these words, "*My beloved is as a bundle of myrrh,*" exhorts his religious to have a great devotion towards the sufferings of our Saviour. "*If you wish to imitate the wisdom of this divine Spouse, let no hour of your life pass in which you bear not on your breast this bundle of myrrh, which ought to be so precious to you. And keep alive continually in your memory, and go over in your mind, what your Spouse has suffered for you, so that you may* say: '*My beloved is a bundle of myrrh. He will rest on my breast.*' *I remember that, at the beginning of my conversion, seeing myself destitute of that abundance of merit which was so necessary to me, I took care to gather up all the afflictions and bitternesses of my Saviour, to make myself a bundle of myrrh, and wear it on my breast. I put into this nosegay the extreme poverty He suffered in His childhood, His labours in His preachings, His fatigues in His journeys, His watchings in prayer, His temptations in fasting, His tears and groans in the compassion He had for sinners. I added the snares His adversaries laid for Him by their deceitful words, the perils to which He was exposed by the treason of false brethren, the injuries with which He was dishonoured, the smitings on the cheek with which He was outraged, the spittings with which He was disfigured, the mockeries with which He was ridiculed, the whips with which He was torn, the nails with which He was pierced, the thorns with which He was crowned, in a word, the torments which mark the whole history of His Passion, whose cruel points have been so salutary for the healing of my wounds. I took care not to forget, amidst this bundle of myrrh, that which was given Him when He hung on the cross, and with which He was embalmed in His sepulchre, knowing that, by the first, He wished to point out to us the bitterness of our sins; and that by the second He has promised us the incorruption of our bodies. These are the wonders of Jesus, which I will publish as long as I live. These are His ineffable mercies which I will never forget, for to them I owe my life. David asked them formerly of God, and asked them with tears, when he said: 'Let Thy tender mercies come unto me, and I shall live.' (Psalm cxviii. verse 77.) And another saint, dwelling on the same subject, exclaimed: 'The mercies of the Lord are great.' How many kings and prophets have wished to see what we see, and have not done so? This bundle of myrrh is reserved for us, we wear it on our breasts, and none can take it from us. It is in this meditation on the sufferings of our Lord that I find the height of wisdom. There is the perfection of justice, the fulness of science, the riches of salvation, and an abundant source of graces and merits. In this meditation I find sometimes a bitter taste, but this bitterness is salutary; and sometimes a balm of which the sweetness fills me with consolation and joy. For this reason the Passion of our Lord is almost always, as you know, on my lips; it is always in my heart, as God knows; and it forms a part of all I write, as you may easily see. The highest and most sublime philosophy is to know Jesus Christ and Him crucified. I do not ask for anything higher. I do not ask with the Spouse where my Beloved rests in the midst of His glory. It is enough for me to contemplate Him as my Saviour amidst the sufferings of the cross. This first view is doubtless more sublime, but the second is sweeter, or at least, it is more proportioned to our needs. I conjure you, therefore, brethren, to gather also for yourselves a nosegay of this celestial myrrh, to keep it always near your hearts, and to wear it as your protection and defence. Do not carry it as a burden on your shoulders, or behind you, but wear it as a nosegay on your breast and before you, for fear lest by bearing it without smelling it, it should weary you by its weight, without rejoicing and strengthening you by its sweet scent."* (Bern., in Cant., ser. 43, num. 2, 3.) The same saint, explaining those words of the Canticle, "*My dove is in the clefts of the rocks,*" (Cant. ii. verse 14,) says: "*This rock is Jesus Christ, and these clefts are His deep wounds. We need not fear that He will reject the soul which desires to hide itself in His wounds, as, on the contrary, He invites us to do so by the words of His prophet: 'Enter thou into the rock, and hide thee in the pit, from the face of the fear of the Lord, and from the glory of His majesty.'* (Isaiah ii. verse 10.) *He thus draws to Himself a soul which is still weak and hesitating, by showing it the openings which are already made in the rock,* so that it may hide itself and get cured, and that, little by little, it may penetrate into the Heart of the Son of God in proportion as it becomes stronger and purer. *What is this rock which has been pierced by the openings made in it? Our Saviour teaches us when He speaks by the mouth of David: 'They have dug My hands and feet.'* (Psalm xxi. verse 18.) *A wounded and languishing soul will be soon cured if she will remain in these openings in the body of Jesus Christ. For what is more efficacious to cure the wounds of the soul, and purify the mind from all impurity, than to apply oneself continually to meditation on the wounds of our Saviour? The spouse says: 'My dove is in the clefts of the rocks.' And the dove says: 'He hath exalted me on the rock.'* (Psalm xxvi. verse 6.) *And it is on this rock, which is Jesus Christ, that a wise architect builds his house, so that he may neither fear tempests nor floods. On this stone I can rest securely. I am strengthened against my enemies; I am firm so that I shall not fall. For all that is on the earth is fragile and uncertain. But being firmly grounded on this rock, I am raised above the earth, and am in heaven, where this stone lives. There is our conversation, our refuge, our sure hope. And, certainly, where can weak souls find strength and rest except in these wounds of our Saviour? I find myself all the more secure in this refuge, as He who hides me in it is the more powerful to help me. The world threatens, the flesh tempts me, the Devil spreads his snares, and yet I do not fall, because I am founded on the rock. Ubi tuta firma que infirmis securitas et requies, nisi in vulneribus salvatoris?"* (Bern., in Cant., serm. 51, num. 3 and 4.)

St. Bernard is not content with exciting Christians in general to have this special confidence in the Passion of our Saviour, but he goes down to those who have lost all grace, and are fallen into great crimes. "*I have committed a great sin,*" he continues; "*my soul is troubled;*

but in this trouble I do not lose hope, for I remember the wounds of my Saviour. He was wounded for our transgressions, and to heal the wounds of our sins. What sin is so mortal that it cannot be cured by the Blood of a God? If, then, I remember so powerful and efficacious a remedy, the violence and malignity of my sin should not make me despair. Therefore he was mistaken who exclaimed: 'My iniquity is greater than that I may deserve pardon.' (Genesis iv. verse 13.) It is evident that he was not a member of Jesus Christ, and did not lean on His merits, with the holy belief that the Saviour's merits were his own, and that he should participate in His graces by the indissoluble union of a head and its members. But for me, the confidence which God gives me results in this, that finding nothing good in myself, I venture to take what I need from the bowels of my Saviour, from whence flows a source of mercy, which I feel He keeps open for me to enter in. 'They have pierced My hands and My feet,' He says; 'they have opened My side with a lance.' It is by these openings that I enter into this mystic stone, and that I suck the oil and the honey. That is to say, that I taste and see how gracious the Lord is. He has only had thoughts of mercy and peace for me, and I knew it not. Who can tell what is hidden in the bosom of God? But now this divine breast is opened for us, that we may find out His will. The lance opens it. His blood speaks. His wounds cry out that God is really in Jesus Christ, and that He is come to reconcile the world unto Himself. The secrets of His Heart are now laid bare. The great mystery of the ineffable goodness of God is revealed to the whole world, and we can penetrate through His wounds into the very bowels of the mercy of our God, wherein He hath visited us, coming down from the height of heaven to save the world." And again in another letter St. Bernard writes: *"Jesus Christ dies, and He deserves to be loved. The Holy Spirit is given to us, and we must love Him. Jesus Christ is worthy to be loved by Himself, and yet we can only do so by the gift of the Holy Spirit. What confusion for an ungrateful soul to see a God dying for him on the cross. And yet man falls easily into this gross ingratitude unless he be touched by the Holy Ghost.*" (Bern., Epist. 107, num. 3.)

It is from this holy unction and grace that our archbishop learned to love and honour the sufferings of Jesus Christ, and not only to honour, but to imitate them. He found in our Saviour's cross an exhortation always to suffer and to work, as well as a consolation in all his labours. Therefore he exclaims in one of his letters, like St. Bernard, "*Ubi fortitudo nisi in Christi Passione?*"

We have seen in his life how great were his corporal austerities. For, not to speak of hair shirts and disciplines, which he used continually, he added the incessant interior and exterior labours of the episcopate, which St. Gregory the Pope calls "*tempestas mentis*," to the rigorous observance of the religious life. He often made his visitations in the midst of winter, when frost and snow were on the ground, and in a country full of rocks and precipices. And though his courage on these occasions made him hard and insensible as regarded himself, his charity gave him the greatest tenderness and compassion for those around him. When he saw them tired and discouraged, he animated them by his cheering words and example, and begged them to consider how much He for whom they laboured had suffered for them, quoting the words of St. Bernard to his monks, "*Mortificamini, sed propter eum que mortuus est pro vobis.*" He never wore gloves, whatever the season might be, and would not even cover his hands with his cloak, but kept them outside, exposed to all the cold of the season. When the cold was extreme during his visitation, he no sooner arrived at the house where he was to stop, than he took great care to see that everybody was comfortable and well warmed, but having done that, he would sit down and set to work at his writing, without ever going near the fire. When his suite used to implore him to warm himself first, and not to let himself die of cold like that, he would reply, smiling: *"That winter had its place in the world like summer, and that the cold praised God no less than the heat."* As to eating, besides the fasts which were habitual with him, he took so little notice of what he ate or drank, that sometimes he was given vinegar instead of wine, and he never found it out. And one of those who was dining with him at the time, having warned the servant of his unintentional mistake, the archbishop excused him by saying, "It was quite good enough for him." He always kept to the rule of never saying if a dish were good or bad, however ill-cooked a thing might be. He used to say: *"That our soul was an angel, and our body a beast, and that we ought to live the life of angels, and treat our bodies as a wise man treats his horse,"* referring again to St. Bernard's words: *"In corpore bestiali angelum vivere."* All this proves that this man of God honoured the Passion of Jesus Christ, not only by continual meditation, but by a faithful imitation of His sufferings and pains, and that he wished to be, like St. Paul, the companion of His tribulations, that he might hereafter share in His glory; so that (as that apostle said of himself,) he wished *"semper mortificationem Jesu in corpore nostro circumferentes."* (II. Cor. iv., verse 10.)

CHAPTER XXVII.

OF THE PROFOUND RESPECT OF THE HOLY PRELATE FOR THE SACRIFICE OF THE MASS.—OF THE SPECIAL GRACES HE RECEIVED DURING ITS CELEBRATION.—HOW HE HONOURED THE VIRGIN AND THE SAINTS.

Devotion to our Saviour's wounds necessarily involves union with Him in the most holy Mystery of the Altar, wherein He gives to each one of us, for the sanctification of our souls, the same Body which was pierced with nails on the cross, and the same Blood which issued from His side for the redemption of the world. Dom Bartholomew had the deepest possible respect for this mystery, as for that of the Passion, both of which were indissolubly united in his heart as they are in themselves. And as he always bore in mind the sufferings of Jesus Christ, he had an equally fervent desire to unite himself daily with Him in the Holy Sacrifice, wherein His Body and Blood become again the price of our sins, the remedy of our wounds, and the nourishment of our souls.

The archbishop, whether at Braga or elsewhere, always regulated his business so as to have time for offering the Holy Sacrifice of the Mass. He used to say that his soul sought daily this divine food to renew that charity and devotion which the continual distraction of business and worldly cares might otherwise cool or destroy. Father Louis of Grenada adds, however, that in spite of the intense affection he had for this mystery, he would purposely omit saying Mass one day in the week, to renew his fear and respect for this adorable and yet awful Sacrament, which proves the extreme humility and veneration of the holy prelate towards Jesus Christ present in this mystery; who, although his life was so pure, and his exercises of penance and charity so continual, thought he ought to deprive himself and his people of this supreme consolation now and then, to impress upon their hearts and on his own the respectful fear which is due to this great mystery. He used to say, "That the little interval which thus elapsed in offering the Holy Sacrifice helped to impress a deeper veneration upon him of this august mystery, and that when on the following day he went up to the altar, it was with a new spirit." And everybody remarked, by his extraordinary fervour, that this voluntary privation had redoubled his devotion, and kindled the warmth of his holy desires. When he did not offer the Holy Sacrifice himself, however, he took care to participate in It by spiritual communion, to which his model St. Bernard exhorts all Christians in the following words: *"There is no one who has any affection for Jesus Christ who does not know how important it is for Christian piety, and how just and advantageous for the servant of God and a slave redeemed by the blood of Jesus Christ, that he should take some hours in the day to meditate with special care on the benefits he has received from our Lord by His passion and death, so that he may taste them in his very heart, and preserve them faithfully in his remembrance. This is eating and drinking spiritually the Flesh and Blood of Jesus Christ, as He commanded all those to do who should hereafter believe in His words: 'Do this in remembrance of Me.'* (Luke xxii., verse 19.) *He who does not fulfil this duty, besides the disobedience he commits, is guilty of gross ingratitude by forgetting the extreme goodness which God has shown him. For it is a crime not to remember One who, in leaving us, bequeathed a special mark whereby we might recall*

Him to our memory. For the adorable mystery of this holy commemoration can be only celebrated in a certain way, at a certain time, and in a certain place, by the small number of those to whom He has confided it. But there is no spot in the whole earth where the effect and fruit of this Sacrament cannot be received as the food of salvation, in the manner I have described, by those to whom it was said: 'But you are a chosen generation, a kingly priesthood, a holy nation, a purchased people, that you may declare His virtues who hath called you out of darkness into His marvellous light.' (I. St. Peter ii., verse 9.) For as he who is well prepared finds his life in this Sacrament, he who approaches it unworthily finds in it only condemnation and death. But as for the effect of the Sacrament, he only profits by it who is worthy and prepared to receive it. If, then, he receives this Sacrament without its fruit and effect, he finds death; but if he receives its fruit and effect, even should he not actually receive the Sacrament, he finds eternal life. If, therefore, you have a hearty desire to bring down this grace into your soul, there is no hour of the day or night when you cannot receive the fruit of this adorable mystery. Each time that you are penetrated with a vivid feeling of faith and love towards Him who died for you, you eat His Body and drink His Blood. As long as you live in Jesus Christ by love, and He in you, by the holy and just works which He enables you to perform, you will be in Him as being of His Body and one of His members. If, then, you really love your life, you should lose and sacrifice it for Jesus Christ; either by martyrdom, if it be necessary to die for God, or by labours and the austerities of penance. For the mortification of the flesh which is made subject to the spirit, is a kind of martyrdom, easier, perhaps, and less terrible than that which cuts off our members and spills our blood, but more trying by its wearisomeness and its long duration." (St. Bern. val al. serm. 2, de Cœnâ Dom. et ad Fratr. de Monte Dei, cap 24.)

Those who have written the life of Dom Bartholomew have remarked something particular concerning the piety with which he celebrated the Holy Sacrifice. "When he had retired to his monastery at Viano, the people of that town conceived an extraordinary veneration for him, and went in crowds to hear his Mass. For he celebrated the Holy Sacrifice with such recollection, such respect and piety, that his devotion was imparted to all who heard him. A great number of sick persons constantly resorted to him, and thought themselves too happy if they could receive his blessing, or if he would make the sign of the cross on their foreheads. At first the humility of the holy prelate made him shrink from these demonstrations of esteem and reverence, and in order to make them go away he would say to them with some severity: 'Why do you seek so earnestly the health of your body, without caring what becomes of your soul?' Or, 'Ask of God that He may cure you, not of your sickness, but of your sins, and that He may give you the grace to use the evils He sends you, to satisfy His justice and save you from purgatory.' Nevertheless his friends entreated him at last to behave towards these poor people with his usual tenderness and charity; and seeing the faith and patience with which they had recourse to him, he granted them all they wished. Many have published the extraordinary cures and graces which they received from his prayers, and especially from his Mass. Nor were the poor the only ones to appreciate his sanctity. When the King of Spain, Philip II., came to Portugal, he showed such veneration for his virtue and piety that he would never miss hearing his Mass if he could help it, with all the first persons in his court. Many strange things happened when he was celebrating the Holy Sacrifice. One day he stopped much longer than usual after the Preface, at the part in which the priest recommends specially to God those for whom he wishes to pray. His server, thinking he was unnecessarily long, warned him by gently pulling his vestments. The holy prelate roused himself as if he had woke from a trance, and continued his Mass with a haste and precipitation which were as unusual as they were extraordinary in him. Those who were present were very much surprised, and their astonishment increased at seeing that, no sooner had he finished it, than he rushed from the church, without stopping a moment for his acts of thanksgiving, but ran quickly up to his cell, where, calling his servant, a man named Ferdinand, he gave him a considerable sum of money, and told him to go as fast as he could to a certain place which he minutely described to him, where he would find a man of a certain age, dressed like a peasant, who was going out of the town with a cord under his arm and a sad and perplexed countenance. That he was to give him this money, and tell him from him (the archbishop) that he was never to despair of the mercy of God, and to believe that He would never abandon those who trusted in Him. Ferdinand started instantly, found the man at the exact place which the prelate had described to him, and recognized him at once by the signs he had mentioned. He gave him the money from the archbishop, and seeing his sadness changed into joy, he asked him where he was going to when he had met him. The poor man replied that, two days before, some one had stolen his two oxen, which were his sole means of livelihood; that he had sought everywhere to find out what had become of them, without obtaining the smallest tidings; that he and his children, of whom he had a large number, were dying of hunger; that the archbishop had already sent him an alms, but that, having sustained so great a loss, and having so many mouths to feed, he had lost all hope and all courage, so that in this extremity he thought his only course was to end his misery with his life. Thus it was discovered that God had revealed to His faithful servant, in the Holy Sacrifice, the sorrow and despair of this poor man, so that he might remedy both one and the other. From that moment the poor fellow was entirely changed; and considering in himself how God had taken pity on and remembered him when he had forgotten Him, he went to see the holy prelate, whom he revered as his father, and became a fervent and exemplary Christian. Thus, by the merit of the archbishop's Mass, and by the tenderness and promptitude of his charity, both the life and soul of this man were saved."

Besides Dom Bartholomew's great devotion towards our Lord in the Holy Sacrifice, he had a tender veneration towards His Virgin Mother. He was strengthened in this feeling by the way in which St. Bernard wrote of her, he being, of all the fathers, the one who has the most strongly recommended to Christians the invocation of the Mother of God in the following words: "*Whoever you may be who recognize that in this unhappy life you are sailing in the midst of storms and tempests rather than walking on the earth, never turn away your eyes from this brilliant star, unless you wish to be overwhelmed by the waves. If the winds of temptation rise up against you; if you are thrown against the rocks of affliction and evils of all kinds: look up at the star, look at Mary. If you find yourself beaten by the waves of pride, of ambition, of calumny, of jealousy: look up at the star, look at Mary. If anger, or avarice, or the concupiscence of the flesh, like so many impetuous waves, dash against the vessel of your soul: look at Mary. If you are troubled at the enormity of your crimes; if the ugliness of your conscience confounds you; and if amidst this horror of yourself with which you have been struck, you begin to let yourself drift into the abyss of sadness and despair: think of Mary, invoke Mary. Let her be always in your heart; and that she may grant you the help of her prayers, take her life as an example and a rule for your own. Thus you will not stray away in following her; you will not despair by invoking her; you will not be deceived in consulting her. As long as she holds you, you will not fall; as long as she protects you, you will not fear; as long as she guides you, you will not weary. And taking advantage of her help, she will make you enter at last into the glory of her Son, who liveth and reigneth for ever and ever, and to all ages."* (Bern., hom. 2, super Missus. num. 17.)

Dom Bartholomew followed exactly this advice of St. Bernard, and especially in striving to follow Mary's example. He thought she was always saying to us in spirit those words of St. Paul: "*Wherefore I beseech of you, be ye followers of me, as I also am of Christ.*" (I. Cor. iv., verse 16.) "And if, in the marriage of Cana, where she became the mediatrix of men, as she obtained from her Son the conversion of water into wine, which marks all the grace of the new law, she said to the officers: '*Whatsoever He shall say to you, do ye,*' (St. John ii., verse 5,) we ought to believe that she says the same thing now to all those who profess to honour her. For if Jesus Christ complained of the Jews in old times, saying: '*Why call you Me Lord, Lord, and do not the things which I say?*' (St. Luke vi., verse 46) we ought to be afraid of her saying to us: 'Why do you call my Son your 'Lord,' and why do you call me 'your Lady,' and your protector, if you do not do what He commands, and what I wish you to do, as it is impossible that my will should not be in entire conformity with His?'" We may indeed say of Dom Bartholomew that he imitated her in all things. For he laboured, like her, to annihilate himself before God; to humble himself the more that God exalted him; to seek for nothing but the accomplishment of His will; to keep alive in his heart the deepest gratitude for all His benefits;

to look upon all that happened to him with an eye of faith; to follow God in all things with an obedience full of affection and peace; to preserve always a uniform disposition of mind in all the chequered events of life; and lastly, to meditate continually on His wonders, and "ponder on them in his heart," as it is said of the Blessed Virgin.

He had a great veneration also for the saints, but espe- for St. Martin. He went into religion on the day of his feast; and when he was raised to the episcopal dignity he considered him as his special model, because he had been drawn, like himself, from the cloister and from solitude, to be made a bishop. He tried to imitate what Severus Sulpicius said of this saint in his biography: "*One may, in a certain way, describe the miracles and actions of St. Martin, but his interior life, his devotion, and his perseverance in prayer, are entirely inexplicable. He never passed a single hour or a single moment of his life which was not full of the thought of God, or of the work of God; and whatever he did he prayed continually. O! truly happy pontiff! always simple and without any disguise; who never judged any one, nor condemned any one; and who never returned evil for evil. No one ever saw him angry, no one ever saw him even troubled, no one saw him either laughing or sad, but remaining always the same, and bearing on his countenance a kind of celestial joy, by which he seemed as if raised above the nature of men. He had always Jesus Christ in his heart and on his lips. And he never had anything but piety, peace, goodness, and compassion in his soul.*" (Sulpit. de Vitâ Beati Martin, cap. 26.)

What we shall have to say in the next chapter of the recollection of Dom Bartholomew, and of his rules as to his words, will show how closely he imitated this great saint, who has been called "*the pearl of bishops*," and whose virtue seemed so extraordinary, that in the praises given him by the Church he is compared to "*the prophets and apostles.*"

CHAPTER XXVIII.

THE GREAT WISH OUR HOLY ARCHBISHOP HAD FOR DEATH.—
OF HIS EXTRAORDINARY ARDOUR TO RECEIVE THE HOLY
VIATICUM.—OF HIS PATIENCE IN HIS ILLNESSES.

St. Paul has said of himself, that "*To me to live is Christ, and to die is gain.*" (Philip. i. verse 21.) "*Mihi vivere Christus est et mori lucrum.*" Dom Bartholomew entirely shared this feeling. He spoke of his tomb as of a place of rest, and as the only dwelling that he desired here below. He often spoke with his friends of the hour of his death as of a happiness which he had waited for with impatience for a long time. A religious of his order having said to him one day that he was astonished that he spoke in this way of death, as every one knew that even great saints, like St. Hilarion, had dreaded this terrible moment, he replied: "I do not wish for death with the idea that I have rendered great services to God, or as if I were worthy of any reward, for the only hope I have of my salvation is founded on the merits of the Blood of Jesus Christ, Who has so loved me, and Who has given Himself up to death for me, as well as on the intercession of His holy Mother and all the saints. If, then, I wish to die, it is to get out of this world, which is so full of corruption, to renounce entirely all that is not God, and to possess Him at last in such a way that I can never more lose Him. For knowing myself to be so full of faults and so great a sinner, I only desire, by wishing to die, to see sin die likewise in me, and to find myself delivered from those troubles which tormen me continually from my fear of having offended so good and loving a Master."

He thus coincided exactly with those old saints who used to say we ought to wish for death rather than fear it, as *death was the end of sin.* "*Mors finis peccatorum.*" For we shall never cease altogether from sin till we die, as death alone can destroy that concupiscence which is the root of all sin. That is what made St. Augustine say: "*We advance in piety in this life by the diminution of concupiscence, and by the growth of charity, but we become entirely perfect in the next life by the destruction of concupiscence and the perfection of charity. Proficimus in hac vitâ, deficiente cupiditate, crescente charitate: perficiemur in alterâ, cupiditate extinctâ, charitate completâ.*" Therefore, a Christian, who lives by faith, must consider that one of the great effects of the Incarnation is, as St. Paul says, "*to deliver those who, through the fear of death, were all their life-time subject to servitude,*" (Heb. ii. verse 15,) and to make all the faithful feel that death is properly the end of sin, and the beginning of life, of justice, and eternal charity.

St. Augustine exhorts all Christians to live in such a way as that they may wish to die; "*for they will only advance in virtue in proportion as they advance in piety. For it is not enough that he should see by faith this celestial abode, where he hopes one day to arrive, but he must besides love it by charity, and already earnestly desire to be there. And it is impossible that he should be in this disposition without being very glad to get out of this life. Therefore it is in vain for those who have already strong faith to say they do not wish to die soon, so as to have more time to become better, as they will only advance in virtue in proportion as they advance in this disposition, which will make them wish for death. If, then, they wish to speak the truth, do not let them say, 'I do not wish to die so* as to have the time to become better,' but rather, '*I do not wish to die, because I am not yet good enough.*' And so, as long as such persons do not wish to die, it will not be a means of acquiring more virtue, but only a mark that they have not yet made much progress. Let those, then, who do not wish to die so as to become more perfect, desire death, and then they will be perfect. *Quod ergo nolunt ut perfecti sunt, velint et perfecti sunt.*" (August. Quest. Evang. I. 1, Quest. 17.)

We find, then, that a good life and the wish for death are inseparable. For, according to St. Augustine, one cannot be really a Christian if one does not love God and that eternal life which He has promised to those that fear Him. We believe in it by faith; we expect it by hope; we love and desire it by charity. In proportion as we advance in the exercise of these virtues, we advance likewise in this holy desire; and the more we wish for eternal life the more we detach ourselves from this earthly life, and the more we feel the advantage of getting out of it, as death alone makes us enter into that life of God which is the object of our piety in this world, and the end of all our desires.

When faith and charity have been perfected, the desire for death increases, and lifts us above this love of life which nature has implanted in us; and to this state our holy archbishop had arrived. St. Augustine says again: " *There are persons who suffer death with patience, and there are others who bear life with difficulty. He who still loves this life suffers patiently the hour of death. He fights against himself to submit to the Will of God; and he would rather yield to whatever He has ordained for him than follow the human inclination of his own will. The love of life struggles in his heart with the necessity of dying, and he arms himself with strength and patience to conquer this wish, and to accept death with submission and peace. He who is in this state of mind suffers death with patience. But he who desires with the apostles the dissolution of his body, that he may be united to Jesus Christ, bears his life with patience and receives death with joy. Ille patienter moritur; hic patienter vivit, et delectabiliter moritur."* (Aug. in Epist. I. Joan. tract. 5.)

This earnest wish which the archbishop had for death gave him great strength and courage in illnesses. When he fell ill, not only he submitted heartily to the will of God, but he felt great joy in the hope of a speedy death. During the plague which raged, as we have described, in his diocese, he one day was seized with violent headache, which every one thought was a precursor of the epidemic. He himself felt persuaded that his hour was come, and trusting in the infinite mercy of God, he disposed himself with joy for the passage. The doctors, however, treated him so skilfully and with such care, that in a short time the malady yielded to their remedies. This holy man felt great sorrow at seeing himself thus saved from the death to which he looked forward as to his rest, and having to go back again to all the miseries of this life; so that, though he was very grateful for the affection of his friends and all the care and devotion of the doctors, he said the following words: "*In this world we do not like those who, by their artifices prolong a trial, and prevent and delay a judgment. Why then are we so anxious to delay a little the sentence by which God ends our life, as we must certainly die? and it is very doubtful whether it be more advantageous to us to die a little sooner or a little later.*" Another time, having fallen dangerously ill, the doctors ordered him a great variety of remedies. He felt great repugnance in submitting to them, fancying that they took too much trouble about his health. But seeing that his friends exhorted him very eagerly to avail himself of them, he said: "If you love me, love also what consoles me, and spare me what gives me sorrow and annoyance. If God has determined to take me out of this world, let me go to Him. For I go with all my heart, leaning on His infinite mercy. Do not oppose yourself to His designs, or deprive me of the accomplishment of my most earnest wishes."

He continued during his illness the same severity against himself which he had used during health. He would not leave off his heavy woollen tunic even in the midst of the most burning fever. He would not allow them even to take off his blanket to give him a lighter covering, and what is still more strange, he made no change in his ordinary diet, unless absolutely constrained to do so by the orders of the doctor and by the violence of his illness. One day, being very suffering and ill, some pious friends of his, seeing him sadly exhausted and weak, conjured him to abate some of his austerities; but he only replied, sighing: "O flesh! how numerous are thy advocates!" All that he cared for during his illness was the presence of Jesus Christ in the Blessed Eucharist, which he justly considered as the only One who by His presence and His help could facilitate his happy passage from this world. The remembrance of this celestial food made him forget all the alleviations of human skill. Once, having a violent attack of fever, he had an interior thirst which burnt him up in such a way that his tongue and his mouth were black with dryness. Nevertheless, when he began to have a little relief, he never complained of this fearful thirst, but thought only of *the Living Water* for which his soul thirsted. He asked eagerly for the Body and Blood of Jesus Christ, and when they entreated him to wait a little and to take some food, he answered with the deepest feeling, and in a way which touched the hearts of all that heard him, "That this was the sole food he wanted, and the only meat he desired."

When his illness left him sufficient consciousness to think at all, his sole idea was conversing with God, and asking Him for patience and perseverance to the end. He esteemed greatly some words of Pope Pius V., (who was of his Order,) which he had spoken in his last illness, when he suffered a perfect martyrdom from stone: "*Domine, adde ad dolorem, dummodo addas ad patientiam.*" In the same way our holy prelate repeated constantly those words of St. Fulgentius on his death-bed: "*Domine da mihi modò patientiam; et postea indulgentiam.*" This Christian disposition shows us that he was indeed of the number of those spoken of by St. Augustine, whose life was the more holy, and whose death was the more happy, as he wished for death and only bore with life, "*Non amant vitam sed tolerant.*" (Aug., in Ep. I. Joan. tract. 9.)

CHAPTER XXIX.

WHAT WERE DOM BARTHOLOMEW'S MERITS AS A MONK.—A MEMORANDUM WRITTEN BY HIM WHEN DRAGGED FROM HIS MONASTERY TO BE MADE A BISHOP.—HIS FEELINGS ON THE PRINCIPAL POINTS OF A RELIGIOUS LIFE.

Having in the preceding chapters shown Dom Bartholomew's perfections as an ecclesiastic, as a bishop, and as a Christian, we will now speak of his admirable spirit as a religious. And we wish our readers to dwell a little on this portion of his life, as there is an intimate connection between this, his first estate, and the second, which was its crown. For whatever was great and illustrious in the episcopate of Dom Bartholomew was founded on the humility and solid virtue he had acquired during the thirty years he spent in his monastery. And in order to prove this, we will give word for word a memorandum he wrote with his own hand on a blank sheet of his diary, which has been carefully preserved by his Order, and which has been removed lately from Portugal to France. It was written partly in Latin and partly in Portuguese, and he mentions some advice which Father Louis of Grenada gave him when he forced him to accept the Archbishopric of Braga, and what he replied to it.

"*In the year 1558, on the 8th of August, all the religious of St. Dominic's Monastery in Lisbon being assembled in the choir of the church, our provincial, Father Louis of Grenada, called me, and told me that the Queen had ordered him to compel me to accept the Archbishopric of Braga, to which she had done me the honour to present me, and which I had refused, although she had deigned to use every argument to persuade me to accept it. And after having talked to me for a long time on this subject, he ordered me to prostrate myself on the ground, and then commanded me, under pain of major excommunication, to receive this archbishopric. Then he gave me three pieces of advice.*

"*The first, not to be attached to my own opinion or my own view of things, but to like to take counsel from others, unless it be a question of tradition or of apostolic truth.*

"*The second was, that I should not be hasty in punishing, but that I should be patient and dissimulate a good deal, not expecting from men of the world conduct as perfect and as spiritual as I should find among religious. But, nevertheless, that I was not to tolerate visible sins, or public and scandalous disorders.*

"*The third, that I should be so circumspect and reserved in my gestures, words, and my whole conduct, that there should be nothing contrary to good breeding, or which should wound the respect due to my episcopal dignity. That with persons of rank I should be grave and courteous; with the poor, open and gentle. In a word, that I should have* humility mingled with magnanimity, and gentleness with gravity and reserve.

"I replied at length to his commands, and I ended by protesting:

"First, that I was resolved to employ the revenue of the Church, which belongs to Jesus Christ, as He Himself had ordained; not to live in luxury and magnificence; or to enrich my relations; or to amass great riches.

"Secondly, that obedience alone constrained me to accept this dignity, which I would not receive from any earthly prince, but solely from her, although in issuing this command she seemed to cast me out of her bosom."

And he added, to show how he valued Father Grenada's advice: "That he entreated him, and whoever was his successor in his charge of provincial, to come and see him at Braga during their visitation; and that he hoped never to fall into such blindness as to despise the charitable advice given him by them or by any one else." To this memorandum he added the words: "My bulls were despatched on the 27th of January, 1559, and I was consecrated on the 3rd of September in the same year."

It was in this way that he entered upon his episcopate, and most faithfully did he fulfil his holy resolutions, as we have seen throughout his life, which was eminently "*humilis et docilis.*" As for his extreme love for the religious life, and the terror with which he looked upon the overwhelming weight of the episcopal charge, he showed it enough by the words he often spoke, and which were inserted in his epitaph: "That having looked upon his monastery as his kingdom, he had been dragged thence by force to make him a bishop as from a throne to a scaffold: *ut de regno ad crucem.*" As long as he remained archbishop he always added his religious exercises to his episcopal functions, and was as perfect in the one as in the other.

He was very particular to avoid that secret attachment which easily insinuates itself into the minds of the best religious, and by which they are so bound to the sole interests of their own community or Order that they have little or no affection for or interest in any other. Our holy prelate took special care not to fall into this snare, or to narrow his zeal and affection for one house or one order. He considered all the religious Orders in the world, and all the monasteries, as if they were his own. He had as great a respect for St. Dominic as for St. Benedict, for St. Bernard as for St. Francis, and the same for all the holy founders of religious orders. And although their respective children may be distinguished by a different habit, or rule, or way of life proper to each, he regarded them all as one in that spirit which unites the whole Church, and he embraced them all equally in his boundless charity, without envy, without ambition, and without self-interest of any kind. With this motive, when bishop, he laboured to introduce certain reforms into the Benedictine Order. Father Alonzo Zorilla, Commissary-general of the Benedictines, having received extraordinary powers from the Pope to reform all the monasteries of his order, and having accordingly passed into Portugal at the request of the king, Dom Sebastian, would not take any steps in so important a matter without having first consulted the holy archbishop, whom he considered the most enlightened person he could find in all matters touching the spiritual and religious life. Dom Bartholomew having had a long conference with him upon the proposed reforms, and the best way of introducing them, strongly advised him not to use his power by doing violence to the opinions and minds of his brethren, but to assemble all the religious of each monastery, and to represent to them with great gentleness and charity that, being all disciples and monks of St. Benedict, they were bound to do all in their power to carry out the rule of their holy founder in all its purity, and to renounce the relaxations and dispensations which the corruption of the age had given rise to, and which had greatly chilled the spirit of charity amongst them. That nevertheless, God wishing to be served in the fulness of love, he would not use the power he possessed to force changes upon any one. That those who felt enough zeal and courage to follow in the steps of the primitive Fathers might begin with him to resume a stricter observance of the rule. That others, who did not think themselves strong enough, could continue to live separately, as they had been accustomed to do. That he would take care that they were always treated with the same kindness and consideration as the rest, and that he hoped that by revering in others the good which as yet they did not think themselves capable of following, and by imploring the help of heaven on their weaknesses, God would strengthen them little by little, and give them the grace to imitate the example of their brethren, so that they might all become in the end perfect followers of St. Benedict."

The general received this advice of the archbishop with great joy and profound respect. He adopted his plan in the reformation of his monasteries to the letter, and it answered so well that, (his charity and forbearance having gained all hearts,) almost all the religious in each monastery adopted the reform, and that the rest, (who were very few,) being quite satisfied with the kindness with which he had treated them, the whole Order of St. Benedict took a fresh start, as it were, and became very soon the most fervent and holy Order in the kingdom of Portugal.

This universal charity of our holy prelate was accompanied by a great love for religious poverty. We have seen in the letter he wrote from the Council of Trent to one of the fathers of his Order, how anxious he was that this spirit should be maintained, not only in the dress, but in the buildings of the Order, and how he would not allow them to break the rule, even for the sake of more beautiful architecture. And in this matter he only followed the spirit of St. Dominic himself, who, seeing that his religious had begun a grand monastery at Bologna, exclaimed: "*Adhuc, me vivente, palatia ædificatis?*" Dom Bartholomew was always on the watch lest superfluous ornaments should be introduced into his monasteries on the pretext that all that was being done there was for God. For he dreaded not only lest the spirit of evangelical poverty should thereby be impaired, but that if the monks embarked in such great expenses, human views would insensibly creep into their souls, and a longing for greater temporal comforts and better accommodation. He feared also lest, in accepting fresh religious into their Order, a less pure intention should be observed than the glory of God alone, and that, without thought, subjects should be preferred who had large worldly possessions, thus preferring earthly treasures to divine. He set great store on the disinterestedness of his monks, and strove with all his might to banish that spirit of pride and ambition which is the ruin of so many houses. Having one day gone on a visitation to one of the monasteries of his Order, he insisted strongly on one point amidst his other instructions, namely, that they should consider themselves always as abjects in the house of God, and be anxious to take the lowest place, unless God Himself were to compel them against their wills to mount higher. And in the midst of this sermon on humility he sighed heavily, exclaiming: "O ambition! how hast thou entered into the house of God, which is the house of the humble in heart! It is ambition, my brethren, which is our destruction. *Ambitio perdidit nos.*" And after having repeated these words with great feeling, he added: "If those who elect or who are elected to important charges have regard to anything, in so grave a matter, but the glory of God and the salvation of their brethren, if the choice of the one be from interested motives, and the promotion of the other from pride or ambition, they will lose themselves and the whole Order, and the piety of their monastery will perish with them."

The holy archbishop exhorted also his religious very earnestly to fly from the world and from secular conversations, and to love rather silence and retreat, and fidelity to their rule in union with God, to enjoy which they had left the world. "Silence," he said, "is the treasure of the soul; it is the father and preserver of all virtue: and by this I do not merely mean bridling one's tongue. A lover of silence and solitude will avoid all visits, active or passive, and will only pay such from some great necessity. A lover of silence not only will not seek to procure, but will fly from permissions or dispensations to go from one monastery to another, or to amuse himself in useless company, where he often loses in a few hours all the virtue and recollection he had acquired in many years. A lover of silence will love and reverence his cell, which St. Bernard called '*his heaven and his paradise.*' This virtue consists in not dishonouring holiness by secular and human intimacies, or by reading profane books, and not to indulge in vain and useless thoughts, either from within or without. In a word, religious silence consists in holding constant communion with God in prayer, in meditation on His word, and holy books, in being occupied solely with Him, and in finding one's pleasure and one's joy in adoring Him without ceasing, with an interior and spiritual worship."

Those who have written the life of Dom Bartholomew

relate that when he was prior of Benefico, finding that he was continually interrupted by visits from the great people about the court, he retired, with some of the most fervent of his monks, to an obscure monastery at some distance off, to live in peace, and be freed from this constant intercourse with worldly people. It was remarked, also, that he avoided with the utmost care losing a moment of time, or the smallest superfluity in talking. Doctor Bartholomew Valla, Archdeacon of Braga, declares that during the twelve years he was constantly living with him, and necessarily speaking to him daily on different matters of business, he never remembers having heard him use one useless or unnecessary word, for his conversation was always limited to the obligations of his charge, the government of his diocese, or to some edifying or pious subject."

As he practised this rule so perfectly, he proposed it also to his ecclesiastics in his book, quoting the words St. Bernard used on the same subject to Pope Eugenius: *"Although the Wise man has said that it is only in quiet that we can learn wisdom, we must take care at the same time that this repose be well employed. Therefore, fly from idleness, which is the mother of frivolity, and the enemy of all virtue. The follies in the mouths of the people of the age are simple follies, but they are blasphemies when they come from the mouth of a priest or a bishop. If it should happen that such things are said before you, it may be wise sometimes to suffer them in silence, but never to encourage them. On the contrary, you should interrupt such conversation by introducing other topics which may be not only useful, but even interesting and pleasant to those who listen to you, and which may draw away their attention from frivolous or improper subjects. You have consecrated your mouth to the Gospel: if you open it to share in such follies, it is a fault and a violation of your duty ; and if you accustom yourself to* such conversation, it is a sacrilege. 'For the lips of the priest shall keep knowledge,' says the prophet, 'and they shall seek the law at his mouth.' (Malachias ii. verse 7.) It is not enough that your lips should be pure from all scandalous words, or from others which are honoured by being called 'bons mots,' or witty sayings, but you should be careful not even to listen to such. It would be disgraceful if you were heard laughing violently, and still more if you were to say things which made others do so. And as for calumny, I really do not know which is most to be condemned: to speak evil oneself of one's neighbour, or to listen to and encourage calumny in others." (Stim. Past., p. 51.)

CHAPTER XXX.

PARALLEL OF DOM BARTHOLOMEW WITH ST. CHARLES BORROMEO.—CONCLUSION OF THIS BIOGRAPHY.

The close intimacy which it pleased God to establish between St. Charles Borromeo and Dom Bartholomew of the Martyrs is one of the most interesting events in the life of this holy prelate. For not only did they live at the same time, but they laboured together in the same spirit for the greatest work which God could give them to do in this world, namely, the defence of the faith and the re-establishment of morals and discipline in the Church at a great General Council. And we have seen that it was by Dom Bartholomew's advice that St. Charles decided to give up his place in the Papal court and devote himself entirely to his bishopric.

We shall see in this parallel how God is pleased to diversify the operations and marvels of His saints, having created these two men, unlike in personal qualities, in the gifts of nature, and in the way in which they were called to the service of His Church; but alike in feelings and in virtue, in conduct, and in the principal actions of their lives; and while He made Dom Bartholomew the witness and admirer of the character of St. Charles, He impressed likewise on the heart of St. Charles the profoundest veneration for the person and the merits of our holy prelate.

They were both born of parents who brought them up in ways of piety. But God placed Dom Bartholomew in a position which had no advantages in the eyes of the world, so that all his greatness should be the effect of His sovereign grace; and St. Charles, on the contrary, was of most illustrious birth, so that his holiness might be the more admirable, as it is rarer in persons of high rank and position than among the poor. The virtue of both was based on the innocence and grace of baptism, which both had preserved. For the Son of God generally lays this solid foundation in those great souls whom He destines to be the support and the glory of His Church.

But God, wishing to sanctify Dom Bartholomew, drew him from his earliest years out of the dangers of the world, to hide him in a monastery. He kept him for a long time in this retreat, to make him grow in grace little by little; and having destined him to so exalted a dignity, in which he was to become one of the great lights of His Church, He willed that he should be prepared and purified for thirty years, so that his virtue might be so thoroughly grounded as to be enabled to bear the weight of this charge, and of the glory which he was to acquire in the fulfilment of his onerous duties.

St. Charles, on the contrary, finding himself a cardinal at twenty-two years of age, nephew of the Pope, Archbishop of Milan, praised and respected by every one, overwhelmed with riches, honours, and dignities, was, at the same time, so filled with God, and so strengthened by His grace, that he preserved the utmost moderation in his great youth, extraordinary humility in the midst of human praise, austerity amid luxury, piety and devotion to prayer in spite of the turmoil of the court, and finally a contempt and aversion for the world in the midst of all that could make it agreeable and attractive to its votaries. The one is like St. Ambrose, who was of illustrious birth like St. Charles, and who was called, like him, in an extraordinary way to the archbishopric of Milan: the other is like St. Basil or St. Gregory of Nazianzum, whom God purified for a long while by the exercises of religious life, because He destined them to become, by their knowledge and dignity, the masters of the whole East. And thus, if the way in which God sanctified the one is more worthy of admiration, that of the other is more useful for imitation.

By the providence of God it was ordained that these two eminent men should meet at the Council of Trent, there to labour together for the good of the whole Church. It was St. Charles who induced Pius IV. to call this Council together. Dom Bartholomew arrived almost the first, and his example attracted the other bishops to attend also. The one gave to all Cardinals a model of the love they should bear to the Church; the other, as was declared by the Cardinals themselves, appeared in their assembly "*as one of the primitive bishops of Christianity.*" Dom Bartholomew proposed the most useful reforms in discipline and morals; but St. Charles laboured to have them approved by the Pope. And both together, on this important occasion, considered *God alone* in their deliberations, and were the principal organs by which the great work of the Council was achieved. After the Council of Trent was broken up they both returned to their dioceses, and appeared as prelates chosen specially by God to set an example to the whole Church. And though they were far removed from one another, one being at Braga and one at Milan, nevertheless the Holy Spirit, who is the same in the hearts of all saints, united them, not only in thought and affection, but even in conduct, in all the most remarkable occasions of their lives.

Both were devoted to the salvation of their people; both were fond of reading and prayer; both occupied themselves continually in preaching the word, and were assiduous in all the duties of their charge. Both endeavoured to carry out in their respective dioceses the spirit of the Council of Trent. Both established seminaries to form ecclesiastical students and prepare them for Holy Orders and other important functions in the Church. Both laboured to banish luxury and ambition from the body of the clergy, and gave them an example of exemplary modesty, enlightened piety, and a charity which was entirely free from envy or self-interest.

Both had a boundless love for assisting the poor; and God permitted that the charity of both should be similarly exercised. Both had the sorrow of seeing their people dying of famine, and made the most extraordinary efforts to succour them. Both their episcopal cities were struck by the plague; and both despised the prayers and entreaties of their friends to save themselves from the danger by not exposing their lives to the infection. Both showed the same vigilant care and prodigious energy and charity in regulating everything in the midst of the general consternation. And during the fearful pestilence, both showed an equal devotion and tenderness towards the sufferers, and an equal indifference to the preservation of their own lives; trembling for their flocks, but never for themselves.

If their charity was so illustrious, not less remarkable were their zeal and courage in maintaining the rights of the Church against those who wished to upset her ordinances. And their apostolic vigour was mingled with so much wisdom and circumspection that even after having exhausted milder methods, and been compelled to resort to excommunications and censures against those who abused the royal authority, they yet always preserved the high esteem and admiration of their respective monarchs, which their consistency and disinterestedness had won for them.

Both laboured to procure for the Church not only exterior reforms; but a solid cure for all her evils. For St. Charles maintained in the Council, "*That they must not fancy they had reformed the Church, and Christians in general, because there were better regulations than before in certain places, but that the morals and piety of the faithful must be tested by the rules of the Gospel.*" And Dom Bartholomew, finding on his return from Rome to Trent that they had decided to weaken the text of the ordinances which had been agreed to be published in far stronger terms, complained to the fathers of the Council on the subject, and exclaimed: "*Far be it from us to have recourse to those glosses and interpretations which destroy the text and the truth; far from us also those reforms and changes which are only nominal, and leave us just where we were before.*" And his words acted so powerfully on the minds of the bishops, that it was finally decided that these ordinances as to the reformation of morals should be even stronger and more explicit than they were at first.

He showed the like zeal when Pius V. wished to examine the proceedings of a provincial council he had held at Braga, in a manner which he thought contrary to the rules of the Church and to the intention of the Council of Trent, and represented to the Pope with great freedom "that he had no doubt he had been misinformed in this matter, and therefore he implored him to change his order," adding the words, "*Absterge illam à tempore Pontificatus tui maculam.*"

Both laboured hard, as we have said, to re-establish morals among the faithful, and St. Charles maintained in the Council: "*That discipline must be re-established by the same means as in primitive times, when it was observed by all the faithful. And that the Council of Trent, having commanded them to restore the ancient discipline, he could not rest till it had been brought back in all its perfection.*" And of Dom Bartholomew it was said: "*Primævum illum ferventum que nascentis Ecclesiæ spiritum tepidis istis frigescentibus que temporibus revocavit.*"

Both were exposed to great persecutions, which they suffered with invincible patience and courage. It is well known that the holy conduct of St. Charles roused against him the anger of the great nobility and ecclesiastics, and even of religious, and what he felt even more keenly, that the malice and calumnies of the envious had made him suspected even in Rome itself, where he was so well known and was so powerful. And having attacked in a special manner the proceedings of his Fourth Council, "*they decried it by so many writings, that scarcely a single clause was left in it entire or without censure; and by their calumnies they so deceived the cardinals, that they were surprised into a judgment which declared that almost every part of it should be changed or suppressed. All the world at that time seemed against him, and they even spread the report that in despair he had left all and gone to be a hermit; so that he was for a while reduced to defend himself solely by prayers and tears before God, imploring His mercy in these words: 'Ut contra fatuas hominum mentes Ecclesiæ laboranti adesse vellet.'*" (Giussano, lib. 6, ch. 1, and Ripamont, lib. 5.)

In the same way Dom Bartholomew was attacked by the great in this world, dishonoured by ecclesiastics, decried to his people, and blackened by atrocious calumnies before the Holy See itself. But though these unjust persecutions greatly tried his humility and patience, we may say that his chief sorrow was to see that the souls whom God had confided to him were being lost before his eyes, without his being able to help them. For when he had laboured with the greatest zeal to show them the true remedies for their maladies, he had the mortification of hearing his people say: "That he was too severe; that it was useless to try and reform the world; that they had always followed their own inclinations, and would go on doing so; and that all his rules would only still further irritate the passions of men, by laying a yoke on them which was quite insupportable," &c. It was this determination to go their own way without thinking of God, and to lead a purely pagan life, (which he remarked in so many,) that formed one of his heaviest crosses. He spoke of it as of a real persecution, not of that kind which kills and tears the body, from which many of God's servants are exempt, but of that in which pity and sorrow for those souls who lose themselves for ever, are like a sword which pierces the heart. "*Gladius transverberans viscera dilectionis,*" as St. Augustine says; and thus he experienced, in a way of which only perfect souls are capable, the truth of St. Paul's words: "*That all that will live godly in Christ Jesus shall suffer persecution.*" (II. Tim. iii. verse 12.)

It seemed as if God in His inscrutable designs had singled out St. Charles to be a model of a holy and penitential life in the midst of the universal relaxation of morals and discipline among ecclesiastics of high position at that time. He had united in his person all those qualities which seemed most opposed to humility and penance, so as to make the example the more striking. For having been brought up in all the luxury of his high birth, and being, through his relationship with Pope Pius IV., overwhelmed with dignities and honours amidst all the pomp and magnificence of the Roman court, he conceived the idea of leaving all, and becoming a simple religious; and when dissuaded from it, he still practised all the austerities of a monk in the midst of the arduous duties of his episcopate. And in spite of his humility, which was very great, he did not think it right to relax any of these penances, (which seemed excessive,) even in deference to the advice and remonstrances of the most pious and learned authorities in the Church, so persuaded was he that he did not do more in this way than what God required of him. Dom Bartholomew rivalled him in austerity of life, and in combining the duties of his episcopate with those of a religious order; but besides the great difference in their birth, it must be allowed that having been accustomed from his youth to monkish discipline, what he did in this way was not so striking and extraordinary as it appeared in St. Charles.

One of Dom Bartholomew's great characteristics was, his extreme veneration for the episcopal dignity. We have seen with what reluctance he accepted it; how he bore the burden for twenty-four years, but under a continual protest; and how he finally obtained leave to relinquish it, not from any want of charity or lack of desire to be of use to others, but simply because he was thoroughly convinced of his utter unworthiness and incapacity for the charge.

If in this matter his humility may appear as excessive as St. Charles' love of penance, we must believe that these two persons were raised above the ordinary standard, to be witnesses for God, and striking examples for the good of the Church: the one, to arrest the stream of luxury and self-indulgence which dishonoured the ministers of Jesus Christ; the other, to remedy the extraordinary blindness of ambitious men, who are ready to thrust themselves into positions which the holiest souls have shrunk from with trembling fear, for the sake of the worldly dignity and emoluments which accompany them.

If we have extolled the spirit of penance of St. Charles as being more remarkable even than that of Dom Bartholomew, we may also say that as regards courage and magnanimity in prelates, the Archbishop of Braga showed a more admirable example than St. Charles, for the very reason that the circumstances of his position made the practice of these virtues more difficult. For to a nephew of the reigning Pope, and a Cardinal of the highest birth, it was not so hard to maintain the cause of the Church with dignity and firmness, knowing that his words would carry weight from the very fact of his rank and relationship. But Dom Bartholomew was a man of humble birth, who had been all his life in a monastery, and had therefore no adventitious circumstances or interest to help him; yet, no sooner was he raised to the episcopate, than he became, as it were, another man, and appeared before all the prelates of the Œcumenical Council, popes, cardinals, and kings, full of that courage and firmness and dignified resolve which were the effects of the episcopal unction, whereby God inspires those whom He has chosen for these high functions with a special grace to tread in the footsteps of the apostles.

Another advantage which Dom Bartholomew had over St. Charles was the leisure he had had during his thirty years' residence in his monastery, to study, not only holy writ, but the writings of the fathers and the decisions of previous councils, all which knowledge must necessarily have been superior to that of St. Charles, who at twenty-two years of age was engrossed by the most arduous business connected with the Church under his uncle's pontificate. It was, therefore, a particular glory to Dom Bartholomew, that by his previous studies he was able to speak before the Council with an authority, an intimate knowledge of the subject under discussion, and a firmness which few others possessed, and which necessarily added great weight to his opinion.

There are certain saints of whom it is remarked that God has sent them into the world for some one particular action. And we think that the merit of Dom Bartholomew must have been singularly great, even if he had done nothing else, when he was chosen by St. Charles among all the prelates at the Council as his director in the most critical moment of his life, and when his very salvation was at stake. It was necessary that God should have put into St. Charles' heart the greatest veneration for and confidence in our holy prelate, and given Dom Bartholomew special lights and discernment to guide so great a soul, and make him understand that he was not called to the religious life, but to the Archbishopric of Milan, where he became so admirable a model to bishops of all succeeding ages.

But St. Charles felt convinced that the Spirit of God spoke by Dom Bartholomew's mouth, and that in following his guidance he was simply fulfilling God's will concerning himself. Yet it required extraordinary enlightenment and divine prudence for any one to advise St. Charles under the circumstances in which he was then placed. All-powerful in Rome, charged with a great archbishopric, loaded with riches and honours, and only twenty-three years of age, the more dazzling was his position, the more was he surrounded by snares and dangers. At the same time he felt a strong interior call to prefer his salvation to everything else, and to seek safety and repose far from the world in a monastery. Who would not have thought that he ought to encourage so salutary a fear and so holy a resolution? This makes one realize the more the enlightenment and piety of Dom Bartholomew, which made him discern the finger of God in the course he was to point out to St. Charles, and assure himself that he could not judge of his case by ordinary rules. He told his illustrious penitent, therefore, that God called him to the government of His Church, and not to the religious life, and that he must believe that, feeling himself free from all ambition or self-interest, He who had laid this charge upon him would preserve and guide him, and would give him sufficient grace and strength to save himself while he saved others. St. Charles, thoroughly persuaded that God had sent him Dom Bartholomew, as He had formerly sent Ananias to St. Paul, and St. Ambrose to St. Augustine, unhesitatingly followed his advice, and ever after conceived the deepest respect and affection for his person. This he expressed in a letter he wrote to him from Rome, when Dom Bartholomew had told him of the grave difficulties he had had with his chapter. *" If the envy of men,"* (he writes,) *" should have raised a thousand calumnies and false reports against you, your virtue is raised so far above the suspicion that there could be a shadow of truth in any one of their accusations, that there is no fear that they will diminish the least in the world the esteem which His Holiness has for your merits."* This was the judgment pronounced by Pope Paul IV. on the character of Dom Bartholomew. Let us now hear that of St. Charles himself: *" But what shall I say of my own feelings in the matter? I, who have you always present in my mind and heart, and who propose no other model of imitation to myself than you and your virtue? Do you wish me to say what I think? I do not believe, then, that there is anything in the Archbishop of Braga which is not eminent and worthy of the highest praise. And I feel that he is so not only from his dignity as primate of a particular kingdom, but that by his virtue he soars above all other prelates in Christendom."*

These praises are very strong in themselves, but they are without comparison stronger when we consider who it is who has made use of them. For if we are to measure praise by the greatness of him who bestows it, we see that Dom Bartholomew was judged worthy of such encomiums by the first person and the greatest saint then existing in the Church. We can add nothing to such testimony as this, and we feel we cannot better conclude the life of this holy prelate than by entreating our readers to follow the judgment of one whom the Church admired during life, and now reveres on her altars throughout all ages. We do not think there is any bishop in the world who would not do well to regulate his conduct by the example of Dom Bartholomew if he wishes to acquit himself worthily of the duties of his office, remembering that St. Charles said: "*That he was the only model he proposed to himself to follow.*" We hope also that those who have studied this biography will own the truth of my first statement, namely, that whether they be ecclesiastics, religious, or people in the world, they will find in the actions, sufferings, and feelings of this holy man, and in the words of the holy Fathers which he has quoted in his book, many things which may enlighten them in their conduct, console them in their troubles, and animate and strengthen them in their pious desires. This is the principal fruit which the Church wishes us to draw from the lives of persons of extraordinary virtue, whom God sends upon the earth from time to time. It rests with the Sovereign Pontiff, as the Vicar of Jesus Christ, to place them, when he thinks fit, (after a careful inquiry into their merits,) in the catalogue of saints, and to make them the object of public worship and of the general prayers of the faithful. But the Church wishes us specially to revere the divine qualities in such persons, so that they may excite us to virtue by their examples, and that, recognising that they have been, in a more excellent manner than others, members of our Lord, and organs of His Holy Spirit, we should render to God all the glory of their great deeds, as coming from Him who sanctified them by His grace, who enlightened them by His wisdom, and who, according to the words of St. Cyprian, having retraced in their persons the life which He led on earth, "*crowns Himself in crowning them.*"

THE END.

www.ingramcontent.com/pod-product-compliance
Lightning Source LLC
Chambersburg PA
CBHW031941290426
44108CB00011B/638